Pioneering Family Firms' Sustainable Development Strategies

NEW HORIZONS IN SUSTAINABILITY AND BUSINESS

Books in the New Horizons in Sustainability and Business series make a significant contribution to the study of business, sustainability and the natural environment. As this field has expanded dramatically in recent years, the series will provide an invaluable forum for the publication of high-quality works of scholarship and show the diversity of research on organization and the environment around the world. Global and pluralistic in its approach, this series includes some of the best theoretical and analytical work with contributions to fundamental principles, rigorous evaluations of existing concepts and competing theories, stimulating debate and future visions.

Pioneering Family Firms' Sustainable Development Strategies

Edited by

Pramodita Sharma

Schlesinger-Grossman Endowed Chair in Family Business, Grossman School of Business, University of Vermont, USA

Sanjay Sharma

Dean and Professor of Management, Grossman School of Business, University of Vermont, USA

NEW HORIZONS IN SUSTAINABILITY AND BUSINESS

Cheltenham, UK • Northampton, MA, USA

Published by
Edward Elgar Publishing Limited
The Lypiatts
15 Lansdown Road
Cheltenham
Glos GL50 2JA
UK

Edward Elgar Publishing, Inc.
William Pratt House
9 Dewey Court
Northampton
Massachusetts 01060
USA

Paperback edition 2022

A catalogue record for this book
is available from the British Library

Library of Congress Control Number: 2020952389

This book is available electronically in the **Elgar**online
Business subject collection
http://dx.doi.org/10.4337/9781789904420

ISBN 978 1 78990 441 3 (cased)
ISBN 978 1 78990 442 0 (eBook)
ISBN 978 1 0353 0676 3 (paperback)

Printed and bound by CPI Group (UK) Ltd, Croydon, CR0 4YY

Dedicated to
our daughter Smita
and
all families building a better world

Contents

Contributors

Francesco Barbera is Senior Lecturer and Co-Director of the Family Business Education and Research Group at the Adelaide Business School. His research interests encompass a wide range of issues applied to family business, entrepreneurship, small business management and family business education.

Yashodhara Basuthakur provides research assistance to the Thomas Schmidheiny Centre for Family Enterprise at the Indian School of Business. She holds a post-graduate degree in management (strategy and entrepreneurship) from the Indian School of Business. She is interested in research in the area of strategy, sustainability and family business.

Tatiana Bouzdine-Chameeva is Senior Professor of Information and Decision Sciences at KEDGE Business School, Bordeaux, France and holds a PhD in applied mathematics from Moscow State University. Her research is on performance management, the wine supply chain and logistics, sustainability and innovations in the wine sector as well as wine distribution channels and wine tourism experience. She has authored several case studies on wine and spirits as well as the tourism industry (for France, Japan, Italy and Russia). Bouzdine-Chameeva has received honorary membership and awards from the prestigious Japan Society for the Promotion of Science. Her research works have received numerous best papers awards in international academic conferences. She has published in journals such as *Decision Sciences*, *European Journal of Operational Research*, *International Journal of Wine Business Research*, *Journal of Retailing* and *Supply Chain Forum*.

Gary Bowman is Associate Professor of Global Strategy at Bond University, Australia. He has held academic positions at the University of Cambridge (Judge Business School) and the University of St Andrews (School of Management) in the UK. He is Director of Bond Business School's MBA program and leads the 'Transformational Business' research group. Bowman's academic publications, teaching cases and research focuses on global aspects of risk and strategic planning.

Michael Browne, a Fellow Chartered Accountant, is a PhD student at the University of Adelaide having commenced his PhD after retiring as a partner of the Big 4 accounting firm PricewaterhouseCoopers in Australia. His research interests include the creation of non-financial wealth in family business and how this relates to socioemotional wealth. This research extends his professional practice experience in the area of privately owned business, including family business. Michael also continues to consult to privately owned business and is a member of the Advisory Board of the University of Adelaide's Family Business Education and Research Group.

Justin B. Craig is Professor of Entrepreneurship and Family Enterprise at Bond University, Australia. He has held faculty positions at Oregon State University, Northeastern University in Boston, and the Kellogg School of Management at Northwestern University (where he holds a visiting professorship). He has co-directed the Australian Centre for Family Business at Bond University (with Ken Moores) and the Centre for Family Enterprises at Northwestern University's Kellogg School of Management (with John Ward). Craig has authored 49 peer-reviewed academic publications, numerous book chapters and teaching cases, and has co-edited several books, all aimed at better understanding the challenges of entrepreneurial business-owning families across the globe.

Rocki-Lee DeWitt gained her PhD at Columbia University and is Professor of Management in the Grossman School of Business at the University of Vermont. She studies the innovative and resilient behaviors of family businesses, especially those who compete in industries where sustainable land use matters. Her family business research, representing a mix of case and panel methods, has been published in *Family Business Review*, *Case Research Journal*, *Journal of Real Estate Research* and in edited volumes. Other publications that address business distress can be found in the leading peer-reviewed management journals. She is a member of the editorial boards of *Family Business Review* and *Academy of Management Learning and Education* and the former chairperson of the North American Council of STEP.

Vanina Farber is the Elea Chair for Social Innovation at IMD, Switzerland. Her research focuses on scaling up social businesses and on innovations in inclusive value chains, especially last-mile distribution. Prior to IMD, Vanina was Professor and Chair of Sustainable Entrepreneurship and Social Inclusion at Universidad del Pacífico, Peru, where she also was the Dean of the Graduate School of Business from 2014 to 2016. Vanina has worked as a researcher and consultant for different international organizations and national institutions in the USA, Switzerland, European Union and Peru.

Associate Professor **Chris Graves** is the Director and Co-Founder of the University of Adelaide's Family Business Education and Research Group (FBERG). His research on the strategic behaviour, governance and performance of family enterprises has been recognized with awards from leading international institutions such as the Family Firm Institute and the International Family Enterprise Research Academy. Chris has "real-life" experience in working with family businesses as an accountant in public practice, and more recently, through his consulting work as a result of completing a clinical graduate diploma in family therapy and systemic practice.

Stuart L. Hart is Professor and Steven Grossman Distinguished Fellow in Sustainable Business at the University of Vermont's Grossman School of Business and Co-Founder of the School's Sustainable Innovation MBA Program. *Bloomberg Businessweek* has described him as "one of the founding fathers of the 'base of the pyramid' economic theory." He is also the S. C. Johnson Chair Emeritus in Sustainable Global Enterprise at Cornell University's Johnson School of Management, Founder and President of Enterprise for a Sustainable World, Founder of the BoP Global Network and a Net Impact board member. His over 100 articles and nine books have received more than 40,000 Google Scholar citations. His article "Beyond Greening: Strategies for a Sustainable World" won the McKinsey Award for Best Article in the *Harvard Business Review* for 1997 and helped launch the movement for corporate sustainability. Hart's best-selling book, *Capitalism at the Crossroads*, is among Cambridge University's top 50 books on sustainability of all time.

Joerg S. Hofstetter is Associate Professor, Operations and Supply Chain Management at KEDGE Business School Bordeaux, President of the International Forum on Sustainable Value Chains, Lecturer at the University of St Gallen's School of Management, Business School Lausanne and Leuphana University Lüneburg and Fellow of the Center for Organization Research and Design at Arizona State University. He has consulted the World Bank Group, various national and supranational government organizations as well as over 100 private and public companies, and is non-executive board member in the private sector. He is a member of Future Earth's working groups on global value chains, circular economy and post-Covid-19 transition, and a member of the Green Growth Knowledge Platform's Trade and Competitiveness Research Committee. He holds an MSc in mechanical engineering from the University of Stuttgart and a PhD in management from the University of St Gallen.

Sarah Jack is Professor at the Stockholm School of Economics (SSE) and the first holder of the Jacob and Marcus Wallenberg Chair in Sustainable and Innovative Business Development at SSE, Sweden. Before joining SSE, Sarah was a professor at Lancaster Management School, UK. Her research focuses on entrepreneurship and social networking; in particular the relationship between entrepreneurs and their context and how this impacts entrepreneurial businesses. Her research interests also include issues such as sustainability, innovation, family entrepreneurship and the role of higher education in entrepreneurship. Sarah holds editorial roles at *Entrepreneurship Theory and Practice* and *Entrepreneurship and Regional Development*. She is currently Program Chair of the Academy of Management's Entrepreneurship Division. Sarah's research projects include social innovation in marginalized rural areas), leading work on innovation actions through the delivery of social innovation on the ground and Recirculate (a global challenge project aimed at building capacity within Africa to solve the continent's water crisis).

Mattias Nordqvist is Professor of Business Administration with a focus on Entrepreneurship at House of Innovation, Stockholm School of Economics, Sweden. Previously, Mattias was a professor at Jönköping International Business School (JIBS), where he also served as the director for the Center for Family Enterprise and Ownership (CeFEO). He is still affiliated with JIBS and CeFEO. Mattias has served as a co-director of the Global STEP Project and a visiting scholar at Babson College. His research focuses on entrepreneurship, innovation and ownership/governance in different types of family firms and in other private companies. He has published widely in these areas and was involved in the start of the *Journal of Family Business Strategy* as a founding associate editor. He currently serves on several editorial boards of leading journals. Mattias is a frequent key-note speaker and guest lecturer globally on topics within his fields of expertise. Mattias is also active as an advisor and coach to business leaders.

Maria José Parada is an Associate Professor of the Strategy and General Management Department at ESADE Business School. She has PhDs from Jönköping International Business School and ESADE Business School. She has been visiting researcher of the INSEAD Global Leadership Center, France, and visiting scholar at HEC, Paris. She has the advanced family business advising certificate from Family Firm Institute. Maria José teaches family business management and strategy. Her research about governance, professionalization, values and next generation development has been published in various academic journals, such as *Entrepreneurship Theory & Practice*, *Human Resource Management Review*, *Family Business Review*, *Journal of Family Business Strategy*, *Journal of Organizational Change Management*, *Harvard Deusto Business Review* and *Entrepreneurship Research Journal*, and book chapters. She has co-edited two books, one about transgenerational entrepreneurship and another about family business groups. She is part of the editorial board of the *Journal of Family Business Strategy*. Prior to her academic career, Maria José worked for a multinational corporation in the telecom industry and in her family business in the tourism industry. She served as chair of the EU STEP council and has been a board member for three years. She currently serves as board member in her family-owned business.

Kavil Ramachandran is Professor and Executive Director of the Thomas Schmidheiny Centre for Family Enterprise at the Indian School of Business. He earned his PhD from the Cranfield University, UK and is involved in extensive research on family business, entrepreneurship and strategy. He trains and consults family businesses in India and outside.

Alyssa Schuetz is a production associate and sustainable fashion advocate based in New York City who works with a high-end designer to develop and manufacture seasonal collections. Alyssa graduated with her MBA, focused on sustainable innovation from the Grossman School of Business, University of Vermont. She also holds a BSc in design and merchandising and a certificate in writing and publishing from Drexel University.

Caroline Seow is a catalyst and change agent at Family Business Network, where with purpose-driven family business leaders she co-created Polaris – a framework to enable family businesses to accelerate their sustainability practices and create a shared prosperity for all. She is also an ardent advocate of the B Corp movement and co-founder of B Market Builder in South-East Asia. Caroline started her career as a systems engineer with IBM. Her last corporate role was head of marketing, Apple Asia Pacific. After spending two decades in multinational corporations and recognizing the importance of cross-sector collaboration, Caroline ventured into the family business, impact and non-profit space. With graduate degrees in sustainability leadership from Cambridge University and education from Monash, Australia, she is an ambassador and contributor to the Cambridge Institute of Sustainability Leadership.

Pramodita Sharma is Professor and the Schlesinger-Grossman Endowed Chair in Family Business at the Grossman School of Business, University of Vermont, and is a visiting professor at the Kellogg School of Management and the Indian School of Business. She has a PhD from the University of Calgary and honorary doctorates from the Jönköping University in Sweden and the University of Witten/Herdecke in Germany. She has studied succession, governance, innovation, next generation commitment, entrepreneurial leadership in family firms and the role of spirituality, philanthropy and sustainability on strategic decisions of family business leaders. This research has been published in over 50 scholarly articles and 10 books including: *Entrepreneurial Family Firms* (with Hoy), *Sage Handbook of Family Business* (with Melin and Nordqvist) and *Entrepreneurs in Every Generation* (with Cohen) and her recent work with Sanjay Sharma, *Patient Capital: The Role of Family Firms in Sustainable Business*.

Sanjay Sharma is Dean of the Grossman School of Business at the University of Vermont since 2011. His research has been published in the *Academy of Management Review*, *Academy of Management Journal*, *Academy* *of Management Discoveries*, *Strategic Management Journal*, *Journal of Marketing* and the *Academy of Management Executive*. His publications include nine books on corporate sustainability. His book *Competing for a Sustainable World* was a runner up for the Best Book Award at the ONE Division of the Academy of Management meetings in 2015. His most recent co-authored research monograph is *Patient Capital: The Role of Family Firms in Sustainable Business* (2019). In 2016, he received the Distinguished Scholar Lifetime Achievement Award from the ONE Division of the Academy of Management. Before pursuing an academic career, he was a senior manager and chief executive officer with multinational corporations for 16 years.

Rosemarie Steenbeek is a junior researcher at the Dutch Centre of Expertise in Family Businesses at the Windesheim University of Applied Sciences in the Netherlands. She holds a BSc in entrepreneurship and management studies (Windesheim University of Applied Sciences) and an MSc in business and organizational studies (VU University Amsterdam). Her research focuses on religious family values and the role these values play in sustainable entrepreneurship.

Alexa Steiner holds a BA in political science and sociology (Western University), a diploma in communications and public relations (MacEwan University), and she most recently completed her MBA at the University of Vermont, with a focus on sustainable innovation. Prior to pursuing her MBA, she worked in government communications and strategy for a municipal sustainable development department. She currently works as a sustainability and corporate innovation consultant and splits time between New York City and Canada, working across industries. Her consulting portfolio includes startups in sustainable fashion, as well as large cultural institutions; she is helping these organizations embed sustainability and corporate social responsibility into business strategy. Alexa is very grateful for the opportunity to be published alongside distinguished researchers and authors, and to write about an incredible family business, Rocky Mountain Soap Company, from her beautiful home province of Alberta, Canada.

Judith van Helvert is Associate Professor at the Dutch Centre of Expertise in Family Businesses, Windesheim University of Applied Sciences, the Netherlands. She holds an MSc in international business studies (Maastricht University) and a PhD in business administration (Jonkoping International Business School, Jonkoping University). Her research focuses on the role of advisory boards in family firms and the ways in which these advisory boards operate and potentially provide value for the firms, the families and the owners.

Marta Widz is Research Fellow at IMD Business School, Lausanne, Switzerland, working on the world's most prestigious accolades for family businesses: the IMD Global Family Business Award, sponsored by Pictet, and the IMD-Pictet Sustainability in Family Business Award. She serves as a non-voting jury member for both awards and heads the evaluation committees. Marta embraces the worlds of research, advisory and teaching in the family business field. She has worked with many global, multigenerational, as well as first-generation family businesses in developed and emerging markets. Marta serves as Co-Chair of the Program Committee of the 2020 Family Firm Institute Global Conference and "Learning and Exchange" Track Chair at 2020 International Family Enterprise Research Academy Conference. She is a frequent presenter for the Family Business Network, the Hénokiens and the Institute for Family Business. She has written a number of practitioner articles, book chapters, case studies and peer-reviewed articles on family business. Marta obtained her PhD from the Center for Family Business at the University of St Gallen, Switzerland, is an alumna of London School of Economics and Political Science, CEMS Global Alliance in Management Education, IMD Business School, Warsaw School of Economics, and brings multiple years of international experience from the finance and pharmaceutical industries.

PART I

Introduction

1. Pioneering business families committed to sustainable development

Pramodita Sharma and Sanjay Sharma

This book is about cases of pioneering *business families* whose leaders have *core values* that consider it their responsibility to contribute to sustainable development via their operating *family enterprise(s)*. For example, the Griffith family of Illinois has operated their animal and human food ingredients company Griffith Foods "as a force of good" since 1919. With core values of being "duty bound" to innovate for the betterment of society, four generations of the Griffith family have invested time and efforts in their business to expand its reach to over 30 countries, exceeding a billion dollars in revenues. A second-generation American family, the Nelsons of Kemin Industries, values its "moral obligation" to use its knowledge of food science and nutrition business to avoid the global challenge of widespread starvation. The Nelsons have grown their food ingredients family business from a farmhouse in Iowa to serving over 4 billion humans in 120 countries around the world. Driven by the clarity that radical innovation is needed to avoid global starvation since new cultivable areas are unavailable, in 2010, this family established a grand purpose to *double the food* produced by 2050. A fourth-generation Dutch company in the paints and coatings industry for over a hundred years, Royal Van Wijhe, continues to innovate environmentally friendly long-lasting paints and coatings. In order to reduce their carbon footprint, the Van Wijhe family leaders have established a purpose of seeing that all 10 million buildings in The Netherlands use durable paints made from bio-based renewable materials using a circular-economy process. This is core to their values of leaving "a better world for the next generation."

The *business families* represented in this book carry *core values* that consider it their moral obligation or responsibility to leave the world a better place by using their business as a force of good for society. The *family enterprises* run by these *business families* have been successful in translating their values into a clear purpose of addressing one or more major sustainability challenges, e.g., doubling food production by 2050 or ensuring that all 10 million buildings in The Netherlands use bio-based paints made from renewable materials.

This book shares in-depth experiences of such remarkable family businesses that are sustainable development leaders in their industries and regions. It is evident that in investing significant time and resources to embed sustainability principles in the core decisions and strategic choices of their business(es), each family continues to identify a universe of opportunities for new products and markets as well as efficient and effective processes, thereby reaping significant economic advantages. Pioneering family-controlled and -run companies such as Tahbilk of Australia and Thermax of India reinforce that achieving the triple outcomes of healthy people, healthy business and a healthy planet applies across a wide array of industries and regions of the world. With annual revenue growth rates exceeding their respective industry norms, even first-generation pioneers like Biofilter of Hungary, Rocky Mountain Soap Company of Canada and Supreme Creations of the United Kingdom (UK) shatter the myth that being environmentally friendly and socially conscious is a cost with negative impact on profits for younger companies. Before we describe each company, let's step back to briefly reflect on the sustainable development journey of the business sector during the past three decades.

The concept of *sustainable development* was introduced by the World Council of Economic Development (WCED) in its 1987 report: *Our Common Future*. This milestone report based on a 900-day international exercise integrating insights from scientists, governmental and non-governmental experts, industrialists and public hearings brought to global attention the concerns of depletion of non-renewable resources, rising population and income disparity. It concluded that only the "development that meets the needs of the present without compromising the ability of future generations to meet their own needs"[1] is sustainable. Thoughtful scholars and practitioners embraced the concept with an aim to understand how businesses could contribute to sustainable development while simultaneously securing their economic performance and longevity. Concepts like triple-bottom line,[2] corporate sustainability, impact investing, environmental/social/ governance investing, corporate social responsibility and stakeholder capitalism have since filled the lexicons of business journals and practitioner discussions. Following the WCED Report, in the early 1990s researchers, educators, businesses, government and civil society formed partnerships such as the Greening of Industry Network to focus on the role of business organizations in environmental and societal resilience and health, while businesses created associations such as the World Business Council on Sustainable Development to help support each other on their sustainability journey. Such efforts began to yield insights from entrepreneurial founders as well as later generational family business leaders who pursued sustainable development goals through their enterprises while simultaneously achieving economic success. For example, the experience of Yvon Chouinard[3] in building his outdoor apparel company Patagonia based on his environmental beliefs suggested the necessity of an unwavering *purpose* toward sustainable development goals in the successful launch and growth of a new venture. A closer look at the journey of Ray Anderson[4] in transforming his existing carpet tile manufacturing business, Interface, to embed sustainability principles through product and process redesign aimed at minimizing negative impacts on the environment, revealed the challenges and opportunities of balancing economic and non-economic goals over the short and the long term.

Family firms that were successful in addressing sustainability challenges while simultaneously generating profitability and shareholder value were not only the domain of visionary first-generation entrepreneurs such as Chouinard and Anderson but also that of large multi-generational family firms that successfully outperformed their peers. For example, in their 1995 book, *Managing for the Long Run*, Danny Miller and Isabelle Le Breton-Miller compared 24 family-owned and non-family firms identifying four differentiators of high performers: a shared dream, a competent team rallied around that dream, decision-making freedom and strong linkages with the larger society. While the focus of their book was on financial performance differences between family and non-family firms, the winning family firms included the third-generation family business, L. L. Bean of the United States (USA), built on the principles of environmental conservation, as well as IKEA of Sweden and Michelin of France for whom relationships with their employees, customers, suppliers and community transcended generations.

The importance of the values and beliefs[5] of the dominant coalition of a family to use its business as a vehicle for achieving sustainable development goals[6] is even more critical in small and medium-sized firms given their limited resources. Our 2019 study of *Patient Capital*[7] investments by family and non-family wineries suggested that while external forces such as regulations, powerful suppliers and customers, media and reputational concerns can pressure business family leaders to pursue sustainable development investments, the potency and effectiveness of such exogenous forces is weak as compared to that of endogenously held values of the *business family* and the driving purpose of the *family enterprise(s)* controlled by them. A recent study[8] of 500 Standard & Poor firms reveals that family firms with active corporate social responsibility strategies spend at least 95 percent less than their non-family counterparts on corporate political activities, indicating that investments toward achieving sustainable development goals reduce the need to expend time and resources in the hopes of garnering political favors. Instead, the family pioneers featured in this book work in close partnership with their communities and regulators to develop meaningful metrics and policies to make progress on sustainability goals for their regions and industries.

Individual entrepreneurs and business families vary significantly in their values to use their firms to address societal challenges by enhancing social justice and preserving the environment. Some multi-generational family firms with deep traditions and legacy find it easier to compartmentalize their social impact goals and business goals separately. Jaffe and colleagues studied such large centennial family firms that have created significant financial and societal impact over three generations of family leadership through their philanthropic efforts. Their 2019 report confirms the critical role of a shared purpose for *Social Impact in Hundred-Year Family Businesses*. While we acknowledge the important role of philanthropy and impact investing in sustainable development goals, this book focuses on business families that have embedded or transformed the core operations and strategies of their family enterprises to achieve sustainable development goals, even though some may also additionally invest in philanthropic ventures.

The family firms in our book are certainly not situated at the *reactive* end of the sustainability strategy continuum where they may be content to comply with existing regulations and the demands imposed by powerful external stakeholders like their customers, suppliers and special interest groups. Short-term financial returns dominate the attention of such reactive firms. These families run their business with some success while continuously playing catch-up to exogenous factors.[9] Rather, the cases in this book are of family enterprises that are at the *proactive* end of the sustainability strategy continuum. Such firms invest significant time and resources to develop processes, products, business models and solutions to address the grand challenges of environmental preservation and social justice. These far-sighted family business leaders find ways to balance their short-term productivity and profitability objectives with transgenerational societal value creation goals. By integrating societal and environmental concerns in strategic investments and operations of their firms, they make patient capital investments with uncertain economic returns and time horizons to develop innovative market solutions aimed at addressing grand societal challenges. These enterprising families often find themselves in unexplored territories not yet addressed by public policy, regulations, or by other firms in their industries. Sometimes, they lead or contribute to scientific knowledge in the domain of their business or industry even though returns on investments are uncertain and unknowable.

The cases identify six factors essential for successful pioneering sustainable family firms (Box 1.1). Three are in place for the *business family*: *commitment*, *control* and *continuity*; and three are critical for the *family enterprise(s)* used as vehicles for the achievement of sustainable development goals: *purpose*, *professionalism* and *partnerships*. We briefly explain these concepts below before we provide an overview of the cases in this book that exemplify the six factors.

BOX 1.1 SUCCESS FACTORS FOR PIONEERING SUSTAINABLE FAMILY FIRMS

Business Family

- Commitment driven by core values to use the family business as a force of good for society.
- Control to implement strategic decisions and resources in the family business.
- Continuity of the family business beyond the tenure of the incumbent generations.

Family Enterprise

- Purpose to achieve sustainable development goals.
- Professionalism embedded in accountability of self and others that sparks innovation via the development of unique capabilities and the appropriate organization design and structure.
- Partnerships with multiple stakeholders to jointly achieve sustainable development goals.

THE BUSINESS FAMILY: COMMITMENT, CONTROL AND CONTINUITY

It is critical that the controlling owners of the business family are able to focus their core values that consider it their moral obligation or responsibility to do good for society into a *commitment* to use their family enterprise(s) as a force of good to achieve specific sustainable development goals.[10] As patient investments of time, effort and resources are inevitably required to integrate sustainable development goals into new startups or to reimagine existing legacy companies,[11] it is further important that family leaders and the dominant coalition (decision makers) have *control* to make related strategic choices and investment decisions for their business(es). Long leadership tenures with generational overlaps ranging from one to three decades provide the time period that the family firm needs to build the unique capabilities required to simultaneously achieve financial, social and environmental outcomes[12] and embed such values, commitments, traditions and networks across generations. This transgenerational *continuity* of *commitment*, and *control* drives the proactive pursuit of sustainable development goals in pioneering family enterprises. Research[13] suggests that leaders of business families with an expectation to continue their business beyond their tenure invest more in research and development (R&D) activities, including those directed towards proactive environmental strategies such as adopting eco-certifications in the winery industry.[14] Long leadership tenures accompanied by control over the business strategy and decisions, a deep commitment to use their business as a vehicle to address sustainable development goals and family involvement in the continuity of the business helps to overcome any emerging doubts and trials along the way.

THE FAMILY ENTERPRISE: PURPOSE, PROFESSIONALISM AND PARTNERSHIPS

Establishing a new enterprise or transforming an existing business by embedding sustainability principles often requires a great deal of innovation and change, which in turn is resource intensive and involves patient investments with uncertain and long-term paybacks, testing the resolve of business family leaders. Returns from investment in sustainability initiatives take time, and pressures from non-believers to reverse strategic directions can hinder progress. Even when the controlling owners of such business families have strong values and a deep *commitment* for environmental preservation and social justice, these values-driven commitments need to be translated into a strong driving business *purpose* for the family enterprise(s). Examples of such purposes include: the doubling of the global food production by 2050 (the Nelson Family), achieving a toxin-free lifestyle for personal skin care (Birch and Baty of Rocky Mountain Soap Company) or eliminating plastics from our oceans (the Sriram Family).

It is not enough to have the motivation to achieve certain goals in a business through values, commitment and purpose; the family's enterprise must also build the capacity to achieve these goals by developing unique organizational resources and capabilities that can help the business reconcile its economic, social and environmental goals and innovate products, services and business models to achieve these goals,[15] and ensure the appropriate organizational design and structure that motivate its employees to generate innovative ideas and solutions.[16] For family enterprises, the development of organizational capacity accompanies the pivotal process of *professionalization*[17] to successfully develop new products and technologies, and enter entirely new markets. It is even more important when family firms enter unknown territory where they need to integrate sustainable development goals into their operations. The professionalization of a family business does not necessarily require the hiring of external business professionals to lead the firm, but the appropriate education, training and external internships of family members can also inject, and add to, professionalization into the family enterprise.[18]

Professionalism is cited by the Sriram family of Supreme Creations as the secret of its scaling up, innovation and success, driven by the founder who has many years of professional experience with multinationals. Similarly, the founder of Biofilter is professionally trained and experienced. Each used their professional background to set up the architecture – systems and structures – of their family firm. Karina Birch and Cam Baty, the founders of Rocky Mountain Soap Company, did not have prior business experience when they started, but early on they fulfilled their commitment and purpose toward a toxin-free world by hiring professionals that included an experienced chemist to add world-class expertise in formulating their toxin-free products. Kemin and Griffith used their own professional training and the hiring of experienced business professionals to embed R&D practices into their companies with the most appropriate structures, internal innovations and acquisitions. Similarly, Jebsen & Jessen formalized professionalization in governance structures, etc. All the firms in our cases have relied on non-family professionals to embed sustainability into their entrepreneurial ventures and innovations.

Scientific knowledge at the interface of business and the environment and society is in a state of flux and constantly evolving. Sustainable development is a complex phenomenon and a long journey that no firm is able to achieve on its own.[19] Going it alone is not an option if the aim is to make a significant impact. The family firm needs to engage and *partner* with a wide range of stakeholders not only to avoid the risks and pitfalls of undertaking this journey but also to develop the knowledge that will help it to build a competitive imagination of products, services and businesses for a sustainable future.[20] The firms in our cases partnered with other companies, customers, suppliers, regulators, bankers, non-governmental organizations (NGOs), United Nations (UN) agencies, academic institutions, industry associations and organizations such as the Family Business Network (FBN) and other key stakeholders to achieve sustainable development goals while delivering investor value.

Escalating global sustainability challenges of climate change, depletion of clean water, social injustice and destruction of habitats leading to viruses such as Covid-19 jumping species, signal the urgency and necessity of firms to become vehicles to offer business solutions by integrating social and environmental goals and metrics in their performance. Those families or family firms with a steadfast commitment and purpose to tackle such challenges have the opportunity to develop the competitive imagination of new products, services and business models that can offer significant first-mover advantages.[21] At the same time, as concerns of a backlash from regulators, powerful suppliers, consumers and special interest groups escalate,[22] an increasing number of business leaders feel compelled to embark on this journey but they risk becoming followers while the proactive firms achieve unassailable competitive advantage via products and business models that are relevant for an increasingly sustainable society.

Even when the necessary conditions to pursue sustainable development goals are there, and business families' *commitment*, *control* and *continuity* and their business enterprises' *purpose*, *professionalism* and *partnerships* are present, the practicalities of how to balance the short-term profitability goals with the long-term investments in sustainability are far from clear. What specific goals to focus on and metrics to use? How to engage and ignite the interest of powerful stakeholders to develop a shared sustainable development vision for their entire value chain? How to develop and integrate holistic strategies that balance the triumvirate goals of people-planet-profits? What decision-making structures and processes are useful to embed the sustainability mindset into their enterprise? Is it more efficient and effective to embark on a sustainability journey alone to gain first-mover advantages or is it better to join forces with other stakeholders in ones' region or industry to make quick progress or spread the risk? What type of unique capabilities do firms need to build in order to reconcile their economic, social and environmental goals? What changes need to be made in the organization structure and design to ensure the professionalization of the firm to foster innovation? Decision makers wrestle with a great deal of uncertainty in the domain of sustainable development.

To shed light on such practical issues, 22 researchers collaborated to identify and develop 12 in-depth case studies of pioneering business families with a commitment to use their enterprise(s) as a force of good to address sustainable development challenges. Each enterprising family has invested significant resources and time to reinterpret the economic focus of their industry to reimagine market solutions that also address specific environmental and societal challenges relevant to their business. Each case provides a deeper understanding of *how* family firms undertake patient investments to develop long-term proactive sustainable development strategies. Which types of defining moments propel a family enterprise to embark on the sustainability journey? How are the economic, social and environmental performance goals set and reconciled at different stages of development? Does one type of goal take priority over the others? What is the role of controlling and minority owners, non-family professionals, board members and advisors in these companies? Do founder-led firms face different sorts of challenges if they choose to engage in sustainable development goals than descendant-led family firms who must innovate through legacies and traditions?[23]

In 2015, the 193 member nations of the UN ratified the Sustainable Development Goals for 2030 (SDGs) (Figure 1.1). While eight SDGs are primarily focused on the people or social justice dimension of sustainability (1, 2, 3, 4, 5, 8, 10, 16), five focus on ecological or environmental sustainability (6, 9, 13, 14, 15) and the last four (7, 11, 12, 17) address both people- and planetary-related goals. The same year that the SDGs were ratified, the FBN – a global organization of 4,000 business families spanning 65 countries, launched its Polaris[24] initiative to enable the sustainable development journey of its members. Four companies featured in this book – Biofilter of Hungary, Jebsen & Jessen of Singapore, Royal Van Wijhe of The Netherlands and Thermax of India – are FBN members. A closer study of pioneering business families of sustainability reveals the various possible ways to integrate the sustainability-related aspirations of business families into the core strategies, operations, lived behaviors and communications of their enterprises.

Figure 1.1 *The United Nations Sustainable Development Goals*

ABOUT THE CASES IN THIS VOLUME

The cases presented in this book can be classified into three types of pioneering business families that have successfully embedded the SDGs (whether explicitly calling them SDGs as in the case of the members of the Polaris initiative of the FBN, or implicitly naming global sustainability challenges in all other cases) in their businesses to achieve triple-bottom-line success (Table 1.1). In the cluster of firms in Part II – Designed for sustainability – there are three young entrepreneurial companies from Canada, the UK and Hungary. Founded in 2000, 1999 and 1990, respectively, these first-generation family firms were established with sustainable development principles deeply embedded into values, commitments, purpose and operations. In the cluster in Part III – Transformed for sustainable development – there are seven family enterprises run by the descendants of founders. These later-generation family leaders have successfully reconceptualized and reinvented their traditional businesses to embed sustainability principles into core operations. Established between 1860 and 1966, multiple family members and generations are actively

Table 1.1 *Pioneering sustainable business families: demographics of the cases*

Firm (family name)	**Head office**	**Industry**	**Number of employees**	**Founded**	**Controlling owners' generation**	**Generation championing sustainability initiatives**
			Designed for sustainability			
Rocky Mountain Soap Company (Birch/Baty)	Canada	Personal skin-care products	180	2000	1st	1st
Supreme Creations (Sriram)	UK	Reusable ethical carry bags/designer face masks	800	1999	1st	1st
Biofilter (Deák)	Hungary	Recycling food, plant and animal waste	~ 100	1990	1st (majority) & 2nd	1st
			Transformed for sustainable development			
Thermax (Bhathena (G1), Aga (G2), Pudumjee (G3))	India	Energy, environment, chemicals	~ 4,200	1966	2nd and 3rd (62%)	1st – social justice; 2nd and 3rd – environmental
Kemin Industries (Nelson)	USA	Human and animal nutrition ingredients	2,800	1961	1st and 2nd	1st 2012
State Garden Inc. (DeMichaelis)	USA	Organic produce	900	1937	3rd	3rd 1998
Griffith Foods (Griffith)	USA	Food science: ingredients	3,800	1919	3rd and 4th (majority)	4th 2013

Firm (family name)	Head office	Industry	Number of employees	Founded	Controlling owners' generation	Generation championing sustainability initiatives
Royal Van Wijhe (Van Wijhe)	The Netherlands	Paints and coatings	230	1916	3rd (10%) and 4th (90%)	3rd Early 1980s
Jebsen & Jessen (Jebsen and Jessen)	Singapore	Conglomerate	7,100	1895	3rd	3rd 1992
Tahbilk (Purbrick)	Australia	Winery	~ 230	1860	4th and 5th	4th 1995
Institutional leadership for sustainability						
Vignobles Bardet (Bardet)	France	Winery	~ 200	1704	9th or 10th	1994
Château Pontet-Canet (Tesseron)	France/USA	Winery	~ 300 Bordeaux ~ 500 California	Early 1800s	2nd	2nd 1994
Château La Grâce Fonrazade (Bon)	France	Winery	~ 50	1992	1st	1st 2010
Wallenberg Group (Wallenberg)	Sweden	Conglomerate	~ 40% of Sweden's industrial employees	1856	5th	2nd – social causes 1900; 5th 1990s

involved in the leadership of these family enterprises that are located across four continents. Establishing close partnerships with non-family professionals and industry experts, companies in this part of the book invest significant resources to innovate and stay at the forefront of the technological advances in their industries. In the cluster in Part IV – Institutional leadership for sustainability – there are three business families from France and one from Sweden that have leveraged their position and networks to collaborate with other stakeholders in their regions to engage and energize several other business families in the sustainable development journey, thereby magnifying the collective impact. One of these families tracks its roots to 1704, two others go back to the 1800s, and the youngest is Château La Grâce Fonrazade, a first-generation family winery from France established in 1992.

Part II: Designed for Sustainability

Rocky Mountain Soap Company of Canada, Supreme Creations of the UK, and Biofilter of Hungary are three first-generation companies in this part. While Biofilter and Supreme Creations were established by entrepreneurial leaders with several years of professional experience in other companies, Rocky Mountain Soap Company was co-founded by a young husband and wife team only a few years after their graduation from college. Deeply moved by a grand sustainability challenge facing humanity and the environment, these founders with strong core values and a commitment to address these challenges used their talents, interests and networks to build a business to translate their values and commitments into a strong purpose of addressing these challenges. In introducing each company, we highlight the major motivator of each company and its primary contributions to the SDGs.

Rocky Mountain Soap Company, Canada

Karina Birch and Cam Baty, a husband and wife team, established the Rocky Mountain Soap Company in 2000 to prioritize sustainability in every aspect of their personal skin-care business. This pioneering family business, nestled in the serene Canadian mountain town of Canmore, Alberta, is founded and run with the family's core values of loving nature and encouraging and educating consumers to choose a toxin-free lifestyle. With complete decision-making control, Birch and Baty have built their company reflecting their mission to eliminate all toxins and artificial ingredients from personal skin-care products and contribute to environmental sustainability. According to Karina Birch, chief executive officer (CEO), their industry uses over 85,000 chemicals and only a fraction of them have been tested for their long-term health effects. Rocky Mountain Soap Company's products are developed with no animal testing and it uses 10 or fewer all-natural ingredients in each of its formulations. Sustainable design is used in all aspects of operations including physical space. Workshops and stores are filled with recycled and eco-friendly materials. Reclaimed marble, LED lights, low VOC paint, recycled carpets, salvaged and reclaimed wood are used throughout the company's retail spaces and the corporate office is powered by renewable energy.

The family has patiently invested its capital and has hired professionals in areas of product formulation and marketing for the dedicated achievement of its purpose of a toxin-free future for personal skin care. Rather than focusing on short-term financial returns, it has reaped above-industry average growth and performance by focusing on the long term. The next generation is still in school and thus far has limited engagement in the business.

By focusing on building a toxin-free wellness community via ingredients, products and education, this pioneering company contributes to SDG 3 of promoting good health and well-being. Related to this goal, it also sponsors an annual Women's Wellness Run and Walk. Rocky Mountain Soap Company contributes to SDG 7 by using renewable energy in all operations and retailing, and minimizing energy use by locally sourcing ingredients. It contributes to SDG 8 via its employees volunteering in Africa to help foster entrepreneurship amongst the poor, fostering fair-trade sourcing of ingredients and aligning employee values with business, and its inclusive work culture. Rocky Mountain Soap Company's contributions to SDG 12 are in the form of education related to wellness and healthy consumption, and a circular business model aimed to reduce or eliminate packaging. Its contribution to mitigating climate change (SDG 13) is via its use of renewable energy and reliance on ingredients that do not harm the environment in their extraction. It protects life on land (SDG 15) by ensuring that its products are not tested on animals, ingredients are sourced respecting and preserving biodiversity and by ensuring that extraction does not use environmentally harmful processes. It partners with environmental NGOs such as the Suzuki Foundation and other environmental working group NGOs focused on environmental preservation (SDG 17).

Supreme Creations, UK

Established in the UK in 1999 by Ram SriRam, Supreme Creations is the world's largest ethical manufacturer of eco-friendly reusable shopping bags for the grocery and retail industries. The company also produces sustainable packaging and luxury goods for health care, cosmetics and beauty and fashion industries. Equally focused on its founding core values of professionalism, ethical treatment of stakeholders and eco-friendly products, this second-generation family business is headquartered in London and has its principal manufacturing facilities in southern India. With over 800 employees, Supreme Creations serves over 60,000 clients globally. Supreme Creations is wholly owned by the Sriram family. Ram Sriram and his daughter, Smruti

Shriram, run the business, while his wife Rajni runs the family's charitable venture, Wings of Hope. The singular driving purpose of this company is to help reduce single-use plastics in the world replacing them with innovative, ethically produced, eco-friendly products. In addition to its well-known retail customers such as Debenhams, Tesco, John Lewis and Selfridges, Supreme works with the British Fashion Council and several top European designers to create fashionably designed tote bags, designer face masks and other utility products featured in the London and Berlin Fashion Weeks and touted as collectible items by global brands like Topshop and Zara, among others.

Since 2000 Supreme has helped to reduce the distribution and circulation of over 5 billion plastic bags. The business family believes that its commitment to building a professional, ethical and green company that treats its employees and suppliers with dignity and respect is good business. It also has a deep commitment to ethical relationships with stakeholders and uses fair-trade practices in its supply chain. In 2009, Supreme received the His Royal Highness the Prince of Wales Business in the Community Award that recognizes responsible British companies committed to improving their impact on the environment and society.

Supreme contributes to multiple SDGs: by hiring underprivileged segments of society in its factory including over 90 percent women and paying above market living wage to the workers (SDGs 1, 5, 8 and 10); by providing world-class working facilities at its factory in India and pivoting during the Covid-19 pandemic to produce medically designed reusable ethical cloth masks it contributes towards SDGs 3 and 8; by educating the lower socioeconomic segments and the underprivileged via its charitable venture (Wings of Hope) and the adoption of schools in India and Malawi it aids towards SDG 4; by producing innovative fair-trade, eco-friendly jute bags and other products to tackle plastic waste at point of sale and with a mission to free our oceans of plastic waste to protect marine life it attempts to contribute towards SDGs 9, 12 and 14; and, by partnering with retailers and distributors and establishing a charity to extend its stakeholder network it aids in SDG 17.

Biofilter, Hungary

György Deák, a Hungarian aeronautical engineer, established Biofilter in 1990 with the purpose of building a viable business to reduce and redirect environmental organic waste from landfill towards renewable energy while minimizing emissions during transportation or processing. Using the principles of the circular economy, Biofilter collects and processes used cooking oil from the hotel, restaurant and catering industries, as well as food, animal and vegetable waste from the fast-moving consumer goods sector, and processes it to convert and sell usable energy, heat or electricity. The launch of Biofilter pre-dated sustainable development discussions in Hungary, posing significant challenges to establishing a new venture in an undefined industry and requiring tenacity to open a new industry sector in its country. György's two daughters Dóra and Brigitta are major shareholders in the company. Dóra handles the strategic business development while her younger sister is responsible for marketing and sustainability.

With a workforce of over 100 employees and 4,500 contracted partners, Biofilter covers 70 percent of the Hungarian market. In 2019, the company collected 17,000 tons of organic waste thereby saving 24,000 tons of carbon dioxide from reaching the atmosphere or keeping 5,000 cars off the road for a full year. It generated over 14 million kilowatts per hour of energy that serves the needs of 7,000 Hungarian households. As the first B-Corp certified company in its region and an active member of the FBN's Polaris initiative, the Deák family is committed to the principles of stakeholder capitalism in its region. In 2015, Biofilter joined the national chapter of the World Business Council for Sustainable Development, a CEO-led business organization focused on helping businesses to explore, develop metrics and deliver on the SDGs with measurable impacts. The company pledged to take action on five SDGs – 2 (zero hunger), 6 (clean water and sanitation), 8 (decent work and economic growth), 12 (responsible consumption and production) and 13 (climate action). While all pioneering businesses featured in this book have a clear purpose and are making notable contributions to several SDGs, this is the only company with formally stated plans to achieve the SDGs.

Summary: Part II

The experiences of these three young enterprising families confirm the necessary conditions of a strong and shared *commitment* to use their family enterprise as a vehicle to address grand societal challenges, and the importance of the ability to *control* the strategic decisions of their enterprises in order to invest patiently in sustainability-focused initiatives. In the case of these companies, tight ownership and decision-making control lies with one to three members of the founding nuclear family. Commitment towards the SDGs and *continuity* of decision-making control provides the willingness and ability[25] to establish an entrepreneurial family business as a sustainability pioneer in its industry and/or region.

These business families have achieved operational success by translating their values for a sustainable world into a clear *purpose* to address specific sustainability challenges via their business (toxin-free personal-care lifestyle, elimination of plastics and eliminating organic waste from landfills). Their clear purpose serves as a reference point for strategic decisions including the location of the manufacturing facilities, hiring and investments. Either they have family members with significant professional experience and/or they have engaged experienced non-family *professionals* who complement the interests and talents of family founders. In addition, they have ensured the professional training and experiences of family members as in the case of the next-generation members of the Sriram and Deák families. Moreover, these families have established trusted *partnerships* with important external stakeholders including customers, suppliers, NGOs, etc. to enhance not only the networks but also the knowledge base of the enterprising family seeking to address sustainability challenges. The business families' commitment, control and continuity and the clear purpose, professionalization and partnerships of their enterprise have enabled them to make progress on multiple SDGs.

It is interesting to note that in all three cases, female family members hold the current chief operating officer or CEO position: the co-founder and CEO of Rocky Mountain Soap Company is female and the founder's daughter is leading Supreme Creations, while the next-generation female family members are in senior leadership positions at several firms. Perhaps this is an idiosyncratic coincidence of case selection, or it reinforces previous research[26] findings from large Fortune 1000 publicly listed companies that female board members of the controlling family who are actively involved in business operations have a significant positive impact on the corporate social performance.

In terms of challenges faced, the liabilities of newness, particularly with the evolving knowledge about sustainable development, poorly developed supply chains and regulations, and the lack of role models to enable mimicking of existing "best practices" force these pioneering family firms to carve their own niche not only in the marketplace with customers and suppliers, but also with regulators and the local community. Nevertheless, first-mover advantages certainly favor these companies as they are held up as exemplars in their respective industries and/or regions, gaining attention from the highest ranks through awards and visibility opportunities like the Prince of Wales Business in the Community Excellence Award for Supreme Creations and the 2016 listing of Biofilter among the Top 10 European businesses in environment and corporate sustainability. Furthermore, each company continues to experience above-industry financial performance and a plethora of opportunities to grow its business into new market segments and regions, confirming that what is good for the people and the planet is also good for profits for these firms.

Part III: Transformed for Sustainable Development

This group of seven business families have transformed their already successful and well-established enterprises to embed sustainability principles in them. Thermax of India established in 1966 is the youngest company in this part and is the only publicly listed company, although majority ownership and voting control including the leadership of the board lies with the founders' descendants. At the other end of the age spectrum is Tahbilk of Australia tracing its roots to 1860 and is led by fourth- and fifth-generation members of the Purbrick family.

The themes of tight control of ownership and strategic decision making and continuous innovation and professionalization, observed in Part II, are even more deeply embedded and nuanced in this set of family businesses that collectively employ around 20,000 people. Female family members lead Royal Van Wijhe and Thermax, and are the rising next-generation leaders in Kemin and Tahbilk. In the other three cases, the current leadership control lies with male descendants whose children are in school and have yet to decide on their career goals. In terms of the SDGs, the planetary concerns are the primary drivers for Jebsen & Jessen, Royal Van Wijhe, Tahbilk and Thermax, though each company also contributes significantly toward social justice and the health and well-being of its communities. Similarly, while concerns for human health drive the products and processes of the three food ingredients and processing companies – Griffith, Kemin and State Garden – planetary issues are equally important motivators for these three American families.

Thermax, India

Founded in 1966 by A. S. Bhathena, Thermax is a third-generation publicly listed Indian family business operating mainly in the energy and environmental sectors and to a lesser extent in the chemical industry. With a robust R&D center and 14 manufacturing facilities, 10 of which are in India and one each in Denmark, Germany, Indonesia and Poland, its 2018 revenues exceeded 800 million US dollars and the company employs over 4,100 people.

Originally set up to manufacture hospital sterilizers and fowler beds, environmental sustainability principles are deeply embedded in Thermax as illustrated by its vision statement established in 1980, "To conserve energy and preserve the environment." It is notable that this mission pre-dates the introduction of the concept of sustainable development by the WCED in 1987. Throughout its history, Thermax has continuously redefined its business to meet emerging market needs. During the oil crisis in the early 1970s, it transitioned from manufacturing oil-based boilers to solid fuel-powered boilers. Growing concerns about non-renewable resources and pollution motivated it to expand its portfolio of boilers that used renewable and waste materials such as biomass and industrial waste heat. While not an engineer himself, the founder institutionalized high standards of professionalization via technical excellence. At the same time, the Bathena family enhanced its focus on social justice in its charitable activities and its business. The second-generation family leader Aga, the founder's son-in-law, and later Aga's wife Anu, embedded a commitment to environmental preservation and social justice within the business. The founder's grand-daughter Meher continues the Thermax tradition of staying at the forefront of sustainable development with a clear purpose of combating climate change via carbon emissions reduction, energy-efficient processes, products and services, even when faced with short-term set-backs in profits.

With its focus on eco-friendly power, water recycling, waste heat energy, cooling from waste, emission controls and solar energy, Thermax is largely focused on SDGs 5, 7 and 13. In addition, the controlling family actively contributes to social justice via equitable and inclusive high-quality education and lifelong learning opportunities for Indians (SDG 4).

Kemin Industries, USA

Established in 1961 by R. W. Nelson and Mary Nelson as a manufacturer of anti-oxidants, flavors and crop preservations, today Kemin is a global manufacturer of over 500 specialty ingredients used in human nutrition, textiles and animal feed. While manufactured in 10 countries, the company's products are consumed in 120 countries. Over 20 years ago, Kemin started developing products from sustainable plant materials with a stated purpose to "sustainably transform the quality of life of 80% of the world's population by 2030." An individual who consumes Kemin's products at least five times a day is considered "sustainably transformed" by the company. Concerned about predictions of population growth and food shortages by 2050, second-generation family leader, the current president and CEO Chris Nelson reflects the family values that "those who have knowledge of nutrition and the ability to make an impact, have a moral obligation to meet this challenge."

Three generations of the Nelson family are actively involved in the leadership of this privately held family business with over 2,800 employees. Servant leadership values and stalwart business practices such as tiptoeing into markets and establishing sales before making permanent investments have put Kemin in a strong financial position. Signaling the transgenerational continuity of the Nelson family, Chris Nelson, the second-generation family leader, noted that "We have a plan in place to keep Kemin as a seventh-generation family business. At that point, we will celebrate our 200th anniversary." Ending hunger, promoting good health and well-being and responsible consumption and production (SDGs 2 and 3) are the driving forces for Kemin Industries, and constant innovations to develop eco-friendly consumables (SDGs 12 and 15) are equally important.

State Garden Inc., USA

The DeMichaelis family of Boston has followed over three generations their core value of "doing right by our people" regardless of whether they are employees, growers, suppliers, customers or members of their community. This value has been the foundation of its success and unstinting support of generations of loyal employees, suppliers and customers. The family's business – State Garden Inc. – was started by Giovanni DeMichaelis who migrated from Italy to the USA only a few months before the stock market crash of 1929 and the decade-long Great Depression. Now run by the third generation of this business family, it is the leading provider of organic and conventional tender leaf salads, spinach and celery hearts in the eastern USA with its own brands and with private label brands to stores such as Whole Foods. Each week, State Garden processes over a million pounds of produce grown on 6,000 acres in western USA, in its 170,000 square feet premises that encompass a state-of-the-art processing facility and cold and dry storage areas in Chelsea, Massachusetts.

The business is controlled by the third-generation DeMichaelis brothers – John III,[27] Mark III and Kevin III – who share an office, continue the family's eight decades' old deep commitments to building and maintaining authentic social networks and stakeholder relationships, while running their business with principles of continuous innovation, financial prudence and patient reinvestment. A combination of persistent hard work, integrity and an ability to build and maintain professional relationships has enabled this 900-employee company to be a successful attentive innovator, pursuing opportunities presented by changing societal needs and customer preferences. While all three brothers have worked in the business since they were young children, Mark III who received his professional training at the University of Vermont acquired a passion for sustainability and safe healthy farming and food while living in Vermont. The family's values translate into a deep commitment to integrate the 3Ps of sustainability – people, profits and planet. The fourth generation of the family has begun to enter the business, ensuring transgenerational continuity.

The company contributes towards SDGs 3 and 12 by helping hundreds of farmers with techniques and processes of cultivating organic produce with above-industry standards and safety protocols, and SDG 12 by providing consumers with opportunities for healthy consumption via wide distribution of safe, high-quality and chemical-free produce. State Garden contributes to SDG 8 through its loyalty to its employees and families by providing consistent financial support during downturns and difficult times. It contributes to SDG 4 via its charitable activities in educating the underprivileged and enhancing the health and well-being of children.

Griffith Foods, USA

Griffith Laboratories was founded in 1919 by a Chicago salesman Enoch Luther Griffith (E. L.) and his pharmacologist son Carroll Ladd (C. L.) Griffith. The duo aimed to use food science and technology to improve food safety and taste, while reducing wastage through production efficiencies. E. L. expanded the company beyond the US borders to North, Central and South America through extended family members. In his tenure of over 60 years, the third-generation family leader, D. L. (Dean Griffith) consolidated the company's ownership.

After this, he followed a focused growth strategy to revolutionize the food industry with new processes, ingredients and innovative machines. This resulted in further expansion of Griffith product lines and markets beyond the Americas. Great-grandson Brian Griffith became executive chairman in 2015 after working five years outside his family's business and 20 years at Griffith. In close partnership with like-minded, talented, non-family executives, and light-touch encouragement by his son, Brian is deeply committed to embedding the sustainability lens throughout Griffith Foods.

In 2019, Griffith's annual sales exceeded 1 billion dollars and the company operated in over 30 countries. Stretch goals like achieving sustainable sourcing from 10,000 farmers before 2030 are set to anchor Griffith to continue on its legacy values and commitment of using its business as a "vehicle for greater good." About 9 percent of the voting control of this private company is dedicated to the Employee Stock Ownership Plan such that employees who retire or leave can sell their shares back to the company. Similar to the Nelson family of Kemin, the purpose of Griffith is to end hunger, promote good health and well-being and responsible consumption and produce (SDGs 2, 3, 12). In addition, working in partnership with the Rainforest Alliance, Griffith has developed sustainable farming capabilities of small-holding farmers by educating and helping them convert from traditional to sustainable farming practices. Thus, Griffith aims to simultaneously improve the livelihoods of farmers and the health of the land, thereby aligning with SDGs 15 and 17. The ultimate goal of Griffith is to source 100 percent of its spices, herbs and botanicals from sustainable farmers.

Royal Van Wijhe Coatings, The Netherlands

Royal Van Wijhe is a medium-sized Dutch family business that produces its innovative high-quality paints and coatings using sustainable materials. Led by two third-generation sisters, Marlies and Marijke, since 2000, Royal Van Wijhe has owned its production facilities, 15 trading stores and two research facilities. Focused on business-to-business sales, the company's products are available in several European countries. Van Wijhe received the "Royal" predicate in 2016 when it celebrated its 100th anniversary as an independent Dutch manufacturer of quality products.

In 1916, two paint store employees – Dirk Hendrikus Van Wijhe and Derk Vermeulen – pooled their savings to establish a wholesale paint business in Zwolle in The Netherlands. When Derk passed away in 1928, Van Wijhe's sons Bertus and Jan joined the company. The trio invested in R&D focusing on decorative paints and coatings. In 1935, they invented a unique cold-water paint that became a hallmark of their company. In 1946, another innovation, an oil-based paint for raw wood, was released. This was a well-timed product as the demand for paints was high during the post-war reconstruction phase in

The Netherlands. Even at this time, Van Wijhe was well known for providing good retirement plans and old-age provisions for its employees when no national pension programs existed. Dick, a third-generation member, joined in 1960 and worked closely with his father before ascending to the helm in 1971. In addition to enhancing system efficiencies and expanding the product range through innovations and acquisitions, he directed the Van Wijhes' business purpose towards developing environmentally friendly paints with fewer solvents. The fourth-generation family leaders' purpose has been defined to develop paints that can be safely flushed through the sink without harming people or the environment. Today, Van Wijhe's two R&D labs remain at the core of its business as efforts continue to make water-resistant paint from environmentally sustainable materials like duckweed.

Like Biofilter, Van Wijhe is a B-Corp and an active member of FBN's Polaris initiative. Planetary-focused SDGs 9 and 14, people-focused SDGs 3, 5 and 6 and SDGs 11, 12 and 17 that are focused on both people and the planet are important for this company that partners and collaborates with NGOs, scientific institutions and governments to encourage sustainability practices in other businesses in its region.

Jebsen & Jessen, Singapore

The business was founded in 1895 as a trading company by Jacob Jebsen and Heinrich Jessen. The group is now managed and owned by the third generation's two principal family shareholders, Hans Michael Jebsen and Heinrich Jessen. In 2019, the company generated over 3 billion euros in sales and employed over 7,100 people. Its international footprint spanned 20 countries around the globe.

Jebsen & Jessen is the only pioneering company in this book that has been jointly governed and owned by the descendants of two founding families for three generations. Inspired by the time-tested "one ship, one captain" concept of principal shareholder from its shipping roots, Jebsen & Jessen is a loose federation of independent business units, each with one principal shareholder and decision maker, while the other family or non-family professional managers own minority shares. Clear, simple and practical shareholder agreements govern the maximum allowable dividend levels and most profits are reinvested in the business. Upon exit from an operating business, the family and non-family members must sell their shares to the principal shareholders. Only one principal shareholder from each family holds the majority position and this individual must bring something to the table to earn this position. Upon retirement, the shares of the principal shareholder are bought by the next-generation family principal and it often takes over a decade to buy these shares using returns from dividends.

The sustainability journey of Jebsen & Jessen began with the low-hanging fruit tied to core business challenges like eliminating toxic chemicals and plastics. However, efforts intensified when the third-generation leader Heinrich Jessen, who has strong core values and professional training related to sustainable development, came to the helm to embed social and environmental initiatives throughout the company. The case features the sustainable transformation of GMA Garnett, one of Jebsen & Jessen's operating businesses, into a closed-loop operation based on circular economy principles, thereby maximizing the life span of a non-renewable natural resource. The primary contributions of this company are focused on the planetary SDGs 9, 12 and 15.

Tahbilk, Australia

Established in 1860, Tahbilk is a fifth-generation family business and the oldest company in this part of the book. Australia's largest and "greenest" winery is located on the 1,214 hectare Tahbilk Estate with 11 kilometers of shore line on the Goulburn River, eight kilometers of wetlands and 200 hectares of vineyards. The high ferric oxide sandy loam vineyard soil enables the cultivation of several high-quality grape varietals. Up to the late twentieth century, Tahbilk's focus was on crop yield as the land was worked hard with liberal usage of synthetic fertilizers and pesticides. Environmental impacts were not considered in decision making until the 1990s, when the Purbrick family turned 350 hectares of unproductive farmlands into wetlands based on a commitment that it was the "right thing to do." As this project grew, the family began to reap unanticipated financial and non-financial benefits through eco-tourism initiatives like the Wetlands Café, eco-trail walks and boat cruises. Today, the triple-bottom-line concept is embedded into Tahbilk's sustainable business model that guides strategic decisions, operational practices and performance evaluation at all levels of the organization.

Viewing itself as the caretaker of the business charged to preserve the estate for future generations, the Purbrick family considers the impact of every decision on all three of the people, the environment and the viability of the business. A well-developed governance structure oversees the dual goal of maintaining family legacy and pursuing ambitious growth. Similar to Jebsen & Jessen, the "no-greed" family policy is perpetuated across generations leading family members to favor reinvestments in sustainability initiatives over dividends. Working closely with fourth-generation family CEO Alister Purbrick, who initiated the wetlands project, fifth-generation family member Hayley Purbrick leads the sustainability initiatives making sure to gain the approval of the Tahbilk board and the Advisory Committee. Tahbilk is Australia's only winery to be carboNZero certified, an accreditation recognized in over 60 countries. The planet-focused SDGs 12, 13 and 15 are closely aligned with the goals and efforts of the Purbrick family.

Summary: Part III

A review of these seven cases of multi-generational family enterprises that have transformed their core business to address and contribute to the SDGs, reinforces similar factors for success of the sustainable family firms that emerged in Part II. For the business family, the first is a strong *commitment* to using its business as a force of good. The second is an ability to *control* the strategic decisions including major patient investments by the company. The maintenance of control gets tricky over generations as the number of family members and the scope of business adds more complexity. Each family has developed its unique way of retaining (or regaining) decision-making control using its unique mix of ownership, management and governance practices. For instance, while Thermax chose to retain the chair position of the board and majority ownership of its publicly traded family business, in State Garden ownership is equally divided between three siblings, one of whom serves as the CEO while unanimity in decisions guides strategic actions and investments.

In addition to commitment and control, with the passage of time and age, a third necessary condition emerges in Part III that is less evident in Part II of younger family firms where the founder is still actively engaged: the desire of the controlling family/ies to *continue* the family business beyond the tenure of the incumbent generation. The companies in this group range from 55 to 160 years of age. It is interesting that while the same business entity has continued in all seven cases the meaning of "sustainability" has changed over time. The fourth-generation family leaders of Royal Van Wijhe were most explicit about this evolution. For their founding generation, sustainability meant survival of the business, while for the second generation it meant a focus on people, which changed toward environmental sustainability in the third and fourth generations.

For the family enterprise run by the business family, three factors – *purpose*, *professionalism* and *partnerships* – are not only reinforced but amplified and more nuanced in this group of firms with greater complexities and diversified operations. More confident in the legacies of transgenerational success and longer productive life spans of each generation of family leaders, the Part III companies develop generational depth of purpose to pursue sustainable development goals by translating their family commitments and values. For instance, in Jebsen & Jessen, the *purpose* of using its business operations to achieve the SDGs draws upon its shared heritage of seafaring and close proximity with the natural environment. While most firms are addressing several SDGs, they may not specifically cite the SDGs and each company may use its unique narrative to express these goals.

In terms of *professionalism*, the education and experiences of family member leaders in these enterprises is further enhanced by educating and training their family's younger generations professionally and by working closely with carefully selected non-family *professional* managers to co-create and guide the SDGs and strategies of these companies. Long-term orientation of the controlling family in their relationships with non-family professionals is evident in each company.

Partnerships with external stakeholders play a significant role in Part III companies with family member leaders taking on the role of active boundary spanners and being highly authentic in their contributions to their industry associations, regional governance and at times in charitable endeavors of their families. For example, third-generation family leaders – Anu Pudumjee of Thermax, Mark DeMichaelis of State Garden and Marlies Van Wijhe of Royal Van Wijhe – invest significant time and effort to actively develop and deepen their relationships with customers, suppliers, competitors, regional and national leaders, research scientists and other external stakeholders. These efforts position them and their companies in a continuous learning mode, modifying their sustainable development reference points.[28] In turn, this enables them to innovate and seize opportunities as they emerge.

With the passage of time, most business families featured in this part became more thoughtful about their transgenerational continuity ambitions. It is interesting to note the extended periods of time, often in excess of one to two decades, when two and sometimes even three generations work together in the business. This important overlap phase ensures an organic transmittal of traditions, values, commitments and networks across generations. It allows time for a subdued and gradual change in culture facilitating the absorption of changes and modifications in the company. In turn, it enables the accumulated resources and competencies to be leveraged to develop future-focused innovative market solutions to address global sustainability challenges.

Part IV: Institutional Leadership for Sustainability

The families in this part of the book are encapsulated in two cases. The first case about institutional change in the Bordeaux wine industry features three business families. Two of these families – Bardet (Vignobles Bardet) and Bon (Château La Grâce Fonrazade) – led the process of rapid institutional change by building consensus amongst all estates in all four wine-producing appellations (Appellation d'Origine Contrôlée) of Saint-Émilion to mandate sustainable wine farming and production by 2019. This process involved multiple stakeholder engagement including regulators, industry associations, merchants, small and large estates. The third family, the Tesseron (Château Pontet-Canet), sells a classified Fifth Growth prestigious high-priced wine. By transforming its estates to be fully biodynamic while boosting its quality and profits, this family led by example. These (and other) families have set into motion the transformation of the entire Bordeaux region toward sustainability and the change is now spreading rapidly across France.

The second case is that of the Wallenberg family of Sweden, which due to its size and influence has the power to bring about institutional change in the country. The Wallenberg family has controlling ownership in most large Swedish industrial groups including Ericsson, Electrolux, ABB, SAAB, SAS Group, SKF, AIK, Atlas Copco and Nasdaq, amongst others. During the 1990s the Wallenberg family enterprises represented around one-third of the Swedish gross domestic product.[29] Hence, the commitment of the Wallenberg family to societal responsibility and sustainability has had a major institutional influence in the Swedish business sector.

Vignobles Bardet

The Bardet family traces its history in the wine business to 1704. The previous generations of the Bardet family were merchants and brokers, though they had a vineyard and were making wines for their own needs. Philippe Bardet, the ninth-generation family member and head of the family winery since the 1980s, decided to focus mainly on wine producing and extended the winery from 9 to 90 hectares making it one of the largest Bordeaux estates spread across the three appellations of Saint-Émilion, Castillon and Côtes de Bordeaux. With its motto of "respect for the terroir and the ambition to pass it down," the Bardet family has always valued its environment and the preservation of land. Hence, when lab tests revealed that the river that ran through the family estate had micro pollutants in the form of pesticides and other wastes and discharges, Phillipe Bardet developed a commitment to use the family business to eliminate all chemicals, pesticides and fertilizers not only from his estates but from all the winery estates in the four Saint-Émilion appellations. To this end, Phillipe acquired institutional leadership by becoming the president of the Technical Commission of the winery industry association and took an active leadership role in its sustainable development projects including the creation of sustainability certification of Bordeaux wines. During this process, he partnered with other families (especially the Bon family) to lead institutional change which resulted in a mandate for sustainable farming of all wines produced in the Saint-Émilion appellations. The Bardet estates are wholly owned by Phillipe, his wife Sylvie and his two sons (tenth generation) who are now actively engaged in the operations of the business after professional business education and training in the wine business. All of their operations are 100 percent organic and have received the most rigorous sustainable agriculture certification in France.

Following a relentless purpose of eco-system preservation by ensuring the purity of the river and elimination of all chemicals from the region, the Bardet family contributes to SDGs 3 and 6 by removing cancer-causing chemicals and toxins from water and soil, SDGs 12 and 13 in terms of sustainable production, SDG 15 for eco-system protection and restoration and SDG 17 by entering into multi-level partnerships to lead institutional change.

Château La Grâce Fonzarade

This is a smaller family-owned and -controlled estate in Saint-Émilion owned by the husband and wife team of François-Thomas and Benedicte Bon who bought their estate in 2010 in a deteriorated and half-abandoned state. In 2013, the property started its second life with new modern cellars and meeting the technical requirements of biodynamic certification. François-Thomas Bon has over 20 years of international professional experience in Chile, Argentina, Australia and China in wine making and consulting. He is driven by a strong commitment to environmental preservation and is actively engaged with the small and medium-sized enterprises association and in consulting for a large number of estates all over the Bordeaux region to convert them to sustainable practices and help them with certification. François-Thomas Bon worked tirelessly alongside Phillipe Bardet to engage various stakeholders and partners to bring about the institutional change and mandate for sustainable farming and production in the Saint-Émilion appellations. The business contributes to SDGs 3 and 6 by eliminating cancer-causing chemicals and toxins from water and soil, 12 and 13 via sustainable production, 15 via eco-system protection and restoration and 17 via building partnerships and leading institutional change. François and Benedicte have transgenerational intentions, though their children are young and still at school.

Château Pontet-Canet

This is a prestigious Fifth Growth classified estate that was established in early 1800 and classified in the original French ratings of 1855. Its vintages are pre-sold two years in advance at premium prices. The estate is 100 percent biodynamic and does not use any fossil fuel energy in its operations, which is very rare for an estate that is so large by the standards of Bordeaux (with 81 hectares) and with such prestigious high-priced wines. In 2010, Château Pontet-Canet became the first major Bordeaux wine producer to earn the official French Agence Bio organic certification. Its other certifications include organic certification awarded by Ecocert and biodynamic certification from Biodyvin.

Alfred, the second generation of the Tesseron family, took over the estate in 1994, and reflecting his family values, established a purpose of 100 percent conversion to biodynamic operations and to embed sustainability into all aspects of operations including eliminating fossil fuels from operations. The estate began the process of conversion to being biodynamic in 2004. Alfred Tesseron relied in a major way for this conversion on Jean-Michel

Comme, a professional estate manager recognized as one of the world's foremost experts in biodynamics. The Tesseron family owns and controls the business. Third-generation members, Alfred's daughter Justine and his niece Mélanie, joined the family business in 2015 and 2005, respectively. In 2016, the family purchased the 600 acre estate of the late actor, Robin Williams, in the Napa Valley, renaming it Pym-Rae and converting it to 100 percent biodynamic. The close connection between the Tesseron and Comme families extends into the future as Jean-Michel Comme's son, a trained professional viticulturist, now works on the California estate with Justine Tesseron, ensuring continuity of the family's commitment to eco-system protection and restoration.

The family's commitment was clear when hot and humid weather in 2018 led to an aggressive mildew infestation in Bordeaux and destroyed 75 percent of the Pontet-Canet grapes, Tesseron refused to spray chemicals because any usage would have set the biodynamic process back many years and because the family (and Comme) very strongly believe that such incidents build the natural immunity of the vines and the eco-system. The quality and price of its wines have increased dramatically since it became biodynamic. Pontet-Canet's success as a sustainable biodynamic estate with high quality and prices has inspired other similar classified estates to follow its example, setting institutional change toward sustainability amongst prestigious estates in Bordeaux. The business contributes to SDGs 3 and 6 by removing cancer-causing chemicals and toxins from water and soil, SDGs 12 and 13 via sustainable production systems and 15 via eco-system protection and restoration.

The Wallenberg Group

The Wallenberg family's commanding position in the Swedish business sector accords it major institutional influence to bring about change, not only within its own businesses but also amongst other businesses that seek to emulate the group. The Wallenbergs *control* their business enterprises via 15 non-profit foundations and industrial holding companies—Investor AB (public) and FAM AB (private – owned by foundations controlled by the family) with their respective holdings, including ABB, AstraZeneca, Atlas Copco, Electrolux, EQT, Ericsson, Nasdaq, Saab AB, SAS, SEB, SKF, Stora Enso, Wärtsilä (all public) and Höganäs and Mölnlycke (private). In addition to the three fifth-generation cousins—Jacob, Marcus and Peter, Jr. Wallenberg—who lead the family enterprises, four other fifth-generation cousins are involved mainly in the governance of the family's non-profit activities. The Wallenberg family has a deep commitment to sustainable development and chooses to run its many businesses by hiring the best world-class professional talent. Eighty-three percent of their companies have signed the UN Global Compact and 74 percent of them contribute to the UN SDGs including SDG 7 via major investments in clean energy, 12, 13, 14 and 15 in the domain of energy, environment and climate change, 11 via the major investments made in social welfare and charities to help people and communities, 4, 9 and 17 via innovation, research, academic partnerships focused on addressing climate change and sustainability challenges and 16 via a focus on business ethics and governance in their corporations, in society and nationally.

Summary: Part IV

The Bardet and Bon families realized that the sustainable transformation of their own estates was not sufficient since the Bordeaux appellations share common resources and eco-systems and chemical contamination by one estate can affect the others. At the same time, they all had strong values that sustainability was critical for the long-term health of the families, the workers, the communities and consumers of their wine, as well as the reputation of Bordeaux wines. Hence, it was important to bring about institutional change via collective action. The Tesseron family led by example showing that transforming operations in a major way by deeply and completely embedding sustainability did not compromise the centuries-old finely tuned wine-making processes, and in fact raised the quality of wines as well as the prices that consumers were willing to pay. Its success sparked institutional change amongst the other prestigious classified estates. The Wallenbergs have a commanding presence in the Swedish economy and their integration of sustainability principles influenced other families, companies, regulations and public policy in Sweden. All these families exhibited a commitment to use their enterprises for social good, had control over decision making and had transgenerational continuity aspirations. Their enterprises had a driving purpose to achieve several SDGs and were professionalized with top talent from within and outside the family. Most importantly, they focused on broader institutional change through partnerships with industry associations, standards bodies, research institutes, regulators, suppliers, merchants and competitors.

IMPLEMENTING A COMMITMENT TO A BETTER WORLD

As discussed above, the younger business families in Part II set up their ventures designed for sustainability. For the others, the focus evolved from survival and building the business for the first-generation entrepreneurs in the early years, to continuity in later years as they negotiated their legacy business amidst continuously evolving competition and shifting consumer needs. In parallel, health concerns caused by global pandemics such as Covid-19, deteriorating natural environment, water shortages, rising temperatures and devastating weather events resulting from climate change led to greater attention to societal challenges.

The trade-off between people, planet and profits is never straightforward for any company as the three dimensions are integrated and interdependent, necessitating continuous alertness, flexibility and creativity of business leaders to strike a delicate balance between their company's performance on each of the three dimensions and to ensure its longevity and success. For example, a profitable company that reduces its negative environmental impacts while treating its employees unjustly will be regarded as unethical or *unfair*, limiting its ability to attract or retain talented and motivated professional employees without whom it cannot function. Another family business that treats its employees well and is focused on its environmental responsibilities at the expense of maintaining its position in the market with products and services that meet the needs of its customers is likely to be *unviable* in the long run. And, one that is only focused on its people and operations without paying attention to its environmental footprint will feel the wrath and pressure of regulators and special interest groups, which in turn may negatively influence consumers' interests in its products or services. Thus, for the sustenance and longevity of a family enterprise, it is essential to develop a strategy and capabilities to balance performance on all three metrics effectively. A simplified version of the importance of balance between people, planet and profits is represented in the sustainable development models used by two pioneering families in this book: the Nelsons of Kemin Industries and the Purbrick family of Tahbilk Estate (Figure 1.2).

The Wallenberg family of Sweden regards sustainability as a broader concept that defines its relationship with society. The fifth-generation family leaders note that since the establishment of their company in 1856 their compass has been set toward the broader society rather than just their business ventures. With its roots in banking, the family believes that the only way to deliver sustained economic returns to shareholders is by relating to all important stakeholders including its employees and society at large. This notion of stakeholder capitalism is reinforced by the following quotes from two other companies in Parts III and IV, respectively:

> It is not possible to choose just two of three goals to work with. By that you are basically saying that you want to drive electric, but you do not care about the little children mining the heavy metals for it. (Ron Hulst, R&D Manager, Royal Van Wijhe)

> I do not forget that we are a commercial company and we need to make money. The best approach to do so is to make the best wine. Being a certified growth, we have higher prices and the goal for us is to have the highest price. (Jean-Michel Comme, Estate Manager, Château Pontet-Canet)

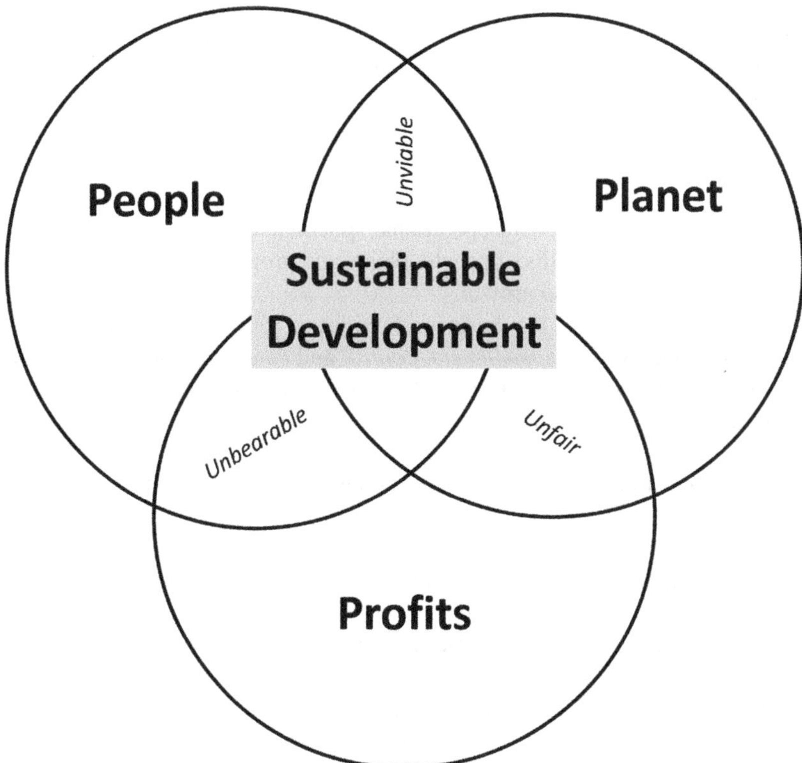

Figure 1.2 *Integrating people-planet-profits to achieve the Sustainable Development Goals*

While striking a balance between the triple-bottom-line performance metrics is challenging, each pioneering business family finds pragmatic ways to build valuable and difficult-to-replicate organizational capabilities and unique competitive advantage.[30] For example, by separating the Tahbilk legacy estate from its high-growth initiatives, the Purbrick family found ways to distinguish itself in the cluttered Australian wine market, gaining economic as well as non-economic reputational benefits. Similarly, Jebsen & Jessen invested efforts to adopt a comprehensive sustainable development strategy in the GMA Garnett business first, and only when it was comfortable with the success of such an approach and had gained valuable insights from transforming this business, did it implement sustainability in all of the other Jebsen & Jessen companies. Others such as State Garden and Griffith Foods transitioned from ingredients based on traditional agricultural practices involving chemical pesticides and fertilizers towards those with organic sustainable farming practices. Each company invested significant efforts to provide expertise to traditional farmers to enable their transition as organic suppliers. Supreme Creations geographically separated its design and marketing in London from its manufacturing facility in India to reap supply chain advantages. The design activities worked closely with global clients, mostly in the Western world, and the manufacturing activities were embedded close to raw materials and manufacturing expertise. This operational split enabled it to manage high performance related to the 3Ps of people, planet and profits thus positioning itself strategically for sustained growth.

As discussed above, the business families in our cases exhibited three necessary conditions of *commitment*, *control* and *continuity* (3Cs) for the successful pursuit of proactive sustainable strategies to implement the SDGs and triple-bottom-line performance.

Commitment to Use the Family Business as a Force of Good for Society

With clarity of the critical importance of stakeholder capitalism[31] for the longevity of a family enterprise, virtually all of the cases presented in this book did not wait for regulations or other exogenous pressures to nudge them to start paying attention to social justice and environmental preservation. Instead, fueled by their commitment to use their business ventures for the benefit of society, they adopted proactive strategies, often changing the rules of the game and helping to establish standards and metrics working with regulators, customers, suppliers and other powerful stakeholders. For example, Biofilter's founder György Deák started collecting used oil from Hungarian restaurants for environmentally safe disposal even before there was an awareness of environmental issues in his country, facing significant challenges as he describes:

> Nobody in Hungary was dealing with used oil in restaurants and hot kitchens at that time, nor was anyone concerned with its environmental impact. I felt compelled to start my own collection process. Most caterers were reluctant to give away or sell the used cooking oil as they were accustomed to throwing it down the sink. (György Deák, Founder, Biofilter)

Similarly, customers for garnets did not understand the value of recycling this natural resource and other suppliers did not want to reduce the sales of virgin materials. Torsten Ketelsen, the entrepreneur who developed the concept of recycling garnet and who worked closely with Jebsen & Jessen to scale this operation, shared the skepticism he faced as follows:

> When I started the recycling concept 20 years ago, everyone said I was crazy to promote recycling because we would sell less virgin garnet. Instead, in the long run,

the customer base has increased greatly due to the additional product value and cost savings for the customers. (Torsten Ketelsen, Jebsen & Jessen)

Firm believers in the coexistence of economic development and environmental protection, the family behind Thermax took its responsibility to support national energy conservation and environmental protection efforts very seriously. Although the industrial regulations for air, water and environment protection were fairly lax in India, Thermax set its own standards based on those used in advanced countries and launched its Enviro division to manufacture air pollution control equipment in 1979, two years before the enactment of the Air Prevention and Pollution Act in India. The Bathena family leaders partnered with the government to help enact air pollution-related policies and regulations. A second-generation family leader remarked that:

> We firmly believe in and support a national effort at environmental protection, in which we have to play a significant role by developing or acquiring appropriate technologies, promoting general awareness, aligning our priorities with those of society and providing a service to industry which enables it to produce in an uninterrupted and yet pollution-free manner. We also strongly subscribe to the view that economic development and environmental protection are not antithetical. (Rohinton Aga, second-generation family member, Thermax)

The Bardet and Bon families in Bordeaux fundamentally changed centuries-old wine-making practices not only for their own estates but for all others in their region while helping to establish standards, appellation regulations and policies and marketing practices. The Tesseron family helped redefine viticulture and viniculture practices radically by showing how well it was able to balance people, planet and profits. Each of these pioneers ended up launching new industry segments and leading the regulations in their regions, thereby enjoying significant first-mover advantages. While family leaders of these pioneering companies achieved remarkable financial and non-financial outcomes, this was possible because each had an unequivocal control to make related strategic decisions and patient investments.

Control to Implement Strategic Decisions in the Family Business

While a commitment to use their family enterprise to achieve the SDGs signals the family leaders' motivation, it is equally necessary that they have decision-making control to allocate resources and make investments to accomplish the desired goals. Each of our pioneers mentioned the critical importance of retaining effective ownership control within a small group with a shared commitment to accomplish sustainable development goals through the family enterprise. In addition, simple and clear rules guide the decision-making authority and responsibility within the ownership group.

Each pioneering firm uses the combination of ownership–management–governance that fits its unique context. For example, similar to the "one ship, one captain" principle of Jebsen & Jessen, Kemin uses the *controlling owner to controlling owner*[32] model of ownership transition from one generation to the next so that there is only one principal shareholder per generation, who is the chief decision maker for the business enterprise. Long periods of overlap between generations exist in which the ownership is slowly transitioned across generations. The DeMichaelis and Van Wijhe families of State Garden and Van Wijhe, respectively, moved from a *controlling owner* to *sibling partnerships* model with clarity of leadership hierarchy in the sibling group. Both companies established clear decision-making processes to ensure the continuity of efficient and effective strategic decision making. For example, Marlies, the older of the two sisters of the fourth generation of the Van Wijhe family, is the CEO who reports to the supervisory board with three external members and her father, while her younger sister takes the meeting notes. This ensures all three family owners are equally informed, which in turn helps with fast and efficient decision making. In the case of State Garden, when the second-generation family leader called his three sons to select a president, the eldest and the youngest brothers quickly agreed on their middle sibling: "Mark is the most qualified of the three." In turn, the siblings established the following decision-making system:

> We would talk about growth plans and if there was something that we don't all agree on, we wouldn't proceed. It's not worth driving any type of wedge between us. So, we usually do things unanimously. (Mark DeMichaelis, President, State Garden)

In the case of Rocky Mountain Soap Company, a husband and wife-founded startup, Cam (the husband) is the chief operating officer. He explained that they felt it was better to have "a formalized structure in case a difficult decision needed to be made, so that's why Karina is CEO. At the end of the day, titles don't matter to us that much. It's a really collaborative environment and we all work together to achieve what we need to every day," but if there is a difference of opinion it is her responsibility to make the final decision.

Clear separation of ownership and governance from the management of the operating enterprises is used by the Wallenberg Group of Sweden and Thermax of India. Family members do not directly work in the operating companies. Instead, they exercise their direction and control as actively involved board members. The Wallenberg Group has had a well-established separation of ownership and management over generations. The three current fifth-generation cousins explained how their governance process helped to embed sustainability thinking into their companies. Each of them is the chairman or a board member of a few of their companies. The three of them meet regularly with one or two topics of discussion. Subsequently, these topics are discussed on each board to identify the current thinking and related initiatives in progress. At their next meeting, the cousins discuss these ideas, thereby facilitating cross-business unit learning. Regular follow-up by family leaders on agenda items ensures continued engagement of management and progress on key items.

The Thermax case, on the other hand, provides a glimpse of how a second-generation family leader separated ownership and management in her family business. Anu Aga, the founder's daughter, had to step up to the leadership role when her husband who had worked for many years with her father and had taken over the leadership died unexpectedly of heart failure. Relying on the services of a well-regarded consulting company, she took the bold step of separating ownership from management based on her belief that while skills could be hired, a family leader needs to show wisdom which cannot be hired. The new board had four independent members, three non-executive family directors including her daughter (future chairperson) and her son-in-law, and a non-family executive director. Nine executive directors had to be persuaded to step down and even her family members had to decide whether to retain their board or executive positions as they could not be in both roles simultaneously.

Perhaps the most intriguing combination of ownership–management–governance control is used by Jebsen & Jessen as this company has been jointly controlled for three generations by the descendants of the co-founders from two separate families. They have established simple yet effective rules to promote entrepreneurial growth and maintain decision-making unity, while ensuring each family has significant latitude of control. Instead of one holding company for the group like the Wallenbergs, Jebsen & Jessen is a conglomerate of several autonomous companies, each with one principal shareholder and key decision maker who is either from the Jebsen or the Jessen families. Each company has an independent board chaired by the principal shareholder. Members from the other family or employees can only hold minority-share positions until they retire or exit, at which time the minority shares must be sold to the principal shareholder. This concept of *temporary partial ownership* draws on the time-tested principles from their shared legacy in shipping that required the ship's captain to own part of the cargo he carried. There can only be one principal shareholder from each family. This person must work in the business and be accepted by all other shareholders. As it takes over a decade to pay off the previous principal shareholder of one of the families, moving from working in the business to shareholding is seen as a big step. Other pioneers have developed their own programs that align with the motivations of principal and minority owners, with non-family professionals. The concept of partial temporary ownership underlies the phantom "Stakeshare" program of Kemin. Based on the performance of a group of 20 Kemin customers, this program gives selected employees an annual bonus and shares redeemable upon their exit or retirement from the company, thereby providing a short- and long-term incentive while aligning the company with their customers.

Thus, each pioneering family has developed its unique combination of ownership–management–governance to ensure it is well positioned to make the necessary decisions and investments to accomplish its aspired sustainable development goals. At times, significant effort and energy had to be expended to prune the family ownership tree to reset it for such decision making. In Griffith, for example, Dean Griffith, the third-generation family leader, spent over 10 years and 15 million dollars to negotiate complex buyouts of extended family shareholdings to consolidate ownership and decision making of the company. Brian Griffith, the fourth-generation family leader, feels that due to his father's efforts, he inherited "a much cleaner, better structured company" that made it easier for him to focus on the sustainable development goals, signaling the importance of *control*, *commitment* and *continuity* of thought and action across generations.

Continuity of the Family Business beyond the Tenure of the Incumbent Generations

In comparison with their non-family counterparts, the primary reason that family firms are better positioned for high performance on corporate social responsibility dimensions is their long-term orientation and transgenerational continuity.[33] Short leadership tenures in non-family firms often lead to changes in core mission, strategies, and hence the commitment to use the business as a force of good. Non-family firms managed by a top management team with short tenures (averaging around 4.6 years for *Fortune 500* firms) usually lack a patient long-term strategic horizon. The non-family publicly listed dispersed ownership firms are also responsive to quarterly financial reporting requirements and financial analyst pressures, and have their compensation tied to stock options with an option to sell at short notice. Hence, they are reluctant to undertake such long-term investments in sustainability initiatives.[34] One can only speculate whether Dean Griffith would have invested the efforts or funds in the enterprise's strategic direction if he had not consolidated ownership of the company and if he had not felt it would continue beyond his tenure. In fact, several of our pioneers explicitly state the importance of generational continuity in their planning.

François-Thomas Bon, the founder of Château La Grâce Fonrazade winery in Bordeaux, explained that becoming organic took time as patient investments of time and money are necessary to develop knowledge and technical expertise to convert a traditional vineyard into an organic one. Philippe Bardet of Vignobles Bardet, the current family leader of a winery that traces its history to 1704, reflected on the necessity of family continuity in their industry by explaining that unlike manufacturing of a product like the Airbus where parts manufactured in different parts of the world can be assembled in one place, the terroir of each vineyard is unique and the only way to understand it is by living and working in the fields. A family can pass on this tacit knowledge and experience during table conversations or when working together in their fields, fueling transgenerational ambitions and respect for their terroir. Similarly, indicating the longevity aspirations of the Purbrick family for Tahbilk, the current family leader Mark says they consider themselves the caretakers of the business for future generations. As the family has no intention to sell, it does not matter how much the business is worth since it believes it will be there forever.

Many of our pioneers engage the next-generation members when thinking about the future direction of their companies. Fifth-generation member Jacob Wallenberg shared that he works a lot with the sixth generation, and when the junior generation were asked what they would like the company to focus on, sustainability emerged as the primary response. This further reinforced the family's traditions of running their companies "with a mind, with a conscience, and do what they can when it comes to how they work with their employees, for the environment and for the general development." Kemin's Chris Nelson shared that they "have a plan in place to keep Kemin as a seventh-generation family business… we will celebrate our 200th anniversary."

Transgenerational continuity, more than any other factor, is the unique advantage that family firms have in making patient investments that may take several years or more to pay back and have an impact. The continuity also helps build unique organizational capabilities for innovation, efficiencies and effectiveness that are hard to replicate by competitors. This advantage is known as *time compression diseconomies*, i.e., building some capabilities that need learning and experience over a minimum period of time and investing greater resources over a shorter period of time will not yield the same level of capabilities.[35] Dierickx and Cool discuss this concept and illustrate it with the following story about a dialogue between a British Lord and his American visitor:

How come you got such a gorgeous lawn?
Well, the quality of the soil is, I dare say, of the utmost importance.
No problem.
Furthermore, one does need the finest quality seed and fertilizers.
Big deal.
Of course, daily watering and weekly mowing are jolly important.
No sweat, jest leave it to me!
That's it.
No kidding?!
Oh, absolutely. There is nothing to it, old boy; *just keep it up for five centuries*.[36]

In short, organizational *control* by a dominant coalition with a shared *commitment* to sustainable development, and *continuity* with long leadership tenures, facilitates the patient investments necessary for achieving sustainability goals. In contrast, dispersed control combined with disparate values, visions and high turnover in leadership hinders progress, as in the case of non-family firms. Business families with a long-term orientation and an expectation of transgenerational *continuity* of their enterprise are more likely to make significant investments to pursue sustainability strategies even when the nature and timing of economic returns of such investments is uncertain.

In addition to the three necessary conditions of *commitment*, *control* and *continuity* for pursuing sustainable development goals, the pioneering business families ensure that their family enterprises have three facilitating conditions in order to successfully implement their commitment to the SDGs and to scale and accelerate the intended positive impact of their sustainability performance. These three conditions are (a) the clarity of *purpose* with specific sustainability goals; (b) *professionalism* embedded in accountability of self and of others that enables the enterprise to build the appropriate capabilities and organizational structure and design to implement a sustainability strategy; and (c) *partnerships* with multiple stakeholders to generate the complex knowledge necessary to simultaneously achieve performance on people, planet and profitability dimensions.

Purpose Based on Controlling Family's Values and Commitment

Purpose is a long-term forward-focused intention to accomplish goals that are meaningful to self and of consequence to the world.[37] It provides inspiration and a sense of direction for organizations including long-lived enterprising families and their employees.[38] Clarity of purpose guides strategic investments and enables efficient decision making for business families by providing a strategic focus to double down on opportunities aligned with overarching goals. Clarity of purpose helps to engage and energize current family members and next generations who relate to and connect with the stated purpose.[39] As organizational purpose is aspirational, the tenure and the contributions of each generation are viewed as the next step towards an incompletable and worthy family mission.[40]

While all long-lasting family businesses have a purpose that emerges from their family values to energize them generation after generation,[41] what is distinctive about the pioneering sustainable business families is that their values emphasize using the business to address societal challenges and hence the emerging purpose focuses on the SDGs relevant to their business domain. The purpose helps them develop clear objectives, measures and targets to embark on the less traveled journey toward a sustainable business undeterred by nay-sayers.

The themes of frugality and simplicity, care for people and environment run through all pioneering companies. Simple statements like helping customers prosper (Kemin Industries, State Garden), encouraging consumers towards a toxin-free lifestyle (Rocky Mountain Soap Company), eliminating plastics from oceans or toxic paints from The Netherlands (Supreme Creations, Royal Van Wijhe), minimizing landfill waste (Biofilter, Jebsen & Jessen), or fostering a healthy living eco-system (Pontet-Canet), provide the foundation that signals the purpose at the core of the enterprise's mission. The purpose provides a clear direction to link the selected SDG with organizational strategy, operations and activities and make difficult decisions with uncertain outcomes. For example, Karina Birch, co-founder of the Rocky Mountain Soap Company, shared that:

> Our industry uses over 85,000 chemicals and only a fraction of them have been tested for their long-term effects, I don't think that's good enough, and our industry needs to change. It's my personal vision, and the mission of our company to be unwavering in our commitment to toxin-free, so you can shop with the freedom of knowing that everything we make is safe and good for you… We don't believe our products are truly natural if the packages are not 100% natural.

The values and commitment to *toxin-free skin-care products* established the aspirational purpose for this young company that set its goal to use 10 or less 100 percent natural ingredients in all its products. This was when the industry norm was to label products as "natural" if a majority of the ingredients used came from natural sources. Making skin-care products based on all-natural ingredients was challenging as the customers were accustomed to the fragrance, color and texture of a product not only at the point of sale but many months (or years) after they had bought the product. Birch and Baty employed experienced research scientists to help accomplish this goal and took the risky step of discontinuing some of their most popular chemically fragranced products, despite significant push-backs against this move from retailers, industry experts and even some employees. In addition to developing such products, significant efforts were devoted to educate the customers, retailers and employees of the rationale behind this move. Co-founder Cam Baty shared their feelings and outcomes as follows:

> we were tiny, and terrified about the impact removing that scent could have on our sales. In the end, it actually did not hurt us. It just increased the trust our customers had in us. (Cam Baty, Chief Operating Officer, Rocky Mountain Soap Company)

With time and experience, following the classic principles of management-by-objectives[42] and S.M.A.R.T. goals[43] (specific, measurable, assignable, realistic, time-related), some pioneers have begun to articulate challenging purpose-driven stretch goals with clear metrics. For example, Griffith has stated its aim to engage 2,000 sustainable farmers by 2020, 7,000 by 2025, and 10,000 before 2030. Pioneers don't hesitate to stretch these goals further once they have accomplished what they set earlier. As an example, following its core purpose of serving others through scientific innovations in food ingredients, when Kemin reached its goal of its products touching 3.8 billion people every day two years ahead of target in 2017, it created a new stretch goal of sustainably transforming the daily quality of life for 8 billion people or 80 percent of the world by 2042.

Jebsen & Jessen finds the carbon neutrality benchmark helpful as it spans its entire organization as every business unit can be analyzed for its current footprint and related stretch goals can be established and accomplished in time with focused efforts. Developed and refined over 160 years and five generations of family leadership, the six guiding principles[44] of Wallenberg capture the *compass* that underlies all their decisions and behaviors. The compass includes principles of a commitment to Sweden, focusing on getting the job done, innovation and renewal, the right person in the right place at the right time, financial vigilance and research excellence. This iconic group relies on the metrics developed by the Global Compact of the UN and has identified four areas within sustainability to focus on – environment and climate, people and communities, innovation and research, and business ethics and government.

Working in conjunction with the B-Lab, the Polaris initiative of the FBN has developed an assessment tool[45] for its members to benchmark their family enterprise's current performance on the SDGs with others in their industry and region. The FBN members – Biofilter and Royal Van Wijhe – have completed this assessment which helps them to determine where additional efforts are needed as they progress on their sustainability journey. To further advance sustainability practices, the Polaris initiative is now working with the UN Conference on Trade and Development to develop capacity training programs and family business sustainability indicators for family businesses globally.[46] Other pioneers are working to develop their own metrics to track their performance and progress along their aspired goals. As more attention is devoted to finding ways of linking family values, aspired purposes and goals, further refinement of these metrics can undoubtedly be expected.

Professionalism Embedded in Accountability of Self and Others

Energized by their clarity of purpose to address sustainability challenges, our pioneering family leaders feel the urgency to scale the impact of their efforts and the necessity of holding themselves and their organizations to the highest professional standards. Professionalism is critical for developing the innovations necessary to reconcile profitability with social and environmental goals. Such innovation requires complex knowledge and technology development, the development of unique capabilities and adopting the appropriate organization design and structure to motivate the creativity and innovation necessary.

As Hungary was preparing for its freedom and opening its borders to chain restaurants like McDonalds, Biofilter's founder György Deák felt the urgency to find efficient and effective ways to avoid large quantities of used cooking oil finding its way into landfills and polluting the idyllic environment of his beloved country. Based on his professional engineering training and work experience that extended through MALÉV Hungarian Airlines, the army and at Budapest's Environmental Institute, it was clear to him that to curb deterioration of the environment, setting up professional systems and processes was as important as ensuring high standards of accountability for himself and others in Biofilter.

For Ram Sriram of Supreme Creations, the temporal urgency of the challenge and the related opportunity of using eco-friendly "bags of ethics" to replace plastic single-use bags was driven by the Courtauld Agreement that challenged the British grocery industry to achieve measurable waste reduction targets within five years from 2005 to 2009. From his professional experience working for large multinational companies, he knew that large sustainability-conscious companies would work only with ethical suppliers who held themselves to the highest professional standards. Thus, Supreme Creations had to exceed labor and health safety standards for its employees, and find ways to build a reliable supply chain of organic cotton and jute farmers using Fairtrade practices. Not only did Supreme Creations acquire and develop state-of-the-art manufacturing, design and technological capabilities, it made sure to hire only those employees who were "fully focused on both the PEOPLE and the PLANET aspects of sustainability… who are invested in long-term sustainability and don't consider it a passing fad."

In legacy companies like Jebsen & Jessen, when the third-generation family member, Heinrich Jessen, a tropical biologist and industrial environmental management studies graduate with work experience at the World Wildlife

Fund in Italy and a rainforest project in Papua New Guinea, asked his father if the environment and business could be combined in their company, he reset his family company on its sustainability journey. Such subtle yet powerful course-changing influence of next-generation members in gently nudging their family enterprises towards sustainability and professionalism is noticeable in other pioneering companies too. Griffith Foods provides a nice example. Brian Griffith, the current president and fourth-generation family member, shares that their family's interest in nature and sustainability did not find its way to their company until his thirteenth year at Griffith. His son Colin, an environmental science major in college, would send books on sustainability for him to read. In going through them he began to feel that sustainability was not a pesky nuisance as was perceived by their senior management team. Instead, it was a powerful connection to the company's core purpose of their business as a "vehicle for greater good" and a pragmatic bridge with their legacy as they propelled their company forward. As the company transitioned to its sustainability journey, non-family managers who were not as deeply passionate about sustainable development goals were gently replaced by those with strong sustainability convictions.

In addition to heavy reliance on formal education, broad scope work experience outside their family company and extended periods of transgenerational working-together phases within family enterprises, sustainability pioneers rely on setting up professional systems to evaluate performance at individual, organizational and board levels. Family and non-family members in leadership positions devote extensive boundary-spanning efforts to engage with a wide range of stakeholders and ensure the different business units or departments in their company remain aligned with their sustainable development goals. Many are deeply embedded in their external environments including local communities, governing bodies and professional associations, thereby facilitating the transmission of current knowledge into their organizational discussions. When such boundary spanning is supported by an organizational architecture of systems and processes adept at integrating new knowledge into strategic and operational decisions, a virtuous cycle of high performance is established.

Partnerships with Multiple Stakeholders

Scientific knowledge on the role of business in addressing sustainable development goals is evolving and there is an urgency to develop new business models with triple-bottom-line outcomes. Going it alone is not an option if the aim is to make a rapid and significant impact. The entire spectrum of our pioneering sustainability firms from Part II first-generational entrepreneurs, to legacy families of Part III and institutional champions of Part IV, rely heavily on partnering internally with competent, non-family professionals with a deep commitment to sustainable development goals, and externally with other companies, customers, suppliers, regulators, industry associations, policy makers, NGOs, UN agencies, the FBN and other key stakeholders.

Institutional champions like the Wallenberg Group as well as legacy companies like Kemin and Griffith work collaboratively with research scientists to develop sustainable solutions. Institutional change agents such as the Bardet and Bon families of Bordeaux work with industry associations, regulatory bodies, certification bodies and research institutions to change the landscape. Royal Van Wijhe and Rocky Mountain Soap Company have in-house research labs focused on new product and process developments with sustainability goals. State Garden and Supreme Creations work closely with organic and Fairtrade farmers for their supplies. The conversion of farms to organic or biodynamic requires over three years and carries a major financial risk as evident in the investments made by Vignobles Bardet, Château La Grâce Fonzarade and Château Pontet-Canet. Finding seed varieties to grow in different climates is challenging. The leaders of Griffith Foods have worked closely with the Rainforest Alliance to enable similar transitions for farmers who are their suppliers. Biofilter and Royal Van Wijhe work closely with the FBN leading efforts to build and support other companies in their country on their sustainability journey.

Given the newness of sustainable development ideas for many consumers, some pioneering family leaders devote considerable efforts to educate their communities and consumers. Biofilter's website (www.kornyezetert.hu) features education on environmental pollution including a video that portrays how a single drop of used oil could pollute a thousand liters of water with damaging impact on wildlife. Here are two other illustrative comments of attempts to educate customers:

> we have always tried to educate the customer that shipping on ocean is much better than putting it on the airplane. Ten years ago, customers were quite happy receiving a product in 8 to 10 weeks. But now customers are more and more eager to receive their product quickly. (Smruti Sriram, CEO, Supreme Creations)

> We can paint a wooden window frame at least eight thousand times before the paint has a bigger negative impact on the environment than the microplastics in the plastic window frame. (Ron Hulst, R&D Manager, Royal Van Wijhe)

Not only do consumers need to be educated regarding usable sustainability knowledge but governmental agencies also need some assistance. Our pioneers step up to help in this regard as well. For example, Rohinton Aga of Thermax chaired the Energy Committee of the Confederation of Indian Industry, the apex industry association in India, while Anu Aga served on the National Advisory Council and the upper house of the Indian Parliament, to catalyze discussions related to standards and regulations on environmental sustainability. With his scientific background and expertise, Chris Nelson of Kemin has been deeply engaged with the World Food Programme, and has helped to develop the Scientific Certification System for rosemary, spearmint and potatoes, creating a major point of differentiation for farmers and users of these crops. The Purbrick family members of Tahbilk have been extremely active in their community and industry, and have helped establish the "Take-2" sustainability initiative of the government in the state of Victoria in Australia. The Bardet and Bon families changed centuries-old wine-making regulations in the Saint-Émilion appellations via collective action to mandate that all wine sold would have to be made from grapes that were sustainably farmed.

In addition to active engagement with external partners, each sustainability pioneer champion found unique ways to engage their employees in the goal-setting process and sensitized them to the driving purpose of their organization and the rationale behind it. In order to develop their vision statement, Chris Nelson of Kemin personally interviewed 200 employees or 10 percent of the workforce to understand how they envisioned the company in 20 years. In some cases, professional managers and employees may need some help understanding the broader sustainability vision, so family leaders invest efforts to create awareness and excitement, while offering career development opportunities for their people. The authentic and deep relationships with employees visibly touched next-generation members and employees in several companies. For example:

> many (employees who work in manufacturing) came as young girls, got married, had children and have spent their life with our business. (Smruti Sriram, CEO, Supreme Creations)

The long-term commitment towards employees is evident in pioneering family firms, which in turn leads to a virtuous cycle of trust and engaged and motivated contributors. Ken Reagan was only in his second year as the vice-president of sales and marketing at State Garden when he suffered a heart attack and was incapacitated for several months. The DeMichaelis family made sure he stayed focused on his health while receiving a regular paycheck. Griffith, Kemin and Rocky Mountain Soap companies take pride in their companies as a place for continuous learning and professional growth. Marcus Wallenberg, the fifth-generation family leader, sums up the essence of a company's relationship with its people as follows:

> You must take care of people. My grandfather always said: "it's not their fault if you appointed them to a job – you did it." So, you have the responsibility to move the person if it doesn't work out and to take care of them. It is not their fault. Try to help them into the next thing… No business is so bad that it cannot be put back on its

feet with the right leadership, but no business is so good that it cannot be destroyed by a bad leader.

HELPING TO BUILD A SUSTAINABLE WORLD: A UNIVERSE OF OPPORTUNITIES FOR FAMILY ENTERPRISES

To stimulate actions that are critical to the future quality of life, health and existence of the human race and our planet, in 2015 the 193 UN member countries adopted a global agenda of 17 SDGs for 2030. The International Chamber of Commerce[47] and the Business and Sustainable Development Commission stated that the SDGs enabled "companies to better manage their risks, anticipate consumer demand, build positions in growth markets, secure access to needed resources, and strengthen their supply chains, while moving the world towards a sustainable and inclusive development path." It was estimated that within a 15-year time frame, SDG-related pursuits by business organizations can potentially generate savings and revenues exceeding 12 trillion dollars and create 380 million new jobs.

Global corporations such as Unilever[48] have revamped their business models with sustainability principles at the core. Smaller companies such as Patagonia and Interface (mentioned earlier), Ben & Jerry's, Seventh Generation and many others have been set up with sustainability embedded in their operations. Family-controlled companies such as Walmart[49] have undertaken comprehensive sustainability audits of their suppliers. The FBN established its Polaris[50] initiative to enable the sustainability journey of its members.

While there are three decades of research on understanding the interface of business and society and the natural environment, family business was not part of these investigations despite an alignment in transgenerational ambitions and core values of many family businesses. The family firm and business family context has only recently begun to be studied and we captured the state of knowledge and practice about the role of family firms in sustainable development in our research monograph – *Patient Capital*.[51] In this monograph and other publications, we argued that with their unique histories, accumulated path-dependent valuable resources, tacit knowledge, relational and learning capabilities, combined with transgenerational long-term aspirations, family businesses can help to accelerate the accomplishment of the SDGs.[52]

While the overall relationship between foundational values and aspired purpose, through strategic and operational decisions and performance metrics, and supporting organizational structure and design, has been part of strategic management discourse since the 1960s,[53] it is not easy to transform an economically successful family enterprise built on the fundamental tenets of investor and shareholder supremacy that have guided management thinking since the publication of *Capitalism and Freedom* by Nobel Laureate Milton Friedman in 1962, to a multi-stakeholder mindset necessary for successful alignment of economic, societal and environment performance dimensions. Traditional thinking and mindsets that have led to organizational success in past contexts are embedded deep in the mindsets and operational capabilities of long-serving family and non-family businesses alike. It is important to understand the defining moments and inflexion points that motivate long-lived family firms to make major strategic changes from a shareholder to stakeholder mindset. Perhaps, long-lived family firms owe their success to a quiet and covert focus on multi-stakeholder capitalism that needs to be unpacked and explained. What processes of change are used to convince the dominant stakeholders—not only family and non-family members within the business, but also external powerful stakeholders like major suppliers, customers and communities – to partner in undertaking the patient investments necessary for a sustainable journey? How do public policies and institutional environments hinder or drive such investments and changes for family enterprises?

To begin to understand these questions, this book features 15 families in three parts of first-generation founders (Part II), multi-generational legacy firms (Part III) and institutional champions of sustainability (Part IV). As we retrace the experiences, motivations and accomplishments of these pioneering business families that have successfully pursued sustainable development goals, it becomes clear that their success relies on continuous learning and innovation aptly symbolized by Jebsen & Jessen's "Three Mackerels"[54] that must "stay in motion to stay afloat." We find that enterprising families with a *commitment* to use their business as a force for societal good, *control* to make strategic decisions and patient investments in their business and a desire for transgenerational *continuity* are more likely to undertake the challenges of a sustainability journey. Within this group, those that invest the necessary time and effort to develop a clear statement of *purpose* for their business enterprise(s) that aligns with family values, embed *professionalism* in people, systems and processes in the business and build enduring *partnerships* with internal and external stakeholders can accelerate on this journey, build competitive advantages and reap significant financial returns. The three necessary business family conditions of *commitment*, *control* and *continuity* help to kick-start the sustainability journey, and the three critical family enterprise conditions of *purpose*, *professionalism* and *partnerships* fast-track this progress.

Once a family enterprise begins the sustainability journey by focusing on the SDGs, it moves beyond legitimacy or societal acceptance concerns into a universe of business opportunities in areas such as clean energy, clean water, Fairtrade supply chains, human health and hygiene, poverty reduction, etc., opening up new markets and industry segments. For example, when garnet recycling provided a novel business solution to maximize the life span of a non-renewable natural resource while at the same time increasing cost-effectiveness for garnet users, Jebsen & Jessen expanded its supply and production capacity to incorporate alluvial, crushed and recycled garnet, incorporated these circular economy principles in its ilmenite mines in South Africa and started providing specialist advice on recycling and its products in more than 80 countries. Cross-unit synergies between the heat generation process and energy conservation opened new markets and enhanced value creation for Thermax using its current infrastructure and assets. For Tahbilk, the wetlands conservation project opened unanticipated eco-tourism opportunities. Leveraging insights from helping farmers convert to organic practices, Griffith, Kemin and State Garden are well positioned to not only grow such agricultural practices but also their product lines. While the paint industry was still concerned about an annual sales decline of 30 percent a year of conventional paints, Royal Van Wijhe family leaders were already investing in new application opportunities for the next 50 years.

At the time of writing, as the world paused for the global Covid-19 pandemic in 2020, State Garden was energized in exploring opportunities to convert post-processing waste into usable products including vegetable juices and frozen products. With the rapid spread of the deadly virus, there were shortages of personal protective equipment. There were desperate pleas by governments for the business community and scientists to help with this dire state of affairs. Supreme worked with medical experts and the British Design Council to mass produce British-designed, Indian-made reusable eco-friendly face coverings[55] that went on sale with its partner retailers within a few weeks of the pandemic's onset. This rapid pivot was not easy since an entire line of new machines had to be procured, transported, installed and commissioned quickly, products designed and approved, materials acquired and staff trained – all amidst lock-downs in the UK and in India. As women are over 90 percent of its manufacturing staff this helped support the livelihoods of its families at a time when the pandemic hit hard both in India and in the UK. From the founder's perspective, this was simply the natural next step:[56]

> We have always been at the forefront of supporting the public through mass behavioral changes in positive and useful ways. Since the early 2000s we helped supermarkets, and retailers reduce their single-use plastic bag consumption by over five billion units through sustainable and reusable bags. A new challenge arose with the Coronavirus pandemic. Our aim is to manufacture high quality reusable non-medical face coverings designed by great British designers and in line with our scientific community. We hope to support the health of the British population and our government, whilst having a positive effect on both people and planet.

These pioneering business families provide lessons for other family and non-family firms seeking to transform their business into a force of good for society. While non-family firms have great strengths in professionalism and partnerships, they may need to find ways to develop the same level of continuity of commitment and purpose as well as the control to make patient investments without distractions of demonstrating short-term quarterly returns. For family enterprises desirous of longevity, our pioneers illustrate pragmatic ways to accomplish transgenerational aspirations while building an economically robust business that helps to sustain the environment and communities.

NOTES

1. World Commission on Environment and Development (1987). *Our Common Future* (Brundtland Report), vol. 383. Oxford: Oxford University Press.
2. Elkington, J. (1994). "Towards the sustainable corporation: Win-win-win business strategies for sustainable development." *California Management Review*, Winter: 90–100.
3. Chouinard, Y. & Stanley, V. (2012). *The Responsible Company: What We Learned from Patagonia's First 40 Years*. Ventura: Patagonia Books.
4. Anderson, R. (1998). *Mid-Course Correction: Toward a Sustainable Enterprise: The Interface Model*. London: Peregrinzilla Press.
5. Rau, S. B., Schneider-Siebke, V. & Gunther, C. (2019). "Family firm values explaining family firm heterogeneity." *Family Business Review*, 32(2): 195–215.
6. Sharma, P. & Sharma, S. (2011). "Drivers of proactive environmental strategy in family firms." *Business Ethics Quarterly*, 21(2): 309–32.
7. Sharma, S. & Sharma, P. (2019). *Patient Capital: The Role of Family Firms in Sustainable Business*. Cambridge: Cambridge University Press.
8. Combs, J. G., Gentry, R. J., Luz, S., Jaskiewicz, P. & Crook, T. R. (2020). "Corporate political activity and sensitivity to social attacks: The case of family-managed firms." *Family Business Review*, 33(2): 152–74.
9. Sharma, P. & Sharma, S. (2011). "Drivers of proactive environmental strategy in family firms." *Business Ethics Quarterly*, 21(2): 309–32.
10. Ibid.
11. De Massis, A., Frattini, F., Kotlar, J., Petruzzelli, A. M. & Wright, M. (2016). "Innovation through tradition: Lessons from innovative family businesses and directions for future research." *Academy of Management Perspectives*, 30(1): 93–116.
12. Sharma, S. & Vredenberg, H. (1998). "Proactive environmental responsiveness strategy and the development of competitively valuable organizational capabilities." *Strategic Management Journal*, 19(8): 729–53.
13. Chrisman, J. J. & Patel, P. C. (2012). "Variations in R&D investments of family and nonfamily firms: Behavioral agency and myopic loss aversion perspectives." *Academy of Management Journal*, 55(4): 9760997.
14. Delmas, M. A. & Gergaud, O. (2014). "Sustainable certification for future generations: The case of family business." *Family Business Review*, 27(3): 228–43.
15. Sharma, S. & Vredenberg, H. (1998). "Proactive environmental responsiveness strategy and the development of competitively valuable organizational capabilities." *Strategic Management Journal*, 19(8): 729–53.

16. Sharma, S., Pablo, A. & Vredenburg, H. (1999). "Corporate environmental responsiveness strategies: The role of issue interpretation and organizational context." *Journal of Applied Behavioral Science*, 35(1): 87–109.
17. Martínez, J. I., Stöhr, B. S. & Quiroga, B. F. (2007). "Family ownership and firm performance: Evidence from public companies in Chile." *Family Business Review*, 20: 83–94.
18. Hall, A. & Nordqvist, M. (2008). "Professional management in family business: Toward an extended understanding." *Family Business Review*, 21(1): 51–60.
19. Sharma, S. (2014). *Competing for a Sustainable World: Building Capacity for Sustainable Innovation*. Sheffield: Greenleaf Publishing.
20. Hart, S. L. & Sharma, S. (2004). "Engaging fringe stakeholders for competitive imagination." *Academy of Management Executive*, 18(1): 7–18.
21. Ibid.
22. Carney, M. & Nason, R. S. (2018). "Family business and the 1%." *Business and Society*, 57: 1191–215.
23. Dick, M., Wagner, E. & Pernsteiner, H. (2020). "Founder-controlled family firms, overconfidence, and corporate social responsibility engagement: Evidence from survey data." *Family Business Review*. https://doi.org/10.1177/0894486520918724
24. www.fbn-i.org/communities/polaris
25. Chrisman, J. J., Chua, J. H., De Massis, A., Frattini, F. & Wright, M. (2014). "The ability and willingness paradox in family firm innovation." *Journal of Product Innovation Management*, 32(3): 310–18.
26. Cruz, C., Justo, R., Larraza-Kintana, M. & Garces-Galdeano, L. (2019). "When do women make a better table? Examining the influence of women directors on family firm's corporate social performance." *Family Business Review*, 43(2): 282–301.
27. Their actual names are John S., Mark and Kevin. To distinguish them from family members in other generations who have the same first names, we used III for the third-generation brothers.
28. Nason, R., Mazzelli, A. & Carney, M. (2019). "The ties that unbind: Socialization and business-owning family reference point shift." *Academy of Management Review*, 44(4): 846–70.
29. https://en.wikipedia.org/wiki/Wallenberg_family
30. Barney, J. (1991). "Firm resources and sustained competitive advantage." *Journal of Management*, 17(1): 99–120.
31. Freeman R. E. (1984). *Strategic Management: A Stakeholder Approach*. Boston, MA: Pitman Publishing.
32. Gersick, K. E., Davis, J. A., McCollom Hampton, M. & Lansberg, I. (1997). *Generation to Generation: Life Cycles of Family Businesses*. Boston, MA: Harvard Business School Press.
33. Cruz, C., Larraza-Kintana, M., Garces-Galdeano, L. & Berrone, P. (2014). "Are family firms more socially responsible?" *Entrepreneurship Theory and Practice*, 38(6): 1295–316.
34. Bansal, P. & DesJardine, M. R. (2014). "Business sustainability: It's about time." *Strategic Organization*, 12(1): 70–8.
35. Dierickx, I. & Cool, K. (1989) "Asset stock accumulation and sustainability of competitive advantage." *Management Science*, 35, 1504–11.
36. Ibid., 1507.
37. Damon, W., Menon, J. & Bronk, K. C. (2003). "The development of purpose during adolescence." *Applied Developmental Science*, 7(3): 119–28.

38. Damon, W. (2008). *The Path to Purpose*. New York: Free Press; Jaffe, D. T., Lescent-Giles, I. & Traeger-Muney, J. (2019). Social impact in hundred-year family businesses: How family values drive sustainability through philanthropy, impact investing, and CSR. Working Paper 6: 100 Year Family Research Project.
39. Sharma, P. & Irving, G. (2005). "Four bases of family business successor commitment: Antecedents and consequences." *Entrepreneurship Theory and Practice*, 29(1): 13–33.
40. Ward, J. L. (2004). *Perpetuating the Family Business: 50 Lessons Learned from Long-Lasting, Successful Families in Business*. New York: Palgrave Macmillan.
41. Cohen, A. R. & Sharma, P. (2016). *Entrepreneurs in Every Generation: How Successful Family Businesses Develop Their Next Leaders*. San Francisco, CA: Berrett-Koehler Publishers.
42. Drucker, P. (1954). *The Practice of Management*. New York: Harper.
43. Doran, G. T. (1981). "There's a S.M.A.R.T. Way to Write Management's Goals and Objectives." *Management Review*, 70(11): 35–6.
44. www.wallenberg.com/en/family
45. Assessment link: Polaris Impact Assessment. www.fbn-i.org/sustainability/measure-your-impact
46. https://fbsd.unctad.org
47. https://iccwbo.org/media-wall/news-speeches/business-stepping-transformational-partnerships/
48. www.youtube.com/watch?v=85EuBUJ_Cww&feature=youtu.be
49. https://corporate.walmart.com/global-responsibility/global-responsibility-report-archive
50. www.fbn-i.org/sustainability/thought-leadership
51. Sharma, S. & Sharma, P. (2019). *Patient Capital: The Role of Family Firms in Sustainable Business*. Cambridge: Cambridge University Press.
52. Sharma, P. & Sharma, S. (2019). "Ideas in local spaces: Sustainability and family enterprise." In *The Oxford Handbook of Management Ideas*. Oxford: Oxford University Press.
53. Andrews, K. R. (1971). *The Concept of Corporate Strategy*. Homewood, IL: Richard D. Irwin; Ansoff, I. H. (1965). *Corporate Strategy: An Analytical Approach to Business Policy for Growth and Expansion*. New York: McGraw Hill.
54. www.jebsen.com/Jebsen/media/Jebsen/Three%20Mackerels/Three-Mackerels-Book-English.pdf?ext=.pdf
55. www.supreme-creations.co.uk/customized-reusable-face-mask.html
56. www.yorkshirepost.co.uk/lifestyle/shopping/british-designer-face-masks-go-sale-ps15-three-aid-nhs-charities-2875715#gsc.tab=0

PART II

Designed for sustainability

2. Sustainability comes naturally at the purpose-driven Rocky Mountain Soap Company

Pramodita Sharma, Sanjay Sharma and Alexa Steiner

Karina Birch and Cam Baty are the husband and wife team behind Rocky Mountain Soap Company (RMSC), a leader in the Canadian natural personal care industry. Based in Canmore, Alberta, Karina and Cam have owned and operated this first-generation family business for almost two decades. Cam grew up in Manitoba, Karina in Alberta and they met in the 1990s at an Arctic fishing lodge in a remote part of Canada. At that time, Cam was managing the lodge and hired Karina over the phone:

> It all started at that fishing lodge. The lodge really attracted like-minded people with connections to the natural world. I grew up on a family farm, and Cam grew up outdoors, hunting, so we've both been connected to nature throughout our lives. Our common connection to land, adventure and the outdoors is a big reason why we're now based in Canmore. (Karina Birch, Chief Executive Office)

Each with a business degree, Karina's from the University of Alberta and Cam's from Ryerson University in Toronto, in late 1999, the couple was looking for an opportunity to start a business. A chance gift purchase, from Cam to Karina, of soap from a local grocery store, spurred the opportunity that would define the couple's future. Owning a soap business was not necessarily the plan, but Karina and Cam have been paving the way as a sustainable family business since they took a risk and bought the small business two decades ago:

> Blind optimism fueled the first few years of the business, but perseverance and a great team helped us grow the company to what it is today. (Karina Birch, CEO)

Handmade products with a limited number of 100 percent natural, simple ingredients, is the mantra of RMSC. The foundation of the business has always stemmed from the couple's core purpose: to love nature and encourage more educated consumers to choose a toxin-free lifestyle.

Since 2000, Karina and Cam have grown their employee base to 180, with products being sold online and in over 100 retail locations. Currently, the company's annual growth rate is 15 percent, growing even more rapidly than the Canadian conventional beauty industry, that grew 9.4 percent as a whole, in 2017.[1] All the while, the couple has grown its nuclear family to five, with three children, now ages 14, 11 and 8. They have taken time to explore the world with their kids, leaving Canmore twice for extended trips to spend a few months in Europe. Taking this time off to enjoy with their family has helped to strengthen their leadership team and business:

> When we made the decision to travel with our kids, we wanted to test and see if the team could run the business effectively without us. They succeeded! The business continued to grow in our absence. (Cam Baty, Chief Operating Officer (COO))

> They were still checking in, so they weren't totally gone. The time went by quickly, but there was something really nice about when they came back – they are the business. Though it ran just fine while they were away, it was nice to have their physical presence back when they returned. (Jane Doyle, Retail Director)

A strong mission is the core of the company. Purpose-driven companies have proven over time to continually outperform their peers.[2] While continuing to build their purpose-driven business, Karina and Cam hope to pass along their beliefs and instill the love for the business and the natural world in their children.

COMPANY HISTORY

Before Karina and Cam purchased the company, it was a tiny, single-employee, home-based business that had been founded in Canmore three years earlier. The previous owner had just opened a small 450 square foot retail location in downtown Canmore and annual sales were about 80,000 dollars. Karina and Cam contemplated purchasing the company in December 1999, after Cam had discovered the product in a grocery store in Edmonton and gave it to Karina as a gift. She loved the product and they became regular customers of the brand. They became loyal followers and began even gifting RMSC products to their friends. Upon receiving consistent raving feedback, they recognized that the product was so good that people were hooked! Not long after, they started looking into the company as a potential business opportunity.

At the time, the couple was dating but lived in different cities. They had an interest in building a business together as they both had completed undergraduate degrees in business just a couple of years prior. Purchasing an existing business was an option, as was starting their own, and thus they saw the opportunity that this small company provided:

> We phoned a friend in Canmore, who happened to be the landlord for the existing retail location. We wanted to ask him what the town needed because we wanted to open a business in Canmore that filled a need. He put us in touch with the woman who owned Rocky Mountain Soap Company. She was looking to sell, so we went in to see it, and one month later we owned it! (Cam Baty, COO)

The entire purchase process took less than six weeks. During this time, Karina and Cam recognized the immense potential of the product but were also acutely aware of the existing deficiencies, such as the packaging, marketing and sales strategy. Despite these deficiencies, they knew why this product was so valuable; it was different from any other personal care product that was available at the time. Natural products were not popular or trendy in 2000; it was a niche market, and Karina and Cam had the foresight to recognize what was to come. The couple's passion for the natural world and its benefits, as well as Karina's background in aromatherapy, lent itself well to the industry they decided to enter.

Knowing that they had an incredible product was not enough. The business was losing money in the years before the purchase and their accountant advised Karina and Cam not to buy the sinking ship. Nevertheless, they decided to take a risk, and within a year, they had turned the business around. Karina and Cam purchased the store for about 45,000 dollars with a combination of personal savings, a 15,000 dollar bank loan and a personal line of credit. The initial founder of the company stayed on for about two weeks to hand over the business and provide them some training, but after that, the business was up to Karina and Cam.

One sticking point for the couple, when they bought the company, was the marketing of an "all-natural" product that was not truly all natural. At that time, some of the products contained artificially fragranced oils that rendered the product less than 100 percent natural. For example, their berry scent was their top-selling scent across the product line at the time, but it contained a fragrance oil that was not 100 percent natural. Karina and Cam sat down with their employees to discuss this issue. In the early 2000s, no one in the industry knew how to formulate a 100 percent natural personal care product, mostly because saying that a product had 85–95 percent natural ingredients had proven to be "good enough" for consumers. As most customers did not ask questions about ingredients, brands did not have to adjust themselves to demands for transparency, as is the case now. Most of RMSC's contracted suppliers and chemists did not support going 100 percent natural. Karina and Cam faced a lot of pressure to follow the prevalent industry standards, but their own beliefs and a strong support from their employees led them to reconsider their product formulations to achieve 100 percent natural ingredients. This led to the discontinuation of some of the company's most popular products. They did so based on their core principles even though it was clearly not the smartest financial decision as their most popular products were the chemically fragranced ones:

> We were tiny, and terrified about the impact removing that scent could have on our sales. In the end, it actually did not hurt us. It just increased the trust our customers had in us. (Cam Baty, COO)

Decisions like these are the bedrock that a company stands upon. Even though to this day there is debate in the personal care industry regarding the necessity of 100 percent natural formulas,[3] Karina explained the rationale for their decision as follows:

> Whether it was mashed avocado on my face or an egg in my hair, I've loved experimenting with natural ingredients since I was a little girl. I have always believed that if it came from nature it was the best you could get. I believe that the earth provides more than enough natural ingredients to give us beautiful and healthy skin for life. I believe that body care should provide more than a sweet-smelling experience, it should be beneficial to our health and our psychological well-being. I believe that parents deserve peace-of-mind when choosing products for their families. Shopping for skin and body care should be a purely joyful experience.
>
> **Today, our industry uses over 85,000 chemicals and only a fraction of them have been tested for their long-term effects, I don't think that's good enough, and our industry needs to change. It's my personal vision, and the mission of our company to be unwavering in our commitment to toxin-free, so you can shop with the freedom of knowing that everything we make is safe and good for you. (Karina Birch, CEO)**

Having made the commitment to make 100 percent natural products and support a toxin-free environment, RMSC adopted a patient capital strategy of investing in further research and development (R&D) for natural product formulations. However, to remain competitive in the marketplace, it made the difficult decision of maintaining the same pricing strategy, while also trying to maintain production costs.

Much to Karina and Cam's surprise, loyal customers praised them for making that decision and appreciated the evolution of the brand to be even more honest than the market demanded, and go above and beyond industry standards:

> Karina actually overheard some customers talking about this change on the street outside the store. They were praising us for the decision we made. To hear that was

really validating that there really was an audience for the mission we were sticking to. (Cam Baty, COO)

To support their efforts, their customers purchased more of the truly all-natural products and began recommending the company's products to others. Sales began to increase, energizing RMSC to double up its efforts towards 100 percent natural product development:

> Especially living here in the Rockies, we are constantly reminded how fragile the environment is and we want to help embrace and celebrate it. (Karina Birch, CEO)

THE NATURAL PERSONAL CARE PRODUCTS INDUSTRY

Globally, the organic and natural personal care market was estimated at 13.33 billion United States dollars in 2018. The projected compound annual growth rate is 9.4 percent from 2019 to 2025. North America leads in this category and the trend is expected to continue over the next six years. Increasing consumer awareness is the driving factor for the demand for these types of products. Consumers are becoming more aware of the benefits of natural and organic products in comparison to chemical or synthetic alternatives, and thus the demand for personal care products has increased. The rising desire for environmentally friendly and cruelty-free products is expected to continue to increase product demand.[4]

Kline Research conducted a study in 2016 that concluded a growing number of consumers are willing to pay a premium for products that are natural or perceived as natural. Realizing this, large cosmetic companies have begun to spend significant dollars on R&D to develop new organic product offerings and are trying to play in the natural space.[5] Because of this recent focus from larger companies, the natural personal care market has become a focus of the industry over the past few years. This trend is not expected to slow, as consumers become more educated and pay more attention to the ingredients that they are using on their bodies each day.

Larger personal care companies that have begun to change their strategy toward more environmentally friendly operations are focusing their efforts on strategic acquisitions of natural and sustainable companies to learn, build expertise and add natural lines of products. With evolving consumer consciousness, these larger companies are looking to gain further core competencies in ethical production. According to CB Insights, 62 privately held beauty companies were acquired in 2016, 38 percent more than the previous year. In recent years, Clorox purchased Burt's Bees, and Colgate acquired Tom's of Maine. These are just a few examples of the significance of the strategic acquisitions in this market. Bigger businesses are making these power plays for sustainable businesses to acquire the knowledge and expertise of smaller firms. The larger companies are continually evaluating what new brands could strategically fit within their portfolio and add value to the core competencies of the business.[6]

The current emphasis on all-natural and organic beauty products has opened an opportunity for new entrants to emerge in the personal care industry with better versions of products catering to consumer needs; however, with the entry of these new companies, it has become increasingly more difficult to create a brand with a solid reputation, and achieve economies of scale. Capturing significant market share in this industry is a challenge for smaller companies with smaller budgets to spend on marketing and advertising. Constant innovation and investment in technology are necessary. Small-scale competitors, such as RMSC, create value-added products and have gained deep customer loyalty, and hence have continued to gain market share.[7]

OPERATIONS

When asked about the structure and governance of RMSC, Cam Baty noted:

> The first person we hired was a woman named Judith, who we hired in 2000. She worked part time in retail and part time in production. It was all six of our hands-on deck back then. After about a year, retail separated into its own department and Judith went on to manage that area. After retail and production employees, our next areas that we hired for were shipping and accounting. We were figuring it out as we went, and now we have a thriving employee base with a little bit more structure.

While functioning as co-entrepreneurs early on, Karina and Cam eventually agreed that Karina would be the CEO and Cam would be the COO. Cam explained how this decision came to be as follows:

> When we bought the company, I was working elsewhere. Within nine months of owning RMSC, I was full time here. Ten years later, after we had kids, Karina was coming back to work full time. She had worked during the early years we had kids, but in 2012 she came back full time. At that time, we had a different CEO, and Karina came back to manage that person. I was working on other projects around that time as well. In 2013, we both decided that we both wanted to be back at RMSC full time and we changed the structure to reflect more like what you see today. We knew we needed a formalized structure in case a difficult decision needed to be made, so that's why Karina is CEO. At the end of the day, titles don't matter to us that much. It's a really collaborative environment and we all work together to achieve what we need to every day. (Cam Baty, COO)

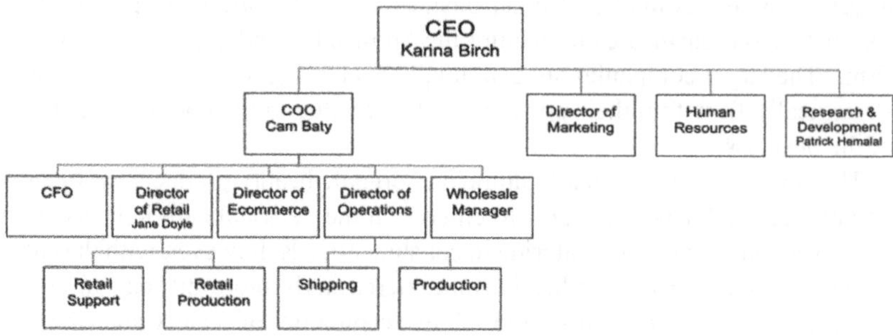

Figure 2.1 *Rocky Mountain Soap Company organizational chart*

The structure of the company is simple (Figure 2.1). In addition to the couple as CEO and COO, the top management team includes the three directors of marketing, human resource management and research and development, all reporting to both Karina and Cam. There are additional directors or managers responsible for operations, retail, e-commerce and wholesale operations, reporting to the COO, Cam Baty. The structure is fairly lean and flat and enables close coordination, for example between retail and production and shipping. Each director has a technical specialist working with them, with the exception of retail, as the retail director oversees all of the retail location managers. The company is currently seeking to hire a vice-president to lead new market development. This experienced professional will help them grow the business both in physical locations as well as online:

> **Our current web developer started as a soap maker 15 years ago. There's room for upward mobility here and we like to foster our employees' professional growth and support it however we can. *Longevity matters to us.* Jane, our current Retail Director, has been with us for over 12 years. (Karina Birch, CEO)**

With Karina in charge of product development and marketing, and Cam handling production and capital investment, there is a clear division of labor and responsibilities. Although there is general alignment of values and overarching vision, at times there are disagreements among the leadership. RMSC values an inclusive decision-making process and holds monthly board and leadership team meetings where important decisions are discussed. This team includes the CEO, COO, chief financial officer (CFO), head of R&D, director of marketing, director of retail, web strategist, operations manager and sometimes the product innovation team. Quarterly strategies are determined by this team and are communicated to all employees:

> Ultimately, when it comes to stalemate decisions, Karina has the final say as the CEO, though I don't believe she has ever had to use that power. (Cam Baty, COO)

RMSC's goal is to not be a command and control organization and there is an emphasis on a flat rather than a hierarchical organizational structure. There are two human resources employees, one who has quarterly conversations with the executive team about leadership and outlines clear performance management goals for all employees, while the other is a recruiter and works on the hiring process. As with many companies, Cam notes that there is a culture and communication gap between the headquarters and the retail stores; however, the team is actively trying to bridge that gap in creative and authentic ways.

Currently, RMSC has about 180 employees all over Canada. Early on, RMSC developed a core purpose and five values that govern the way it does business and the way it recruits, trains and retains its employees. These values are "Positivitude," "Give it a go," "Be kind," "Customer service is an extreme sport," and "Cultivate team spirit," and are visibly written on the walls of the business (Figure 2.2).[8]

Figure 2.2 *RMSC's core values on the wall of its head office*

Karina and Cam strongly believe that their hiring practices and the entire employee experience should reflect these values. Culture is important for them. In their regular *Monday morning meeting with all corporate employees, each member shares stories sharing an example or two that links their past week experience to one or more core values.* The company's elected "culture mayor" is in charge of creating fun activities and events that keep the core values alive. These events are mostly for corporate employees and retail managers, though some invitations are extended to retail staff:

> Our Culture Mayor recently planned our awesome 20th anniversary winter celebration, which was a big holiday party in the new year, with a ski day, dinner, ceremony, and party. She also leads the culture team of five employees who take turns planning the AGM, organizing fun activities in the office like "yoga in the workshop" twice a week, fitness classes like spinning and Crossfit. (Cam Baty, COO)

> At RMSC, leadership is about conversation and asking questions. We have a training, onboarding, and leadership book and each new employee is given a copy. There is a strong focus on team happiness and the relationship between company culture and leadership development. We want to foster an environment where people are excited to come to work because they are passionate about the product and feel supported by the company. (Karina Birch, CEO)

Alongside the core values, innovation and wellness are big pieces of the culture puzzle at RMSC. The company also hosts a semi-annual retreat in Canmore for managers and assistant managers of the retail locations. Impressively, the employee turnover rate is less than 10 percent, and exit interviews are conducted with every employee that leaves.

Employees flock to RMSC not just for a paycheck, but for alignment with their values and lifestyle. Jane Doyle, the retail director shared:

> I started at RMSC in 2008. Something that has always mattered to me is working with a company guided by purpose. I met Karina and Cam and had a feeling that there was a soul, a purpose to what they were trying to do. When I came to RMSC, there was a culture and environment that encouraged creation and innovation. There was no manual to tell me what to do, so there was an opportunity to create, which was honestly challenging at times. Through that, the purpose of the business never changed – Karina and Cam never swayed from their ethics and that is really important to me. (Jane Doyle, Retail Director)

Patrick Hemalal, the R&D director, added:

> In 2015, while I was working for Colgate Palmolive, Karina was looking for a chief Chemist, someone to lead the research and development area. One of my friends connected me to Karina via LinkedIn. I was in Sri Lanka at that time, where I am originally from. In January of 2015, I came to Canmore for an interview. Karina was

> so nice to me, driving me to and from the bus station. Not long after, in May, I ended up in Canmore. We both took a great risk, that has paid off and I am now a Canadian permanent resident. This is a small company with great potential. I get to work for really nice people every day, in an entrepreneurial environment, with autonomy to make decisions. Plus, I get to live in Canmore. (Patrick Hemalal, R&D Director)

Over the years, RMSC has received business advice and guidance from outside sources. Cam and Karina looked for guidance from Sean Durfy, former CEO of WestJet. He came on board with RMSC as a mentor for a few years. Cam says they learned a lot from him and his business experience, and now, years later, WestJet purchases RMSC products wholesale for use on planes.[9] Another, more informal, mentor is Mark Wolverton, the co-founder and CEO of Lush North America. Cam and Karina have called him up over the years with questions about the industry. Lush is a personal care brand, originally founded in the United Kingdom, which was licensed by Mark Wolverton for North America and is based in Vancouver. It is about 10 years older as a company than RMSC.[10] Cam stresses how important it is to have people to trust as mentors and advisors, both from the industry one is in, and outside of it:

> For the last three years or so, we have been working with Glenn Huber, the Founder of Chrysalis Capital. He has extensive experience in private equity, business, and financial advising. He is actually the first member of the advisory board we are in the process of building. That board is in really early stages, currently in the planning phase. He is helping us build it out. (Karina Birch, CEO)

The company has worked with outside consultants in the past particularly to help its branding and marketing efforts, though the preference of Cam and Karina is to do everything they can in-house to ensure consistency and inclusivity.

In terms of the supply chain, sourcing high-quality natural ingredients is a priority for Karina and Cam. RMSC's products use plant-based natural ingredients sourced from around the world. Canadian food distributors are the company's primary source of ingredients, except shea butter that is sourced directly from an organic supplier in Africa:

> Sourcing locally is a priority for us and we try to do it whenever we can. It's not always realistic, so we maintain transparent and ethical sourcing practices as we gather ingredients from producers around the world. (Karina Birch, CEO)

RMSC uses all-natural ingredients and prides itself in its transparency and commitment to quality. All ingredients used in its products are 100 percent natural, that is, extracted and processed from the earth without any negative environmental impact:[11]

> Credibility to our customer is important to us. Early on, we did not have a proper check list for our suppliers. We developed a science-based vetting process for our supply chain with factors including sustainability considerations, process, safety, environmental damage. All of our ingredients must be natural and we were willing to make business sacrifices along the way to ensure that we live up to this commitment to our customers. (Patrick Hemalal, R&D Director)

All products are made in small batches to maintain freshness and ingredient lists are kept small, usually under 10, to maintain transparency. Simpler formulations and small batches allow RMSC to choose ingredients deliberately for quality and benefits. Unlike conventional personal-care products, fillers are never used in its products. Sustainable sourcing practices are prioritized as well. Organic ingredients are used whenever possible and RMSC prioritizes working with local farmers, growers and wild foragers across Canada. A list of Canadian sources can be found on the RMSC website. The company will not purchase ingredients from any source that has negative impacts on any animals or species habitats or the environment in general:[12]

> The evolution of the products has looked more like a circle than a line. (Cam Baty, COO)

When they purchased the company, the recipes were very basic and simple, with no water or preservatives. As the product offerings evolved, so did the need for more complex formulas, some involving water. As these complexities developed, external chemists were hired to manage the process and provide recommendations. Eventually, chemists, now led by Patrick Hemalal, were hired internally to continue innovating with new ingredients and formulas:

> In more recent years, we discovered that we had an ingredient in our shampoo that just wasn't sustainable. I remember us all sitting together and deciding that the right thing to do was take it out, despite that product accounting for about 10% of our sales. (Jane Doyle, Retail Director)

Around 2015, the discussion turned to having a mantra of "10 ingredients or less." It was becoming more difficult to stick to smaller ingredient lists as the product lines expanded, and Karina, Cam and their leadership team wanted to make a strong commitment that could guide them through the product innovation process. Thus, the "10 ingredients or less" mantra came about. This mantra does not come without its challenges, as it is difficult to make products like face care and body lotion with just 10 ingredients:

> **Making something look and feel right for the customer is still so important. So this 10 ingredients or less rule poses an interesting challenge for us with more complex products.**
> We are working every day to make sure that our products are simple, natural, but also feel and look right for our customers. They also need to preserve well, so that adds an extra layer of complexity! We have incredible professionals working on these innovations. (Cam Baty, COO)

> I am a chartered chemist, majoring in chemistry and specializing in natural products. My doctoral degree was to architect biologically active molecules for commercial use. After my PhD, I worked for a few corporations, including Colgate Palmolive, and now I am here, working with natural ingredients all the time. (Patrick Hemalal, R&D Director)

SALES AND MARKETING

Within the first year of purchasing the company, in 2001, Karina and Cam moved the retail location to Canmore's main street that attracted more tourist traffic. This move proved to be prudent as retail sales jumped from 80,000 to 250,000 dollars within a year. Soon, they opened a second retail location just down the road in another popular tourist mountain town, Banff. This was RMSC's first step in becoming a multi-unit retailer.

The Canadian Rockies are Alberta's most iconic attraction, and one of Canada's most sought-after travel destinations by fellow Canadians as well as international travelers. Canmore's economy, like other Alberta mountain towns, Jasper and Banff, relies heavily on the tourism sector.[13] Companies like RMSC benefit from the heavy foot traffic on Canmore's main street, the economic center of the town.

The company now has 12 company-owned retail locations throughout western and central Canada, along with a few temporary pop-up stores that stay open for a short period of time as a trial run for a potential long-term location. The products are also sold at over 100 other retailers across Canada. RMSC retail locations in Alberta are quite successful, pulling in the highest number of sales for the company. RMSC has a strong reputation and a loyal customer base in Alberta. Word-of-mouth marketing has been a significant contributor to the success of the business within the province:

> Two franchises were opened in the early 2000s. One stayed open for three years, and the other for six. Honestly, we didn't like having franchises and are staying away from that model now. The risk you think you are avoiding, you are still faced with. The responsibility is still there because our name is on the lease, but we don't get the

> reward or the control. Investors have approached us wanting equity in our company over the years, but we just haven't entertained those offers. (Cam Baty, COO)

Expanding outside of Alberta has posed issues. One store and two pop-up shops were opened in Toronto (about 3,500 km away from Canmore), but all closed within six months of entering that market. Because of these lessons, long-term planning for retail locations outside of Alberta is a priority that Karina and Cam are focusing efforts on now:

> We've been in Alberta for 20 years, so just through that, we have basic brand awareness. What we've seen in other cities is customers coming in, but they aren't quite sure, so they come in and buy maybe one soap. The trust isn't there yet, so they are seeing if we are who we say we are. Brand awareness takes time. (Jane Doyle, Retail Director)

Natural and organic have become lifestyle terms, reflecting aspirations for good health, hygiene and beauty. The popularity of these products has led to an increase in the distribution channels and ease of access. E-commerce has created even more access to different types of products, allowing companies to reach consumers that were once geographically unattainable, and vice versa. The growing need for convenience and personalization of products has given brands and retailers the opportunity to expand digital footprints and grow their customer base.

RMSC was ahead of the curve with online presence, creating its company website in 2002, though it was never a major priority. Online sales grew slowly but steadily at about 20 percent annually. Less than a decade ago, the company prioritized the website and the potential for increasing online sales. Employees were hired to run e-commerce, and today online sales account for 22 percent of RMSC's business. It is a big growth channel, and the company is starting to now prioritize social media and digital marketing as well. RMSC products are available through the company website, as well as through Canadian online retailer Well.ca, Canada's largest e-commerce provider of natural brands:[14]

> I'd say 60% of our marketing at this point is digital. We are still investing the other 40% in more traditional methods. The lines are blurry with our marketing budget, as efforts in each category can bleed into the other, though we have increased our online and digital budget significantly over the last couple of years. (Cam Baty, COO)

As new technologies provide for more personalized experiences, direct marketing will continue to disrupt the traditional retail distribution network. Direct-to-consumer brands saw a significant increase in market share in 2017. According to a study carried out in 2017, 90 percent of consumers prefer to buy directly from a brand if they have the option. This new strategy of direct marketing, selling directly to the consumer and bypassing traditional distribution networks, is changing the industry. Direct-to-consumer marketing is one of the main forces changing the industry right now. The fragmented, unconsolidated and highly competitive marketplace allows for smaller brands to utilize social media and digital, direct-to-consumer marketing strategies to break down traditional marketing and distribution barriers to entry.[15]

Early in 2020, e-commerce made up 22 percent of RMSC's sales, while 10 percent came from wholesale, and the majority of sales, 68 percent, came from retail. The ratio changed as physical retail operations were shut down during the 2020 Covid-19 pandemic. During the lock-down of the retail operations, RMSC's loyal customers raised its online sales by eight-fold. It will be interesting to see how this ratio stabilizes as retail operations gradually open up as the Covid-19 virus is brought under control during 2020–21.

The growth of business-to-business (B2B) e-commerce had also emerged in recent years and a study in 2016 concluded that almost half of Canadian B2B sellers generate 25 percent of their business online. A study in the United States suggests that B2B e-commerce will account for 1.2 trillion United States dollars by 2021, which is double the size of the American business-to-consumer e-commerce market.[16] Interestingly, more than half of Canadian small businesses do not have an online presence to conduct sales, and shipping across the country can pose issues for smaller businesses. Small Canadian businesses also lose because more than 33 percent of Canadian consumer e-commerce transactions occur with American businesses.[17] Currently, wholesale is not a big part of the business. Karina and Cam tend to think of wholesale or B2B as more of an awareness channel, where consumers who would not normally be exposed to their products get to test them out. A good example of this is their recent partnership with WestJet airline as the airline's soap provider.

RMSC has already done the work in prioritizing natural and toxin-free products, and has continued to research and innovate in this space. Because of this, the company does not need to change its business drastically to reflect changing consumer preferences for natural ingredients and environmental preservation, the way other existing businesses need to. However, the market is becoming increasingly saturated with healthier, toxin-free options and innovation is key to maintaining relevance and market share. RMSC is differentiating itself by prioritizing sustainability in every aspect of the business, but will need to continue to grow market share to compete with American brands that are permeating the Canadian market.

Lush, the Body Shop and Saje Wellness are RMSC's biggest competition in the Canadian market. These competitors also have brick-and-mortar stores in Canada. To the very astute customer, RMSC is the *only one* of those options that makes *truly 100 percent natural products*. However, most customers are less knowledgeable and liken the value proposition of these brands similarly to that of RMSC.

ENVIRONMENTAL AND SOCIAL SUSTAINABILITY: CORE VALUE AND CORPORATE PURPOSE

In Canada, the market for natural personal-care products is almost 1 billion Canadian dollars. At more than 10 percent annual growth, the Canadian market is growing at a slightly faster rate than the United States market. Consumers are looking for products that provide multiple benefits and are made from more natural ingredients. A study in *Cosmetics Magazine* indicated that the top three determinants of consumer trust are a company's ability to respond to issues and provide product information and transparency about how products are made. Canadian consumers are making smarter choices and holding companies to a higher standard than consumers in most other countries.[18] This bodes well for an already transparent and responsible company like RMSC, but also means that other companies are beginning to rise to the occasion and address consumer demands. As these larger companies look for "greener" alternatives and regulations are slowly catching up in countries like Canada, consumers are also becoming more adept at spotting attempts to greenwash, that is, when a product or brand projects itself as more environmentally responsible than it truly is.

Part of what makes RMSC sustainable is its commitment to its values and purpose that is kept alive through strategic as well as operational decisions. From the ingredients in its products to the onboarding process, purpose is instilled in everything it does. The company values are quite literally written on the wall.

While RMSC measures and prioritizes environmental impact, Karina and Cam work hard to extend their impact to include the broader definition of sustainability, with a focus on community engagement and corporate social responsibility. Responsibility is embedded in the core of RMSC's business strategy and drives the purpose.

RMSC prioritizes sustainability in its physical spaces. Its workshop and stores are filled with recycled and eco-friendly materials. Salvaged and reclaimed wood make for excellent display cases. Marble, light fixtures and carpets, all reclaimed, create texture and character throughout the spaces. LED lights and low VOC paint are used for the most sustainable spaces. The corporate office and retail space in Canmore are powered by renewable energy by Bullfrog Power and rooftop solar panels.[19] In the spirit of true transparency, tours of the Canmore-based factory are offered to the public to see how the products are made. These tours are equally popular with locals and tourists.

Although the only mention of the tours is on the company's website and no advertising efforts are made, approximately 2,500 people take the tour annually, and several come back multiple times with family and friends.

Packaging is one of the more challenging areas in achieving the family's core values and corporate mission of sustainability. This is a challenge for all companies in the consumer packaged goods.

Most products, even natural ones, come packaged in plastic that is used once, and then sits in landfill for 100+ years.

Karina and Cam acknowledge the gap that exists in the beauty industry between how long a product lasts and how long the packaging lasts. These concerns have troubled them since the inception of RMSC as they strongly believe that good-quality packaging does not have to be indestructible. Incremental adjustments have been made towards more sustainable packaging choices. Examples include updating soap recipes so there is no waste, using biodegradable edible packing peanuts instead of the more wasteful, non-biodegradable option, choosing recyclable or compostable packaging and reusing shipping boxes and materials. RMSC is also conscious of not using extra packaging, meaning that there are no extra boxes involved – no product inside of a box, inside of another box – a practice that is common amongst other consumer packaged goods brands. For example, according to RMSC, the cardboard that most personal-care products are surrounded by contributes to the loss of 18 million acres of forest each year.[20] The commitment to sustainable packaging is clear when walking into any RMSC retail location. Most of the soap is presented without any packaging, and almost everything else has only one layer of packaging. The company follows its mantra of "what you see is what you get:"

> Customers were saying for years that they wanted a refill program, so we put one in our Canmore store. As of now, not many people are using it. It's interesting because the usage of this program is less than the perceived demand. Customers feel good about us as a brand doing the refill program, but they are still buying off the shelf. That's what we're seeing, but are hoping that will slowly start to change. (Jane Doyle, Retail Director)

As it inches closer to the ambitious goal of eventually becoming a zero-waste company, the goal of diverting all waste from landfills is not easily achievable. More recently RMSC has attacked this issue head on becoming even more innovative with its packaging decisions. For example, its Lip Quench product container is completely biodegradable and it has launched recycled (non-virgin) plastic packaging. The physical appearance of more sustainable packaging poses an interesting dilemma as a recycled plastic bottle has a slight yellow tinge and is not as clear or transparent as traditional packaging. As consumers are used to purchasing products with attractive packaging, the larger and more influential consumer packaged goods product manufacturers have resisted such changes. Thus, RMSC and other environmentally conscious companies face an inherent risk in choosing more sustainable packaging as it may be less appealing to certain customers. Perseverance and commitment to innovation and sustainability is tested with every batch of product that leaves its manufacturing facility. The family's patient capital philosophy is evident in the risk that it is willing to take, as noted by Cam:

> **We don't believe our products are truly natural if the packages are not 100% natural.**

RMSC has worked extensively with the Sustainable Packaging Coalition in the last six years on packaging options for its other products. This research indicated that paper is the most sustainable option, with post-consumer recycled plastic coming in second. Glass scored lower in many of the categories of research and generates more emissions in shipping due to weight. RMSC is currently working on switching over to the best plastic options, like using bio-based and post-consumer resins. It is also working to eliminate the need for most plastic by offering more refillable options as well as non-packaged options like shampoo bars (Figure 2.3):

> An exciting newer sustainability initiative is the pilot returnable refill program. We have bins in stores where a customer can bring back their one liter bottles. We take those bottles, clean them, refurbish them and put them back on the shelf. People have really been supportive and have been buying the refurbished bottles. So currently, we are trying to figure out the details with this one liter program, work out the kinks, and roll out the same idea with other sized bottles. We're always rethinking sustainability in our packaging. (Cam Baty, COO)

In terms of production, the following sustainability principles are followed by RMSC when deciding on the ingredients in its products:

- Guaranteed to be found in nature and good for you.
- As organic and local as is available.
- Will not be produced or extracted through environmentally harmful processes.
- Will not have harmful impacts on your body.[21]

The formulation and creation process for the products is taken seriously, and it often takes a few years to get a combination right. The formulas are designed by chemists and tested scientifically and extensively to ensure the best and safest product for consumers. RMSC products are never tested on animals, nor will the products harm natural habitats or aquatic life when they go down the drain and out into the environment. Not only does this require patience from the owners as coming up with usable products takes time and scientists must be

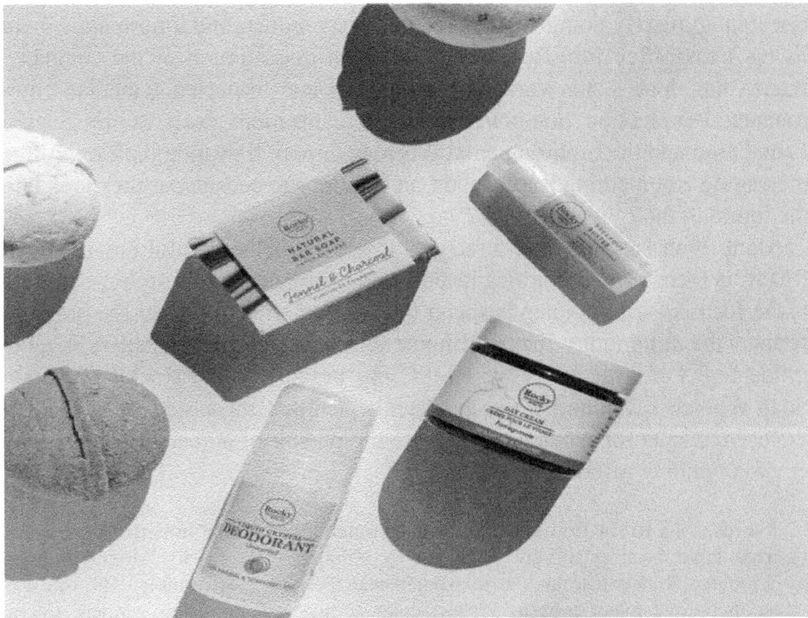

Figure 2.3 *A sampling of RMSC products like bath bombs, lip balm and deodorant in different types of packaging*

paid regularly, but there is an inherent risk of intellectual property theft. Cam explains the process and risks as follows:

> We have IP [intellectual property] trademarks on our name and logo but there is no protection of our formulas. We have been so focused on getting them right and staying committed to our mission of natural.

The company is also doing its part to ensure consumers are educated about ingredients. On RMSC's website, there are two lists, the "Red List" and the "Green List," consisting of exactly what one would imagine lists with those names would contain – ingredients that are used in Rocky Mountain Soap products, and those that will never be used. Each of the "green" ingredients has an explanation of why it is used. Also available online is the company's "Naturalpedia," a platform where it shares its knowledge about fresh, natural ingredients and benefits.[22] RMSC has yet to complete life-cycle analysis of the products. This may be something it considers as the product offerings grow and there is naturally less direct oversight and management of where the ingredients are coming from.

RMSC's toxin-free community is a promotional program that customers can sign up for. By doing so, they receive free products and information about living a toxin-free life. Because of the toxin-free mission of the company, Karina has done some work with prominent and respected Canadian environmental protection non-governmental organizations such as the Suzuki Foundation and the Environmental Working Group. Elevating their toxin-free messaging is something Karina and Cam continue to consider as they look into the future of their business.

Along with sustainability strategies that protect the natural environment, RMSC is focused on promoting healthy and well-balanced lifestyles. Canmore is the focus of the company's social impact as Karina and Cam are proud to support the community they call home and in which their business is quite influential. For over 10 years, RMSC has organized The Rocky Mountain Soap Women's Run and Walk, an annual event that encourages safe, fun and inclusive events for women that inspire the pursuit of an active, healthy and environmentally responsible lifestyle:

> It's inspiring to see how running brings women together and how many women's lives have been positively impacted by running. The Rocky Mountain Soap Women's Run is a testament to women and the power of running. The run was an incredible experience in a spectacular setting with amazing women! (Vera, Women's Run Participant)

The event builds a community platform that offers knowledge and expertise of wellness professionals and supports charitable organizations each year. Well-being stations are available at the post-race reception and RMSC is proud to sponsor this event every year creating an unforgettable experience for women of all ages and fitness levels. The event is widely attended, with people visiting Canmore from surrounding towns and cities, like Calgary, to participate.[23]

Aside from the clear environmental mission and this annual run event, Karina and Cam have implemented other corporate social responsibility initiatives as well. They sponsored a Canadian Olympian who competed in the biathlon in the most recent Olympic Games. Also, since 2015, the company has sent three staff members to communities in Liberia in Africa and India to teach soap making. The hope for these visits is to teach skills to help locals create business opportunities in communities in developing nations. As the company grows, there will be further opportunities to extend social impact.

THE FUTURE

> Building trust with our customers – that is our focus. (Cam Baty, COO)

There are obstacles that the business will need to overcome in the coming years. Karina and Cam have mentioned their intention to expand the scope of the leadership team to add an expert in larger-scale consumer packaged goods as a permanent leadership team member to help grow the business across Canada. They understand that better strategy needs to be in place to expand the brick-and-mortar stores, and bringing in someone with expertise would be a healthy first step:

> In another ten years, I think the heart of the company will still be the bath and body products, though distribution channels may be changing. It will be interesting to see the market demand for natural products and how we react to it. It would be great to think that Cam and Karina's children might be involved in the business. Their oldest actually sat in on one of our strategic planning sessions, so the seed is being planted young. What I know is that Karina's passion for natural and toxin-free will continue to be the guiding light. (Jane Doyle, Retail Director)

With the increasing popularity of the direct-to-consumer market, especially in the personal-care industry, RMSC's leadership team recognizes the opportunity to expand the company's digital presence and create a more robust social media strategy. For example, currently, RMSC has about 30,000 followers on Instagram, in sharp contrast to the 220,000 followers of Saje Wellness, a direct competitor.[24] As consumers increasingly continue to shop online,[25] RMSC has an opportunity to expand its e-commerce presence and could consider expanding to retailers with broader online markets like Grove Collaborative or Sephora. As noted by Patrick Hemalal, the R&D director:

> The business will grow as the demand for natural products is growing. Premium sub-branding may happen as well – you never know. The market will grow and we will hopefully expand across Canada, the US and Europe.

As mentioned above, during the Covid-19 pandemic in 2020, as physical retail operations were shut down, online sales increased eight-fold, and it will be interesting to see how the ratio of physical retail sales and online sales stabilizes once the pandemic is brought under control. It is very likely that the ratio of online sales will stay much higher and continue to grow in the future.

Branding is a huge part of this challenge. As RMSC continues to grow, the leadership is reconsidering the branding of the company as a soap company. Right now, the company is somewhat limited by its name, as some consumers might hear "Rocky Mountain Soap Company" and make incorrect assumptions about what kind of products might be available there. The leadership is discussing the idea of keeping the flagship brand and expanding with sub-brands for hair and skin-care lines. Another option is a complete rebrand, though that would be a huge challenge to regain brand recognition with its existing customer base. Partnerships, certifications and advocacy work are all avenues that the leadership is exploring for the company's future and to expand RMSC's network.

The future is bright for RMSC. Twenty years ago, Karina and Cam bought a small failing company and entered a niche market. Now, green businesses are part of the mainstream in Canada and the United States. Innovation will continue to determine the company's path forward. RMSC chemists will continue to work on emerging technologies, and have hopes to discover new active molecules to be able to invent new plant-based formulas and products. There is a network of chemists in Canada working with local plants on the science of formulation and RMSC hopes to integrate even more local Canadian ingredients into its product lines. Karina and Cam aspire to enter new markets, and potentially develop sub-brands, beginning with the potential for an all-natural skin-care line and continuing the company's innovative work on a natural hand sanitizer:

> I feel very lucky to work for Cam and Karina. I love that we are still growing and innovating and we won't settle. There's something amazing when you have a group of people that have the same belief, the same reasons why, and where that can take you. To be able to be challenged every day – I feel blessed to be a part of it. (Jane Doyle, Retail Director)

Taking a next-generation approach, Karina and Cam are eager to educate their children about the business, but are also supportive of their kids forging their own paths, just like they did. The future of this business being run by one of their kids is uncertain, though their oldest daughter has expressed interest in expanding her business education:

> We are thinking about the future of the company, but aren't making a specific plan. Right now, our kids are interested in what we do, but we don't want to count on them wanting to run it. We want them to do what they want to do. We will see what happens! (Cam Baty, COO)

For now, Karina and Cam intend to continue in their leadership roles, spread the company's mission and help the business flourish even more. Who knows what the future will hold, but one thing is for certain, over the last 20 years, RMSC has developed into a sustainable family business with purpose and passion behind every step:

> When I think about RMSC 10, 20 years down the line, I picture a successful expansion throughout Canada, maybe Asia and the US, with a strong online presence. I have hopes that we will still be based out of Canmore, and will still be a private company, run by family. Ultimately, our goal will still be to provide the best natural, toxin-free options to our customers. (Cam Baty, COO)

Figure 2.4 *Karina and Cam with their three children*

CONCLUSION

It is often argued that it is easier to start a sustainable company with a clean slate than it is to transform an existing company. While this argument has merit, the case of RMSC shows that even when a new business is started with core values and principles of sustainability, it is not an easy path and numerous difficult choices have to be made. Most of these choices involve sacrificing short-term profits and returns for patient investments in products, markets, educating consumers, supply chains and operations that pay off only in the long term – in the case of RMSC, its growth rates show that payoff has been above-industry averages. What keeps such businesses on the path is an unflagging and uncompromising commitment to its core values of sustainability – both environmental and social. Such commitment is more possible in family businesses because the business is an extension of the family values and not just a commercial operation, and they keep their eyes steadily on the future not only for the business, but as in the case of RMSC, for a toxin-free healthy community and society. This is the story of one such pioneering sustainable family business that exemplifies patient capital.

KEY INSIGHTS

- Acquisition of a small venture with products aligned with sustainability beliefs of first-time entrepreneurs can provide the necessary foundation to build upon quickly.
- Environmental sustainability is more easily experienced in the natural environment and hence location of the business enables the family to bring environmental sustainability into the core missions and also attract employees with values to find solutions for environmental preservation.
- Internal physical spaces of an organization can be a powerful medium to simultaneously embed the sustainability values in an enterprise and display them externally as lived values.
- With each step integrating environmental and social sustainability principles into operations, it becomes possible for employees to identify the next challenges and explore viable solutions to remain on the path of continuous improvement. Such integration also reinforces employee values and innovativeness for social and environmental sustainability.
- As consumers become increasingly concerned and aware of environmental and social impacts of business operations, transparency of ingredients and activities is critical for gaining competitive advantage and customer loyalty for this segment.
- Social initiatives like the company's Women's Run and Walk help raise awareness about the values of the business and increase customer interest and loyalty toward its core business.
- Carefully planned sabbaticals by family founders that balance the autonomy and accountability of non-family employees can become potent tools to build internal leadership, organizational capabilities and culture.

NOTES

1. Bauer, E. (2017). *Canadian Beauty Industry up by 9.4%: News: NPD Canada.* NPD Group. www.npdgroup.ca/wps/portal/npd/ca/news/press-releases/whats-fuelling-the-canadian-beauty-industry/
2. Serafeim, G. (2018). "Facebook, BlackRock, and the case for purpose-driven companies." *Harvard Business Review*, January 16.
3. Murray, G. (2020). *Natural Vs Synthetic Beauty: Have We Got It All Wrong?* Refinery29.com. www.refinery29.com/en-gb/2017/10/177954/synthetic-natural-beauty-ingredients
4. Delventhal, S. (2019). *Study Shows Surge in Demand for "Natural" Products.* Investopedia. www.investopedia.com/articles/investing/022217/study-shows-surge-demand-natural-products.asp
5. Ibid.
6. CB Insights Research (2018). *13 Trends Shaping the Face of Beauty in 2018.* www.cbinsights.com/research/report/beauty-trends-2018/

7. Ibid.
8. Rocky Mountain Soap (2020). *Rocky Mountain Soap Company – 100% Natural Skin Care*. www.rockymountainsoap.com/
9. WestJet (2020). www.westjet.com
10. Lush (2020). www.lush.ca
11. Rocky Mountain Soap (2020). *Rocky Mountain Soap Company – 100% Natural Skin Care*. www.rockymountainsoap.com/
12. Ibid.
13. Canmore.ca (2020). https://canmore.ca/
14. Well.ca (2020). https://well.ca/
15. CB Insights Research (2018). *13 Trends Shaping the Face of Beauty in 2018*. www.cbinsights.com/research/report/beauty-trends-2018/
16. Digital Commerce 360 (2019). *U.S. B2B E-commerce Is on Course to Hit $1.18 trillion by 2021*. www.digitalcommerce360.com/2017/06/05/u-s-b2b-e-commerce-course-hit-1-18-trillion-2021/
17. Ibid.
18. Behrendt, A. (2019). *Sustainability Is Key in the Canadian Natural Personal Care Market*. Kline & Company. https://klinegroup.com/sustainability-is-key-in-the-canadian-natural-personal-care-market/
19. Rocky Mountain Soap (2020). *Rocky Mountain Soap Company – 100% Natural Skin Care*. www.rockymountainsoap.com/
20. Ibid.
21. Ibid.
22. Ibid.
23. Ibid.
24. Instagram (2020) *Rocky Mountain Soap Co*. www.instagram.com/rockymountainsoapco/
25. When this case was finalized the Covid-19 pandemic had engulfed the world. As with many countries, Canada had restricted travel and movement. All retail operations of RMSC were closed for several weeks, though the online sales had grown eight-fold. The leadership team was waiting to see if the increased online sales would continue once travel restrictions had lifted, and if so, whether retail operations would still remain viable.

3. Supreme Creations and Wings of Hope: A symbiotic care of environment and society

Pramodita Sharma, Sanjay Sharma and Alyssa Schuetz

> We aspire to replace single-use plastic packaging with innovative, ethically produced, eco-friendly products. Working closely with influential retailers like Boots (Walgreen Group), Nike, Sainsbury's, Tesco, The Co-operative Group, and Walmart, since 2000 we have helped to reduce the distribution and circulation of over five billion plastic bags. (Sriram, Founder and Chairman, Supreme Creations)

Supreme Creations is a business-to-business textile manufacturing company specializing in sustainable production and materials. In addition to its retail customers like Debenhams, Tesco, John Lewis and Selfridges, Supreme works with the British Fashion Council and several top European designers to create fashionably designed tote bags and other utility products featured in the London and Berlin Fashion Weeks and touted as collectible items by global brands like Topshop and Zara, among others.

Sriram, known as Sri, is a commerce graduate of the University of Delhi in India. Upon graduation in 1977, he began his career as a management trainee in Modi Enterprises, an Indian conglomerate. In 1983, he moved to London to serve as the resident director of the Birla Group, India's largest industrial group at that time. In 1999, he set up Supreme Creations with an aspiration to build a *professional*, *ethical* and *green* company (Figure 3.1). While he expected to be the controlling owner of his business, he envisioned that an expert team of professional managers would run his manufacturing business. Having witnessed some "hits and misses" in organizations that failed to instill a sense of discipline, accountability and excellence across each layer of management, and neglected to embed policies and procedures to reduce the reliance of the company on any one individual, he knew that professionalism was a necessity to ensure Supreme's longevity, agility and resilience.

PROFESSIONAL

Large Manufacturing Capacity and Expert Team

ETHICAL

Fair Treatment of Employees and Farmers

GREEN

Sustainable Materials and Practices

Figure 3.1 Supreme Creations' brand vision

In Sri's vision:

> **an ethical business that treats its employees and suppliers with dignity and respect is good business.**

This resolve was reinforced in his meeting with a family friend who was a founder of Infosys,[1] an iconic multinational consulting and information technology company that grew rapidly from its base in India to become one of the largest software businesses in the world. When asked why his company had adopted an ethical approach of transparency as its founding principle in an industry known to be secretive, his friend explained that this approach helped Infosys set a high benchmark in their industry. As their competitors struggled to catch up, it gave them an edge in sales, human resources and marketing, making them "the darling of the stock market." In turn, they were able to attract top-quality professionals by offering lucrative stock options who reinforced the positive virtuous cycle leading to their phenomenal growth. Looking to replicate this ethos that aligned with Sri's core beliefs in Supreme Creations, ethical stakeholder relationships were embedded as one of the three founding pillars to guide the company forward. The vision of using ecologically sustainable materials was triggered by the scientific, political and business debates about environmental concerns, and a desire to become part of the solution while capitalizing on emerging market opportunities.

Supreme Creations' strong digital capabilities enable efficient processing and production. With seamless coordination, professional managers in the European sales, marketing and design departments work directly with clients to co-design the products, and also with their manufacturing counterparts in India to produce digital and physical samples giving customers the opportunity to view products before they are mass produced. The company also has a large sampling department offering ready-to-order selections for clients. Many large brands use it as a sub-contractor to test and produce innovative packaging ideas at a fraction of the cost they would incur in producing the same products in Europe. Clients such as Adidas and Nike use Supreme Creations' products frequently, not only as part of their packaging solutions, but also to promote themselves as a responsible brand. As Supreme Creations digitally shares the story of its production process and its positive societal and environmental impacts, its clients can showcase related content on their own social media feeds. This helps to align the company's anchoring principles with the value proposition for its clients.

Over the past two decades, Supreme has expended a significant amount of time, effort and resources to develop the architecture of the business from client-facing sales and the design center to a technically sophisticated knowledge center for market analysis and operations and world-class manufacturing facilities. The knowledge center, based in India, has qualified software engineers and web designers who are able to support digital campaigns. Sri has devoted significant efforts to nurture a capable team of professional managers both in the United Kingdom (UK) and in India. Supreme's talent hiring process places as much emphasis on societal and ecological sustainability as it does on functional expertise. Sri notes:

> **Those who don't understand that we are fully focused on both the PEOPLE and the PLANET aspects of sustainability don't get hired... we only hire those who are invested in long-term sustainability and don't consider it a passing fad. (Sri Sriram)**

A FOCUS ON PEOPLE

Headquartered in London, Supreme Creations' products are manufactured in its state-of-the-art factory in Pondicherry in southern India. Over 90 percent of its 800 employees are female, many of whom are from underprivileged economic backgrounds. Supreme's employees appreciate the combination of job security, above-market wages and the safe, clean and pleasant work environment that the company provides. Turnover is low and morale is high. Seventy percent of its workforce has been with the company for over 15 years. Smruti Sriram, Sri's daughter and the current chief executive officer (CEO) of Supreme Creations, was clearly moved when she reflected on the average tenure of their employees. She noted that "many came as young girls, got married, had children and have spent their life with our business."

Supreme Creations looks for individuals who "live and breathe" sustainability in their daily lives such as being vegetarian, cycling to work or actively contributing to their community. Attention to detail is a key competency looked for in the hiring process, as the company views itself as not simply selling a product, but as a trusted sales advisor responsible for bringing its experience and knowledge to the benefit of its clients. Its goal is to understand the clients' needs and collaborate to design and manufacture solutions to exceed expectations.

In 2020, in addition to the controlling owners Sri (67 percent) and his wife Rajni (33 percent),[2] the top management team of Supreme Creations included CEO Smruti Sriram (the second-generation family leader), 12 general managers including Ram Naidu (finance and operations), Muthu Kumar (knowledge center), Ghanesh N. (finance) and Selvam Marimuth (merchandising), Dhana Sekhar (factory manager) and several long-tenured functional heads. This team of professional managers and world-class designers enables Supreme Creations to effectively serve thousands of clients in a plethora of industries, with orders ranging from 500 units to well over a million. Invitingly, the company's website assures potential clients that "no project is too big or too small"[3] for Supreme.

BEHAVIORAL SHIFT AND ENTREPRENEURIAL OPPORTUNITY

In 2001, when *Blue Planet*[4] – the BBC documentary narrated by Sir David Attenborough – was aired in Britain, Sri had launched his trading company Supreme, after culminating his professional management experience as the managing director of the UK operations of the Birla Group. Using his personal savings and professional contacts, he commenced a jute trading business, acquiring materials from India and Bangladesh and selling them to carpet manufacturers in the UK. He also continued to represent his previous employers' interests. Based on their trust in him, suppliers would offer favorable credit terms and buyers would expedite their payments. This helped him to procure materials on credit from buyers and settle their accounts after receiving payments from his clients. Fiscal prudence and low overheads were used to reinvest margins to build capital.

Although high-density polyethylene that made it possible to manufacture light and strong plastic bags was invented in 1953 by the Nobel Prize winning chemist Karl Ziegler and his team, these bags did not gain widespread acceptance until the 1980s when grocery chains, department stores and other retailers replaced paper bags with cheaper, more versatile and durable plastic bags. The convenience factor and economic gains of plastic bags did not take into account the sustainability of the planet and the limitations of its non-renewable resources until Attenborough's documentary brought images of struggling turtles and other marine life tangled in the floating debris of micro plastics in the "Great Pacific Garbage Patch"[5] to dinner conversations in the UK and around the world.

The Sriram household was no exception as Sri, Rajni and their only child Smruti, then a high school student, would discuss how rapidly the world had embraced the throwaway culture and started treating plastics as disposable rather than as a valued reusable resource. Concerns were raised that plastic waste led to clogged waterways and sewers that became breeding grounds for mosquitoes and, in turn, increased the transmission of vector-borne diseases such as malaria, particularly in highly populous countries like India. The image of turtles, dolphins and other ocean species struggling with blocked airways and stomachs because of mistakenly ingesting plastic bags as food captivated the Sriram family, who turned their attention to considering how Supreme Creations could become part of the solution. The turtle in Figure 3.2 became the company's informal mascot.

Figure 3.2 Supreme Creations' informal mascot

While the need to decrease reliance on single-use plastics was clear, grocery and chain stores in Britain (and around the world) continued to provide plastic bags for free. Hence, customers did not take the issue of plastic waste seriously. To develop pragmatic, environmentally sustainable waste management solutions, in 2001 Tony Blair's government[6] set up the Waste and Resources Action Programme (WRAP) with a mandate to work collaboratively with leading retailers, suppliers and manufacturers to improve resource efficiency and reduce waste within the UK grocery sector. Leading grocers like Sainsbury, Tesco and Walmart, who were dispensing billions of plastic bags a year, were invited to help develop solutions to the environmental issue at hand with a goal of moving towards a "zero waste economy" and reducing greenhouse gas emissions.[7] From WRAP came the first Courtauld Pact[8] – a voluntary, self-regulating agreement between the UK government and over 40 major retailers like Cadbury, Mars, Nestlé, Tesco, Cooperative Food, etc. – to develop solutions across the supply chain to reduce household packaging and food waste. The government committed its support to those who contributed towards these objectives.[9]

As he followed these events in the news and in public discourse, Sri continued to trade textile raw materials. In 2004, one of his clients in the north of England went bankrupt. When Sri went to meet the owners to discuss their outstanding debt, he saw an opportunity of acquiring the business that manufactured printed cotton bags. Drawing on Supreme's retained earnings, Sri "bought the assets for a very low price from the liquidator" but also convinced the team that ran the business to work for him so he could continue living in London, about 300 kilometers from the factory. This was a desirable outcome for both parties and they agreed to co-develop a professional accounting and reporting system to ensure the ease of coordination between the manufacturing operations near Manchester and the management of orders, sales and accounts from the London office.

With this acquisition, Supreme Creations had inadvertently veered from trading into manufacturing, at an opportune time when the behavioral shift from plastic bags towards environmentally friendly sustainable solutions was gaining momentum. At this time, Supreme Creations had about 25 employees, most of whom worked in the factory. Sri appointed a sales director to supervise and grow the business from London. He continued to devote his attention to growing the trading activities and eventually grew to become the Indian jute and cotton supplier for all major European carpet manufacturers. Alongside these efforts, he continued to develop a professional architecture for Supreme Creations.

With increasing demand for reusable eco-friendly bags, it was becoming increasingly difficult to service the UK market from this small factory in England. The need for increased manufacturing capacity was clear. It was also apparent that scaling up manufacturing in the UK was not feasible due to the high cost of labor and the distance from the raw material sources in Asia. A decision was made to set up a factory to make printed eco-friendly bags and packaging materials in India. After several visits to India a factory was established in Pondicherry, the hometown of Sri's old friend, J. S., who was an experienced textile manufacturing factory manager. While Sri would invest the required capital to launch this factory, J. S. would serve as the general manager overseeing the operations. Sales, marketing and finance would be handled by Sri from London.

Meanwhile, the Courtauld Agreement had challenged leaders of the British grocery industry to achieve measurable waste reduction targets within five years from 2005 to 2009. Time was ticking. Anticipating growing industry trends in favor of reusable eco-friendly bags, Sri knew that Supreme Creations had to quickly retool and expand its capacity. His past experience with multinationals indicated that large sustainability-conscious companies would work only with ethical suppliers who held themselves to the highest professional standards and who were not only in compliance with labor, health and safety laws, but proactively worked to exceed these standards.

WINGS OF HOPE FLY TESCO TO SUPREME CREATIONS

Both Sri and Rajni hail from traditional Indian families that believe in the transformational power of education. They both went to top educational institutions in India and invested in providing the best possible education for their daughter, Smruti, who joined the prestigious North London Collegiate School when she was 11. Once she was in high school, the couple felt the urge to share the gift of education to socioeconomically disadvantaged students. In 2003, the Sriram family established a children's charity, naming it *Wings of Hope* after their shared passion for amateur flying.[10] Following her keen sense of philanthropy and a shared desire to support children's education, Rajni took the responsibility of running the charity, while Sri continued to build Supreme Creations. With the help of local managers, the family identified a small school located near their factory to support. The principal had successfully embedded human values of honesty and universal love in the curriculum for all ages. It was agreed that Wings of Hope would provide the scholarships for students, while the local Supreme managers would oversee the disbursement of funds to the intended recipients.

Smruti was taking a gap year between grade school and university when Sri and Rajni invited a small group of her friends with a keen desire to improve the world to propose ideas to benefit secondary school children. As recent graduates themselves, they felt a vital gap existed for students to express themselves through charitable work while building their skills, proposing a social enterprise program for British students – the Wings of Hope Achievement Awards.[11] Launched in 2005, this national competition invited teams of up to six students from grades 9–13 to compete in fundraising projects to provide educational scholarships to children in India and later in Malawi. The competitors were mentored by the corporate partners of the Achievement Awards that included BBC, British Fashion Council, House of Lords, London Business School and Saatchi and Saatchi, Tatas, among others. Semi-finalists were invited to present their project in the British Houses of Parliament. The winning team was announced in a fun and glitzy event featuring some of the UK's top talent. The winners received an all-expenses-paid trip to a Wings of Hope-adopted school in India or Malawi, where they would spend a week and work on school improvement projects with the local students.

In its first 15 years, 34,200 students from 512 British schools competed in the Wings of Hope Achievement Awards events. Team projects included auctions, bake sales, themed dinner events, beach clean-ups, fitness challenges like cycling or swimming the length of the English Channel in a local pool, seven-hour non-stop drumming, bungee jumping, flying out of an airplane and fashion shows. Notably, artists like the Loveable Rogues, Simon Bird from the television show *The Inbetweeners* and *Britain's Got Talent*'s Gabz appeared in the awards events that were attended by the competitors and their families.

Each year students would invite Rajni and Sri to important fundraising events. A group of two female students from the Francis Holland school in Knightsbridge, London invited them to their event. They were to launch thousands of balloons bought by donors to raise funds for the charity. The parents of the two students and the Sriram family played co-hosts greeting guests including donors and exchanging contact cards. Next day at work, Sri mentioned the successful event to his general manager, Chris Perera, passing him the business card of one of the parents, Clive Humby. After some investigation, Chris found that Humby ran a data analytical business. Given his fondness for data analytics, Chris encouraged Sri to get in touch with Humby, who in turn invited them to his office. The Supreme Creations duo was surprised with the scale and success of Clive's business, dunnhumby, that he co-founded and operated with his long-time business partner and wife Edwina Dunn. In 1995, they helped to launch the world's first mass customization loyalty program Clubcard for Tesco, one of the world's largest grocery and general merchandize retailers. Recalling the meeting, Sri shared that "He [Clive] asked if we did jute bags. And, I said, yes, we did. Before we got to our office there was a call from Tesco to say that Mr. Humby wanted us to contact you for jute bags." Suddenly, Supreme Creations was negotiating for millions of jute bags with Tesco.

While Sri had anticipated a growth in reusable and sustainable bags because of the Courtauld Pact and had aspired to build a large-capacity, professionally managed, green and ethical business, Supreme Creations was not yet prepared to service orders of this magnitude. But this was also not an opportunity to be missed. While some printing machines from the Manchester factory were shipped to India, the majority had to be new acquisitions. Channeling their entrepreneurial spirit, Sri and his team identified and imported screen-printing machines from Australia and stitching machines from Japan. Prominent textile consultants were hired to oversee the printing works. A modern design studio was set up and intensive training in artwork management and digital manipulation was provided to the Pondicherry team. Over 1,500 workers were recruited and trained in printing, stitching and fabrication. Within six months, Supreme was ready to produce over a million units a month and successfully pioneered Tesco's "Bag for Life" program.[12]

Recalling the early days of business to his experience as a pilot, Sri reflects:

> Launching and sustaining a new business is like flying a small plane. It is about A-N-C: Aviating, Navigating and Communicating at the same time. A pilot's top priority is to aviate using flight controls and instruments. Then, you must navigate – know where you are and where you are going. And, third, you must communicate and stay in touch with someone outside the plane so they can guide you as you go along. (Sri Sriram)

These fundamentals are as applicable to business as they are to flying and crashing is often only one error away. As it is a continuous balancing act, having some professional experience is essential for any entrepreneur. He added:

> Contextual factors, both external and internal, dictate the optimal rate of incline for a plane, and similarly the appropriate growth rate for a business. Going too fast or too slow is a recipe for crash-and-burn. Only with industry and contextual experience does one learn the skill to sense the right balance for a particular time and place. (Sri Sriram)

THE MOVE TOWARD FAIRTRADE: THE BAG OF ETHICS

While Tesco was a "commercial retailer," the next defining moment for Supreme Creations came through partnership with an "ethical retailer" – the Co-operative Group (Co-op). This large business originated from the co-operative movement with a deep grounding in ethics and sustainable business. In 2005, Brad Hill, a buyer from the Cooperative Group,[13] approached Sri with a desire to buy Fairtrade eco-friendly bags. So, the Supreme team had to figure out how to source cotton from farmers who only used eco-friendly herbicides and pesticides to grow their crops, and pay fair prices to these farmers. In addition, it had to treat its employees in a responsible, respectful manner paying them above-market wages. Essentially, the Fairtrade movement required its suppliers to be responsible and transparent in their entire supply chain. Going this route was more costly for manufacturers and regular audits of the entire production and supply chain from raw materials procured, manufacturing as well as distribution were conducted.

Sensing Supreme Creations' sincerity towards social equity and ecological sustainability, as well as the professionalism and entrepreneurial will of its leadership, Brad, who had a lot of experience in the banana and coco Fairtrade industries, helped the company to move toward Fairtrade. He made several trips to India to guide the company's efforts to source cotton from Fairtrade farmers, and where needed, helped farmers convert their farms to Fairtrade acceptable levels. It was made clear to the farmers that the company was "trying to do something different and be of assistance to them as well as to the environment."

The Co-op was also keen on building communities so Supreme's decision to predominantly hire women was well received by the group as it was an opportunity to create a lasting impact in the community of their operations. The company would hire a few hundred women at a time and train them for six months. Once one group was trained, the next group would be hired until they reached full capacity. Supreme paid "higher than market wages, though not substantially higher," notes Sri, and provided an exceptional work environment that was "as safe and as friendly as any factory in the UK with airy and well-lit work space, channel music, clean sanitation facilities including shower rooms" (Figure 3.3). Perhaps most importantly, the company provided a sense of security to be treated with dignified respect by the carefully screened highly ethical managers. The workers developed deep bonds of friendship with their colleagues and felt a sense of being part of the Supreme community.

As a privately limited partnership, the external pressures faced by the company don't come from the stock market as is the case in publicly listed companies, but rather in fulfilling and exceeding the needs and expectations of their clients and end customers. Ultimately, it is up to the Sriram family to decide on what basis to build their company and how best to embed their guiding principles within the company.

In pursuit of excellence, efforts were made to continuously automate manufacturing and improve the processing systems. Professional expertise was brought in as needed. For example, a printing technology expert, Bill Hood, was hired from America to help establish systems to enable Supreme Creations to design and manufacture its bags to global standards. He introduced them to the technique of high-quality automated screen printing which needs a 360-degree approach including choosing the appropriate digital software, printing pressure and handling, and using the Pantone Matching System (PMS)[14] color coding system. The PMS identifier is used by notable graphic and fashion designers and printers to match the exact shade of a color in physical and digital formats, and in production and manufacturing processes

Figure 3.3 Supreme Creations' Pondicherry factory

for textile materials. The challenge for Supreme was to find efficient ways to match the design aspirations of customers stationed thousands of miles away through the use of digital technology. Precise shades of black, red or yellow (and there could be hundreds of shades of each color) that their customers' designers had specified were brought to manufacturing systems and processes to deliver thousands of units of final products with precisely those colors. Bill Hood proved an invaluable resource to establish these systems for Supreme Creations.

In the UK, the interest in environmental sustainability continued to attract attention at the highest levels of society. For example, over the years, His Royal Highness Prince Charles has championed initiatives to protect bees and other endangered insects, designed mini townships using sustainable materials and reducing carbon dioxide emissions and supported the planting of fruit and vegetable gardens to provide organic produce to local retailers in the Duchy of Cornwall.[15] An ethical supply chain lies at the heart of these initiatives and is well aligned with Supreme Creations' passion for sustainability. When Prince Charles and Camilla got married in 2005, Supreme Creations was among the companies commissioned to provide eco-friendly commemorative tea towels with the names and pictures of the royal couple and their wedding date – Friday, April 8.[16] But, when the week of the wedding arrived, the date had to be postponed by 24 hours so Prince Charles could attend the funeral of

Pope John Paul II on behalf of the Queen. By then, thousands of Supreme's tea towels had been sold with the original date. Within hours of the date change announcement, the company churned out thousands more towels, thereby gaining the attention of royalty and fashion enthusiasts alike. Tim Steer, then sales director of Supreme, noted there was considerable interest from people who wanted to buy the products with the incorrect date in the hope they would become valuable collectors' items. With the original batch sold out, he joked, "We'll just set up another print run with the old date on." As the "rejected tea towels" became popular collector items, even the Royal household placed an order for them. Subsequently, Supreme Creations received a signed cheque from the Duchess of Cornwall with a thank you card.

By 2008, in addition to supplying bulk shopping bags to commercial retailers like Tesco and Sainsbury's, Supreme Creations became the first London-based company to mass produce Fairtrade cotton shopping bags for the Co-op. When asked to sum up his entrepreneurial journey to date, Sri shared his gratitude towards "Tesco for their trust and large orders, Brad Hill of Co-operative Group for introducing Supreme Creations to the Fairtrade movement, and Boots, the pharmaceutical retailer for instilling the importance of exacting standards in manufacturing systems and procedures."

THE NEXT GENERATION AND ENTRY INTO THE FASHION INDUSTRY

After spending her gap year co-founding the Wings of Hope Achievement Awards with her mother, Smruti Sriram earned a PwC scholarship to pursue a social science degree in philosophy, politics and economics (PPE) from Oxford University. While in college, she was proficient at getting summer internships in corporations like Goldman Sachs, McKinsey, Bains and Saatchi and Saatchi. These experiences helped her to identify that she enjoyed creative work more than working for large banks or consulting companies. However, upon graduating from college in 2008, she followed the typical route of PPE graduates and worked in London's financial district, "The City." After several months of work, she felt unfulfilled in a vast organization and decided to give it up to take some time to reflect. Sri described the contextual environment as follows:

> After the 2007–2008 financial crash and the external environment was very difficult. It was strange that the Tesco's of the world, who were Supreme Creations main customers, lost interest in sustainable initiatives. Large orders were drying up from these big stores with their managers either being fired or moved to different areas. People we knew were being moved around. We had to reinvent ourselves to cope with the new realities of a sudden loss of large business. (Sri Sriram)

Always a source of encouragement and mentorship for Smruti,[17] Sri invited her to come to Supreme Creations until she figured out her next career move. She thought she would "come for 3-months till I figured out my next management career." Sri assigned her a small office and charged her with some basic tasks. He shared that:

> I had no intention of bringing Smruti in the business as I already had an established team of managers who had been with me for many years. I also felt the need to keep my family and the business separate. (Sri Sriram)

Around this time, Supreme Creations was invited to apply for His Royal Highness the Prince of Wales Business in the Community award. Launched in 1997, this award recognizes responsible British companies committed to improving their impact on the environment and society. Smruti offered to complete and submit this application and took a deep interest in it. Inadvertently, she was learning all aspects of their company and taking note of growth possibilities, particularly in the high-end fashion and design industry. When Supreme Creations received this prestigious award in 2009 (Figure 3.4), the decision for Smruti to fully devote herself to her family's company came as the next natural step. The collective efforts of the Sriram family enabled Supreme Creations to establish itself as a multi-generational family business, strategically positioned as the world's largest supplier of eco-friendly ethical bags that had received favorable reviews from the highest rungs of British media and society.[18]

Smruti was appointed as the corporate and new markets manager and given independent charge to find ways to embed creativity and sustainability into the fashion industry. When asked to share her experience from her early days at Supreme, she acknowledged "being on a high-horse" for a short time feeling that because she came from Oxford University she could "help with strategy, whatever that meant." However, she soon realized that "the people in the business were exceptionally smart and humble to take me under their wing. They had not gone to Oxford but they were smart." And her father made it clear that there was going to be "zero nepotism" and she would have to work hard to earn the respect of their "very small and efficient team." Keen to understand about marketing, she first worked with then sales director Chris Perera, describing her experience as follows:

> He [Chris Perera] came from a scientific background and was very data focused. We'd have long conversations and I'd learn from him. I quickly enjoyed client interactions and learning the CRM systems. (Smruti Sriram, CEO)

Her next training stint was with Tim Steer who managed large accounts. With him she learnt how large clients were exacting in their expectations and

Figure 3.4 *Supreme Creations receives the 2009 His Royal Highness Prince of Wales Business in the Community Excellence Award*

pushy in their dealings. To her surprise, her Achievements Awards experience proved "vital to build her skills and confidence in pitching, sales, resilience, and hard work." In 2009, she won her first contract from Top Shop, followed by a string of contracts from Nike, Zara, Adidas and other fashion brands. Sri observed that:

> As she [Smruti] got more involved, she felt more satisfied and the team began to respect her contributions in the fashion field. Since then she took on more and more senior roles in the business. (Sri Sriram)

Working with Top Shop helped Smruti understand that their products were highly desirable for promotion and marketing. Top Shop would get their top artistic team heavily involved in the design of their tote bags and used these bags as an integral part of their marketing campaign. Celebrities like Beyoncé, Jennifer Lopez, Kate Moss, Rhianna and Tom Hanks were featured holding Top Shop tote bags that Supreme Creations had manufactured in India. Londoners began to wait for hours queuing for the next release of the Top Shop tote bags that became "walking billboards," catching the eye of numerous marketing agencies keen on promoting their products. The humble shopping bag had become an imaginative tool of brand promotion. This kind of pizzazz caught Smruti's attention, who began expanding the company beyond the grocery spectrum into the fashion industry.

As the clients in the fast-paced fashion industry needed short lead times, Supreme Creations had to improve the adaptability and agility of its supply chain. It was clear to the leadership team that its supply chain extending from relationships with Fairtrade farmers through its fully owned manufacturing facility located in close proximity to the raw material sources, and its front-facing design and sales offices in London, provided it a unique competitive edge. Furthermore, the perspective of two generations and two genders brought up in different continents provided Supreme Creations a competitive advantage to work with diverse clients, react quickly and keep up with their demands. Smruti explained their unique positioning as follows:

> Very few European distributors in our industry own manufacturing facilities in Asia. Most of our competitors are traders who procure from Asian sources and thus lack an authentic story to tell. We are uniquely positioned to understand the style and design needs of our customers and also manufacture it in our predominantly women-run manufacturing facility in India. Our customers love our story and brand managers trust us to bring out cool impactful eco-friendly products. (Smruti Sriram)

In 2016, Smruti became the first recipient of the "30% Scholarship" to pursue an MBA at the world-renowned London Business School.[19] Set up by the British government, this scholarship aims to prepare young British women for board positions in the UK, in order to achieve the overall goal of having at least 30 percent of women on each board. Reviewing Smruti's explanation of how she would use her graduate education signals her ambitions for Supreme Creations as well as the goal alignment between the two generations of the Sriram family:

> I want to use my MBA to follow my ambition of leading ethical businesses – both starting and growing them – and to lead innovations in youth education.
>
> **My compass is set towards growing Supreme Creations through diversification and acquisitions of socially conscious ventures, empowering young people across the world, and being a thought leader on enterprise and development. (Smruti Sriram)**

While pursuing her graduate studies, Smruti worked part time at Supreme Creations to integrate her classroom learning in the family business. Over the years, her responsibilities have continued to increase and in 2013 she was appointed the CEO for Supreme Creations (Figure 3.5), spending 60 percent of her time and effort on sales, marketing, public relations and social media; 20 percent on human resources issues managing teams in India and the UK; and another 20 percent on operations to ensure coordinated effort across different teams. In 2014, 28-year-old Smruti Sriram was honored with Britain's "Top 35 women under 35" award[20] for running the "world's largest ethical manufacturer of reusable bags and eco-friendly packaging."

Figure 3.5 *Smruti Sriram, CEO of Supreme Creations*

When asked what "being ethical" means to her, she explained that, "it is always a work in progress and a balancing act." While Supreme Creations has always focused on people and has used biodegradable materials for a long time, its attention has now turned towards repurposing previously used plastic or wood. And, it must continuously educate their clients. For example, in terms of transportation and the supply chain:

> **we have always tried to educate the customer that shipping on ocean is much better than putting it on the airplane. Ten years ago, customers were quite happy receiving a product in 8 to 10 weeks. But now customers are more and more eager to receive their product quickly. (Smruti Sriram, CEO)**

Although there is more awareness about environmental challenges now, customer attention is fickle and easily swayed by the news of the week. For example, when Stacey Dooley's BBC documentary[21] on cotton production in Kazakhstan was aired, British press and customers alike were deeply concerned about how 68,000 square kilometers in the Aral Sea, full of fish and wildlife in the 1960s, had turned into a dusty, barren, motorable seabed by 2018 because of water diverted for cotton farming. Supreme Creations was flooded with calls from concerned clients to inquire about its cotton sources and their impact on water sustainability. However, as shared below:

> The Aral story does not reflect the full story of cotton farming and the impact of water used. Most of the cotton is grown in areas with substantial rainfall and the excess rain causes havoc to vast swathes of land. Cotton farming is an income source for millions of farmers. (Sri Sriram)

Resonating her father's sentiment, Smruti added:

> Switching overnight from one material to another is not only impossible, it can absolutely decimate thousands of cotton farmers in India. As we are as focused on the people side as we are on the environment, the trade-offs are never straightforward.

2020 AND BEYOND

By 2020, Supreme Creations was supplying ethically produced, eco-friendly bags and promotional products to over 60,000 clients including retailers like Sainsbury, Tesco, Co-op and Walmart, and fashion houses like Christian Dior and Jimmy Choo. Each Supreme product could be reused over 5,000 times, enabling the company to help reduce the circulation of over 5 billion plastic bags that could otherwise have found their way into the oceans and waterways of the world. The Wings of Hope charity supported the education and skill development of over 34,000 students in the UK, India and Malawi. Supreme Creations had become a first mover and trendsetter in reusable eco-friendly utility bags and the fashionable promotional marketing segments. With automation and technological advancements, the number of Supreme Creations employees has dropped from its peak of 1,500 in 2008 to 800 though the tradition of hiring over 90 percent women employees continued.

The tight-knit Sriram family works harmoniously with each member clear about his or her role. Sri and Smruti focus on Supreme Creations, while Rajni devotes herself exclusively to Wings of Hope. With many new initiatives introduced for UK students like speed mentoring, workshops by leading employers and guiding students eager to pursue academic careers, the charity continues to grow. With the integration of fashion and design as an integral part of Supreme Creations, its renewed philosophy is articulated as follows:

- Don't (create) waste
- Don't be boring
- Don't forget the humans
- Be flexible
- Be technical

When asked about the dynamics of working with family, Smruti shared:

> Even though I came from an Indian background and a business started by a man – my father, never never never have I felt that because I am a girl that I am not pushed. When it comes to work, I have no gender. And, this is because of my dad. I know so many other kids who are from patriarchal family. I think it could not have been easy for him. (Smruti Sriram)

From Sri's perspective:

> Having my daughter in the company (instead of a male child), allowed for a "yin and yang" balanced leadership as diverse experiences and perspectives pushes us to make better decisions. We are both leaders and have a mutual respect for each other. (Sri Sriram)

Noting the severity of the negative impact as it specifically correlates to single-use plastic bags, over 60 countries including Australia, Canada and the UK have implemented bans and taxes to discourage and reduce the single-use plastic bags[22] that had been the favored choice of retailers from the 1980s. From a global perspective, reusable bags have proven their usefulness in utility to consumers, and also as a major component of promotional marketing materials. For instance, apparel retailers from fast-fashion companies like Urban Outfitters to high-end designers like ATM Collection by Anthony Thomas Melillo gave away a branded, reusable bag with every purchase to their customers. The traditional plastic packing industry was poised for disruption by more sustainable alternatives.

Nevertheless, more recent reports on the plastic industry[23] revealed that production and consumption had outpaced recycling and usage substitution efforts. For instance, out of the 8.3 metric tons of virgin plastic produced, only 9 percent is successfully recycled, 79 percent still ends in landfill or in the natural environment, with the remaining 12 percent being incinerated.[24] If current consumption and waste management practices are to continue until 2050, another 12 billion tons of plastic litter will find its way to landfills and waterways. As such, plastics remain one of the most commonly found items in the environment, so the journey towards clean oceans is far from over.

According to McKinsey's *The State of Fashion 2020* report,[25] the fashion industry is going through a transformation. Placed on high alert by sustainability conscious consumers:

> Fashion players need to swap platitudes and promotional noise for action on sustainability measures such as energy consumption, pollution, and waste... The coming year will be tough, as the digital shakeout gathers pace, customers demand more on sustainability, and slower growth puts pressure on margins. However, there will be opportunities. Brands that can align with the dominant trends and continue to innovate are most likely to ride the challenges and emerge ahead of the pack.

Trends point to the materials revolution as companies seek to develop sustainable substitutes. As a supplier within the fashion industry supporting these aims, there is a huge potential for Supreme Creations to grow and become a major player within the fashion system, especially as governments pass new environmentally focused policies. In addition, the company continues to prioritize inclusivity and diversity internally through company culture and in expanding its target markets.

When the Covid-19 global pandemic engulfed the world in 2020 suddenly suspending the economy and shutting down the retail sector, Supreme Creations, a business heavily reliant on promotional and retail markets, came to a crashing halt. Struggling to protect their citizens from this invisible and deadly virus, European governments mandated the usage of face coverings on public transport, suggesting such usage in enclosed spaces as well. Urgent appeals were made to companies with tailoring capacity to help produce such coverings. Meanwhile, images of discarded facemasks on Hong Kong's beaches[26] and headlines like "Will plastic pollution get worse after the Covid-19 pandemic?"[27] served as stark reminders that although managing the health pandemic was a serious immediate concern, finding environmentally sustainable solutions was equally essential.

Never one to back away from an entrepreneurial challenge, the Supreme team joined forces with friends and family in the medical community to successfully design a non-medical-grade face covering. With rapid experimentation, within two weeks a prototype product that not only met the approval of medics, but was also attractive for the design and fashion community was ready. The company worked with the British Fashion Council[28] and six designers to refine the product. By early June, the British Fashion Council was selling the face coverings with pride as it became a best seller at retailers like Boots, Walgreen, Sainsburys, John Lewis, Waitrose and ASOS. The announcement read:[29]

> 'Great British Designer Face Coverings: Reusable, for People and Planet', is a joint campaign with *Bags of Ethics*, to manufacture and retail internationally, sustainable and reusable non-medical face coverings to use alongside existing social distancing measures. Designed in London by six British designers, Halpern, Julien Macdonald, Liam Hodges, Mulberry, RAEBURN and RIXO the project *aims to raise £1 million with 100% of sale profits going to charity* and split between NHS Charities Together Covid-19 Urgent Appeal, BFC Foundation Fashion Fund and *Wings of Hope Children's Charity*.

The non-medical face coverings are *manufactured at Bags of Ethics™ 100% owned partner factories and provide a reusable and sustainable option for the environment with no single-use plastic.* The non-medical face coverings will not deplete healthcare system. The product will be retailed at £15 for three reusable, washable, fabric face coverings with two protective pouches. These non-medical face coverings will be available to buy online through british-fashioncouncil.com and through partner retailers including ASOS, Boots, John Lewis & Partners and Sainsbury's.

From the perspective of Supreme Creations, this was simply the next natural step that Sri explained as follows:[30]

> **We have always been at the forefront of supporting the public through mass behavioral changes in positive and useful ways.**
>
> Since the early 2000s we helped supermarkets, and retailers reduce their single-use plastic bag consumption by over five billion units through sustainable and reusable bags. A new challenge arose with the Coronavirus pandemic. Our aim is to manufacture high quality reusable non-medical face coverings designed by great British designers and in line with our scientific community. We hope to support the health of the British population and our government, whilst having a positive effect on both people and planet.

Over the years, Supreme has continued to push technological sophistication and innovations in materials that are better aligned with its company values and meet the needs of their customers. Sri credits its success with "serendipity and having knowledge of the fibers market." In addition, the giving spirit expressed through Wings of Hope helped the Sriram family to establish networks that are generally beyond the reach of most first-generation immigrants.

Comparing his professional management experience with his entrepreneurial journey, Sri reflected that:

> Life of an entrepreneur is like riding a tiger. If you get down, the tiger will eat you. Your hope is to take the tiger to a zoo that will look after it well and will buy it for a good price. (Sri Sriram)

With the second-generation leader Smruti Sriram comfortably at the helm of Supreme Creations and excited about the future possibilities of her family company, perhaps the zookeeper is his own daughter! From her perspective, by 2030:

> Our team will continue to grow and innovate making design-oriented products with environmentally sustainable materials, while caring deeply about the lives and livelihood of our people.
>
> Supreme's base principles will be there. And, we will remain agile.
>
> We will be the #1 global player in sustainable packaging. I would want us to be a household name. I can certainly make that claim in the UK today. (Smruti Sriram)

KEY INSIGHTS

- Balancing the 3Ps of people–profit–planet is a trilemma that leaves the entrepreneur in a high-alert position similar to that of a pilot who must aviate–navigate–communicate at the same time.
- While stakeholder pressures change with the weekly news, the trade-off of being focused on people and on the environment is never straightforward.
- Social and environmental challenges cannot be integrated in isolation since they are connected: a sustainable company that reduces negative environmental impacts while treating its employees unfairly is not credible. Supreme Creations was able to integrate these principles effectively.
- Companies that start with a big sustainability challenge in mind (in this case the huge global problem of ocean plastics) have a universe of opportunities to innovatively develop products and businesses and also create new markets to address such a challenge.
- An ability to view an opportunity from the perspective of two generations and two genders brought up in different continents can be a distinctive competitive advantage when working with diverse clients in a wide range of industries.
- All successful products eventually attract competition. The success of a competitive strategy is in continuous innovation, continuous value addition and moving upmarket, as Supreme has continued to do with its rapid growth in the high-margin fashion industry.

- Family firms with low overheads, established networks and quick decision-making capabilities are well positioned to pivot to new opportunities in crisis situations like a pandemic.

NOTES

1. www.infosys.com/about/management-profiles/founders.html
2. *Supreme Creations Ltd.* (Shareholders) (2019). Retrieved from D&B Hoovers database.
3. www.supreme-creations.co.uk/about-us/our-testimonials.html
4. https://en.wikipedia.org/wiki/The_Blue_Planet
5. www.nationalgeographic.org/encyclopedia/great-pacific-garbage-patch/
6. www.theguardian.com/politics/2000/oct/24/labour.labour1997to99
7. "Business is Great Britain support, advice and inspiration for growing your business" (n.d.). www.greatbusiness.gov.uk/a-supremely-international-business/
8. www.wrap.org.uk/content/what-is-courtauld
9. www.wrap.org.uk/content/what-is-courtauld. Over the four-year period of Phase 1, 1.2 million tons of food and packaging waste was prevented, with a monetary value of 1.8 billion pounds, and a saving of 3.3 million tons of carbon dioxide, which is equivalent to the emissions from 500,000 round-the-world flights.
10. Sri is an amateur pilot and during their flying trips in various parts of the world, Rajni would serve as the co-pilot or navigator.
11. www.thewingsofhope.org/our-story-and-vision
12. www.managementtoday.co.uk/smruti-sriram-ceo-supreme-creations/article/1301791
13. https://en.wikipedia.org/wiki/The_Co-operative_Group
14. www.pantone-colours.com
15. www.duchyofcornwallnursery.co.uk/about
16. "Charles and Camilla give boost to promotions firm" (2005). *Incentive Today*, *20*(5), May, 5. http://link.galegroup.com.ezproxy.uvm.edu/apps/doc/A132842408/ITOF?u=vol_b92b&sid=ITOF&xid=a7bdcbc5
17. Sriram, S. (2015). "What glass ceiling?" *Management Today*, 22. https://search-proquest-com.ezproxy.uvm.edu/docview/1680758082?accountid=14679
18. www.supreme-creations.com/about-us/awards-accreditations.html
19. Sriram, S. (n.d.). www.london.edu/masters-degrees/student-alumni-and-ambassadors/smruti-sriram
20. "35 women under 35: Don't hold us back" (2014). *Management Today*, 40. https://search-proquest-com.ezproxy.uvm.edu/docview/1545528024?accountid=14679
21. Sanghani, R. (2018). "Stacey Dooley: Are your clothes wrecking your planet?" www.bbc.co.uk/bbcthree/article/5a1a43b5-cbae-4a42-8271-48f53b63bd07
22. Dal Porto, L. (2018). Singling out plastic. *Quality Progress*, 51: 10–12. https://search-proquest-com.ezproxy.uvm.edu/docview/2131174042?accountid=14679
23. Geyer, R., Jambeck, J. R. & Law, K. L. (2017). "Production, use, and fate of all plastics ever made." July 1. https://advances.sciencemag.org/content/3/7/e1700782
24. Ibid.
25. Amed, I., Balchandani, A., Berg, A., Hedrich, S., Poojara, S. & Rölkens, F., *The State of Fashion 2020.* Business of Fashion, McKinsey & Co. www.mckinsey.com/~/media/McKinsey/Industries/Retail/Our%20Insights/The%20state%20of

%20fashion%202020%20Navigating%20uncertainty/The-State-of-Fashion-2020-final.ashx

26. "Discarded coronavirus masks clutter Hongkong's beaches, trails." www.reuters.com/article/us-health-coronavirus-hongkong-environme/discarded-coronavirus-masks-clutter-hong-kongs-beaches-trails-idUSKBN20Z0PP
27. www.euronews.com/2020/05/12/will-plastic-pollution-get-worse-after-the-covid-19-pandemic
28. Smith, S. (2020). "British designer facemasks go on sale for £15 for three in aid of NHS charities." *Yorkshire Post*, June 5. www.yorkshirepost.co.uk/lifestyle/shopping/british-designer-face-masks-go-sale-ps15-three-aid-nhs-charities-2875715#gsc.tab=0
29. www.britishfashioncouncil.co.uk/About/Great-British-Designer-Face-Coverings
30. www.yorkshirepost.co.uk/lifestyle/shopping/british-designer-face-masks-go-sale-ps15-three-aid-nhs-charities-2875715#gsc.tab=0

4. Biofilter: A Hungarian champion for the circular economy and stakeholder capitalism

Caroline Seow and Maria José Parada

György Deák was puzzled: *Why are the workers moving these barrels? Where are they taking them? What is in them?* The young Hungarian engineer was on a study trip with colleagues in Vienna. The group was having lunch at the local McDonald's. He called the waitress over. Charmed by his interest, she explained patiently that the barrels contained the restaurant's used cooking oil for the day and that "someone would be picking them up." The young man's curiosity mingled with his penchant for problem solving. Could cleaning up the environment and reducing waste also be a business opportunity?

This accidental foray into an Austrian fast-food restaurant proved to be a watershed event for György Deák. His spirit of enquiry and journey of exploration would lead to the establishment of Biofilter – one of Hungary's foremost companies dealing with environmental protection.

SETTING THE STAGE

Founded in 1990 by György Deák,[1] Biofilter is a Hungarian family-owned environmental company specializing in the bioenergy sector. The company collects and processes used cooking oil from the hotel, restaurants and catering sector, which is then used as raw material for producing biodiesel at plants in Hungary and neighboring countries. In addition to cooking oil, it also collects and processes food, animal and vegetable waste from the hotel, restaurants and catering and fast-moving consumer goods sectors that can no longer be marketed because it has expired or is not meant for consumption.

The collected waste can be used to generate heat, energy and electricity after it has been processed at biogas plants. One hundred percent of the organic waste collected is used for renewable energy production. Biofilter currently has a national collection and international processing network of more than 4,500 contracted partners. With a workforce of over 100 employees, Biofilter covers approximately 70 percent of the Hungarian market with seven collection points nationwide.[2]

Patriarch Deák is the principal owner, key decision maker and chief executive officer of the company. His wife Mariann and two daughters are also shareholders: older daughter Dóra handles strategic business development while younger daughter Brigitta is a marketing manager and sustainability ambassador (Figure 4.1).

Figure 4.1 *The Deák family (left to right: György, Mariann, Dóra, Hanna (Dóra's daughter), Gábor (Brigitta's husband), Brigitta, Mira (Brigitta's daughter))*

Biofilter is an advocate of the circular economy (Figure 4.2). This business model looks beyond the conventional take–make–waste extractive industrial model and focuses on positive society-wide benefits. It entails gradually decoupling economic activity from the consumption of finite resources and designing waste out of the system.[3] Underpinned by a transition to renewable energy sources, the circular model is based on three principles:

- design out waste and pollution;
- keep products and materials in use; and
- regenerate natural systems.

Since its founding, Biofilter has strived to put these principles into practice and has aligned its strategic and operational goals accordingly. Strategically, Biofilter seeks to keep all collected waste out of landfills and to supply the renewable energy sector with a reliable source of raw materials in the long term. Operationally, it aims to responsibly collect and process organic waste while emitting the least possible amount of carbon dioxide in doing so. Biofilter believes that circularity, innovation and transparency are themes that will dominate tomorrow's business conversation.

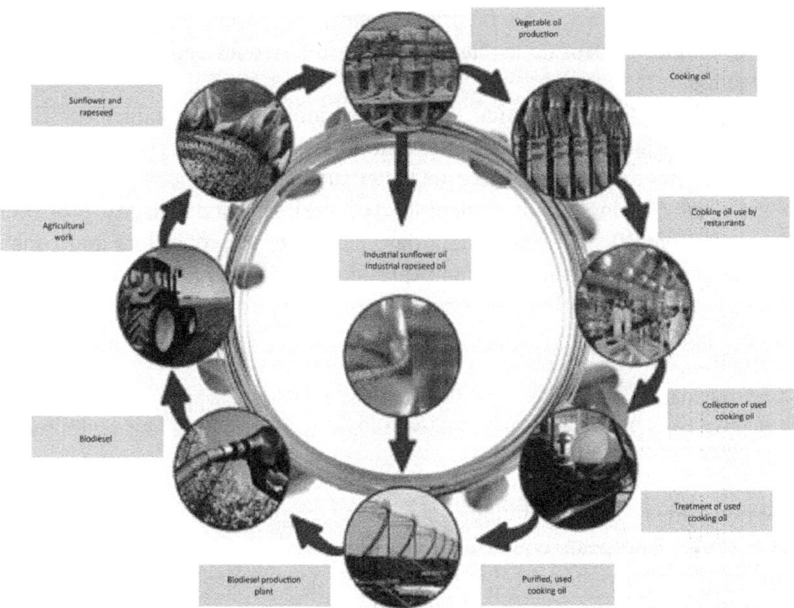

Figure 4.2 *The circular economy in practice: the collecting, processing and recycling of cooking oil*

THE FOUNDER: ENGINEER AND ENTREPRENEUR

György Deák was born in Siófok, a small river city 100 kilometers from Budapest, attractive to tourists for its scenic views and ancient settlements. The historic town on the banks of Lake Balaton served as the backdrop to an idyllic childhood spent with his engineer father, accountant mother and elder sister. The pleasing water landscapes inspired the artist in György who loved playing the piano, particularly the ballads of Schubert and Haydn. The versatile young man was also a keen sportsman, representing and leading his school team to the City Championships in Budapest for volleyball and table tennis. After high school, György moved to the capital, having secured a place at the MALÉV Aeronautical Institute. He graduated in 1980 as an aeronautical engineer and worked a year for the now defunct MALÉV Hungarian Airlines before being conscripted into the army.

For György, 1982 was a watershed year. Through mutual friends in Budapest, he met his wife Mariann. The loving couple were ecstatic when György landed a new job at Budapest's Environmental Institute. He was assigned to study noise protection. Five years into the job, he embarked on what was to become a pivotal study trip to Vienna. He was thrilled to be visiting the "home" of two of his favorite classical composers and had not thought that something as prosaic as "used cooking oil" would end up defining this experience.

Intrigued by his observation of the used cooking oil container barrels in McDonald's during his two-week visit to Vienna, upon returning home, he took a month's unpaid leave to better understand what was being done to the used cooking oil in Budapest.[4] His curiosity and tenacity propelled him to explore 10–15 restaurants a day. He spoke to proprietors and cooks, endured strange looks and puzzled expressions and concluded that the system of removing and recycling used cooking oil he had observed in Austria was non-existent in Hungary. György recalls:

> At that time, eating habits were different. The chefs were happy to put the used oil in the stew or mix it in the mayonnaise. And the food diluted with used oil was well peppered to mask any after-taste.

Where others were oblivious, the young engineer identified a business opportunity. European countries were already dealing with environmental issues and György thought this could be an appropriate time to bring these practices to Hungary. The first McDonald's had opened in Hungary in April 1988 to great fanfare. This was the very first fast-food outlet behind the Iron Curtain, and customers travelled from all over the communist-controlled Eastern Bloc to wait in line, sometimes for hours, to get a burger, fries and a "real" Coke. Over 10,000 patrons were served in the first 14 hours of opening.

The Ronald McDonald on the street corner posing for pictures with Slovakian and Bulgarian tourists sparked an insatiable appetite for French fries. György foresaw that the corresponding proliferation of used cooking oil would be an emerging environmental concern. However, acting on his instincts proved surprisingly challenging. When György approached the Hungarian Department of Environmental Issues to enquire about the reporting and removal of waste such as used oil and baking fat, he was met with blank stares. The authorities declared that "as there was no such type of waste in their system, there was nothing to report."[5]

Undeterred, György pressed on. He began collecting used cooking oil on his own while still working for the Institute. He was convinced that the removal of used cooking oil was a needed new business. So, at the end of 1988, with the 100,000 Hungarian forints he raised, György left his stable job at the Institute to establish the foundations for Biofilter. He recalls his meetings with the Hungarian authorities as follows:

> We tried, but our meetings with authorities met with little success. They revolved around "but there is no waste" conversations. Nobody in Hungary was dealing with used oil in restaurants and hot kitchens at that time, nor was anyone concerned with its environmental impact. I felt compelled to start my own collection process.

THE EARLY YEARS OF BIOFILTER AND THE HUNGARIAN MARKET ECONOMY

Armed with a waste collection license from the city council, György invested in his first vehicle – a German Wartburg.[6] The entrepreneur and his trailer would make their rounds of the city collecting barrels of used cooking oil. He procured the house next door and used it for a workshop and storage area. Daughter Brigitta recalls, "We had a swing in our garden, and it faced the factory. We could see all the work that was being done. The smell of grease was all around us."

The first challenge György encountered was to find food outlets that were prepared to allow him to collect the used cooking oil. He would sit by the telephone with an open phone book and systematically dial all the restaurants in Budapest. Most caterers were reluctant as they were accustomed to throwing the used oil down the sink. One of his earliest clients was the legendary Kisrabló restaurant in Budapest. György was now collecting used cooking oil either for free or for 3 forints a liter.[7] This lukewarm start provided an opportunity to road-test the operational procedures he had designed.

The beginnings of Biofilter ran parallel to Hungary's independence. Once part of the Austro-Hungarian Empire, Hungary emerged from 45 years of communist rule to become fully independent in 1990. The early 1990s saw Hungary's market economy take off, and the Hungarian fascination with fried food and French fries spilled over from restaurants to hotels and homes. This had significant effects on kitchen culture and Biofilter's prospects:

- New deep fryers were installed in commercial and domestic kitchens, and more oil was used.
- Customers became aware of the health hazards of fried food, and restaurants were pressured to change their oil more frequently.

- The huge volumes of used oil generated could not be disposed of by mixing with batches of pre-made foods. Commercial outlets discovered they had nowhere to "dump" their used oil.

Mindsets in commercial kitchens shifted. They were now prepared to pay for the removal of their used cooking oil – the volumes generated rendered "pouring down the sink" unfeasible. Biofilter's business began to grow. However, the slim margins in oil collection motivated György to identify additional opportunities to keep the business going. At that time used cooking oil was used almost exclusively for pet and farm animal food. Enterprising György identified every company in this market, and offered them the used oil as raw material for their pet food production. His persistent search for customers led him to Monori Allami Gazdasag, the largest pet farm in Hungary. The company contracted to pay 16 forints per liter for the oil. György was elated!

In the first year, György sold 20 tons of used cooking oil, followed by 50 tons in the second year. To transport the oil from collection point to selling point, György required a second vehicle. As the business expanded, a Barkas truck, IFA truck and other commercial vehicles were added to Biofilter's fleet. It was in 1989[8] that Biofilter signed its first large multi-contract for used cooking oil and garbage collection with McDonald's. Back then, the fast-food behemoth had only the one outlet on Régiposta Street. Prior to this, Biofilter was shipping waste out of the city once a day. However, the growing popularity of restaurants like McDonald's and the accompanying waste volume generated rendered this insufficient. Biofilter ramped up operations and its Barkas trucks soon started making an average of five trips a day.

Biofilter was on a growth trajectory. In 2002, the company moved its headquarters to Törökbálint, a town in Pest county, approximately 15 kilometers west of Budapest. It continued to innovate and streamline operations. Biofilter invested in its own cleaning and recycling facility and the collected cooking oil was purified in-house before shipping to the animal feed processing facility next to Monori Allami Gazdasag. As the business expanded, the rented feed processing facility was purchased in 1996. Towards the middle of the 1990s, the company was collecting 1,000 tons of oil annually. No other company in Hungary had yet entered the market. Biofilter was ahead of the curve.

THE TURBULENT YEARS: RISKS, RESILIENCE AND REWARD

The promising beginnings of Biofilter were shaken in the spring of 1999 with the unravelling of the dioxin crisis in Belgium. The Dioxin Affair, as it came to be called, started with complaints from chicken farmers alarmed by the unexplained deaths of their newborn chicks. The media reported increased incidences of chicks with nervous system problems and eggs which failed to hatch.[9] Laboratory analysis confirmed the presence of dioxins – highly toxic environmental pollutants, well above acceptable limits in the eggs, tissues and feed of the affected birds. The presence of the cancer-causing dioxin was traced to pet food containing recycled oil sold by Verkest, a fat and oil processing plant and animal feed manufacturer based near Ghent in northwest Belgium. Industrial oil had been mixed with the used cooking oil. The contaminated fat was processed as animal fat and used to make animal feed. Verkest had supplied this contaminated fat to Belgian animal feed manufacturers, as well as French and Dutch manufacturers. This feed from Verkest and from the other manufacturers was then sold to egg, broiler chicken, pork and beef producers.[10]

Media reports estimated the carcinogenic compound had leaked into nearly 150,000 tons of feed.[11] The damage amounted to hundreds of millions of euros. Over 2,500 farms had been contaminated; 7 million chickens and 50,000 pigs had to be slaughtered. The Dioxin Affair erupted into a major political and health scandal for the Belgian government. European Union (EU) counterparts were scathing of Belgium's handing of the crisis; it was deemed to lack urgency and transparency.[12] The fallout extended beyond Belgium's borders. Several hundred farms in Holland, France and Germany were placed under surveillance to check for contamination. In The Netherlands alone, over 400 pig farms were placed under quarantine order.[13]

Within two to three weeks following the first announcement of contamination, at least 30 countries including Australia, Canada and Hong Kong banned imports of Belgian agriculture products. Some countries banned just poultry while others banned all meat, dairy products and animal feed. As the crisis unfolded, anxious countries added more products to their lists of banned goods. This included the famed Belgian chocolates and other processed foods that could have contained contaminated chicken or eggs. Some countries banned imports from France, Germany and The Netherlands as well. The United States and Singapore took it one step further and temporarily banned all European poultry and pork products.

Fearful of what this meant for European exports, the EU passed resolutions banning the use of frying oils in animal feed and imposed more stringent regulations on the largely unregulated feed production and fat-processing industries.[14] At that time, Hungary was not yet a part of the EU and the ban on used cooking oil lasted only a month. Further analysis had determined that the source of contamination was not the used cooking oil per se but machine oil that had been mixed with the animal fat. In 2009, a court in Ghent sentenced two businessmen in Verkest for knowingly selling contaminated fat driven by their "lust for profits."[15]

Yet, this was a critical juncture for Biofilter. It had invested heavily in cleaning and recycling facilities; selling used cooking oil to pet farms formed the core of Biofilter's business. However, the experience of unscrupulous animal feed manufacturers and contaminated frying oil potentially affecting farms and livelihoods across Europe as well as the possible repercussions on human health weighed heavily on György. It led him to re-examine his business and contemplate a major transformation to his operating model. He needed to identify other applications for the used cooking oil. His options were direct disposal to landfill, chemical feedstock or the production of biodiesel.

Production of biodiesel aligned with Biofilter's values on "circularity." At that time, Hungary was making plans to join the EU. The production of biodiesel from used cooking oil was gaining traction across the continent. Several biodiesel factories were being built in Hungary, but many were not operational because they lacked qualified specialists. Keen to embark on this low-carbon journey, Biofilter crossed the border to sell frying oil to biodiesel plants in Austria. However, the growing popularity of biodiesel meant that the waste material was now being sold to the highest bidder. The pollutant was now a valuable input and what György called "Cooking Oil Wars" ensued – collectors like Biofilter had to pay increasingly higher prices to commercial organizations for the used oil.

The accession of Hungary to the EU in 2004 presented learning and business opportunities for Biofilter. On account of the first African swine fever epidemic and other calamities, health authorities banned the recycling of food waste for animal feed across the EU. Hungarian companies needed to comply with these stricter European regulations. As Biofilter's core purpose was to keep waste materials in circulation and out of landfills, the company began to explore alternate avenues for kitchen waste. In that year several biogas plants in Hungary started testing new types of fermenters with food waste proving to be an excellent raw material for biogas production.[16] By leveraging off its network of restaurants, hotels and caterers, Biofilter became the first company in Hungary to enter the food waste and biogas industry in 2004.

THE GROWTH YEARS: REGIONAL EXPLORATIONS AND PATIENT INVESTMENTS

Over the years, Biofilter diversified into related areas, but György admits that not all of them were successful. Building on Biofilter's success in Hungary, he reasoned that it would be opportune to replicate operations in other European markets. With his trademark efficiency and diligence, György embarked on a fact-finding mission to neighboring countries. In 1998, after three months of research, armed with an initial investment of around 10 million forints, the family established an office in Thessaloniki, Greece's second major economic, commercial and political center.

Biofilter was the first company in the Greek city to focus on the collection of cooking oil and György was convinced that the long-term prospects were good. However, a few years into the operation, structural weaknesses in the Greek economy emerged. It transpired that when Greece was accepted to the European Monetary Union in 2001, it did so under false pretenses as its deficit and debt were nowhere within the Maastricht Treaty guidelines.[17] In 2004, the Greek government openly admitted that its budget figures had been doctored to meet the entry requirements for the Eurozone's single currency, with hopes that its premature entry into the European Monetary Union would boost its economy, enabling the country to deal with its fiscal problems.[18] The debt crisis of the Greek government dealt a severe blow to the economy and the ensuing reforms and austerity measures led to severe loss of income and property and ultimately impoverishment for large swathes of the population. Not unexpectedly, this catastrophe crushed the tourism and restaurant industries. After 10 tumultuous years, Biofilter shuttered its Greek operations.

Elsewhere, attempts to expand internationally also proved a struggle as different overseas markets had markedly distinct patterns. In Croatia, Serbia and Slovenia, culinary and hospitality practices were such that not enough cooking oil was generated for the waste to be worth collecting in an organized fashion. Although the business did not take off, Biofilter made contacts with many European biodiesel plants and gained valuable insights.[19]

Undeterred, György continued strategizing to expand the family business. Opportunity presented itself when a trusted business associate asked György to buy his shares in Greenpro – a manufacturer of grease and oil filters. The long-time business partner was Greenpro's major shareholder and he was looking for a synergistic and natural partner for his five-year-old company. Greenpro had business relationships with Hungary's largest retail chains. In addition to manufacturing filters, it was also in the business of collecting expired groceries from supermarkets and stores, a valuable raw material used in biogas plants. The decision to purchase Greenpro in 2011 as a patient investment proved to be a shrewd strategic move. György knew that it was important to balance the short-term return on this investment against the longer-term value. He foresaw that acquiring Greenpro would enable Biofilter to offer a complete waste management service, thus redefining itself as a total circular economy business. Greenpro was already profitable at the time of purchase. By the end of 2019, Greenpro had doubled its revenue, reaching a turnover of 1 billion forints. The Greenpro acquisition represented an expansion of the Biofilter enterprise and a way to vertically integrate the business, allowing more efficient and effective delivery of its service and products.

THE NEXT GENERATION MAKE THEIR MARK

György's vision of a circular economy business is deeply ingrained in the second generation of Deáks who embrace the sustainability mandate of the family business. Sensitized to ecological issues from an early age, both Dóra and Brigitta aspire to embed sustainability not only in environmental practices but also in the culture of their company. "When we were in high school, we did holiday internships of one to two weeks to get to know the company and its working from the inside… It was a tremendous learning experience," reflected Dóra.

Dóra majored in finance and marketing and worked outside the family business before joining Biofilter full time in 2010 as a customer relationship manager. Her prior experience in banking and finance enabled the resourceful 25 year old to develop sound relationships with Biofilter's diverse customer base. Four years into the family business, she had her first child and took time off to be a full-time mother. Coming back to the business after a year of maternity leave, Dóra focused on modernizing the family enterprise. Her time away had allowed reflection and she subsequently implemented practices to professionalize the business. Leveraging off her experience, she put in place a modern customer relationship management database. She also introduced *Lean* methodology principles in the plants to improve efficiency and eliminate waste. The far-sighted Dóra appreciated the importance of good governance and recognized that Biofilter would benefit from the shared wisdom of other business families. In 2014, Dóra mobilized the family to join the Hungarian chapter of the international Family Business Network (FBN).[20] Founded in 1989, FBN brings together over 4,000 business families from across 65 countries. The world's leading family business organization, FBN provides a safe, shared learning space for enterprising families. Learning from experts and peers, Dóra initiated a process in the family business that led to the development of Biofilter's family constitution, which provided greater clarity on ownership roles and responsibilities.

Dóra's younger sister Brigitta studied tourism and hospitality and worked abroad in Brussels and Malta before she went to Vienna to pursue her MBA, majoring in sustainability. The subject had always resonated with her as she cared deeply about the impact a business could make on society and the environment. Brigitta recalls how Al Gore's *An Inconvenient Truth* moved her:

> Al Gore's first movie represented a turning point for me. It was in 2006 and I was just 18 years old and very idealistic. It made me understand that the world is far from idyllic. Our Earth is in a crisis and we need to take action. It moved me to focus on the sustainability field.

Like elder sister Dóra, Brigitta had opportunities to participate in paid internships in the family business. In 2013, Brigitta joined Biofilter full time as a trade assistant. Her experience over the ensuing two years exposed her to the company's different partners and helped hone valuable marketing skills. She noted, "It was a great start for me, because this trade position allowed me to learn the details and processes of the company. I was fortunate to have a manager who was supportive and encouraged creativity within limits. This manager was the right-hand person for my father, and she was very knowledgeable."

Encouraged by elder sister Dóra, Brigitta started attending FBN Next Generation activities. Given her passion for sustainability, Brigitta became very engaged in Polaris[21] – FBN's movement of leaders – championing *Family Business as a Force for Good.* Named after the north star, Polaris aims to build resilient, purpose-driven family businesses by advancing sustainability practices and creating shared prosperity for all.

Brigitta's involvement in Polaris gave her the opportunity to meet her "hero of the environment," Al Gore, when she successfully secured a place in the hugely oversubscribed *Polaris Training with Al Gore* in 2017. Competition to attend had been keen and participants were encouraged to complete FBN's Polaris Impact Assessment (PIA) – a tool to help family businesses measure, benchmark and improve the sustainable practices related to their region and industry.[22] Brigitta's passion for "making the world a better place" made her the lead person driving sustainable practices in Biofilter. She is, in effect, Biofilter's honorary sustainability ambassador. Constantly in search of solutions that can reduce the company's carbon footprint, she works on communicating these efforts to raise awareness among their key stakeholders.

György had always made it optional for his daughters to join the business. While he had been careful from the start not to impose the family business on them, he is delighted that they are both invested in Biofilter. He also recognizes that Dóra and Brigitta's skills and passion complement his engineering expertise and values the strengths that each brings to the business. Like many founding entrepreneurs, György is accustomed to being the sole decision maker for the business. While he considers the input from his team of professionals, including his daughters, and shares his business plans with them, he is still the key decision maker for major investments, acquisitions, growth and divestments. He assumes the risks and responsibility of his decisions, and entrusts his senior management team with the execution.

More recently, György has empowered his daughters to strategize on Biofilter's sustainability trajectory and develop policies and programs that will advance Biofilter's practices and further embed sustainability into Biofilter's operations. This is yet another indication of György's appreciation of patient capital investments. He understands that sustainability measures are for the long term whilst providing intangible short-term benefits. Indeed, Biofilter initiatives such as a greener fleet, a paperless office, recycling projects and the *Move it Bio!* [23] health-care and environmental program are building a more resilient operation while contributing to employee and community education, engagement and empowerment.

CIRCULAR ECONOMY: GIVING NEW LIFE TO WASTE

Throughout its 30-year history, Biofilter has striven to be a socially and environmentally responsible business. Since its founding, the central mission has been to collect waste and turn it into a valuable product. The company has achieved this goal of becoming a zero-emissions company through its circular economy activities. In 2016, Biofilter collected and processed more than 13,000 tons of organic waste, generating savings of approximately 19,000 tons of carbon dioxide emissions. These savings are able to offset the emissions of almost 4,000 cars driving non-stop for one full year! This trajectory is embedded in the business model with year-on-year improvements. In 2019, the amount of organic waste Biofilter collected rose to an impressive 17,000 tons (Figure 4.3). This translates to saving 24,000 tons of carbon dioxide from reaching the atmosphere – the equivalent of keeping 5,000 cars off the road for a full year.

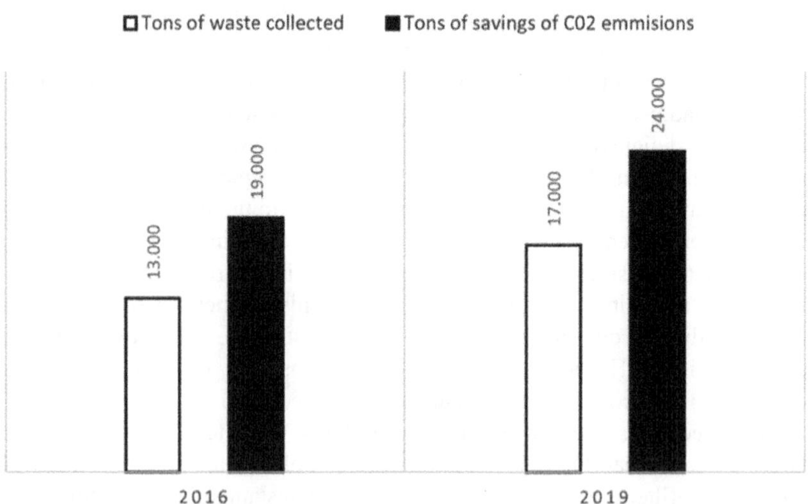

Figure 4.3 *Waste collected and corresponding savings of carbon dioxide emissions in 2016 and 2019*

To better measure and manage these emissions, Biofilter joined the French Clim'Foot Program[24] in 2016, a European system for carbon footprint calculations. According to 2016 data, Biofilter emitted 1,555 tons of carbon dioxide in total. The largest part of these emissions came from deliveries and logistics (64.6 percent) and the second largest from energy usage (27.8 percent). The rest of the emissions came from the transportation of employees and guests (4.6 percent), from generated waste (2.6 percent) and other input materials (0.3 percent). To reduce its logistics emissions, the company continuously improves its car fleet with hybrid vehicles and modern, higher euro-level trucks – a European-wide emissions standard aimed to curb pollution.

As its production process evolved, Biofilter realized that after the cooking oil is purified, only 90 percent of it can be used by biodiesel plants. So they explored innovative solutions for the remaining 10 percent. Their hard work paid off as they discovered that this leftover substance is an ideal raw material for biogas production. Today Biofilter recycles 100 percent of cooking oil for bioenergy generation in its plants.

The circular business for recovered cooking oil is replicated for kitchen waste as depicted in Figure 4.4. Biofilter is primarily working with the

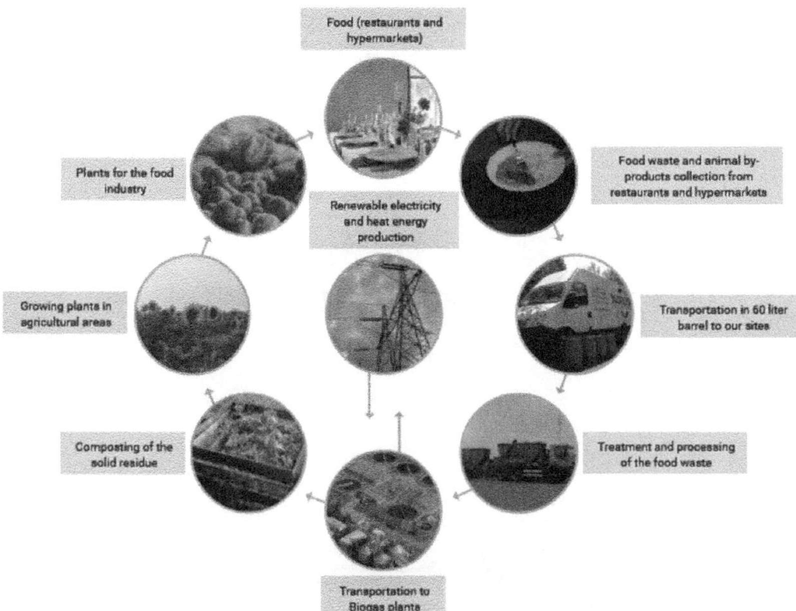

Figure 4.4 *The circular economy in practice: the collecting, processing and recycling of food waste*

South-Pest Wastewater Treatment Plant to "feed" its biogas fermenter. The plant generates enough electrical and heat energy to completely cover its energy usage. In 2016, the food waste used for biogas production generated more than 8 million kilowatts per hour, which covers the yearly energy usage of approximately 4,500 households. Operations have improved year on year. In 2019, the business generated more than 14 million kilowatts per hour - equivalent to the yearly energy usage of approximately 7,000 Hungarian households.

Biofilter's commitment to reducing waste both at source and in the hotel, restaurant and catering sectors was acknowledged in the 2018 *Report by the Embassy of the Kingdom of the Netherlands in Budapest, Hungary* on the state of food waste in Hungary.[25] This report surmised that underdeveloped logistics and processing sectors contributed to Hungary's close to 2 million tons of annual food waste. It recognized Biofilter as a key player in the private sector for its initiative in addressing this issue, commending its efforts to collect expired food and waste and turning this resource into biogas.

Greenpro has similarly evolved to become an innovative circular business. Since its acquisition by the Deák family in 2011, the 50-person cleaning and collection company has expanded its fleet to 25 vehicles and developed a national collection network of over 1,600 partners. The animal by-products,

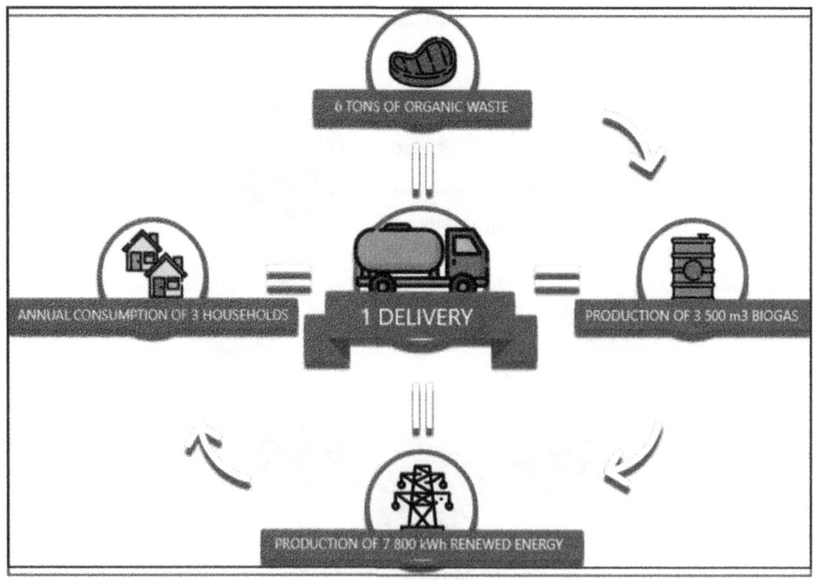

Source: www.greenpro.hu.

Figure 4.5 The impact of one Greenpro delivery

food waste and oils and fats from grease traps collected by Greenpro are recycled 100 percent for biogas production. With biogas, Greenpro partners are able to generate electricity and heat from renewable sources. The numbers tell the story of positive ecological impact as depicted in Figure 4.5.[26] On average, one Greenpro truck collects six tons of organic waste per delivery. From this, 3,500 cubic meters of biogas is produced. This volume of biogas in turn generates 7,800 kilowatts per hour of electricity – an amount sufficient to cover the total yearly energy requirements of three households in Hungary.

Biofilter has shattered the myth that being environmentally friendly and socially conscious is a "cost" with negative impacts on profit. Since the early days when the young engineer made his rounds in his trusted Wartburg, the company has demonstrated steady growth as depicted in Figure 4.6. The 2019 revenues are estimated to be upwards of 3,200 million forints, an increase of approximately 18 percent over six years.

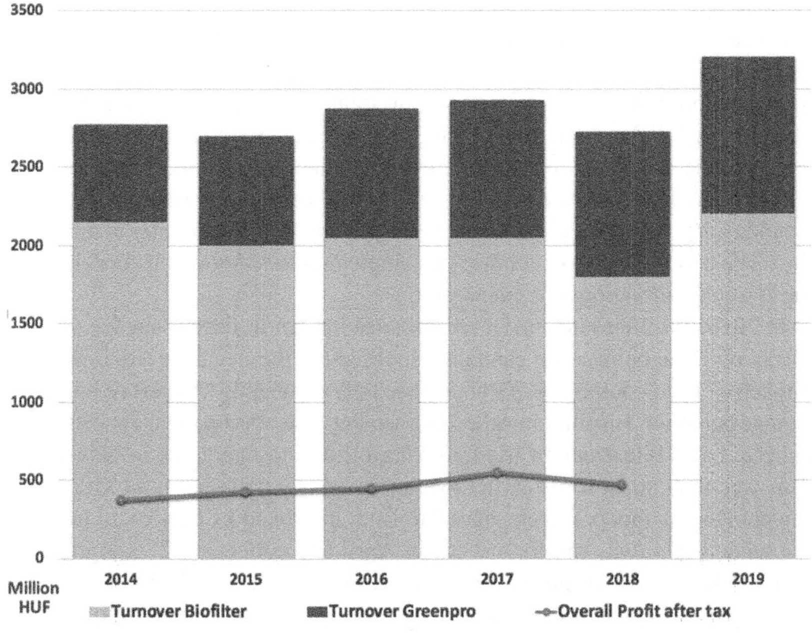

Note: The 2019 profit numbers were not available at the time of publication.

Figure 4.6 *Financial information for Biofilter and Greenpro (in million Hungarian forints)*

BIOFILTER IN THE COMMUNITY

The world is facing a climate crisis. In its quest to care for our planet, Biofilter is keen to engage with partners in the eco-system. It is leveraging its leadership in environmental sustainability and partnering with like-minded businesses, non-governmental organizations (NGOs) and foundations to educate, initiate and implement programs to raise awareness of this crisis and spark action for change. In 2014, Biofilter created a website to raise awareness of environmental issues specific to restaurants, offices and organizations (www.kornyezetert.hu). This website features content that educates and campaigns that engage the community. One video portrayed how a single drop of used oil could pollute 1,000 liters of water with damaging impact on wildlife. Other content focuses on food waste, plastics and packaging and climate impacts. Through these efforts more businesses and consumers are becoming aware of the importance of the proper disposal of used cooking oil, the relevance of recycling and the positive impact of circular solutions.

Since moving its headquarters to Törökbálint, Biofilter has earned the social license to operate in the community. In 2015, Biofilter reached out to Kerekdomb Association, a local environmental NGO. They agreed on a long-term collaboration to jointly develop and implement new projects in the area to raise awareness of environmental challenge and impact. Since 2015, Biofilter has supported the Association's annual community run by sponsoring running gear, visibility vests for race officials and a digital counter at the finish line. The company also encourages its employees to support and participate in the Association's programs every year.

In 2016, Biofilter launched a recycling campaign to further engage the residents of Törökbálint. The campaign highlighted the negative environmental impacts of used cooking oil if not disposed of responsibly. As part of its aim to change behavior, Biofilter installed convenient collection points. The first pilot collected 129 kilograms of used cooking oil during one week in November. This was in contrast to its earlier average weekly collection of 34 kilograms. Encouraged by this promising start, Biofilter improved its campaign. In 2017, the second pilot was run for a week in April and collected 227 kilograms of used cooking oil, a 76 percent increase. Biofilter now schedules semi-annual campaigns – in spring and autumn – to engage more residents and educate them on ecological issues and responsible oil disposal. Environmentally conscious residents have the option of disposing of their used cooking oil at Biofilter plants throughout the year.

To reach the community at large, Biofilter is supporting several associations and non-profit organizations such as the Heroes of Responsible Dining Foundation, which has the mission to make all restaurants in Hungary "green."

The company also partners with the Messzehangzó Tehetségek Foundation which supports underprivileged youth in the community by organizing special training and fields trips in the areas of information technology, natural history and the arts.

BIOFILTER'S JOURNEY TOWARDS B CORP CERTIFICATION

As a market leader in this industry, Biofilter believes it has a responsibility to demonstrate that embedding sustainability is not just a "feel-good" factor or "nice-to-have" achievement, but it is good for business. Many businesses in Hungary view sustainability as a "cost" and Biofilter aims to shatter this myth by being more transparent and public facing.

Brigitta's involvement in FBN's Polaris movement motivated her to take, on behalf of Biofilter, the PIA. The PIA is a customized version of B Lab's Impact Assessment (BIA), specifically tailored for family businesses who want to measure, benchmark and accelerate their sustainability performance. The standard version of the BIA is well established globally and has been taken by more than 50,000 companies in over 60 countries to drive sustainability. It has been shown to have positive impacts.

Brigitta first completed the PIA in March 2017 and it afforded Biofilter a first-hand look at how its family business was doing in the areas of governance, workers, community, the environment and family engagement. The family engagement section covered areas such as the family constitution, responsible ownership and investing in the next generation. Biofilter's completed PIA reflected that the family business had a clear purpose and direction and that it took an active leadership role in the community. Eager for constant improvement, Brigitta did a detailed analysis of Biofilter's performance and identified specific areas for furthering the company's positive impacts. These included developing a supplier code of conduct (community section), a more streamlined employee satisfaction process (workers section) and increasing transparency (governance section). Biofilter's transparency score was a composite of indicators that included questions on mission statement characteristics, social and environmental engagement, social and environmental key performance indicators and impact reporting (Figure 4.7).

The PIA data highlighted that when benchmarked against other businesses globally, Biofilter outperformed its peers in mission statement characteristics, social and environmental key performance indicators and stakeholder engagement, but there was a significant improvement opportunity in the area of impact reporting. Like many private companies, Biofilter, despite its focus on the environment and circularity, did not have a public-facing report detailing its mission-related or sustainability performance. This realization motivated

Companies in Benchmark	Companies in Network
9,477	1

Legend: Above Average, Average, Benchmark

Summary	% of Points Earned	Benchmark
Mission Statement Characteristics	100%	35%
Social & Environmental Internal Engagement	33%	11%
Social/Environmental Key Performance Indicators	100%	17%
Impact Reporting	15%	10%

Source: B Analytics, September 2018. Polaris (2018). *Shaping the Future We Want*, p. 20, available at https://www.fbn-i.org/sustainability/thought-leadership.

Figure 4.7 Biofilter's transparency performance benchmark

Biofilter to strive for B Corp certification – a little-known program in Hungary but a growing global phenomenon among purpose-driven businesses. On completing the full self-assessment, companies get a "score." Only companies with a verified score over 80 are certified. The process involves virtual meetings with B Lab staff to review the completed BIA and submission of confidential documentation to validate responses. To maintain certification, B Corp updates their BIA and verifies their updated score every three years. The B Corp movement has gathered accolades in mainstream and business media, with *Fortune Magazine* positing "Be like a B Corp is one of 5 business trends to master" and *Harvard Business Review* advancing that "It pays to become a B Corp."[27]

Biofilter's B Corp journey was led by Brigitta and involved engaging with the different areas of the business to fully understand the operations, challenges and obtain the requisite data. By using a systematic process to identify areas of improvement in governance, workers, community and environment, and making the necessary business transformations, Biofilter attained B Corp certification in 2018 – joining a global movement of businesses that meet the highest standards of verified social and environmental performance, public transparency and legal accountability.[28] That same year, Biofilter published its first public-facing sustainability report. As Brigitta explains, "This is important to the continued evolution of the company because sustainability reporting has a significant impact on corporate transparency which is one of the most important core values of Biofilter besides 'circularity' and 'innovative culture.'"

Not content with being the first B Corp in Hungary, Biofilter is now aiming to partner with like-minded organizations to bring the B Corp movement to the region and make visible a group of values-driven enterprises that are redefining success in business and building a more inclusive and sustainable economy.

SHAPING SUSTAINABILITY IN HUNGARY

György is optimistic for the future. As someone who has worked closely with the restaurant industry for decades, György sees two distinct trends – both related to higher disposable incomes and greater purchasing power. First, people are eating out more and there is a rise of fast-food chains and an accompanying increase in used cooking oil. And, second, greater affluence has led to an increase in fine dining outlets with its accompanying themes of healthy, organic and multi-sensory dining experiences. More demanding clientele also means that restaurants no longer tend to save costs through the multiple reuse of cooking oil. There is increased waste as restaurants discard "ugly" food and tend to use only selective parts for cooking or plating. The irony that more waste in the system could be advantageous for environmental companies like Biofilter is not lost on György. He notes, that:

> while the increasing trend of eating out in fast food chains and fine-dining restaurants means more raw material for Biofilter, this is short-term thinking. Our ultimate goal is to reduce the volume of organic waste that arrives to landfills. Being faithful to our philosophy, we are constantly working to improve our processes and to recycle the waste in a more environmentally conscious way, ensuring that it will re-create an economic value.

To this end, Biofilter is also taking action on the United Nations Sustainable Development Goals (SDGs). Ratified by 193 member countries in 2015, the 17 SDGs were developed with the business community and encompass economic, infrastructural, social and environmental dimensions. The goals are expansive and aspirational and place business at the center stage, presenting a historic opportunity for businesses to engage as a strong and positive influence on society.

Biofilter joined the Business Council of Sustainable Development Hungary (BCSDH) in 2015 and signed an Action 2020 plan. BCSDH is the national partner organization of the Swiss-based World Business Council for Sustainable Development (WBCSD), a chief executive officer-led business organization focused on how business can deliver on the SDGs. Working with the scientific, NGO and business communities, BCSDH identified the most important business sustainability risks and opportunities in Hungary. It sought to explore, develop and raise awareness about existing business solutions, as well as to measure and collate their results and impacts. In support of this nation-wide initiative, Biofilter pledged to take action on SDGs 2 (zero hunger), 6 (clean water and sanitation), 8 (decent work and economic growth), 12 (responsible

Table 4.1 Biofilter's commitment to Hungary's Action 2020 goals

BCSD and WBCSD Hungary Biofilter Action 2020 goals and sub-goals		
Goal 2	Zero hunger – food and feed	https://action2020.hu/en/cel/food-and-feed/
	• Less food waste	
	• Sustainable value chain	
Goal 6	Water	https://action2020.hu/en/cel/water/
	• Water efficiency	
	• Water quality	
Goal 8	Employment	https://action2020.hu/en/cel/employment/
	• Fair wages	
	• Lifelong learning	
	• Equal employment	
	• Women leaders	
Goal 12	Sustainable lifestyle	https://action2020.hu/en/cel/sustainable-lifestyles/
	• Life-cycle development	
	• Balanced lifestyles	
	• Empower consumers	
Goal 13	Climate change	https://action2020.hu/en/cel/climate-change/
	• Climate change risk mitigation	
	• Clean technologies	
	• Clean energy	

consumption and production) and 13 (climate action)[29] as listed in Table 4.1. The company is making progress on this journey. In 2018, Biofilter took home the Business Solution Prize awarded by WBCSDH. The Council deemed Biofilter's *Circular Approach in Digital* as an innovative, far-sighted exemplary program, noting that "Beyond regular business considerations, Biofilter continues to expand its own responsibilities and thus contributes to meeting the Action 2020 Hungary and United Nations' Sustainable Development Goals."[30]

One of the objectives of the Action 2020 program is to explore, develop and raise awareness of business solutions that go beyond business as usual to contribute towards meeting the Hungarian SDGs. The interpretation of "business solutions" includes business models, systems and technologies which are effective, adaptable, quantifiable and progressive.[31]

A ground-breaking project that has emerged out of Action 2020 is the Circular Economy Platform. Officially established in November 2018, this platform is a joint initiative of Hungary's Ministry of Innovation and Technology, the Embassy of the Kingdom of The Netherlands and the BCSDH. The platform aims to play a key role in creating a change of mindset about linear versus circularity and in sharing business solutions that bring about real change.[32] The Circular Economy Platform published its first report in January 2020 and highlighted the current thinking and practices of the Hungarian circular economy. It outlined three key actions for the country – more innovation, increased education and the need to share best practices. Biofilter was highlighted as one of the ten companies in the "Businesses that already have Solutions" and stood proudly among sustainability giants like Unilever, Nestlé and Tesco.

LEADING CHANGE, REDEFINING SUCCESS

In addition to supporting Hungary's national sustainable development aspirations, Biofilter is examining the SDG framework as it plans for its future. It seeks to identify specific SDGs aligned to the company's risks and opportunities and adopt meaningful near-term targets that include both the societal progress they intend to achieve and the positive impact on Biofilter. To make progress on this journey, Biofilter will leverage B Lab's SDG Action Manager – a platform launched in January 2020 and developed in partnership with the United Nations Global Compact. B Lab's SDG Action Manager is designed to enable businesses to get a clear view of how the business operations, supply chains and business models can simultaneously build resilience, identify opportunities and create positive impact. The online tool leverages the World Benchmarking Alliance's market analysis and has, as its starting point, a baseline assessment, which will help a company identify areas of risk and opportunity. Hence, according to the responses provided, companies will be advised on the SDGs most material or relevant to their business. Biofilter has taken the baseline assessment and were encouraged to focus on SDGs 7 (affordable and clean energy), 9 (industry innovation and infrastructure) and 13 (climate action).

Biofilter intends to embark on this journey in late 2020. Its B Corp certification is up for renewal in 2021 and the company plans to take this opportunity to update its BIA given that there is some overlap in questions with the two platforms. What is new for Biofilter is that the SDG Action Manager will enable the family business to build a long-term plan to further identify, take action and track progress on the SDGs with the most impactful opportunities. The company is also exploring with like-minded peers how to build awareness of the B Corp movement and the SDG Action Manager in Hungary.

Next-generation Brigitta is also part of FBN's Polaris Steering Group, which is driving an FBN–United Nations Global partnership to empower family businesses to deliver on the SDGs. Following FBN's participation at the United Nations World Investment Forum in 2018,[33] the United Nations Conference on Trade and Development has reached out to the network to develop a Family Business for Sustainable Development Global Initiative. Using the SDGs as a framework, this is designed to accelerate sustainability practices for all family businesses, more effectively deliver on the SDGs and create a shared prosperity for all. James Zhan, director at the United Nations Conference on Trade and Development and convenor of the World Investment Forum, noted that:

> FBN has provided visionary leadership. To maximize the potential of family firms, they need to be empowered to seize the untapped opportunities associated with embracing the sustainability agenda. We are pleased to share best practice derived from our global network of investment development stakeholders and offer the family business community an international platform to discuss and showcase their contribution to sustainable development.[34]

Biofilter is excited about this development as it presents a tremendous opportunity for family businesses to contribute to and lead sustainable development. György and his family have always understood that with their intrinsic intergenerational nature, the needed shift from *shareholder primacy* to *stakeholder capitalism* is well served by the family business model. Indeed, delivering for all stakeholders, investing in people, dealing fairly and ethically with suppliers and taking action to protect our climate have long been the principles and practices of Biofilter.

Throughout its 30-year history, the Deák family has aspired to build a business aligned with its values. Family control, long-term thinking and patient capital have enabled Biofilter to embed sustainability practices into the core of its operations and led to value creation over decades rather than focusing on one quarter to the next. External factors such as the Dioxin affair and the Greek debt crisis were weathered by the founder's clarity of vision and adherence to ideals of circularity, innovation and transparency. These efforts have been widely recognized with awards and accolades from national and international communities. An illustrative list is provided in Table 4.2.

Biofilter's journey of resilience, inclusive growth and purpose is a testament to the spirit of entrepreneurship and stewardship epitomized in the Deák family. Like its peers across the globe, family businesses like Biofilter are playing a key role in driving the circularity and sustainability agenda – redefining success in business for society and across generations.

Table 4.2 Biofilter's awards, certifications and recognition

Awards, certifications and recognition	Organization	Year
Businesses that already have solutions	Circular Economy Platform report	2020
Best for the World honoree – governance	B Lab Impact Assessment	2019
Addressing Food Waste in Hungary – Private-Sector Initiative	The Netherlands Embassy, Hungary	2018
Business Solution Prize	Business Council of Sustainable Development Hungary	2018
Rising Stars award	European Business Awards	2018
B Corp certification	B Lab Impact Assessment	2018
Top 10 European Business in Environment and Corporate Sustainability	European Business Awards	2016
Business Ethics award	Hungarian Piac and Profit Magazine	2016
Business Ethics award	Transparency International	2015
International Sustainability and Carbon certification[1]	ISCC	2014

Note: [1] Globally recognized sustainability and carbon certification that covers the entire supply chain, available at www.iscc-system.org.

KEY INSIGHTS

- Biofilter's success as a pioneer in the circular economy is *by design.* The company has, from the onset, embedded sustainability into the core of its business. Unlike many enterprises where "sustainability" is a public relations tool or "bolt-on" extra, concepts and practices of environmental stewardship and social responsibility are integral to Biofilter's operations.
- Clarity of purpose is a critical ingredient for long-term value. This is evidenced by Biofilter's commitment to its credo of "circularity, innovation and transparency" which has enabled it to develop a patient capital mindset and approach to operations, investments and expansion.
- Businesses that embrace a stakeholder worldview of capitalism are more willing to embark on entrepreneurial ventures that are less traveled. Undeterred by nay-sayers, György identified opportunities while others saw problems and with tenacity and patient capital has emerged as one of the pioneers of the biodiesel, biogas and circular economy for the region.
- Sustainability is a driver of innovation, growth and success. Contrary to perceptions that sustainability is a "cost," "feel-good" factor or just a "nice-to-have" achievement, Biofilter has shattered this myth by demonstrating that it is good for business. In addition, it has done this not by just

rhetoric or platitudes but by being transparent as evidenced by its sustainability reporting and B Corp certification.

- By sharing his values and aspirations with his family, György's vision of a circular economy business is deeply ingrained in the second generation of Deáks. Furthermore, his empowering of his children to lead and shape the sustainability mandate of the company will further embed this strong sense of purpose in the culture of Biofilter.
- We are living in volatile, uncertain and complex times. Crises such as climate change and global pandemics are upending markets and disrupting traditional businesses and whole industries. In its 30-year history, Biofilter has weathered turbulent storms and faced massive disruption. Clarity of purpose, innovating for impact and patient capital have been critical to Biofilter's progress and will be strategic for the family business's onward trajectory.

NOTES

1. This case is based on in-depth interviews with György Deák and his daughter Brigitta. The authors are especially grateful to Brigitta for being our translator and key resource person over this 12-month period. In addition, information was gleaned from news articles, sustainability-related portals, the FBN Polaris case study and the BCSD Hungary website.
2. Polaris (2018). *Shaping the Future We Want.*
3. Ellen MacArthur Foundation, 2019.
4. G7, 2019. https://g7.hu/
5. Boom Magazine, 2019.
6. A three-cylinder, two-stroke engine car with only seven major moving parts manufactured in East Germany since the 1950s.
7. Attila, J. (2019), "Business families." Forbes, January.
8. This contract was signed by György Deák, the self-employed entrepreneur, who was collecting used cooking oil before Biofilter, the private limited company, was created.
9. Lok, C. & Powell, D. (2000). "The Belgian Dioxin crisis of the summer of 1999: A case study in crisis communication and management (monograph on the internet)." University of Guelph, Ontario. Department of Food Science.
10. Ibid.
11. G7 (2019). https://g7.hu/
12. IHT (1999). www.wsws.org/en/articles/1999/06/belg-j08.html
13. Lok, C. & Powell, D. (2000). "The Belgian Dioxin crisis of the summer of 1999: A case study in crisis communication and management (monograph on the internet)." University of Guelph, Ontario. Department of Food Science.
14. Ibid.
15. Flanders Today (2009). "Sentences in dioxin case."
16. Polaris (2018). *Shaping the Future We Want.*
17. European Central Bank (2017). "5 things you need to know about the Maastricht Treaty."
18. Investopedia (2020). "Understanding the downfall of Greece's economy."

19. G7 (2019). https://g7.hu/
20. Family Business Network, www.fbn-i.org
21. Family Business Network, Polaris. www.fbn-i.org/sustainability
22. Polaris Impact Assessment for Family Businesses, www.fbn-i.org/sustainability/measure-your-impact
23. "Move it Bio" is a health-care and environmental program that includes a series of sporting and environmental activities for employees and the community.
24. www.climfoot-project.eu/en/description-program-france
25. Embassy of the Kingdom of The Netherlands (2018). "The state of food waste in Hungary."
26. www.greenpro.hu
27. Stammer, R. (2016). "It pays to become a B Corp." *Harvard Business Review*, December.
28. B Lab (2020). www.bcorporation.net/about-b-lab
29. Biofilter (2020). www.biofilter.hu/rolunk/korforgasban-a-kornyezetert
30. WBCSD (2019). www.bcsdh.hu/sustainable-future-prize/the-winners/the-winners-in-2018/
31. BCSDH (2020). https://action2020.hu/en/uzleti-megoldasok/
32. WBCSD (2020). www.bcsdh.hu/projects/circular-economy-platform/
33. FBN Polaris (2020). www.fbn-i.org/sustainability/voice-family-business
34. Polaris (2019). "Redefining success across generations." FBN.

PART III

Transformed for sustainable development

5. The evolution of a sustainable energy family business: The case of Thermax

Kavil Ramachandran and Yashodhara Basuthakur

INTRODUCTION

> My vision is not to build a dynasty but to build an institution. (Rohinton Aga)[1]

As 2019 came to a close and a new decade approached, Meher Pudumjee, chairperson of Thermax, a leading Indian engineering company, prepared her message for employees with Warren Buffet's "moat" principle[2] in mind: what was the "moat" or competitive edge that differentiated Thermax from other companies in the energy and environment engineering space? The company had performed well on many parameters over the years, but what stood out to Meher were the values of social good and environmental sustainability that her grandfather, A. S. Bhathena, her father, Rohinton Aga, and later her mother Anu Aga had ingrained in Thermax's DNA decades earlier. These values had guided the family for three generations and driven its many pioneering and game-changing initiatives, setting Thermax apart from, and often ahead of, its competitors.

Thermax, a multi-generational family business operating in the areas of energy, environment and chemicals, was headquartered in Pune, Maharashtra, in western India. The company had 4,110 employees and a revenue of over 61 billion rupees in the fiscal year 2018–19. Originally a part of National Steel (India) Private owned by A. S. Bhathena, the business unit was set up to manufacture hospital sterilizers and fowler beds. Later, in the 1960s, the company collaborated with Wanson Belgium to manufacture baby boilers and hence Wanson India was born. Bhathena brought in a dynamic youngster, Rohinton Aga (who later became his son-in-law), initially as a senior executive and later as a member of the board of the newly formed company.

The company's first environmental sustainability initiative was precipitated by the oil crisis of the 1970s, when it developed a boiler called Multitherm that used locally available biomass as fuel, marking the company's entry into the solid fuels. This was an important step for the Indian industry towards energy conservation. Under Bhathena and Aga, Thermax also expanded into auxiliary offerings including chemicals, water treatment and air pollution control.

Bhathena instilled the values of social service and individual responsibility across the organization. The deepening focus on environmental sustainability took shape in the second generation of the family business in the 1980s, led by Aga. Bhathena was supportive of Aga's initiatives. During the 1980s and 1990s, Aga defined the green initiatives of the firm and made environmental sustainability an integral part of the company's value and mission statement. He recruited high-caliber engineers from the premier technical institutes of India and gave them freedom to innovate and come up with energy-efficient and environmentally friendly solutions. Some of the key professionals, like N. D. Joshi and R. V. Ramani, grew to become "intrapreneurs" and worked very closely with him to diversify the company into waste heat recovery, absorption cooling and captive power generation.

This was also the period during which Thermax forged critical technology partnerships with global players and became a public company. Under Aga, the company became, and remained, a powerful advocate for sustainability at the industry and national levels, helping to shape environmental policy and leading by example. The human values and business ethics that Bhathena and Aga had embedded in the management practices of the organization were carried on by their successors and professionals.

Appendix 5.1 provides a synopsis of the sustainability journey of the family across the generations.

Arnavaz (Anu) Aga, Bhathena's daughter and Aga's wife, took over as the executive chairperson at Thermax in 1996 after the sudden death of her husband. During her tenure, she reinforced the company's social initiatives with a focus on educating the underprivileged. She also played a critical role in turning around the organization. In 1988, she became the non-executive chairperson and professionalized the family business. Her daughter Meher, who took over in 2004, continued the family legacy of environmental and social responsibility. Along with the top management team, she launched organization-wide initiatives to further innovation and operational excellence. She was a clean energy crusader and pushed forward this agenda through green product offerings and sustainable building design by incorporating energy and environment standards such as site planning, water and energy conservation at their manufacturing facilities. Like her mother, Meher truly believed in ethical business practices and the positive role that industry had to play in social uplifting.

The story of Thermax and its controlling family presents an opportunity to study the factors that contributed to the success of a socially and environmental sustainability-oriented family business in an emerging economy over three generations. The experiences and decisions of the family leaders of Thermax will offer useful insights for other family firms that are pursuing long-term, environmentally sustainable growth and success.

The next section traces the evolution of Thermax, describing the sustainability vision and values of three generations of the family and how these were embedded in the organization's culture, and its process and product offerings over the years. The section discusses the source of the company's sustained competitive advantage which led to transgenerational perpetuity; traces the company's response to various internal and external shifts and challenges and how it shaped the company's culture, strategy and focus; and highlights the family values of sustainability that played a key role in leveraging patient family capital in a market that was yet to evolve. This section is followed by a review of the company's recent performance, the future outlook for Thermax and, finally, key insights and takeaways for other family businesses.

THERMAX THROUGH THE YEARS

The Early Years under A. S. Bhathena (1966–81)

A. S. Bhathena was born into the small but influential Parsi (Zoroastrian) community in Maharashtra. He worked for a time at Godrej & Boyce, a steel furniture manufacturer, before quitting his job in 1947 to start his entrepreneurial venture in the export–import business. The company, National Steel, manufactured adjustable hospital beds called "Fowler beds." These specialty beds had to be imported from the United Kingdom before Bhathena began manufacturing them indigenously. His experience with the hospital equipment business helped Bhathena diversify into several related product lines. He started manufacturing sterilizers and other types of hospital equipment and, in 1966, entered a collaboration with Wanson (Belgium) to manufacture "baby boilers" named "Vaporax" under a new company name, Wanson (India). Bhathena set up the company's first manufacturing plant in Mumbai (formerly Bombay). The plant was later relocated to Pune.

Bhathena had two sons, but neither was interested in joining Wanson India (later Thermax, as the company will be referred to hereafter). His younger son, Daravus, took over the family business, National Steel, that Bhathena had set up, and his older son Jamshed settled abroad. Prior to leaving for the United States, in 1962, Jamshed invited his friend Aga, a Cambridge-educated economist who had worked at multinationals such as Burmah Shell and Duncan Brothers, to join National Steel as a senior executive. It was a move that would have a profound and lasting impact on the family and the business. Bhathena's association with Aga was strengthened in 1965 when Aga married his daughter Anu. In 1966, Aga became a director at Thermax.

Bhathena articulated the human and social values of the company at the very early stages of its formation. He was a strong proponent of equal opportunity for everyone, irrespective of their social or cultural standing. He believed in integrating people across communities and regions. In a 1970 letter to fresh recruits, Bhathena described the qualities and traits he believed every employee should cultivate, being "earnest, competent, mature, sensitive to their surroundings, pleasant and positive in their attitude towards life, with a capacity to laugh at themselves, and above all show evidence of management muscle at senior levels"[3] (see Appendix 5.2). He considered the firm a "human enterprise" that empowered every employee to take decisions and actions responsibly, advocated freedom of thought and expression and fostered relationships based on mutual trust and respect. Though neither Bhathena nor Aga had an engineering background, they built a successful engineering company, thanks to the freedom, empowerment, responsibility and accountability they gave to their leadership team. The company did not have rules and regulations that stifled people's imagination and innovativeness. He called upon his employees to become warriors against poverty and social injustice. He eschewed extravagance and set an example for his employees and the organization on the importance of frugality, simplicity and moderation. Over time, these values became institutionalized in the company.

Thermax's early environmental sustainability initiatives were triggered by the oil price shock and global economic slowdown of the early 1970s, which affected countries like India that depended heavily on imported oil. The crisis also sparked discussions about alternative sources of energy with a strong emphasis on local availability to ensure energy security. Thermax seized this opportunity to redefine itself. It redesigned its energy-related products that were dependent on oil into products that harnessed solid fuels such as coal, wood and husk. This transition led to the development of unique, organization-specific capabilities such as in decision-making processes based on deep insights into the application of sustainability and an organization culture that endorsed the importance of sustainability. These capabilities contributed to improving the competitiveness of the firm. When the company developed India's first solid fuel-powered water tube boiler Multitherm, which could use different sources of energy such as coal, wood or husk, it became a trendsetter in the industry. Aga wrote:

> The first oil crisis in 1973 could have been our Waterloo because we were manufacturing only oil-fired boilers. We reacted fast, coming out with the country's first packaged coal-fired unit, well before the competition; this has since been a bestseller.[4]

Thermax went on to build complementary process capabilities at various stages of value addition in the new technologies and products. It developed synergies focused on environmental sustainability over the next few years, extending into water treatment systems and chemicals for boilers and air pollution control to reduce boiler emissions. In 1976, Thermax acquired Tulsi Fine Chemicals, which later became the chemical division of the company. The division manufactured a range of resins and specialty chemicals used in water and wastewater treatment. It then diversified into construction, paper and pulp, oil refinery operations and the sugar industry. The company launched its Enviro division to manufacture air pollution control equipment in 1979, even before the Central Pollution Control Board, set up in 1974, became an active player with the enactment of the Air (Prevention and Control of Pollution) Act 1981. The comprehensive environmental legislation on protecting and improving environment quality was enacted much later in 1986. Though the industrial regulations for air, water and environmental protection were fairly lax and discretionary during that period in India, Thermax set its own higher standards. Aga wrote:

> We firmly believe in and support a national effort at environmental protection, in which we have to play a significant role by developing or acquiring appropriate technologies, promoting general awareness, aligning our priorities with those of society and providing a service to industry which enables it to produce in an uninterrupted and yet pollution-free manner.
>
> **We also strongly subscribe to the view that *economic development and environmental protection are not antithetical.***[5]

At that time, most companies had smoking chimneys and made perfunctory use of emission control equipment to keep regulators at bay. The emission dust particles (particulate matter) in India ranged between 700 and 800 mg/Nm^3, far below the standard of 250 mg/Nm^3 that existed in advanced countries then and 30 mg/Nm^3 or below adopted by most advanced countries and India today. The Enviro division was instrumental in partnering with overseas companies and developing best-in-class industrial pollution control filters and solutions. Thermax's air pollution control products, which catered to Indian and global locations, surpassed the local norms and matched up to global emission norms. The company played an active role in partnering with the Indian government to formulate policies on air pollution in the 1980s.

Environmental Sustainability to the Forefront under Rohinton Aga (1981–96)

In 1980, the collaboration with Wanson came to an end, and the company was officially renamed Thermax Private Limited. By this time, the company had established itself as a boiler manufacturer and expanded to the overseas market. Its vision statement in 1980 read, "Conserving energy, preserving the environment."[6] Aga was appointed chairman and managing director of the newly christened Thermax in 1981.

In 1982, Aga suffered a massive heart attack and had to undergo bypass surgery. During the procedure, he also suffered a paralytic stroke. Through sheer determination and will power, he recovered almost fully in two years and returned to lead Thermax. It was during this time that his wife Anu officially joined Thermax in the human resources department, where she later introduced several human resources management initiatives such as Open Forum, a platform for employee–management dialogue; skill-building programs for women employees and workmen; and educational programs for the children of employees.

Aga, like Bhathena, believed in "business with a purpose." He knew that industrial activity and the energy generation business would be unsustainable if the environment was not given due attention and care early on. He was the visionary behind Thermax's sustainability efforts and aligned the company's business goals with the broader national pursuit of greener and more sustainable energy sources.

Aga continuously redefined the business to meet emerging market needs, and with help from his intrapreneurial team, expanded the product portfolio from energy-related products such as boilers to products that used sustainable forms of energy, such as biomass, industrial waste heat and absorption cooling. He was a pioneer in starting India's first wind energy business in the 1980s. This business did not take off immediately in the absence of policy stipulations needed to encourage green energy development.

During these years, the concepts of climate change and sustainability were little understood in India. Aga knew that sensitization and communication both internally and with external stakeholders was important to get them on board with the company's sustainability goals. Initially, Thermax had difficulty marketing its pioneering solutions such as harnessing steam from factory smoke and reusing waste for energy generation. Aga was critical in changing the prevailing industry mindset by propagating knowledge, technology and product offerings within the industry and convincing stakeholders of the benefits of environmentally sustainable solutions. For instance, in the 1980s, rice milling was a proliferating business in India. However, in the process, rice mills accumulated huge amounts of rice husk as waste. Thermax's engineers came up with an innovative solution to generate heat from rice husk. The steam produced from the waste husk was sufficient for the entire process requirements of the rice mills.

Another challenge during the early days was the dearth of technology and know-how in the country for the design of efficient boilers and chillers and the high cost of green energy operations. This was because the cost of setting up green energy technology was expensive besides achieving the same level of technical and cost efficiency as fossil fuels. Aga and his team began looking for international collaborations to bring in the necessary expertise. In 1986, Thermax collaborated with GE Environmental Services Incorporated (United States) to bring state-of-the-art particulate emission control technologies to India and enhance the capabilities of the Enviro division and its air pollution control product offerings.

At this time, Thermax was far ahead of the competition in India on its environmental sustainability initiatives. In fact, various national-level environmental policies came into existence well after Thermax had taken a lead in this arena.

In the international arena, in 1987, the Montreal Protocol was taking shape to regulate the global production and use of chemicals, namely chlorofluorocarbon (CFC), hydro-chlorofluorocarbon (HCFC), carbon tetrachloride (CTC) and halons, which depleted the earth's ozone layer and harmed the environment. India became a signatory to this treaty in 1992. As a signatory to the Montreal Protocol in 1987 and Kyoto Protocol in 1997, India's global commitment was to phase out the use of HCFCs by 2030. The Indian industry had to realign its goals to meet the targets of the international agreement.

Aga and his management team proactively responded to global developments on the elimination of ozone-depleting chemicals. Under his leadership, Thermax collaborated with Sanyo (Japan) in the late 1980s to design vapor absorption chillers that offered a CFC-free air conditioning and refrigeration solution. Thermax went on to further develop the technology indigenously. The cooling solution used absorption technology with pure water as the refrigerant instead of hazardous greenhouse gases such as CFCs. The chillers utilized waste heat from industrial processes. These chillers consumed only 5 percent of the power consumed by an electrical chiller of similar capacity, thereby saving energy and reducing carbon emissions. In 1988, Thermax entered into a joint venture with Babcock and Wilcox (United States) to design and manufacture steam generation plants with capacities of up to 300 tons per hour and heat recovery steam generators. Aga wrote in the company magazine, "Most of the products and technologies accord with our national priorities of conserving energy, preserving the environment."[7]

For most of his tenure, Aga operated in a closed economy with restrictive trade practices and almost negligible awareness of environmental sustainability in business practices. The Monopolies and Restrictive Trade Practices Act 1969 put severe restrictions on the quantities and types of goods or services that could be produced by the private sector. Private firms had to obtain licenses or permits to expand or start new businesses. Because of these constraints, firms pragmatically focused on diversifying only into areas where they were able to acquire the required licenses. Aga navigated through the maze of licenses by focusing on diversification into areas where he saw a market need and alignment with the firm's existing values and capabilities in energy and environment sustainability. Aga wrote:

> Our strategy of diversification was four-fold: First, we were quick to react to events and opportunities as they unfold themselves. Second, defining and redefining our business to be in the area of conserving energy and preserving the environment. If you can re-define your business in terms of the market need you fulfill, the canvas is limitless. Third, to move into areas which provided a synergy in terms of the technology, or the market, or both. From process heat generation (boilers) to energy conservation is a diversification where both the technology and the market are familiar. Fourth, the choice of products which makes it possible for us to use the same assets and infrastructural facilities to serve a variety of markets.[8]

The liberalization of the Indian economy in the early 1990s resulted in the removal of import restrictions on technology and had a positive impact on the company's acquisition, internationalization and technology collaboration strategy. In February 1995, Thermax became a public company on the Bombay Stock Exchange. Aga noted:

> We perceive a tremendous potential in our core areas of energy, environment, and related technologies, thanks to the opening up of the economy.[9]

Aga's pioneering role in the energy and environment space, and specifically in green industrial development, was appreciated, and he led the energy delegation of Indian industrialists to the United States in 1995. He was also the chairman of the Energy Committee of the Confederation of Indian Industry, the apex industry association in India. He once said: "For the economic progress of our country, industrial growth is essential, and yet it has to be sustained at ecologically acceptable levels."[10] He put his words into practice by defining Thermax's energy-efficient product portfolio to service heavy engineering and manufacturing industries such as refineries, cement, paper, thermal power plants and steel.

Professionalization and Continuation of the Legacy under Anu Aga (1996–2004)

In 1996, Aga suffered a second and fatal heart attack in Mumbai, as he was getting ready to pick up Anu from the airport. Anu was returning from the United Kingdom after a six-month visit to their daughter Meher, son-in-law Pheroz and newborn grandchild.

On Aga's passing, Anu was appointed chairperson by the board of directors. With no time to mourn or cope with her loss, Anu had to take over the leadership mantle of a company that was facing growing competition. As she later recounted, she was not at all prepared to lead the company but did not have many options since the family held 62 percent equity in Thermax and she felt responsible for the several families that were dependent on the company.

Anu had grown up in Mumbai in an upper-middle-class Parsi family where, as she later wrote, "The message was drummed in my mind that as a woman, I ought to marry and start a family first."[11] She had never been groomed to enter and lead a business. She earned her undergraduate degree in economics and political science from St. Xavier's College, Mumbai, and pursued a master's degree in medical and psychiatric social work at the Tata Institute of Social Sciences, Mumbai. She eventually married Aga and had two children, fulfilling the role that was expected by her family and community. It was Aga who encouraged Anu to join the human resources department at Thermax and channel her talent in people management. With the leadership of the company suddenly thrust upon her, Anu leaned on "the core values and business practices so successfully ingrained by R. D. Aga over the last 29 years."[12]

Though she may have been a reluctant leader to begin with, Anu immersed herself in the business and was determined to carry on her husband's legacy. She continued the work on the research center for energy and environment-related technologies that her husband had begun; the Energy and Environment Research Centre was inaugurated in December 1996. The center developed and adapted technology for various uses; for example, it introduced the process of co-generation, i.e., simultaneously generating power and steam from boilers for industrial use, which became a major part of the company's energy portfolio.

A little over a year after Aga's death, Anu suffered another personal loss when her 25-year-old son, Kurush, died in a car accident. These were difficult times for the business as well. Within the first four years of Anu taking over the reins of the company, the Indian economy witnessed a downturn, and Thermax's share price plummeted from 420 to 36 rupees. The company posted an operational loss for the first time in its history. Investors were distressed by the company's performance; in fact, Anu received an anonymous letter from one of the shareholders who wrote, "Mrs. Aga, I don't know your financial condition, but you have let me down."[13] Anu had always believed that it was the leadership's responsibility to protect the interests of employees, customers, family members and minority stakeholders. It was the family's deeply ingrained belief that it had to shoulder all fiduciary responsibilities towards its investors and stakeholders irrespective of difficult personal or economic circumstances. Anu wanted to preserve the family legacy in Thermax and nurture and protect it for her children and future generations. It was a challenging time for her, and she turned to meditation to find the inner strength and confidence to cultivate her talents and lead the business. She said, "I cannot keep comparing myself with my husband and feel inadequate and small."[14]

Anu orchestrated a comeback in the face of adverse market conditions and skepticism from Thermax executives. She believed that "skills can be hired, but the leader has to show wisdom – that cannot be hired."[15] She took the bold step of hiring the services of Boston Consulting Group to assist in restructuring the business, redefining the board structure and further professionalizing the family business by separating management from ownership. Anu said, "I realized that as a public limited company, we had to protect the interests of the minority shareholders who had placed their faith in Thermax. I was convinced that our management was out of its depth and needed outside help. My senior executives resisted the idea."[16]

The new board had four independent directors; three family members as non-executive directors, namely, Anu, her daughter and future chairperson Meher Pudumjee and son-in-law Pheroz Pudumjee; and one full-time executive director (managing director). The decision to restructure the board was not easy for Anu. She had to persuade nine executive directors who had long tenures with the company to step down, which they graciously accepted. She gave Meher and Pheroz the option to decide whether they wanted to be on the board or retain their position as executives. Anu recalled, "At that time, [Meher and Pheroz] were a little upset with me. They were used to managing the business."[17] They were not fully convinced of the soundness of Anu's decision but ultimately decided to continue on the board with no executive responsibilities.

Apart from implementing organizational changes, Anu also followed Boston Consulting Group's advice on restructuring the business portfolio. The new structure had four core businesses: boilers and heaters, absorption cooling, water and wastewater management, and chemicals. Thermax divested non-core businesses and joint ventures such as software, electronics, surface coating, a joint venture with Fuji, a joint venture with Culligan for drinking water and redefined its focus to only energy and environment solutions. During this time, Thermax set up fully-owned subsidiary operations in the United States. The company's business in wastewater treatment and energy co-generation continued to make steady progress. Anu and her team (headed by Prakash Kulkarni as managing director) succeeded in turning around the company's financial performance by 2002.

During her tenure on the board of Thermax for over two decades, profitability was not the only thing on her mind. Her instincts for public service, nation building and philanthropy ensured that she conducted the business ethically and with empathy. She followed a transparent, moral and value-based approach to managing the company, connecting with her employees and other stakeholders.

Protection of the environment was close to her heart. In Anu's words:

> **The disastrous consequences of the world's climate change offer just such an opportunity to link business with the wellbeing and security of nations and future generations. Unless we step out of the paradigms of limitless growth based on unchecked exploitation of hydrocarbon fuels and curb our wasteful energy use patterns, we would soon be crossing the point of no return.**
>
> Can we, as business leaders, contribute in our individual ways to reduce our energy intensities and reduce our carbon footprints? More importantly, can we voice our concern in industrial forums and bring pressure on our respective national governments to frame and implement economic and industrial policies that arrest and reverse our suicidal rush in the name of development? Can we redefine success as not what we create for ourselves but the legacy we leave behind for our future generations?[18]

All her life, Anu had demonstrated a passion for social service. For many years, Anu had divided her efforts among a wide range of social issues, such as river cleaning, adopting a village and setting up watershed facilities for the village. However, after she lost her son, who had been keen to reach out to the poor and needy, she collaborated with Akanksha, a reputed non-governmental organization started by Shaheen Mistry, that offered educational support to poor children. Anu was invited to join the Akanksha board.

Later, Thermax Foundation (founded in 2007) started to train government school teachers in Pune who were capable and wanted to give their best, but did not have the right opportunities and training in harnessing their individual strengths. Anu said, "Unfortunately in India, the quality of education is deteriorating every year. Thermax Foundation focuses on training the teachers very effectively. The teacher training institutes are inadequate and corrupt, and quality of education is bound to suffer."[19] In 2007, long before India had made corporate social responsibility (CSR) mandatory for companies through the Companies Act 2013, Anu had decided to allocate 1 percent of the company's profits to CSR initiatives through the Thermax Foundation, with an exclusive focus on education.

Anu retired from the position of chairperson in 2004 at the age of 62 and the board appointed Meher as chairperson at Thermax. Anu continued as a member of the board but focused on philanthropy and social causes as a member of the National Advisory Council and later as a member of the upper house of the Indian Parliament. She was awarded the Padma Shri, the fourth highest civilian award in India, in 2010 for her contributions to the social sector.

The Third Generation: Perpetuating the Family Business and Values under Meher Pudumjee (2004–present)

Meher, the third-generation leader of Thermax, joined the company as an engineering graduate trainee in 1990 after earning a master's degree in chemical engineering from the Imperial College of Science and Technology, London. She worked in various capacities across Thermax's businesses. Meher said, "The best legacy an outgoing family leader can bestow on the next generation is to ground them in the values cherished by the family, and that is valued as the hallmark of that organization."[20]

Meher, who joined the organization in 1990, and her husband Pheroz continued the family legacy of embedding environmental sustainability in the company's business practices as articulated in its vision statement "To be a globally respected high-performance organization offering sustainable solutions in energy and the environment."[21] Thermax adopted a triple-bottom-line framework to assess its social, environmental and financial performance. In 2004, under Meher's leadership, the management hired the services of McKinsey and Company and launched Project Evergreen to strategize Thermax's position in India and the international market and propel growth. They decided to focus on the domestic dominance, selective internationalization, innovation, people development and services.

Meher started her leadership tenure term in a world that was more aware and vocal about environmental sustainability. Thermax recognized that "climate change and a strong impetus on reduction in carbon emissions are shifting the world focus to clean and efficient technologies."[22] She explained:

> In the years to come, with climate change and the population increasing faster than our resources can cope, we need to conserve energy and preserve our environment. Also, with oil prices ramping up and fossil fuels running out, it only makes sense to develop alternative forms of energy.[23]

In the boiler and power generation domain, Thermax once again collaborated with global industry leaders such as Babcock & Wilcox to enhance operational and technical know-how. These technologies offered higher efficiency, resulting in better energy output from the same coal or fuel input, thereby helping to reduce carbon emissions. Unfortunately, the market did not develop as anticipated. Moreover, the offerings moved from boiler only to boiler turbine generator to engineering procurement construction, and hence Thermax decided to close the joint venture.

Meher was keen to set up a solar energy business in 2008 in the face of rising oil prices globally. Shortly thereafter, Thermax entered into a public–private partnership with the Department of Science and Technology, Government of

India, to establish a solar power generation plant. There was a dilemma about the extent to which green energy should be pursued, as sometimes environmental sustainability comes at the cost of profits. Notwithstanding, green technology development was driven by Thermax.

During the financial crisis in 2008–2009, Thermax launched Project Ever-Lean to "eliminate waste, streamline processes and systems and reduce costs."[24] This initiative, in conjunction with an organization-wide focus on operational excellence, resulted in the creation of better and more robust processes and systems. As part of Project Ever-Lean, various steps were taken to reduce power consumption at Thermax facilities, including installing energy-saving devices, such as energy-efficient high luminosity lighting and auto-controlled real-time clock timer units for streetlights and fans, and modernizing plant machinery. Thermax harnessed solar energy to augment power demand at a few of its locations. Every effort was taken to ensure that Thermax did not become a wasteful organization. M. S. Unnikrishnan, managing director and chief executive officer of Thermax, said, "Everyone avails the economy class for domestic air travel and stays in company guest houses. Also, employees are encouraged to avail rideshare services wherever possible."[25]

Thermax had already started to implement a zero-waste policy at its plants. It had set up rainwater harvesting, water recycling and treatment facilities at all of its premises towards waste minimization. All of its plants offered a safe and healthy working environment and all newer manufacturing locations of the company complied with stringent green-building norms.

Thermax continued to add green and energy-efficient systems, products and services to its portfolio, enabling its customers to achieve higher productivity and efficiency while maintaining a cleaner environment. For example, Thermax offered a total heating, cooling and power generation solution to an Indian multinational. It transitioned the company from fossil fuel to a 100 percent biomass-fired boiler, resulting in fuel cost savings of 45 percent. The steam generated by the boiler was used in the manufacturing of potato chips and instant noodles. Thermax's ultra-low pressure vapor absorption chiller extracted waste heat from potato fryers, noodle steamers and snack fryers to provide air conditioning in the production area. Its absorption heat pumps reduced the energy required to heat water by nearly 40 percent through waste heat recovery.

In 2010, Thermax opened a wholly-owned subsidiary, Thermax Onsite Energy Solutions (TOESL), which was entirely focused on supplying "green steam" to customers. The steam generated for this business was derived exclusively from biomass. The company management had initially proposed the use of fossil fuel also for steam generation since it would allow the business to grow at a much faster pace. However, Meher and the majority of the board were committed to the use of clean and green alternatives and held their ground. Meher said, "I was particular that our subsidiary, TOESL, should continue with clean energy solutions. That decision has obviously put limitations on its growth. We are prepared to live by that decision even if it means short-term setbacks."[26]

Meanwhile, on the research and development front, the research center, which had been upgraded and named the R. D. Aga Research, Technology, and Innovation Center (RTIC) in 2007, had been developing a number of indigenous products and solutions. For example, in 2011, RTIC developed a first-of-its-kind technology that used solar energy to create efficient and eco-friendly cooling systems. It also collaborated with eminent institutions at home and abroad to develop solutions for energy, water and waste solutions, chemicals and air (see Appendix 5.3).

The Enviro division continued to offer innovative and customized solutions to diverse industries. For example, Thermax collaborated with Marsulex Solutions (United States) to bring flue gas desulphurization emission control technologies to India, supporting the Indian government's mandate for all the thermal power plants in the country to reduce sulfur oxide emissions to below 100 mg/Nm^3. Initiatives such as these helped Indian industry meet India's pledge at the Paris Climate Summit (2015 United Nations Climate Change Conference or COP21) and advanced the Indian government's efforts to reduce greenhouse gas emissions.

Meanwhile, the social initiatives of the company continue to focus on improving the quality and reach of school education. Anu and Meher are active in the Thermax Foundation which continues to work with leading non-profit organizations in the education sector like Akanksha and "Teach for India" and helps provide free education to economically underprivileged children. A few employees of the company are also actively involved in its philanthropic initiatives. Some take time off during weekends to mentor students, while a few have applied for "Teach for India" fellowships, where they serve as full-time teachers in government and under-resourced schools for two years. In 2011–12, the company increased its CSR contribution to 3 percent of its net profits, even before the Companies Act 2013 mandated a 2 percent contribution.

During Meher's tenure, Thermax cemented its position as a sustainable energy and environment solution provider (see Appendix 5.4 for sustainability awards received by the company over the years). The company's tagline was "Conserving Resources, Preserving the Future" – conservation of not just energy, but water and other resources that need to be conserved on our planet. Meher's favorite quote is: "We have not inherited this earth from our forefathers but borrowed it from our children." Meher was actively involved in the activities of Shakti Sustainable Energy Foundation, a non-governmental organization that worked towards facilitating India's transition towards clean

Table 5.1 *Financial performance 2013–19 (in million rupees)*

Year	2013	2014	2015	2016	2017	2018	2019
Sales	45,650	41,680	45,440	42,740	36,770	37,840	50,980
Profit before tax	5,160	4,070	4,970	4,230	2,750	3,780	4,444
Profit after tax	3,500	2,530	3,360	2,970	1,450	2,380	2,750
Earnings per share	293.7	212.3	281.9	249.7	121.5	199.9	231.0

Source: Thermax Annual Report 2018–19.

energy by aiding the design and implementation of policies. Thermax was well positioned to continue to partner with the government, private industries and global firms to build a cleaner and greener business. It was the accredited "Channel Partner" of the Indian Ministry of New and Renewable Energy for off-grid and decentralized solar installations.

RECENT PERFORMANCE

In 2018–19, Thermax has subsidiaries, sales and service offices and channel associates located across Asia, Europe, Africa, the Middle East and the Americas. It has a robust research and development center and 14 manufacturing facilities – 10 in India and one each in Denmark, Germany, Poland and Indonesia. All these sites adhere to stringent global standards and international codes. In all, Thermax has seven wholly-owned domestic subsidiaries and 21 wholly-owned overseas subsidiaries.

Meher's family (the controlling family) holds 62 percent equity in Thermax, and public shareholders hold most of the remainder. Its equity shares traded at 1,100 rupees in January 2020. The company continues to innovate in the areas of energy and the environment by providing sustainable, energy-efficient, environmentally friendly products.

The company recorded a 33 percent growth in revenue in 2018–19 after three consecutive years of declining sales (Table 5.1). The earnings per share also improved in 2018–19 after two consecutive years of decline.

Thermax is a capital goods company subject to business cycles. In 2014, after a decade of impressive growth, Thermax reported fluctuations in financial performance primarily due to difficult macro-economic conditions that led to a slowdown in investments in the manufacturing, infrastructure and power sectors. To mitigate the cyclical vagaries of the capital goods sector, the leadership team strategically spread Thermax's products and services across different sectors and focused on entry into select international markets. Meher continued to push green energy initiatives through renewable energy projects. In her words:

> **As an energy and environment company, we should be at the forefront of [combating climate change and carbon reduction].**[27]

The economy continued to be sluggish in 2017–18, with muted investment in core sectors, which resulted in lower order booking in the international and domestic markets. The company, however, benefited from the government's emphasis on investment in infrastructure development and an uplift in the domestic cement, captive power plant, chemicals and refining industries. While energy-related products accounted for 80 percent of revenues, Thermax continued the push to build its environment and chemical businesses. Table 5.2 shows segment-wise performance.

In the water, air pollution and emission control areas, where norms were becoming more stringent, Thermax stays ahead of the competition through continuous innovation and technological upgrades. It continues to provide unique solutions and product offerings while maintaining profitability in the regulated market. The solid reputation and goodwill that Thermax has built over many years was evident in the company's share price and valuation over the years on the Bombay Stock Exchange (see Figure 5.1).

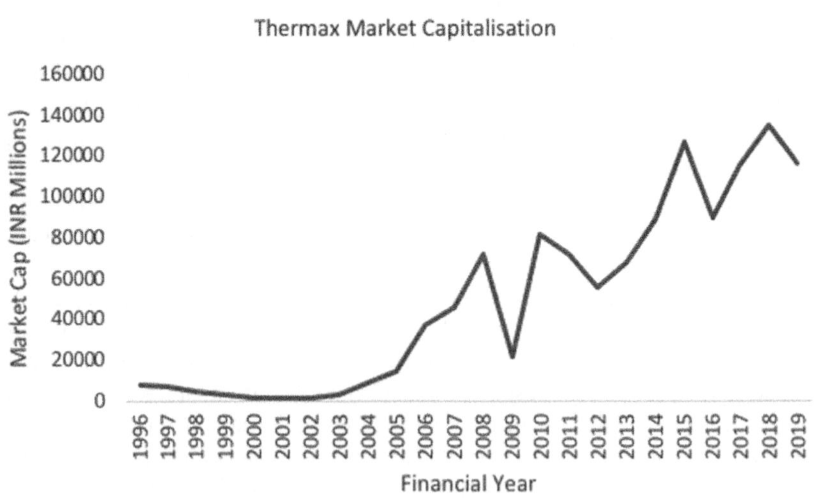

Source: Prowess Database of Center for Monitoring Indian Economy.

Figure 5.1 *Bombay Stock Exchange market capitalization*

Table 5.2 *Financial performance across segments (in million rupees)*

	Split across the three business segments (2018–19)		
	Energy	**Environment**	**Chemical**
Operating profit margin	80.3%	12.8%	6.9%
Net revenue[1]	47,990	8,280	4,150
Profit[1]	3,220	570	620

Note: [1] In water, air pollution and emission control.
Source: Thermax Annual Report 2018–19.

Table 5.3 *Environment, social and governance score, 2015–18*

	2015	2016	2017	2018
ESG disclosure score (1–100)	9.09	15.70	21.90	21.90
Environmental disclosure score (1–100)		2.33	9.30	9.30
Social disclosure score (1–100)		22.81	33.33	33.33
Number of employees		3,872	4,137	4,204
% women in workforce		—	6.62	6.64
Community spending		91.0	87.9	91.4
Governance disclosure score (1–100)	39.29	39.29	39.29	39.29
Size of the board	8.00	8.00	9.00	10.00
Independent directors	4.00	4.00	5.00	6.00
% independent directors	50.00	50.00	55.56	60.00
Board duration (years)	—	—	—	—
Number of board meetings	5.00	5.00	5.00	4.00
Board meeting attendance	95.23	92.50	93.02	97.50

Source: Bloomberg, the disclosure score is calculated based on Thermax's reporting/ disclosure in official reports and channels (annual reports, business responsibility reports, news/ media).

Environment, Social and Governance Reporting

The environment, social and governance (ESG) report for Thermax (Table 5.3) reported by Bloomberg shows progressive improvement in reporting and disclosure of key metrics over a four-year period from 2015 to 2018. The ESG disclosure score is calculated by Bloomberg based on Thermax's disclosures on environment, water, waste, workforce, governance and social data in annual reports, business responsibility reports and other press releases.

FUTURE OUTLOOK

The controlling family of Thermax, across three generations, has demonstrated its belief in the social relevance of business. Its focus on environmental sustainability grew more defined over the years, with Meher eventually emerging as a major champion of the cause. For the family, adherence to the core family values and patient long-term success of the business were always more important than short-term financial gains. The family leaders and board consistently set standards for the business that were well above what was demanded by the competitive and regulatory environment. Patient capital and their 62 percent equity holding enabled them to pursue their commitment to environmental sustainability.[28]

Thermax has evolved significantly as an organization over the past five decades, and particularly in the past 20 years. The company steadily redefined its strategic thrust areas, seizing new opportunities to grow both in terms of products and markets. In the process, the resource basket of the organization became richer and was fortified. The resource basket comprises strategic tangible and intangible resources and capabilities of the firm accumulated over the years. Thermax's tangible resource mix consisted of the innovative environmentally sustainable product offering assets, people and organizational processes imbibed with the family belief and value of conserving and sustaining the environment. The intangible resources comprise the firm's knowledge, organizational learning, competencies and culture. The capabilities are an effective and efficient utilization of the resources in a synthesized way to achieve the organizational goals. With the help of consultants, Thermax brought about major changes in organizational structure, systems and a number of processes, all of which led to the creation of new capabilities in innovation and implementation. Professionalization expanded the talent pool, not only in terms of highly skilled, capable and experienced people, but also brought in a focus on sustainability, largely due to the leadership's persistent efforts in communication and culture building.[29] The restructuring of the board of directors made it easier for the family to build an organization culture that was sympathetic to the cause of environmental sustainability.

The external environment was constantly changing, and as calls to preserve the environment grew louder and more urgent, regulatory standards for businesses became more stringent worldwide. Thermax was at the forefront of these changes; it not only was ahead of the curve among technologically advanced organizations in its green practices and standards, but also actively made use of available platforms to propagate the message of environmental sustainability. Increasing acceptance of higher standards by markets across the world has helped Thermax achieve better growth performance.

Thermax is likely to continue to pursue a strategy of growth by developing and marketing products and technologies that contribute to environmental sustainability. The strong, time-tested commitment of the family to this strategy is a powerful assurance. The alignment of the board, top management and employees to the shared goal of ensuring environmental sustainability while maintaining technological and commercial leadership has been critical to Thermax's success thus far and will continue to be so going forward. Future opportunities in the area of green technologies are likely to grow exponentially, and Thermax's products, technologies and markets will be shaped by its proactive strategies on this front. It can be safely assumed that Thermax will invest in strengthening its pool of resources and capabilities at the business level with strong support from the family[30] and the board for furthering the goals of social development and environmental sustainability. This indicates that the family's and board's commitment to strong governance and reporting practices will continue. The three pillars of business success, namely organizational resources and capabilities, founding families' commitment to values and a favorable environment, are all strong indicators of Thermax's continued pursuit of sustainability.

In 2020, Thermax responded to the Covid-19 crisis very quickly, thanks to the proactive implementation of various measures to ensure employee wellbeing while maintaining business continuity. Leveraging its ongoing digitization drive with a chief digitization officer leading the efforts at the senior management level, the company was able to transition to remote working immediately. To ensure a seamless transition to work from home for the staff, measures such as availability of computer server round the clock, procurement of hardware if required and strengthening firewalls to ensure robust cyber security were put in place. Within one week of the lockdown, more than 30 percent of the staff were able to work from home seamlessly, that steadily rose to 60 percent of all non-factory staff. Thermax was ready with standard operating procedures, including human safety and physical distancing in factories, as soon as the government permitted reopening. They renegotiated with insurance companies to cover Covid-related illness too. Two dedicated teams headed by the chief human resources officer and the chief financial officer had daily phone calls with all their locations across the world. Both Meher (chairperson) and Unnikrishnan (managing director) conducted several town hall talks to motivate and reassure all employees across the globe, besides having review meetings with the dedicated team three times a week. Business leaders and their teams continued to engage with customers and channel partners through remote and continuous onsite support wherever crucial. Thermax has reworked a dynamic business plan for the next year that will help it to respond to multiple scenarios.

KEY INSIGHTS

- Although the importance of environmental sustainability is acknowledged worldwide, not all nations and their leaders, both political and business, are ready to commit to the changes needed to achieve it. In such an environment, Thermax is an example of a business in an emerging market that has proven that environmental sustainability makes good business sense if pursued consistently and with conviction.
- Business families with significant patient capital and a deep conviction in their beliefs, in this case sustainability, must lead the change and invest in technologies and business opportunities that are slowly but steadily emerging across the world.
- Family business leaders, whether operationally involved or not, need to champion their cause continuously as the operating management may not always be ready to see the big picture and the purpose of the organization. Family firms need to invest in sensitizing and persuading professional managers and employees to embrace their sustainability vision and involve them in strategy to create awareness and excitement in the team.
- Significant ownership control is important for the organization to adopt and execute strategies that may not appear immediately attractive financially and may pay back over the long term.
- When environmental sustainability is at the core of any strategic decision making in the firm, the board of directors has a critical role to play in pursuing a less than convincing commercial strategy. Hence, be prepared to reconstitute the board if required.
- The environment is impacted by several factors – competitive, economic, sociopolitical and technological – which are almost impossible for a single firm to tackle singlehandedly. It is important for firms to make use of multiple platforms such as industry associations, international agencies (such as the United Nations) and voluntary action groups to build the argument for environmental sustainability.

ACKNOWLEDGMENTS

The authors gratefully acknowledge the support provided by Meher Pudumjee (chairperson) and M. S. Unnikrishnan (managing director) of Thermax in preparing the case. The authors also gratefully acknowledge the generous assistance received from the Thomas Schmidheiny Centre for Family Enterprise at the Indian School of Business. All errors remain the authors' own.

NOTES

1. Pudumjee, M. (n.d.). “Challenges in corporate governance: A family business perspective.” Company archives. www.thermaxglobal.com/wp-content/uploads/2020/03/corp-gov-challenges.pdf
2. The concept of an economic moat, i.e., a long-term, sustainable advantage that a business has over its rivals, was popularized by Berkshire Hathaway’s chairman, Warren Buffet. In her message to employees, Pudumjee describes her experience of attending Berkshire Hathaway’s annual general meeting in 2018, where she had the opportunity to hear Buffet speak. Pudumjee, M. (2019). “Expressions.” *Fireside*. Company archives. www.thermaxglobal.com/wp-content/uploads/2020/03/Fireside_Vol_49_Issue_4_OCT-DEC2019_Web.pdf
3. Bhathena, A. S. (n.d.). A letter from A. S. Bhathena to new employees. Company archives. www.thermaxglobal.com/wp-content/uploads/2020/03/letter-from-bathena.pdf
4. Aga, R. (1990). “My years with Thermax.” Company archives. www.thermaxglobal.com/wp-content/uploads/2020/03/my-years-with-thermax.pdf
5. Ibid.
6. “Thermax milestones.” www.thermaxglobal.com/about-us/milestones/
7. Aga, R. (1990). “My years with Thermax.” Company archives. www.thermaxglobal.com/wp-content/uploads/2020/03/my-years-with-thermax.pdf
8. Ibid.
9. Aga, R. (1995). “On going public.” *Fireside*. Company archives.
10. Aga, R. (1990). My years with Thermax. Company archives. https://www.thermaxglobal.com/wp-content/uploads/2020/03/my-years-with-thermax.pdf
11. Shah, B. (2016). “Anu Aga, India’s eighth richest woman, says she’s no different than you.” *Your Story*, March 23. https://yourstory.com/2016/03/anu-aga
12. “Anu, Abhay take charge” (1996). *Fireside*. Company archives.
13. Interview with Anu Aga, interviewed by Geoffrey Jones, Mumbai, India, February 14, 2017, Creating Emerging Markets Oral History Collection, Baker Library Special Collections, Harvard Business School. www.hbs.edu/creating-emerging-markets/interviews/Pages/profile.aspx?profile=aaga
14. Ibid.
15. Ibid.
16. Ibid.
17. Ibid.
18. Aga, A. (2011). My perception of leadership. Company archives. https://www.thermaxglobal.com/wp-content/uploads/2020/03/leadership-iese6.pdf
19. Interview with Anu Aga, interviewed by Geoffrey Jones, Mumbai, India, February 14, 2017, Creating Emerging Markets Oral History Collection, Baker Library Special Collections, Harvard Business School. Retrieved from https://www.hbs.edu/creating-emerging-markets/interviews/Pages/profile.aspx?profile=aaga
20. Pudumjee, M. (n.d.). “Challenges in corporate governance: A family business perspective.” Company archives. https://www.thermaxglobal.com/wp-content/uploads/2020/03/corp-gov-challenges.pdf
21. Thermax website. www.thermaxglobal.com/about-us/corporate-philosophy/
22. Pudumjee, M. (2008). “Expressions.” *Fireside*. Company archives.

23. Khan, S. (2011). "Electric woman: Interview with Meher Pudumjee." *India Today*, May 5. www.indiatoday.in/magazine/supplement/story/20110516-electric-woman-745951-2011-05-05
24. Thermax Annual Report 2008–2009. Retrieved from www.thermaxglobal.com/wp-content/uploads/2020/02/2008-09.pdf
25. Unnikrishnan, M. S. (2019, 2020). Phone interview. (K. Ramachandran, & Y. Basuthakur, Interviewers).
26. Pudumjee, M. (2017). "Thermax over the years: Interview with the promoters and the managing director." *Fireside*. www.thermaxglobal.com/wp-content/uploads/2020/03/vol-47.pdf
27. Pudumjee, M. (2015). "Expressions." *Fireside*. www.thermaxglobal.com/wp-content/uploads/2020/03/fireside-oct-dec-2015-lores.pdf
28. Sharma, S. & Sharma, P. (2019). *Patient capital: The role of family firms in sustainable business*. New York: Cambridge University Press.
29. Sirmon, D. G. & Hitt, M. A. (2003). "Managing resources: Linking unique resources, management, and wealth creation in family firms." *Entrepreneurship Theory and Practice*, 27(4): 339–58.
30. Ibid.; Habbershon, T. G. & Williams, M. L. (1999). "A resource-based framework for assessing the strategic advantages of family firms." *Family Business Review*, 12(1): 1–25.

APPENDIX 5.1: SUSTAINABILITY VALUES AND OFFERINGS ACROSS THE THREE GENERATIONS

Years	Controlling family	Family values	Sustainability initiatives				
			Energy heating/cooling/ power/renewables	Water/waste management	Chemicals	Others	Social
Foundational years 1966–81	A. S. Bhathena	Business with a purpose	Multitherm – multiple sources of energy such as biomass		Tulsi Chemicals (resins, specialty chemicals) for waste treatment	Enviro division – air pollution control equipment	Connect with community, equal opportunities
2nd generation 1981–96	Rohinton Aga	Conserving energy and preserving the environment Research and investment on sustainable energy solutions	Reduce greenhouse gas emissions Cogeneration (steam and power) Heat from rice husk/biomass/ other industry wastes Technology collaboration for absorption chillers	Reuse water for energy generation	Invest in chemicals for various industries	Wind power Harness steam from emissions Emission control technology through technology collaboration	Connect with community, employee relations
2nd generation 1996–2004	Anu Aga	Business with responsibility to preserve the environment Continue focus on research Governance	Energy saving Reduce greenhouse emissions Technology collaboration	Wastewater treatment	Investment in research		Philanthropy, Thermax Foundation (focus on education), employee connect
3rd generation 2004–present	Meher Pudumjee	To be a globally respected high-performance organization offering sustainable solutions in energy and environment Conserving resources, preserving the future Continued focus on governance	Solar power for cooling systems, power plants, rural electrification Energy generation from waste Renewable energy Efficient/clean energy/power generation	Water and wastewater treatment Bioenergen for solid waste management	Chemicals for mono ethylene glycol recovery, gold recovery	Reduce nitrogen oxide emission Air quality control (flue gas desulphurization technology)	ESG and CSR initiatives, philanthropy, Thermax Foundation (education)

APPENDIX 5.2: LETTER FROM A. S. BHATHENA TO NEW RECRUITS

A. S. Bhathena
Founder
Wanson (India) Pvt. Ltd

Dear friends,

In welcoming you to our fold let me try and acquaint you with our company's basic philosophy and attitudes to enable you to understand us and enjoy being one of us in the shortest possible time.

Since our company has been getting involved only with essential items needed for the country's economy and as our goal has been clearly defined, we try to encourage entry of only those young men who are earnest, competent, mature, sensitive to their surroundings, pleasant and positive in their attitude towards life, with a capacity to laugh at themselves, and above all show evidence of management muscle at senior levels. The fact that you are now within, our fold would indicate that you do have most of these qualities in good measure.

This being a human enterprise and therefore fragile, we would like to handle it with great care. We generally trust people and like to be trusted; playing the role of a policeman all the time is distasteful to us. Delegation of authority is what we encourage. We like to work in freedom in 'the belief that you would enjoy doing your work in such an atmosphere 'and would like to be trusted with the responsibilities. In such an environment, your contribution is likely to be the maximum and making a living would be incidental.

You will therefore see in Wanson (India) an absence of authoritarian rule long drawn, printed manuals. Incidentally, may I suggest you use your freedom with great finesse, so that eventually you become more conscious of your responsibilities than your rights?

While all of us may not be equal in every respect, we endeavour to give equal opportunity to everyone to grow with our organisation. Accidentally, we may have employed Brahmins or Kshatriyas, Vaishyas or Shudras, Muslims or Christians but we would very much like to see them all turned into Kshatriyas (warriors) in a ceaseless fight against poverty, disease, communalism, despondency and indolence all around us.

We are an expanding all India organisation and our growth rate is rather impressive but please do not let success go to your heads; we have yet to learn a lot. Please, therefore, help us remain students all our lives. Quality of life is what we are seeking. Simplicity and moderation in all walks of life is what we cherish; try to be YOURSELF at all times.

Yours sincerely
for Wanson (India) PVT. Ltd.

Source: Thermax.

APPENDIX 5.3: TECHNOLOGY PARTNERS, GOVERNMENT PARTNERSHIPS AND SUSTAINABLE PRODUCT OFFERINGS

Year	Partners	Products
2018	Defence Research and Development Organization, India	Fuel cells generator
2017	FlowVision A/S, Denmark	Reduce nitrogen oxide emission
2016	Frenell, Germany	Solar thermal power plant
2015	Marsulex Environmental Technologies, United States	Air quality control (flue gas desulfurization technology)
2015	Bhabha Atomic Research Centre and Indian Institute of Technology, India	Wastewater treatment (patented product) – Biocask
2012	Rifox, Germany	Acquisition for steam engineering business
2011	Bhabha Atomic Research Centre, India	Biodegradable solid waste management
2011	Amonix, United States	Solar power generation
2011	Tecnochem Italiana SpA and Gruppo Chimico Dalton SpA, Italy	Construction chemicals
2011	Graver Water Systems LLC, United States	Water treatment at thermal power plants
2011	Fraunhofer Institute, Germany International Advanced Research Centre for Powder Metallurgy and New Materials, India IIT Kanpur, India	Solar-powered, eco-friendly cooling systems
2010	Babcock & Wilcox, United States	Joint venture for higher-efficiency power generation
2010	Danstoker, Denmark	Acquisition to reinforce renewable energy solutions
2010	Lambion Energy Solutions, Germany	Waste to energy
2009	GE Water, United States and Wehrle Umwelt GmbH, Germany	Water and wastewater treatment
2009	Department of Science and Technology, India	Solar power project for rural electrification
2007	Georgia Pacific, United States	Chemicals for paper industry
2007	Balcke-Dürr, Germany	Air pollution control
1998	Kawasaki Thermal Engineering Company, Japan	Vapor absorption division
1994	Struthers Scientific and International Corporation, United States	Heat, energy conservation
1989	Babcock & Wilcox, United States	Joint venture for boilers, captive power generation
1987	Sanyo, Japan	Vapor absorption machines

Source: Thermax website and newsletter *Fireside*.

APPENDIX 5.4: SUSTAINABILITY AWARDS (HIGHLIGHTS)

2019	ACREX Award (Energy Saving)
2018	"Innovative Energy Saving Product": 19th National Award for Excellence in Energy Management at the Energy Efficiency Summit organized by CII
2018	REFCOLD Emersion Award in Industrial Refrigeration (Innovative Products)
2018	Power 100 2018 at the Renewable Energy India Expo
2018	Low Carbon Heroes by SPCA (Sustainable Production and Consumption Association), Istanbul, Turkey
2013	National Intellectual Property Awards (Trademarks), Department of Industrial Policy and Promotion and Intellectual Property Office (Government of India)
2012	Asia Innovator Award (M. S. Unnikrishnan) at CNBC Asia Business Leaders Award
2011	Safety Innovation Award from Institution of Engineers, Delhi, for innovative health, safety, and environment initiatives
2006, 2007, 2010	BRY Awards – Most Innovative Product Design for the research and development team
2006	National award at ACREX for the research and development team for the design of Trigenie chiller (works on exhaust gas and other sources of heat)

Source: Thermax website.

6. Kemin Industries: A sustainable future in focus

Justin B. Craig and Gary Bowman

> As a responsible family-owned-and-operated company, Kemin is committed to sustainability to improve the quality of life now and for generations to come. This commitment is at the heart of our servant leadership approach which compels us to focus on the growth and well-being of our team members, customers and world's population that we serve every day, while safeguarding our planet's finite resources. (Chris Nelson, second-generation leader)

INTRODUCTION

RW and Mary Nelson launched their business on December 15, 1961 in Des Moines, Iowa. Unwavering for over half a century is their zest for, and commitment to, remaining a family business *and* serving their consumers. Their mid-west-rooted philosophies are firmly embedded in the DNA of their global ingredient business, which has grown to amass a team of 2,800 employees, serving more than 120 countries with manufacturing facilities in Belgium, Brazil, China, India, Italy, Russia, Singapore, South Africa and the United States. Over the years they have become accustomed to setting ambitious goals, rallying a global workforce, and dedicated to improving the quality of life around the world. With increased input from, and eventual leadership by, two of their five children, siblings Chris and Libby, the founders have designed their management approach around the concepts of servant leadership.

Despite rapid growth and success, both generations had two overarching concerns. First, they needed to better understand servant leadership and, second, they needed to interpret these concepts to ensure all stakeholders were co-committed to the future sustainability not only of the business but, more broadly, the planet. Though long adopted as the philosophical underpinning of its raison d'être, as the company grew, there was a need to define what it meant to be a servant leader, to understand more specifically what broader cause it was serving. Servant leadership had become the connective tissue that provided the link between the purpose and continuation of the company to a broader, societal mission. In other words, it had to increasingly refine its

Table 6.1 The Nelson family and their Kemin roles

Name	Generation	Education	Role
RW Nelson	1st	BA Biology and Chemistry (Drake University)	Chairman Founder (1961)
Mary Nelson	1st	BSc (Iowa State University)	Vice-President
Christopher E. Nelson	2nd	BSc (Northwestern University); PhD Biochemistry and Biophysics (Washington State University)	President and Chief Executive Officer
Elizabeth "Libby" Nelson	2nd	BA (Washington University in St. Louis); JD (Drake Law School)	Vice-President and General Counsel
Kimberly Nelson	3rd	BA Communication (Northwestern University); MA Luxury and Fashion Management (Savannah College of Art and Design, Hong Kong)	President, Kemin Textile Auxiliaries

commitment to family and business continuity and broaden its servant leadership message to put the future in focus. And, to do that, it required stakeholder[1] buy-in and message clarity.

THE COMPANY

Kemin began modestly in a sheep-buying station owned by Bart Nelson in Des Moines, Iowa. Today, the company has morphed into being among the leading providers of innovative ingredients and solutions to customers in more than 120 countries. A molecular science company, Kemin maintains top-of-the-line manufacturing facilities in which more than 500 specialty ingredients are made for humans, animals and pets in the global feed and food industries, as well as the health, nutrition, textiles and commercial horticulture markets.

VISION AND MISSION

Kemin has always been committed to its customers and has sought to grow, but how it engages with its stakeholders and the scale of its ambition has evolved. Its previous vision was for its products and services to *touch more than half of the world's population every day*. After reaching this vision in 2017 by touching more than 3.8 billion people each day, the company created a new vision in 2019 to "strive to sustainably transform the quality of life every day for 80 percent of the world" and to do so by 2042.

Its mission illustrates the nature of its transforming potential, noting specifically the combination of scientific discovery, an innovative spirit and the essence of servant leadership:

> *Kemin Mission*: Kemin is a global ingredient manufacturer providing local, innovative nutritional and health solutions for a changing world. Kemin will act in partnership with our customers to fulfill their needs and expectations while achieving mutually profitable results. Kemin will achieve our mission by placing the needs of our customers first, creating technology at the molecular level and fostering continuous improvements in our people, processes and products.
>
> **Our commitment to making things better for people, animals, plants and the planet has driven us to new innovations and advancements in science.**
>
> Previously, Kemin reached more than 3.8 billion people every day. As we expand into new areas, Kemin remains loyal to what led us here: our commitment to science, our spirit of innovation and our belief in serving others.

For more than 50 years, Kemin has been investing in generational capital to build the capacity to adapt to the challenges and demands of a changing market. From animal health and nutrition to human nutritional supplements, and now to aquaculture, food technologies and even textiles, Kemin uses molecules and plant-based extracts to enhance the staples of modern society. Set against the environmental threat of climate change and changing consumer attitudes towards food and well-being, today's goals encompass an ever broadening swath of humanity. Chris Nelson, president and chief executive officer of Kemin Industries, says:

> Survival is dictated by what we eat. Kemin can serve that most basic need by improving the quantity and quality of food. Beyond that, we can improve the quality of life by providing beneficial active and functional products to not only the global food supply chain but also in food supplements and food technologies.

The success RW first created as a classic entrepreneur, seizing a market opportunity to grow a firm in the developing world of agribusiness, now allows Kemin's second generation to focus on the world of human nutrition. Says Chris, "Some companies set a goal to manufacture better cars. Our goal is to manufacture ingredients to better human nutrition and do it in the most sustainable way possible."

CHANGE AND CHALLENGES

There is an unusual awareness of the pace and meaning of change at Kemin. It is defined as a "way of life, and a core value of our company." It is also recognized that a significant aspect of change is pure demographics and the challenge that population growth brings. Global population is estimated to reach 10 billion people by 2050. Driven by income growth around the world, this expanded global population will consume two-thirds more animal protein than it does today. Kemin is constantly repositioning itself and adapting itself as a partner to stakeholders to help prepare for such a future: "These changes, and many others, will mark incredible transformations in what you – our customers, partners and stakeholders – need as we work together to help improve the daily lives of people around the globe."

The sensitivity to, and preparedness for change is underpinned by an acute understanding of the future challenges facing the company, and the world. When asked to elaborate on the evolution of its company's guiding principles, particularly as they relate to transformation and sustainability, family leadership was united in its message. The world has a number of challenges ahead and Kemin will be very focused on these. Box 6.1 shows four specific challenges that Chris shared that are a priority and which will guide Kemin efforts for many years to come.

BOX 6.1 CHALLENGES FACING KEMIN

The Challenge of Unprecedented Population Growth

> As far back as the 1960s, pundits warned of the disastrous effects of unrestrained population growth. Consider that there are 7.5 billion people on the planet today; 1 billion of them are hungry. *The amount of food required to feed people in 2050 is predicted to be more than double the food that was produced in 2010.* We can't respond by farming large, new areas of land; it's simply not there to be cultivated... So we must become more efficient at how we grow and process our food and how we convert our crops into good nutrition. If we do not do this, vast numbers of people will die from starvation. *Those of us who have knowledge of nutrition and the ability to make an impact on it, have a moral obligation to meet this challenge.* (Chris Nelson)

Kemin's understanding of nutrition at the molecular level will create many new opportunities to increase productivity and drive down the cost of nutrition. The Kemin food technologies business unit, working alongside Kemin customers and organizations like the World Food Programme, plays a significant role in solving this global problem.

The Challenge to Understand How Food Affects Our Health

The United States Department of Agriculture's MyPyramid (formerly the Food Pyramid) is a well-recognized tool enabling people to design their own healthy-eating plans that provide all the micro nutrients needed to live to their fullest genetic potential. But only 4 percent of Americans consume the MyPyramid recommendations. Unfortunately, this American diet has been emulated in Europe and, increasingly, in other parts of the world. "Much of the world's population is getting adequate amounts of protein and carbohydrates," says Chris. "That's not the issue here. Instead, it's getting people to understand how that food affects their health." In other words, it's not simply eating that enables people to realize their genetic potential; it's what they eat. "We know our body's nutritional needs will change dramatically as we live longer," says Chris. "That longevity means understanding, accepting and responding to the fact that food, indeed, affects health." Kemin's understanding of biochemistry will result in technologies that deliver effective vitamin and mineral supplements to address what people aren't getting in their regular diets. The challenge, then, becomes to identify the critical nutrients in the fruits, vegetables and animal proteins people should be eating and provide those nutrients in effective forms through the products people are consuming.

The Challenge to Change Our Eating Habits

Humans evolved to eat as much as possible, whenever possible, because they didn't know when, or if, they'd get their next meal. Excess calories became fat the body stores as its energy source. Today, millions of people with adequate food supplies are losing their fight against evolution as they continue to accumulate and store large amounts of unnecessary fat. Obesity is the largest single cause of long-term chronic disease in virtually every economically advanced country. Over the next 50 years, it will critically compromise the ability of many to reach age 100. "We need to change our eating habits," says Chris. "But it's a fool's errand to believe someone could convince millions to do this." Discovering new natural molecules that allow us to control and modulate the desire to endlessly consume calories is key to this change in lifestyle. Kemin's understanding of nutrients at the molecular level already has yielded Slendesta®, a natural satiety enhancer to manage hunger while trying to lose weight. "It's a good start," says Chris, "but it's only one product. We need to continue developing and manufacturing products that result in more healthy food options and assist with managing appetites."

The Challenge to Utilize Sustainable Resources

As the human population continues to expand and finite resources are divided among increasing numbers of people, it will become more and more difficult to maintain prosperity and quality of life. As Kemin strives to transform the quality of life, it has a choice between doing so by creating products that utilize limited resources or creating solutions derived from sustainable sources that can be optimized and replenished again and again. Kemin started to develop products from sustainable plant materials more than 20 years ago. Now, many of Kemin's products and solutions are either entirely or heavily plant-based. A focus on optimizing botanicals to produce the active ingredients that improve nutrition and people's quality of life enables the Company to not only develop sustainable materials, but also save contributing limited resources.

Kemin has always thought about the future and about positioning itself to tackle emerging challenges. RW and Mary Nelson noted Kemin's understanding that some products were always ahead of their time: "In the years to come, Kemin expansions will include more inclusive coverage of our current markets and expansion into other global markets once infrastructure is in place and that will increase the benefits the products can offer." As the world's population increases and more land is taken out of agricultural production, efficient crop preservation and utilization will be paramount. RW and Mary explained that the third and fourth generations of Kemin will serve a more diverse company than it is today with expanded areas of expertise that match the abilities of family members. Accordingly, they said, "Our mission will be maintained in placing the needs of our customers first and creating innovations at a molecular level." Further, Kemin "will remain a Company with the values of integrity, hard work and continuous change as a part of life."

The flow of thinking and emphasis on servant leadership between the first and second generations and the need to preserve that for the future is evident in any interaction with the family. Equally evident is the awareness of the need to continuously evolve. Libby Nelson notes the global focus of Kemin and the need to "go off in new directions while staying with its molecular heritage and agricultural roots that now touch so many." Examples were given of cross-platform products (e.g., that have come from chickens and which may move to human pharmaceutical uses, the trace minerals for agricultural production animals that have moved to human applications and the lutein derived from marigolds). They all branch from the same tree: *agrifoods*. Libby states further, "when we start to look at new business opportunities, I think we will look at interesting botanical molecules, other molecules from animals, synthetic molecules and combination products." Kemin's past and future are connected explicitly in the way the family reflects on its past growth and assesses emerging opportunities. Libby conveyed that significance of both foundations *and* change: "the agrifoods side of our business is our heritage and part of our future. We can't reach 80 percent of the world's population without participating in agricultural markets. But we will be different in other ways in 50 years. Definitely."

SUSTAINABILITY ROOTED IN SERVANT LEADERSHIP PHILOSOPHY

RW and Mary, from the very start, were focused on relationships. Originally called Chemical Industries, they worked very closely with an Omaha company (Standard Chemical) and from the very beginning put high value on farmer meetings to understand better how to innovate and provide solutions. Based on customer needs, their initial products were a liquid sheep wormer and mold inhibitors. Then, applicators to spray preservatives on hay and silage. They also relied on the assistance of their banker and lawyers in the early days as it was clear to them that they needed assistance from others and were not afraid to ask for, and take, advice. Both founders commented that the philosophy of servant leadership started on day one in their business but that, in fact, they received this approach from their parents. It was engrained through their Catholic teachings and was how everyone in their community grew up. The notions of respect and humility were basic to them from an early age. And when this evolved into their business, they were committed to reward their employees with a fair wage (always above the minimum wage) and provided them with a community to which they could contribute and be valued.

As the business grew, their commitment to always taking people's advice stayed constant. RW is famous for telling anyone that "I am here to take advice," and he was true to that when the company needed to consider more sophisticated sales techniques. As Mary said, "RW was a good sales guy and I always could count on him from day one to make a sale, but when we hired an experienced sales executive in the sales role, to his credit, RW knew that his role was being redefined."

In unison, the founders commented: "To be a good servant leader you need to know when to step away" and "that is what RW did with Chris when he was in his early thirties," added Libby. At that time, Chris was made responsible for Kemin – a growing company with an annual turnover of 80 million dollars. But, consistent with their servant leadership philosophy, RW stepped back and allowed him to make mistakes and provided oversight to assist him in his leadership role. Chris was given room to introduce new structures and products as the company grew.

Part of Chris' challenge was to continue to define what servant leadership meant to Kemin. It had always been fundamental to the Nelson family but conveying it to different people in different countries was a harder task: "this is an ongoing challenge for us," said Libby, and the founders agreed. "In effect, as it is a philosophy, and something we believe in passionately, it is not the same for everyone."

Part of the philosophy lies in practice. Libby, for example, explained that she does not tell her team "how," rather, she "provides guidance and support – a bit like a soccer team coach. I am responsible for putting the best team on the pitch and providing them with the resources to succeed. They don't need to be the best of friends; they need to have the same values and a common objective." This also extends to building community and the celebration of achievements. It is accompanied by a team-based approach to challenge: "a big part of Kemin's success is that we have always embraced adversity and never been afraid to change, and this permeates the organization."

A LONG-TERM LEADER'S PERSPECTIVE

A Kemin leader who had been with the company for a long period shared: "The key thing I find about servant leadership is that none of us are required to have the answers. Moreover, we commit to hire the right people and provide them with the tools to do their jobs. It really is a matter of working shoulder-to-shoulder to get stuff done." From his perspective, servant leadership is mainly about treating people as individuals and taking the time to understand them and their career aspirations, so they can advance, and hopefully stay with Kemin.

He shared a particularly poignant perspective in his role as a leader of the specialty crops division, that the key to success is continuity of knowledge and that requires keeping people in place and keeping them engaged. He shared that "what is required is a 'patient human capital' approach." Characteristic of loyal employees of innovative family enterprises, he understated his role and contribution. However, his vantage as a long-tenured member of Kemin's key leadership team made his insights additionally pertinent. He personally has become a perpetual student of servant leadership and this requires continual learning. Importantly, the philosophy is embedded throughout the organization to a point now where it is linked to performance and individuals are recognized for their servant leadership behavior. "It is certainly reinforced behavior in practice, but you need to look no further than the founders RW and Mary or their offspring Chris and Libby for exemplars of servant leadership behavior."

The leader also was able to share his journey at Kemin. In his role he lives in a world of "biological molecules in plants that have a wonderful ability to synthesize complex molecules. I have an appreciation for sustainability brought about from my understanding that plants need to synthesize complex molecules in order to survive."

Around 2012, the leader and his team observed how the agricultural and animal nutrition industries were switching from synthetic to natural ingredients. However, at the time most of the ingredients were "in the wild" which meant they were actually farming and waiting for nature to replenish supply, typically in two years. Effectively, they were replacing a problem with a different problem. Kemin saw this as an opportunity to expand cropping systems and began producing other crops, specifically, rosemary. They then made the decision to pursue sustainability accreditation from Scientific Certification Systems (SCS), a conversation and process which at the time was very nascent. "We took a chance as we did not know whether this was worth it – whether customers would value it, if investing the money and considerable time was going to be a waste. We did it because it was the right thing to do," he shared. The relationship they built with SCS helped them understand and develop accreditation standards. When customers genuinely appreciated their endeavors of getting third-party accreditation for their rosemary, they subsequently moved to spearmint and are currently seeking certification for their new potato crop:

> We really didn't know if anyone would care but when our competitors responded enthusiastically, we knew we had "moved the chains up the field" and this was a serious point of differentiation. But, and perhaps more importantly, our initiatives helped elevate sustainability to a point where it is included in our Company vision.
>
> **Sustainability is not something that we pay lip service to, it is the basic fabric of the entire company. It underlies our messages about healthy people, a healthy business and a healthy planet.**

But to understand sustainability, he indicated that it is necessary to understand the Nelson family. "This is a very unique company," the leader shared, proudly. "The Nelsons set the tone. All of them are approachable and genuinely interested in us and our families. They not only talk to you; they are engaged when they talk to you. They are anything but aloof," the leader continued. "And they are all about building a sustainable family business, across generations."

On the topic of having a long-term perspective, Chris Nelson explained, "We have a plan in place to keep Kemin as a seven-generation family business. At that point, we will celebrate our 200th anniversary." Chris said that dedication *by* the family only reinforced *his* dedication to the family. "That to me is sustainability in motion," Chris concluded. Part of the generational change is emerging in the diversification of Kemin's activities. Kimberly Nelson, the first of the third generation, is serving as the leader of Kemin Textiles, a new area of expansion for Kemin in the textile and garment finishing industry.

FROM TOUCHING TO TRANSFORMING: A NEW *SUSTAINABLE* VISION

Chris and his leadership team knew they had set a lofty goal in 1999 by setting their collective sights on "touching more than half the world's population" as part of their strategic vision. It became evident that they were going to achieve this goal two years early in 2017, which created a new challenge. Specifically, what would they now rally around for the new vision? Chris took this challenge personally and traveled around the world to all Kemin locations to get buy in. He personally interviewed 200 people in the organization (approximately 10 percent of the workforce). He asked them a simple question: "Tell me the words that describe best how you see the next 20 years." He then created a Vision Committee and shared the information he had collected and asked the small group to help him craft a vision statement. He started with three examples to give them a start and was amazed by how effectively and efficiently they grasped the task. He took their draft to the board and other team members and the new vision was created:

> We strive to sustainably transform the quality of life every day for 80 percent of the world with our products and services.

When asked about the thesis of the statement, Chris was clear: "We knew we had to have the word sustainable in the vision and, while before we were happy to 'touch lives' now we are committed to 'transforming lives.'" When pressed to explain, Chris clarified how he and his team considered the concept of transformation:

> This became crucial. To transform we need to do more than just touch. To be transformed by Kemin, you must engage with a Kemin molecule at least five times in a day. For example, the clothes you wear; the food you eat; supplements or what you feed your family or your pets. Our strategy is that by 2042, we will transform 8 billion lives of the world's estimated population of 10 billion people.
>
> Currently, we transform 800 million (i.e., the number who come into contact with a Kemin molecule five times a day). My simple message is that we need to grow 10 times. I frame this in my simple story-telling message all we have to do is add a zero.

When asked about how they will build measurement into their triple bottom line (people–business–planet) strategy, he replied that they are establishing three metrics for each pillar. When further pressed about how this longer-term strategic thinking will impact individual incentives he has in play, Chris replied with confidence:

> This is the constant conundrum for family business owners – how to balance long-term and short-term incentives. We have developed a phantom share program we call “Stakeshare.” It is quite complex, but centers on the performance of a group of 20 Kemin customers. We examine their PE [price to earnings] ratio figuring that if our customers are doing well, we are doing something right. We know what our earnings are over the previous two years and give shares, which individuals can redeem or sell at retirement. It is a type of golden handcuffs, so they know they’ll leave some money on the table if they leave Kemin and also an incentive if they stay long-term, they can accrue wealth, as well as their annual performance incentive. This gives them a sense of ownership and motivates them in both the long and short term.

RECRUITING AND RETAINING TALENT IS VITAL

When asked what role a focus on sustainability meant to the recruitment process, leaders responsible explained that this gives prospective hires a preview of what they can expect:

> It is seen as something that we don’t just talk about, we live it. It fits. Sustainability is part of the same conversation as servant leadership. And the family. It is all integrated. Sometimes it is hard for people to understand servant leadership, but what we have now is tangible. They can understand. The family is also a big piece of our talks. Mary and RW are still so involved in their 90s. You still see them in the hallways. We all know that the intent is to keep the business in the family for seven generations and this is something tangible that we can share with potential hires. Incentives are not an issue. It is clear that people believe in what we are trying to accomplish, and it is a simple message focused around our 2042 strategy. We can tell one story: that we are working together to change the world.

The marketing and branding leader who was integral to the repositioning and message delivery reinforced Chris Nelson’s depiction of how the process worked: “We accomplished our previous objective to *touch* half the world two years ahead of schedule, which prompted the question, ‘what’s next?’” The Vision Committee reviewed the information and considered that the previous ambition to touch was good, but *to transform* is so much bigger. Interviews reinforced that there was a need to include “sustainability” in the new vision and strategy so now both – “sustainably” and “transform” – are included to stress that commitment over the long term.

When asked about how the change process was received, the leader responsible commented that:

> we did not get any push back – though change is challenging for people even if it's a great change – and we were conscious of that throughout the process. The concept of sustainable transformation has been a unifier throughout the organization. It is driven by Chris Nelson, but he has been careful to be inclusive. He offers us a seat at the table and listens to what everyone has to say and has acted on this information.

Finally, she observed that "What Kemin does can be complicated to understand and not everyone in the organization is a scientist; what we have with this vision is simple to grasp and something that everyone can get behind."

MORE ON THE HOW: UNDERSTANDING THE IMPORTANCE OF SERVANT LEADERSHIP

Robert P. Neuschel, a pioneering thinker on the topic of servant leadership, considered that "a servant leader by definition leads people in a manner that helps them grow and increases their capacity to contribute." Chris Nelson explained how servant leadership fitted into the new strategy. He put it simply: "Servant leadership is 'The How.'"

The concept of servant leadership has long been fundamental for the Nelson family and Kemin. It is what drives their culture and their shared philosophy of management and leadership. To signal the importance of servant leadership in their organizational fiber, the family leadership team commissioned a study in 2018 to further define servant leadership and establish, then monitor, how it mattered to the company. In other words, while the concept of servant leadership was firmly embedded in the organization, given the evolution to a future-focused global company, and being a science-based organization, the leaders thought it was time to put some science (i.e., theory-based empirical evidence) behind their philosophical approach to commerce.

The researchers first confirmed that, according to the academic literature and extant studies, servant leaders focus on building a loving and caring community, generating a shared vision for helping others and creating the freedom and resources for employees to become servants themselves,[2] as their primary motivation is to serve others.[3] Also, aligned with Greenleaf's warning that servant leadership would be difficult to operationalize, they learned that theoretical development of this construct had been slow partially because it is more than just a management technique but a way of life that begins with "the natural feeling that one wants to serve, to serve first."[4] It was further confirmed that servant leadership is a multi-dimensional construct where the leader places the good of those being led over their own self-interest, emphasizes employee development, displays stewardship of organizational resources, builds community and practices empathy, humility and authenticity.[5] Confirming the "Kemin Way," servant leadership requires social exchanges that are long term, enduring and ongoing, where individuals maintain consistency and fairness.[6] Importantly, and very relevant to the Nelson family, the review of the servant leadership literature highlighted that by building a loving and caring community, servant leaders create a multi-generational legacy of serving others first.

To refine their understanding and application of servant leadership, the servant leadership research team utilized Barbuto and Wheeler's Servant Leadership Questionnaire. The questionnaire identifies five distinct behaviors: altruistic calling (a desire to make a positive difference in others' lives); emotional healing (fostering spiritual recovery from hardship or trauma); wisdom (an awareness of surroundings and anticipation of consequence); persuasive mapping (influencing others using sound reasoning and mental frameworks to conceptualize greater possibilities); and organizational stewardship (taking an ethical responsibility for the well-being of the organization and society). While other instruments exist, it was the inclusion of organizational stewardship that spoke to the researchers and Kemin leadership as this was particularly relevant to their wanting to focus on the future. Organizational stewardship was defined as committing first and foremost to serving others' needs. Servant leaders recognize the role of organizations is to create people who will build a better tomorrow, and therefore, they build "people first" organizations that emphasize service. Organizational stewardship assumes responsibility for the well-being of others and ensures organizational strategies and decisions to make a positive difference. Servant-led organizations act as caretakers and role models working for the common interest of society, developing a community spirit in the workspace, and building a positive legacy. As Greenleaf said, "the only way to change a society is to produce people, enough people, who will change it."[7] To servant leaders, organizations play a moral role in society to give back and make things better than when they found them. (See Appendix 6.1 for a detailed description of the other four dimensions: altruistic calling, emotional healing, wisdom and persuasive mapping.)

MEASURING SERVANT LEADERSHIP AT KEMIN INDUSTRIES

All employees were invited to participate in a comprehensive survey designed to establish servant leadership and its relationship with other constructs, which we outline below. More than 1,000 Kemin employees participated, which represented approximately 52 percent of all employees (334 female, 652 male, 75 unspecified; age: $M = 39.08$ years, $SD = 10.46$ years; 49.67 percent Caucasian/White; 3.02 percent Black; 27.43 percent Asian; 4.90 percent Hispanic/

Latino/a; 1.51 percent Multi-racial; 1.70 percent Other), via email. Participants completed the previously validated Servant Leadership Questionnaire (M = 3.52; SD = .93; α = .97).[8] In this questionnaire, participants rated how well 23 statements described their supervisor (e.g., "My supervisor puts my interests ahead of their own" and "My supervisor does everything they can to serve me"; 1 = *Not at all*, 2 = *Once in a while*; 3 = *Sometimes*; 4 = *Fairly often*; 5 = *Frequently, if not always*).

Participants rated the degree to which their supervisor embodied a servant leadership style, as well as the degree to which their supervisor embodied a servant leadership style. They then completed an assessment of their job satisfaction, well-being and health. The data enabled the researchers to establish the specific influence of having a leader high in altruistic calling, emotional healing, wisdom, persuasive mapping and organizational stewardship. While there was an array of interesting and confirmatory results (see Appendix 6.2) the most notable to the understanding of the role of servant leadership on sustainability was that organizational stewardship was strongly related to greater psychological well-being. As a part of the study, the research team also conducted informal interviews with a sample of employees and members of the leadership team (n = 24) from around the world. A sample of the responses appears in Table 6.2 and captures and reflects the concepts of servant leadership and the shared commitment to transformation and the future.

GETTING STAKEHOLDER BUY-IN FOR SUSTAINABILITY FOCUS STRATEGY AND MESSAGING

With servant leadership firmly embedded in the psyche of the organization, the leadership moved forward to set the organizational compass to the future. As part of this process, it reviewed 23 competitors to gauge how it was messaging its sustainability initiatives. A sample is included in Table 6.3.

This information was collated to develop their revised strategic directive and launch a formalized program, *Seeing Our Future Sustainably*, introduced internally in late 2018 and made available to the public in the 2018 Annual Report.

This strategy committed the company to address global challenges sustainably in order to transform the quality of life now and for the generations to come. Sustainable growth would be realized when three types of factors – *environmental*, *economic* and *social* – are considered together, an approach known as the triple bottom line. At Kemin, these factors were treated as lenses positioned to be the guiding framework to build resilience, innovation and

Table 6.2 *Sample of comments with employees who were asked in semi-structured interviews to explain what servant leadership at Kemin means*

Purpose is to improve quality of life	Values very clear
Trust is key	Transparency is key
Freedom I receive from Nelsons	Ability to empower
No barriers in hierarchy	Lead by example
Mutual respect	Shake hands with Chris Nelson and you feel the science
Owners believe in higher purpose	Servant is MINDSET… Leader is SKILL SET
Lead by example	Autonomy to operate
Founder is ambassador	Discretion
Hiring process is intentionally intense	It's all about changing the world
A noble goal to try and touch half the people on the planet	We have a definitive purpose… comes straight from Mary and RW
People here believe we are making a difference	Have to have high integrity to be in this business
High touch place	"It is the way they raised us" (Libby Nelson)
No one is any higher or lower	Teamwork across multiple business units is key
Everybody matters	The Nelson family care
Vested in community	Personal growth potential
Kemin is big but not huge	This is a family-orientated family-owned company
Feel a part of something	Chris and Libby work harder than any of us
No matter your role you can have a say	RW and Mary also work beyond what they should
It's about people who want to make this a better place	Servant leadership leaders put themselves second
If you are not actively involved, you will be weeded out	They let us know we are appreciated
If I can't do it, I won't ask anyone else to do anything I won't do	They make it clear that family is a priority; satisfying
My name on the email (_____@kemin.com) makes me proud	Family enables you to be more involved
RW and Mary instill the values	Company grows… you grow
Almost like a second mother and father to us	We have a voice
I have been given the opportunity to grow	See it in them, then live it
We are a "startup" every day	Face to face is big here
We as employees are buzzed	
That we may touch half the people on the planet every day still gives me chills	

engagement through the organization. The focus on the health of people, the planet and the business was defined as follows:

- *Healthy people.* Build a culture of servant leadership to engage employees and enhance surrounding communities.

Table 6.3 Competitors (company names deleted)

"A cleaner, healthy environment is important to X not only because it's the right thing to do, but also because it makes good business sense."
"Doing what's right instead of just doing better. We've set our goals in each area based on the best available science to ensure we are operating within planetary and social boundaries and thereby becoming a truly sustainable business."
"Brighter Living Solutions" – products and innovations that are measurably better than mainstream reference solutions for planet and people. Strategy: science-based sustainable and scalable solutions that transform markets.
"Sustainability Priorities Compass" Mission: make a difference, meet growing global need for nutrition and health, create efficiencies to make feed for protein.
"We're taking a holistic approach to sustainability focused on social, environmental and economic stewardship. It's our belief that only by a comprehensive approach can we make transformational and enduring change for our company, our consumers and customers, our team members and our planet."
"One Z Guiding Principle" is to minimize environmental impacts and promote resource Conservation."
"We believe that the essence of sustainability is learning to live within the boundaries of nature. By finding new ways to do so, we can supply high quality and nutritious products while improving our impact on the Earth"

- *Healthy planet.* Reduce Kemin's environmental impact and provide solutions to global challenges with sound science.
- *Healthy Business.* Through innovation and quality processes, realize new growth opportunities, create efficiencies and increase profits.

The thesis is that the three lenses work together to focus the company's sustainability vision. When two lenses overlap, quality is enhanced, and when all three come together, the result is natural opportunities to *innovate, protect* and *nourish* a healthy future. Kemin resolved to integrate this vision into how the company operates and how employees function in their daily lives. With this foundation in place, Kemin would be able to set targets and goals that reinforce its focus on the following three areas.

Healthy People

The sustainability strategy involved the company's people (i.e., the thousands of people who come to work at Kemin and the more than 3.8 billion people who are impacted by its products and services every day) and a commitment to promote employee engagement and achieve social good at local and global levels. Again, Kemin's focus on this component of its sustainability strategy was to further empower employees, partners and fellow community members to contribute to a healthy future and, in doing so, achieve Kemin's vision of sustainably transforming the quality of life. The driving mantra on this lens is simple; *we are all better together.*

Healthy Planet

Focusing on a sustainable future also means understanding that the world in which we operate has finite resources. In other words, appreciating that, when resources are at risk, the sustainability of our business and society are jeopardized. To reduce that risk, Kemin committed to working toward the reduction of its environmental footprint. This was to start by understanding their carbon and water footprint and their waste streams. The driving force behind Kemin's planet-focused lens builds on how it has positioned its commitment to people: *we strive to make a planet that is better for our children and their children – where all needs are met, and life is improved – because we are all in this together.*

Healthy Business

Understanding the impact business has on sustainability and a healthy future is Kemin's third focal lens (Box 6.2). Though long separated from sustainability, acknowledging the value of successful businesses allowed Kemin to articulate the company's belief that cultivating honest, ethical, environmentally and socially conscious companies is critical to transforming the quality of life. Further, Kemin sees its customers as partners in creating a vision for future generations. The mantra related to this was: w*e provide our customers with products and services that help drive the transformation of business today into stewardship of sustainability tomorrow. We will continue to pay special attention to our products and processes that are sustainable and plant based. We transform together.*

BOX 6.2 ARTICULATING FOCUS ON SUSTAINABILITY AND FUTURE

As a company built on exacting science and human imagination, we will use our strengths to *nourish, protect* and *innovate*. These are the areas where our lenses of people, planet and business intersect. Under these actionable pillars, we discover the direct connection of our products, services and processes to sustainability. We begin to tell the story of *Seeing Our Future Sustainably*.

Nourish

Through food, feed and nutrition, Kemin finds ways to nourish people, animals and plants. We understand the importance of nourishing the planet, too, with natural sourcing and sustainable crops. We know how to nourish at Kemin. It's demonstrated by the products and solutions we create and the partnerships we've formed to achieve food security goals.

Protect

Where companies and people come together to form something better, we find our strength to protect. As a healthy business, we believe it is the role of Kemin to protect people and the resources on which we depend. From this responsibility comes our commitment to safety and quality processes, food safety, utilization of antioxidants and antimicrobials, and natural pest control.

Innovate

Our spirit to *innovate* is seen in Kemin products, processes and services where we have applied our scientific expertise to overcome industry challenges for 55-plus years. As we recognize and leverage the fierce interconnectivity between people, planet and business, we discover innovative solutions to improve sustainability. These are seen in our core technologies, environmentally conscious chemistry for garment finishing, plant-based products and holistic approaches to improve animal health without antibiotics.

Our culture, scientific capabilities and global reach make Kemin uniquely positioned to improve the lives of others today while working to help safeguard the health of the planet's resources. *Seeing Our Future Sustainably* will further leverage our commitment to sustainability as a way to improve life today and for generations to come.

When asked if the three circles of their Venn diagram (healthy people, healthy planet, healthy business; see Figure 6.1) are equally prioritized, Libby Nelson replied, "it is all predicated on having a healthy business, and this then allows us to impact people and make longer term investments in planet-related endeavors."

Others agreed. "Being family owned means we can pursue economic and social goals concurrently without too much scrutiny."

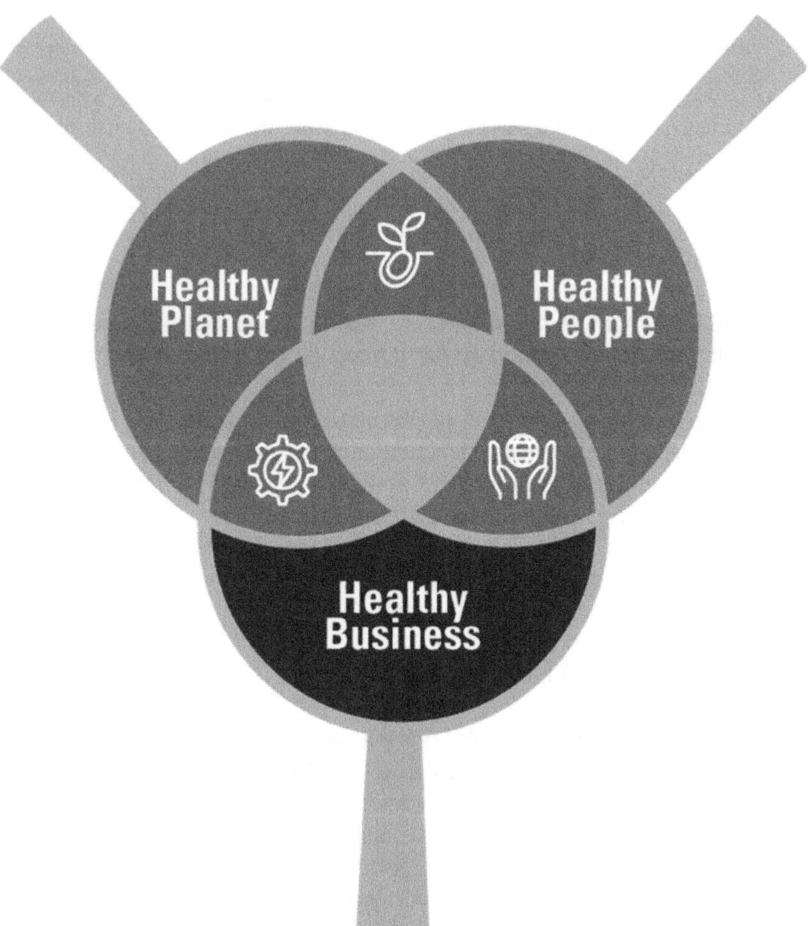

Figure 6.1 *Seeing the future sustainably at Kemin*

RW shared two examples:

In our crop technologies business, we have developed new molecules from plants that enable farmers to improve their income. The Kemin plant-based product provides a positive ROI to the farmer and a profit for us. This is an example of Kemin having a healthy business. The plants used to make these products grow for seven to ten years providing income for the grower, a complex molecule for Kemin and advantage to the end user. There is an added environmental benefit because we are

> using a molecule that came from a plant and can go back into the earth with minimal impact. It all goes together.
>
> Another example is our efforts with African Swine Fever. Many companies put solving this issue in the "too hard" category for multiple reasons, including compliance and regulation. Given our global footprint and understanding of not only the science, but also the societal reliance on pork, we committed to researching innovations and products that may be able to control this virus.
>
> It is the same story as with our Crop Technologies advancements. Our healthy business enabled us to improve the lives of people and sustain the planet. It is also how and why we are involved in the World Food Programme and Habitat for Humanity.

To address African Swine Fever, Kemin developed a three-pronged approach and training program for farmers to take precautions that may reduce the appearance of the virus. Protecting the gut, the feed and the environment of swine is critical to potentially minimizing risk. Kemin also offers products that enhance production animals' immunity and help protect their feed. Kemin-hosted programs throughout Asia and Africa have helped educate governments and farmers on biosecurity practices. Libby summarized, "Fundamentally, if you break down what we are committed to doing, it is about building a community, having people join that community, and being a contributing member of that community."

SYNTHESIS AND LEARNING

While a commitment to sustainability has always been a priority for the Nelson family and Kemin leadership, the decision to "double down" has put sustainability at the forefront in strategic discussions. From an organizational, industry and societal perspective, it was important to refocus attention and develop clear objectives, measures and targets around sustainability. Importantly, Kemin was able to establish a clear link between sustainability and the company's long-held core principle of servant leadership. As demonstrated above, the connections between servant leadership and the *Seeing Our Future Sustainably* program were such that stakeholders needed little convincing that this was a natural next step. Importantly, from a strategic perspective, these approaches are aligned and, unlike companies not family controlled that experience significant changes when new chief executive officers are appointed, the stable tenure of leadership means that a consistent message and messenger is achievable. This all contributes to the family and the growing number of stakeholders being able to tell a simple but effective story about what they do and why it matters.

KEY INSIGHTS

- Establishing a link between the global challenges and responsibilities of a private company or an individual working in it is challenging. Careful conceptualization based on open-minded consultation and logical articulation of the link between global challenges and organizational goals can provide an anchor for strategic investment decisions.
- The Nelson family of Kemin Industries uses the following logic: by 2050, we need double the food produced in 2010. As new cultivable land areas are unavailable, we must become more efficient in growing and processing food and converting crops into good nutrition. Without this, vast numbers of people will die of starvation. Those of us with knowledge of nutrition are morally obligated to meet this challenge.
- Kemin's previous vision was for its products and services to *touch more than half of the world's population every day*. After reaching this vision two years before planned, a new vision created in 2019 states that Kemin *strives to sustainably transform the quality of life every day for 80 percent of the world* by 2042.
- A company's commitment to science and innovation, and a belief to serve others (servant leadership) become the connective tissue to link over generations, products (over 500 specialty ingredients) and locations.
- Phantom share programs, for non-family professionals, centered around the financial performance of key customers of the company is a pragmatic way to align the interests of the controlling owners, its professional executives and its customers. The logic used is that "If our customers are doing well, we are doing something right."
- Stalwart business practices like tiptoeing into markets and establishing sales before making permanent investments are essential to achieve the strong financial position of a company.
- The tri-variate of healthy people, business and planet are an inseparable fabric of a sustainability.

NOTES

1. Interviews were conducted with the following: RW Nelson, Mary Nelson, Chris Nelson, Libby Nelson, John Greaves (vice-president, specialty crops), Heather Christensen (sustainability coordinator), Casey Sciorrotta (human resources director).
2. Parris, D. L. & Welty Peachey, J. (2012). "Building a legacy of volunteers through servant leadership: A cause-related sporting event." *Nonprofit Management and Leadership*, 23(2): 259–76.
3. Greenleaf, R. K. (1977). *Servant Leadership: A Journey into the Nature of Legitimate Power and Greatness*. New York: Paulist Press; Sendjaya, S. & Sarros,

J. C. (2002). "Servant leadership: Its origin, development, and application in organizations." *Journal of Leadership and Organizational Studies*, 9(2) 57–64.

4. Greenleaf, R. K. (1977). *Servant Leadership: A Journey into the Nature of Legitimate Power and Greatness*. New York: Paulist Press, p. 7.
5. Barbuto, J. E. & Wheeler, D. W. (2006). "Scale development and construct clarification of servant leadership." *Group and Organization Management*, 31(3): 300–26; Ehrhart, M. G. (2004). "Leadership and procedural justice climate as antecedents of unit-level organizational citizenship behavior." *Personnel Psychology*, 57: 61–94; Laub, J. A. (1999). "Assessing the servant organization: Development of the Organizational Leadership Assessment (OLA) model." *Dissertation Abstracts International*, 60(2): 308A (UMI No. 9921922); Liden, R. C., Wayne, S. J., Zhao, H. & Henderson, D. (2008). "Servant leadership: Development of a multidimensional measure and multi-level assessment." *Leadership Quarterly*, 19: 161–77; Spears, L. (1995). "Introduction: Servant leadership and the Greenleaf legacy." In L. Spears (Ed.), *Reflections of Leadership: How Robert K. Greenleaf's Theory of Servant Leadership Influenced Today's Top Management Thinkers*. New York: Wiley, pp. 1–16; Van Dierendonck, D. & Nuijten, I. (2011). "The servant leadership survey: Development and validation of a multidimensional measure." *Journal of Business and Psychology*, 26: 249–56.
6. Brashear, T. G., Boles, J. S., Bellenger, D. N. & Brooks, C. M. (2003). "An empirical test of trust-building processes and outcomes in sales manager-salesperson relationships." *Journal of the Academy of Marketing Science*, 31(2): 189–200.
7. Greenleaf, R. K. (1977). *Servant Leadership: A Journey into the Nature of Legitimate Power and Greatness*. New York: Paulist Press, p. 60.
8. Barbuto, J. E. & Wheeler, D. W. (2006). "Scale development and construct clarification of servant leadership." *Group and Organization Management*, 31(3): 300–26.

APPENDIX 6.1

FOUR OTHER SERVANT LEADERSHIP DIMENSIONS

Altruistic calling. Highly distinctive to servant leadership is the willingness to sacrifice self-interests for the sake of others based on the desire to improve others' lives.

Emotional healing. Aligned with helping others first, a servant leader is committed and skilled at practicing empathy, listening and healing, which enables them to foster spiritual recovery from hardship or trauma.

Wisdom. Wisdom is the blend of knowledge and utility. When these two characteristics are combined, leaders are astute at picking up cues in the environment and understanding proactively the implications of an action. Servant leaders high in wisdom are observant and anticipate outcomes well, enabling them to mesh applied knowledge and informed experience to make optimally altruistic choices.

Persuasive mapping. Persuasive mapping is influencing others based on sound reasoning and mental frameworks through conceptualization.

Source: Barbuto, J. E. and Wheeler, D. W. (2006). "Scale development and construct clarification of servant leadership." *Group and Organization Management*, **31**(3), 300–26.

APPENDIX 6.2: RESULTS OF EMPIRICAL STUDY OF SERVANT LEADERSHIP

Respondents = 1,061	**Job satisfaction**	**Perceived stress**	**Subjective well-being**	**Psychological well-being**	**Health**	**Sick days**
Altruistic calling	β = .14**	β = .002	β = .07	β = -.03	β = -.03	β = -.07
Emotional healing	β = .05	β = .06	β = .09*	β = -.06	β = .04	β = .11*
Wisdom	β = .09*	β = -.11*	β = .01	β = .04	β = .05	β = .73
Persuasive mapping	β = .12*	β = .01	β = -.03	β = -.03	β = .01	β = -.14*
Organizational stewardship	β = .11*	β = -.09	β = .11*	β = .25***	β = .08	β = .005

Note: * $p < .05$; ** $p < .01$; *** $p < .001$.

Job satisfaction. All factors of servant leadership predicted significant or marginally significant greater job satisfaction with the exception of emotional healing.

Perceived stress. Having a supervisor high in wisdom appeared to have the greatest impact on reducing stress. Perceiving your supervisor as having greater foresight and anticipatory capabilities appeared to be most strongly associated with reducing individuals' level of stress.

Subjective well-being. Having a supervisor high in organizational stewardship and emotional healing seemed to be most strongly associated with greater well-being.

Psychological well-being. However, psychological well-being was best predicted only by organizational stewardship, which was strongly related to greater psychological well-being.

Health. Although we observed that individuals who reported having supervisors high in overall servant leadership also reported significantly greater health over the previous year, no one sub-component of servant leadership appeared to drive this effect.

Sick Days. Having a supervisor high in emotional healing was associated with taking more sick days, perhaps due to perceiving that supervisor as being more understanding and lenient of taking time off, whereas having a supervisor high in persuasive mapping was associated with fewer sick days, perhaps due to these supervisors being more persuasive in motivating individuals to work through a cold.

7. Social capital as a pathway to sustainability at State Garden

Pramodita Sharma and Rocki-Lee DeWitt

In 2020, State Garden Inc.[1] has established itself as the leading provider of organic and conventional tender leaf salads, spinach and celery hearts in the eastern United States (USA). In addition to its two well-known retail brands of *Olivia's Organics* and *Simple Beginnings*, the company supplies store-brand private-label salads and green leaf produce to grocery chains like Ahold Delhaize and Whole Foods. Each week, State Garden processes over a million pounds of produce grown on 6,000 acres in western USA, in its 170,000 square feet premises that encompass a state-of-the-art processing facility and cold and dry storage areas, in Chelsea, Massachusetts. Third-generation DeMichaelis brothers – John III,[2] Mark III and Kevin III – share an office in the headquarters right across the street from their processing facility (see Figure 7.1 for a family genogram).

Pride in the high quality of their products, customer orientation and a deep respect for the DeMichaelis family can be felt throughout the company's premises that bustle with energetic people walking with a purpose and a smile on their face. State Garden's website invites the visitor to "start a relationship." This warm welcome in the physical and online presence of State Garden feels authentic, as social networks and stakeholder relationships have defined its evolution through continuous innovation, financial prudence and patient reinvestment for nearly eight decades. The DeMichaelis family's philosophy of "doing right by their people," regardless of whether they are employees, growers, suppliers, customers or members of their community, has remained a constant for State Garden. A combination of persistent hard work, integrity and an ability to build and maintain professional relationships has enabled the company to be a successful attentive innovator pursuing opportunities presented by changing societal needs and customers' preferences. An inseparable integration of the 3Ps of sustainability – people, profits and planet – is evident in the evolution of State Garden from its humble beginning in the 1930s to a third-generation company with about 900 employees today.

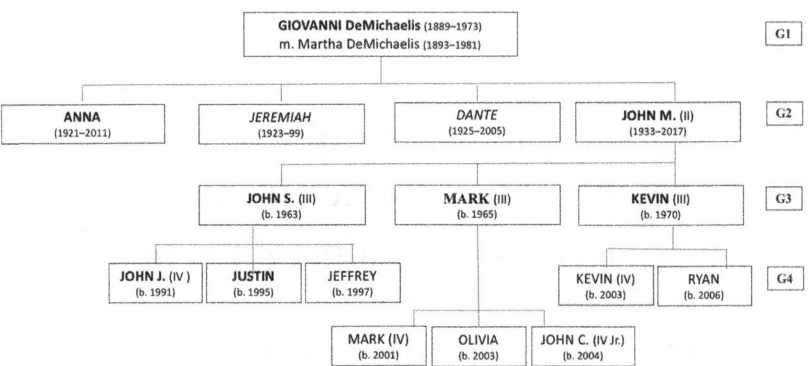

Note: For generations 1–3, this genogram highlights family owners and managers of State Garden since 1937. All children of the fourth generation are listed. Owner-managers are in bold. Family members who owned and managed for a few years but later departed State Garden are in italics. Roman numbers, related to the generation represented by each family member, are used to distinguish between family members with the same name for parsimony though the DeMichaelis family does not follow this practice. When two family members of the same generation have the same first name, the suffix Jr. is added for the younger member.

Figure 7.1 *DeMichaelis family genogram*

1930S TO MID-1970S: THE FOUNDATIONAL DNA OF STATE GARDEN

Born in 1889 in the Abruzzi region of Italy, Giovanni migrated to the USA in 1929. His wife Martha joined him soon after. This was only a few months before the stock market crash of 1929 and the decade-long Great Depression. While he was a hard-working war veteran, the first few years were extremely challenging for the DeMichaelis family. They first lived in the Philadelphia area with Giovanni's sister who had immigrated a few years earlier and he worked in a shoe factory. Later, the family moved to Boston to be closer to their extended family. A chance conversation with an Italian neighbor turned into an invitation to work for a celery company that operated from the historic Faneuil Hall[3] produce market, a meeting place for growers and buyers since 1743. Each bay in this facility was about 18,000 square feet and had loading platforms, offices and refrigerated storage spaces. Traders would hire hundreds of daily laborers like Giovanni to prepare and process the produce for end consumers.

Motivated to provide for his family, Giovanni soon realized that he could make more money processing celery than working for others. Using his experience and relationships cultivated in the produce market, he invested his savings to start State Garden Celery Inc.[4] as a repackaging business in

1938. Each morning he would purchase ten crates of celery from the market, transport it in his vehicle to his home, hand-wash, trim and wrap two bunches per bundle in parchment paper, and secure each package with an elastic rubber band. These packages were sold to wholesalers, who in turn sold them to consumers. The business flourished during the winter season that lasted from October to June but waned in summer as customers preferred the locally grown celery. This ebb and flow of the year enabled Giovanni to spend more time with his family during the off-school summer months. When the frost came, the focus returned to the celery business.

Anna, the eldest DeMichaelis child, is acknowledged to have co-founded the business with her father (see Table 7.1 for timeline). A high school student when State Garden was launched, she would help her father before and after school, joining him full time upon her graduation in 1939. Processing celery was a damp, chilly, laborious endeavor that began at 4 a.m. and continued well into the evening. Father and daughter washed and trimmed the celery by hand to improve its appearance and quality. They would stand in water with celery trimmings at their feet, while the younger siblings collected the waste and Martha tended to the family's needs. Anna would work full time during the day doing a mix of physical and administrative tasks, while pursuing a bookkeeping degree part time in the evenings. She became familiar with, and connected to, their suppliers and buyers, and even inspired other female immigrants to contribute to their family businesses.[5] Her youngest brother John II was clear that if it wasn't for his sister, their father could not have succeeded in the business as he could not read, write or speak English. She opened a bank account for him to buy the product, kept track of receipts and bills and maintained the books. The family took great pride in the quality of its products and were deeply committed to providing exceptional service to its customers.

Jeremiah, Anna's younger brother, joined the business in 1940 and, like his sister before him, worked in the company during the day and took classes at night and on weekends. Dante, the third sibling, joined in 1942. But, within a few months of his working at State Garden, both he and his older brother had to leave to fight in the Second World War. Because of their sudden departure and the needs of the business, John II, the youngest sibling, began working in his family's business before he was 10. During the war, when their father was ill, Anna and John II learned how to drive the truck and move heavy boxes of celery to keep the business going. War-time shortages of rubber necessitated the first packaging innovation of State Garden as they had to purchase a machine to tie celery bundles with a string.

Upon their return from the war in 1945, Jeremiah and Dante rejoined the business. And, a year later, Anna got married to Leonard Geraci. At the behest of Jeremiah, the business was expanded into repackaging fresh spinach. As farmers could harvest two growths of spinach from an established root

Table 7.1 The DeMichaelis family's entrepreneurial itch

Timeline	Family participation and new initiatives/innovations
1930s	State Garden Celery Inc. established by Giovanni DeMichaelis and his daughter Anna (1938)
1940s	Second-generation sons – Jeremiah, Dante, John II – helped in the business part time based on availability between war service and school; youngest son continued at State Garden while the older two boys left to pursue other interests
	Machine to tie celery bundles with a string is purchased to manage rubber band shortages during war
	Business expanded into washing and repackaging of spinach to operate around the year
	Celery processing ceased for two years to focus on spinach processing, until bread-wrapping machine is modified for cellophane packaging of celery
1950s	State Garden relocated to a larger facility in the Faneuil Hall produce market investing $15,000
	First non-family member, a daily wage laborer, employed
	Partial ownership transferred to two second-generation members – Anna and John II
	John II adapts his mother's washing machine to "spin dry" spinach
	Industrial dryers, integrated with a scale and conveyor system and a "merry-go-round" multi-bag packaging machine
1960s	Moved to the New England Produce Center – family investment of $100,000
	Three bays and 15 non-family employees by end of 1960s
1970s	Giovanni (generation 1) passes away (1973)
	Generation 3 siblings John III, Mark III and Kevin III work in the business before/after school and during breaks
	State Garden sells celery and spinach packaged for wholesalers, retailers and food services
	Three bays and 18 non-family employees by end of 1970s
1980s	Third generation joins State Garden full time as each completes his college degree; each third-generation member is paid the same salary; roles and responsibilities clarified
	State Garden becomes area distributor for a company from Buffalo
	Family investment of $200,000 to purchase automated spinach bagging and sealing machinery
	First big deal to supply spinach to a large regional grocery chain, Stop & Shop
	Buy one, get one free program launched
	Addition of a professional accountant and computerized accounting system
	Continued with three bays, 40 non-family employees
1990s	Additional investment exceeding $1.5 million to acquire seven more bays and custom machinery to ensure the highest quality of products and state-of-the-art food safety
	New computer system integrated accounting and supply chain systems
	Mark III elected State Garden's president by his brothers and father
	Acquisition of Bay State, a Boston wholesale fruit and produce business
	14 bays, and about 60 non-family employees; 75% conventional produce, 25% organic food processed

Timeline	Family participation and new initiatives/innovations
2000s	Acquisition of Noreast, purchase and retrofitting of another building ($5 million investment)
	Piecemeal sale of 14 bays to fund growth and ensure food safety
	Started processing of organic ready-to-eat salad
	First company to put spinach and salad into clam-shell packaging
	Ownership transitioned to third generation
	Olivia's Organics (organic brand) and Olivia's Organics Children's Foundation established
	Greenhouse and farm operations in Maine and Florida (piloted for three years before closing)
	120 non-family employees
2010s	Generation 3 passed away – Anna in 2011; John II in 2017
	Generation 4 starts working full time in business – John IV in 2013; Justin in 2017
	90% organic, 10% conventional produce processed
	900 non-family employees; 170,000 square feet total of processing, cold storage, dry storage and head office facilities

system, State Garden was able to expand into a year-round business and serve a broader range of customers including local restaurants and grocery stores. While spinach and celery could be cleaned in the same wash tank, there were significant processing and packaging differences. As compared to celery, spinach required less cutting of the root ends, but its fragile leaves needed greater attention during drying. Moreover, the parchment technique used to package celery could not be used for spinach as it was sold by weight rather than by piece. Instead, cellophane bags sealed with staples were used to package spinach. The task of managing two different products and processing lines proved challenging for the DeMichaelis family. Instead of compromising its ability to fully satisfy its customers, for two years it chose to drop celery processing to focus solely on spinach. However, this changed with the purchase of a bread-wrapping machine to wrap celery in cellophane, expanding its product line to two items again.

Although the family worked hard and long hours, the parents encouraged and supported their children to pursue sports and other pastimes. While Giovanni focused on the business, Martha absorbed the additional work to enable the pursuit of their children's interests. With the support of his parents and siblings, in 1948 Dante left the company to study law. To cope with the increasing growth, in 1950 the family invested 15,000 dollars of their savings to relocate State Garden to a larger facility in the centrally located Faneuil Hall produce market. Shortly after this move, John II was summoned to serve in the Korean War. He had just returned from a two-year war-time service and was contemplating his next move when Jeremiah decided to pursue his entrepreneurial interests outside the family business. This left Anna to assume an even greater role in running the business focusing on billing, payables, supplier and customer relations, while her younger brother John II and their father processed celery and spinach. Even after efficiency-enhancing changes were made to operations some laborers were employed to help. Despite these changes, the physical labor demands and long hours persisted for the family, but they remained steadfast in their commitment to not let their customers down and endeavored to deliver "anything the customer wanted" day after day.

Always on a look-out for ways to enhance their operations and product quality, in the late 1950s John II adapted his mother's washing machine to "spin dry" spinach, thereby improving the quality and shelf life of the packaged spinach. Throughout this period, emphasis was placed on getting the produce appropriately trimmed, washed, dried and packaged as effectively, efficiently and economically as possible. Perishability was, and continues to be, a major risk in fresh produce packaging as labor remains a more manageable expense. Around this time, competitors were making inroads and technology was spreading through the industry. While State Garden's customers were largely wholesale produce companies, some of their competitors were much larger and owned chain stores providing them direct access to end consumers. John II noted that they continued to "slug it out and always managed to make a living" by staying close to their customers and earning a reputation for reliable quality, service and products. Financial prudence came naturally to this family of immigrants.

Giovanni was the sole owner and the controller of the business though he encouraged his children to make decisions. John II reminisced that it was in the mid-1950s when one day without any fanfare their father came to Anna and him and said, "I think it's time," and transferred a quarter of the business to each of them. The duo responded with an equally simple "Okay Pa, whatever you want." Everyday life remained unchanged for the DeMichaelis family as they continued their assiduous pursuit of opportunities to improve their products and services for their customers, while providing the best possible workplace for their employees.

Industrial dryers integrated with a scale and conveyor system and a "merry-go-round" multi-bag packaging machine were added next. In recounting the story of how this came to be, John II recalls loading a truck outside when a man named Victor came to him and said: "'You, State Garden? How would you like to have spinach dried by itself?' I said, What? You are nuts?"

Despite the initial reaction of shock at the idea of self-drying spinach, Victor was welcomed with the customary warmth of State Garden. He demonstrated his mechanized contraption of a conveyor belt connected to a weight-adjustable stainless steel bucket that went into the drier automatically. Washed and wet spinach would be dropped through the conveyor belt to the weight-adjusted bucket and onto the drier that would start at a slow speed and kick up to a high speed. The dried spinach would drop down through one of the 20 funnels arranged in a slowing rotating circle. One person would just put a bag on the bottom of the funnel, pass the filled spinach bag to the next person to weigh it for accuracy, who in turn would pass it to the third person to seal it with a stapler. The spinach assembly line was born! This miracle machine of its time simultaneously enhanced efficiency and quality of the product. According to John II, this capital equipment investment of 5,000 dollars was “a no brainer” for them as it helped to somewhat level the playing field with their much larger competitors. As word of this new machine at State Garden spread across the country, people from the produce industry came from as far as California and Texas to see it in action.

John II worked on the floor and over time became quite an expert in operations, often repairing the machines himself. Anna continued to manage the administrative tasks, while Giovanni oversaw the business. All of them remained focused on serving their customers well. Unfortunately, this relatively smooth run was soon interrupted in 1968 by the Faneuil Hall marketplace fire, forcing State Garden to relocate to the New England Produce Center,[6] which was part of the city’s redevelopment efforts. While the city provided an incentive of 15,000 dollars to relocate, the family invested 100,000 dollars of its savings to move State Garden to 300 Beacham Street in Chelsea, Massachusetts. The company now owned three bays and employed 15 non-family members to process the produce. In John II’s opinion, this was “one of the best things that happened to the produce business in Boston… [they] had more room to operate more efficiently.”

After the DeMichaelis family felt settled into its new premises Giovanni retired briefly, but soon returned back to work, until illness forced him to cease working. He passed away in 1973 leaving Anna and John II running the business as a sibling partnership.[7] Anna and her husband had no children. With her incredible work ethic and financial prudence, she remained the cornerstone of State Garden, always attentive to watch the interests of the DeMichaelis family, its customers and suppliers.

MID-1970S TO MID-1980S: IMPRINTING THE DNA IN THE THIRD GENERATION

Fair stakeholder dealings, financial far-sightedness and unwavering work ethic imprinted on State Garden by the life’s work of Giovanni, Anna and John II left a deep impression on the third generation of the DeMichaelis family – John III, Mark III and Kevin III, born in 1963, 1965 and 1970, respectively. Following the family traditions, they worked in the business part time during high school and summers during college. They would start work with their father at 4 a.m. performing a wide array of receiving, processing and shipping tasks. Ken Reagan, a grocery chain buyer in the 1970s and 1980s, noted that while he had no work relationship with the DeMichaelis family at that time, it was hard not to notice the three boys and their father coming to the produce market day after day. He reminisced:

> the boys were always polite and well-dressed. While the older two were more stoic, Kevin, the youngest, always had a funny comment and called (Ken) the 5th Beatle. That's how the relationship was built – when you see them every day at 3 or 4 or 5 a.m. in the morning, they make an impression on you. Then, you get a relationship going.

Ken eventually joined State Garden as vice-president of sales and marketing in 2005 and describes his time with the company as the "fantastic 14 years of my life" adding "I won't retire from here unless they kick me out. Wouldn't trade this for anything. I just love it here."

Recollecting these early days, John III mused that his father allowed him to come to the market "because he wanted to spend time with his father. And, just through osmosis [he] started to learn at a young age what [his] dad was up against and how difficult the business was from a physical and mental standpoint." He continued, "it was all hands on the deck. We used to do everything and anything just to get through the day, to get the orders out, to keep the customers satisfied."

John II and Anna also established expectations for mutual respect between the next-generation family members and State Garden's employees. Kevin III described the responsibility he shared with his brothers to drive their employees, sharing the following as an example:

> We had an Italian immigrant woman who lived in the North End. It was our job to pick her up from her home in the morning and drop her back when she was done. She had worked for [our] dad for 40 years and we did it out of respect for her but also for him.

John II's and Anna's care for the family and their employees extended seamlessly toward their suppliers and customers, serving as a model for the next generation. In the USA, the largest volume of vegetable production is in California, Iowa, Nebraska and Texas.[8] Thus, the northeastern produce businesses like State Garden are heavily reliant upon the weather patterns of the growing regions to meet their customers' needs. They started purchasing a truckload of produce from these growing regions and smaller quantities from other parts of the country. If a truck was not filled up with celery and spinach, they would ask the supplier to fill it with other items they could sell in their region, thereby expanding the product line to include radishes, turnips and parsnips. Mark III, the current president, recalls his father keenly following the rain patterns in these regions worrying "what he would tell his customers" if the produce did not make it to Boston. He would remind his sons:

> **If *it wasn't for the customers we can't survive.* If there was an issue with a customer, agree with them and make it right and when you hang up the phone, you can call them all the names you want.**

The customer orientation naturally lent itself to care and concern for the growers. Mark III recollected that his father would often go to Texas to visit the growers. And:

> some of the guys took such a huge liking to him that even when pressed by larger buyers to not sell to the smaller State Garden, the grower would say, "I'll never stop selling to him, he pays his bills, and he's a gentleman, he's the nicest guy in the world."

While all three next-generation siblings acknowledge the hard work they put in when working with their father and aunt, each also remembers the business fundamentals they learnt slightly differently. The youngest brother Kevin III started going to work with his father and brothers when he was 10 or 11 years old. He described learning the production, bookkeeping and customer dealing as follows:

> One of my first jobs was to make sure that the bags went through the heat sealer and they were sealed properly. Then, I was at the end of the line putting the product into boxes. Mom would come and pick me up at noon time. I had put in an 8-hour day and would be done.
>
> When I was 14 or 15, I started to get into dealing with the customers, the walk-in trade that would come in. I'd have my Dad or my brother Mark or John next to me filling out invoices, making sales, and quoting prices. They started to wade me into the waters in that respect. And, then I would go and help my aunt with the bookkeeping.

Mark III vividly recalls learning about negotiation as follows:

> Back in the day, when we were getting trailer loads of spinach, it would come in these bushel baskets and my father would have us unload the trucks. It was probably some of the hardest physical labor I've ever done because these things weighed about 30 pounds, everything came packed in ice, was wet and freezing especially if you were unloading them in January.
>
> One of our responsibilities was to hand unload trucks full of produce. It would take about 4 to 5 hours to unload, so if there were 2 of you and you negotiated a $40 unloading fee with the driver, you each got $20 so you are getting $5 per hour for ungodly work.
>
> We would have to negotiate how much we were going to charge the truck driver, and that could be somewhat of an intimidating thing for a 12, 13, 14 years-old kid

> when you have this guy who has driven 5-days with no sleep and we'd say that we want $60 to unload the spinach. He'd say, "No, I'll pay $40," and you start negotiating back and forth.
>
> So, it taught us when you negotiate, you better get what you feel you're worth and try to hold out what it is that you want… some days we got it and some days we didn't.
>
> Those are some of the earliest memories I have of John, Kevin and I having to actually stand there, nose to navel with a truck driver, and saying, "This is what I want."

The eldest son, John III, credits State Garden, his father and brothers with instilling a strong work ethic in him from a young age and notes that "the structured work helped (him) to develop as a person" and establish a sense of equity and shared responsibility in their family. He shared that when Mark III graduated from the University of Vermont in 1987, he had already been working full time at the company for two years. So, his father called him into his office and said:

> Your brother is coming to work full time with us. [John III] said, I was expecting him to. [Father] asked: How much are we going to pay to him? [John III] said, it's your decision. It is not his [Mark's] fault that he was born two years later.
>
> **If we don't get paid the same immediately, when we leave at night how are we going to maintain equality and respect for one another?**

There was no hesitation from his father. A similar discussion ensued between their father, him and Mark when youngest brother Kevin joined after his college graduation. Their father set the expectation for how they would work together. Kevin recalls that their father was very clear that there would be disagreements amongst the brothers in the workplace, but once a decision is made, we don't carry those over, and we keep moving in the right direction.

By the mid-1980s, John II and Anna had run State Garden for over three decades and established it as a specialized celery and spinach company in the competitive Boston market. Despite the full-time addition of the three next-generation family members, they continued to be heavily involved in the business. John III noted that when he joined the company full time his father was only 52 and could work "like a bull." He would do any job needed including loading and unloading thousands of pounds of produce and fixing any machinery in the building. Kevin III reinforced that although their father was in a supervisory role, he worked constantly side by side with his employees and got his hands dirty. Getting teary eyed, he noted that:

> It was a pleasure to work side by side with him. The way that he went about treating people – customers, employees, suppliers, rubbed off on us. My brothers and I didn't know anything else – he is our positive root.

They saw what he was doing and did the same thing.

John III spent more time with his father focusing on the purchasing and packaging side of the business. Mark III split time between the physical work and working with his aunt Anna to become more familiar with the customers, billing, managing accounts payable, bookkeeping and banking. Kevin was in charge of the walk-in trade at the wholesale market and dealt a lot with the wholesalers and supermarket buyers. While their responsibilities were clear, all of them helped to load trucks or whatever else was needed to get the product to customers on time. According to Mark III, their father and aunt let them do the day-to-day work but also alerted them of the "big land mines out there and kept [them] from stepping on these."

By 1987 State Garden was still a small business with three bays and about 40 employees cleaning and packaging celery hearts and spinach for retail and bulk sales. Through astute management of relationships with customers, employees and suppliers and their continued hard work, the company generated enough profits to support the employees, the DeMichaelis family, and make ongoing investments in the business.

MID-1980S TO 2000: SCALING UP WHILE CULTIVATING STAKEHOLDER RELATIONSHIPS

Around the mid-1980s, some major societal and technological changes provided a boost to State Garden. Fruits and vegetables were increasingly being recognized as important components of a healthy American diet[9] and the role of women in the workplace was changing. With these changes, the demand for ready-to-consume healthier meal options was increasing. Simultaneously, food preservation and preparation technology, especially refrigeration, began to draw the attention of consumers away from canned produce and vegetables to packaged fresh produce.[10] Shifting consumer preferences provided opportunities for grocery stores to offer a larger variety of produce and for specialized suppliers like State Garden to grow. For example, between 1994 and 1995, while the sales of State Garden's local competitor – Noreast Fresh[11] – doubled from 8.9 million to 17.9 million dollars, its receipts from spinach had decreased from over 50 percent of total sales to 35 percent, while the salad lines had increased from 10 to 60 percent.

With the increased band width of dedicated family and non-family members working full time in the company, the attention of the DeMichaelis family turned towards expansion and, with it, the acquisition of needed facilities and processing automation. John III shared that his brother:

> Mark was keeping his finger on the pulse of the packaged goods business. [They] were largely reliant on only two products – celery and spinach, and it was scary to

> have such a limited product line. Mark could see the value in the expansion to other packaged produce items.

They persevered following the financial prudence principles instilled in them by their seniors, that is, first grow and manage the demand by increasing shifts and working harder, only invest in new space or equipment after the stability of the market had been tested, and minimize their reliance on borrowed money.

To expand their portfolio, they became area distributors for a company from Buffalo that sold pre-packaged vegetables and convenience food items like broccoli florets, carrot sticks and cauliflower florets. They also considered the addition of packaged salad but were worried about their ability to be competitive as large national companies like Dole and Chiquita were already ahead of them in terms of scale and the learning curve. Moreover, customer tastes were continuing to evolve, making it difficult to establish which sector of the packaged produce business would ultimately be preferred. Instead of straying too far from their core business, Mark started chasing bigger customers aggressively and in 1989 secured their first big exclusive deal with a large regional grocery chain. Mark III explained his thinking as follows:

> There were a lot of big fish [grocery chains] that we weren't selling and [he] wanted to start landing some of these fish. Our success was built on the strong foundation of the 3–5 box customers, but it was time to go after the guys that were buying 300 boxes.

He established a relationship with the vice-president of this regional grocer who gave State Garden a chance to supply a volume of spinach and celery that was significantly greater than anything they had previously delivered to a single customer. Working collaboratively with this new chain store, Mark helped to introduce the first "buy one, get one free"[12] promotion in the fresh packaged produce market. Instantly, the sale of spinach quadrupled and with it the opportunities for the grocery chain, State Garden and its growers. To deal with the consequences of "overshooting," two generations of the DeMichaelis family and a trusted employee, Son Le, worked around the clock to satisfy the customer. Mark III noted:

> We just had no right picking up this big of an account. My brother and I would run the plant from 4 a.m. to 5 p.m., and my father and Son Le would show up around 5 p.m. and run it until around 4 a.m. when we came back in.

Son Le added that he learnt about hard work when he worked all night with John II and began to care deeply for him. Kevin III would help store and slot the produce in the cold storage warehouse and load the trucks. He shared that they were:

> busting at the seams… We had a 10-pallet truck and as the product was coming off the line, [we] were loading and delivering it to the cold storage facility. [Me and my] brother John were just going back and forth, all day, all night, all weekend. That's what [we] had to do. There was no other way it could be done and although the volume was something we had never seen, Mark made a promise to service the customer to the fullest and we weren't going to let them down.

He continued that:

> Everybody [had] the same goals. Customer first.
>
> As it pertains to getting orders and being able to deliver, the customers love watching the owners get their hands dirty.
>
> I can't count how many times one of the local chains would call us up when one of their stores were short on an advertised item and they needed it immediately. We always found a way to get the customer the product they needed. A lot of times we would deliver directly to the individual stores while on our way home from work.

Growth accelerated in the 1990s. And, with it the family's reinvestments in its company. An expenditure exceeding 1.5 million dollars was made to acquire seven more state-of-the-art bays and custom machinery, to ensure that State Garden always provided the highest quality of products to its customers by maintaining exceptional standards of food safety and working conditions. An offer to acquire Bay State Produce, a wholesale fruit and produce supplier located in the same industrial park housed in four bays, came in 1998. The owner wanted to sell his business and retire, and the DeMichaelis family was attracted to the idea of acquiring more real estate. John III recalls that:

> All of [them] were involved in that decision making. Mark spearheaded it as he was on an industry board with the owner of Bay State Produce. We liked the guys there. And, they liked us. This was their opportunity to sell and distribute hundreds of new and unique produce items overnight. The business was turnkey.

Meanwhile, baby lettuce, including spring mix and baby spinach, emerged as frequently demanded items in the restaurant and food service industry. An opportunity to "jump in" to the ready-to-eat salad business was presented to State Garden. Its largest competitor, Noreast Fresh,[13] was struggling as its attempt to compete and scale with larger competitors left it with a heavy financial burden. The Noreast owners approached Mark III to buy them. In 2000, State Garden offered Noreast a graceful exit. This acquisition provided a spring-board into the ready-to-eat salad category known as "tender leaf greens." At this time, Noreast was starting to get into organic spring mix.

While the momentum was building, the DeMichaelis family remained committed to its shared goals of exceeding its customers' expectations and maintaining financial prudence and strong relationships with its employees and other stakeholders. Most of the management team from Noreast was retained as it was felt that this was the right thing to do and there was much to learn from their experiences. John III shared that 20 years later, several members of that management team were still at State Garden.

In reflecting on the shared sacrifices and family's patient investment in its future, John III mentioned that they "never overextended themselves." When making significant investments, they made sure the three brothers were all on board. When asked about the source of funding for growth, Mark III elaborated:

> Our father and aunt were reinvesting financially back into the company at a stage in their lives that is rarely seen. We were proud of the confidence they had in us…
>
> We were all working toward a common goal and trying to establish ourselves in a growing market. Although we couldn't reinvest with monetary funds up-front like our father and aunt, we made up for it with 80–90 hour work weeks knowing we were building for the future. The financial goals would eventually take care of themselves.

State Garden had grown substantially in a few years acquiring and updating property and equipment as needed. John III recalls it being "a little unnerving" as they were managing different locations and product lines. Like other small businesses, they had been running the business with paper, pencils and sales slips. The acquisitions of Noreast Fresh and the wholesale company required the stronger use of information technology. Increased federal regulations and the need for greater traceability of the products required the development of an Enterprise Resource Planning system to handle accounting, financing and inventory control. The company brought in software consultants and certified public accountants to develop a system and process tailored to the needs of the growing company. Change and the transition to automation didn't come easy to the second generation. Kevin III recollected the challenges faced when trying to get his aunt to share the company's financial information with people outside of the family. Kevin recalled one time his aunt holding up her manual ledger and shouting, "No one looks at my books!" The shared goal of continuous improvement to serve their customers well helped overcome her initial resistance to change. The automation served as a signal that State Garden was appropriately modernizing in order to do business with the larger grocers. Competitive intensity had increased as well. Unlike its earlier willingness to share ideas with other folks in the industry, State Garden became more guarded about sharing its unique processes.

As the third-generation sibling team took on more responsibilities, John II started spending his winters in the warmer Florida weather. But he would get right back into work upon his return. The evolution of State Garden's leadership to his sons also required consideration of role transitions and a hierarchy of leadership within the siblings. John III (the oldest brother) vividly recalls when in 1995 their father called the three brothers on a Friday after work and said:

> We need a President of the company. We looked at each other and [John III] said, "Mark is the most qualified of the three of us." Kevin said, "I agree." Dad asked Mark how he felt about it.

Kevin III filled in that it was not even a question and when they told Mark III that they wanted him to be president, he was humbled and embarrassed. And, "that speaks volumes for the type of person he is and how we could all check our egos at the door." Pointing to the benefits of distinct roles Mark III noted that:

> My specialty at the time was customer relationships, identifying opportunities and building revenue. Theirs was the operational part. So, we all had a role, we all had different personalities and that's a good thing. If you all had the same personality in a family business you'd bound to be clashing.

John III added:

> When [Mark III] came in, it added a different dynamic. My brother is probably one of the best at what he does. When he came on, we were doing well but he had ideas, he had visions, he had guts.

And then we started going after business. We would meet and he'd say:

> Hey listen, I'm thinking of going after XYZ account and will try to get half the business to start, and let's go from there. You okay with that? And (we'd) say, Fine. We were good battery mates, backing each other up.

Mark was laying the groundwork and things started to present themselves.

Kevin III's admiration for his brother, Mark III, was evident in our meeting with him as he noted:

> I would work with Mark at the trade shows, greeting customers, just trying to push any type of new products that we had brought on.
>
> He's one of the coolest, calmest, smartest guys I know. As far as his integrity, the type of person he is, his vision for the future, he is constantly looking for ways to improve the company.
>
> He's respected by our competitors. He will do any favor for anybody no matter who it is.

Yet, even with their roles specified, the combination of Mark's talent in seeking and securing business and his consultative approach to problem solving and decision making continued. Skip White, the company's current chief operating officer, described Mark III's role and how the brothers continued to work together:

> He [Mark III] is very visionary. Always out front. Has a great mind for calculating the business model.
>
> Brothers have humility, all are different but value the differences.
>
> I have never felt any sense of division. They are a most collective bunch. They go into a room, never yell at each other, never do.

Reflecting upon his own approach to the role, Mark III said:

> **We would talk about growth plans and *if there was something that we don't all agree on, we wouldn't proceed. It's not worth driving any type of wedge between us.* So, we usually do things unanimously.**

Mark III credits his father and aunt for their role-modeled teachings. Not only did they help him and his siblings understand the risks associated with doing business with some suppliers and customers, they also helped them understand what was expected once a relationship was established. Mark reflected upon his own approach as informed by his father's and aunt's way of doing honest business which has served them well, sharing that:

> **I say to everyone in the company, *if you don't give the customer any reason to leave, they won't.***
>
> In the twenty-five years that I have been here, we have never lost a customer because of non-performance. We may have walked away because it wasn't profitable, but we have never lost business because anyone said or felt that State Garden didn't do the right job or didn't try hard enough.

By the end of the twentieth century, the third generation was in an active leadership role. State Garden had established a strong reputation for its high-quality products, reliable service and a business run with high integrity by a hard-working likable local family and its 60 employees. Through strategic acquisitions, the company had not only grown to 14 bays adding significant processing and warehousing capacity, it had also transitioned from a two-item produce business to a 200-item produce business. At the time, 75 percent of its products were conventionally grown while 25 percent was organic. However, management realized that the latter was not only right for the planet, it was also the faster-growing segment on the produce shelves.

2000S ONWARDS: SHIFT TOWARDS ORGANIC

As the business continued to evolve and grow over the next two decades, Mark III's approach to leadership did not waver. Nor did the family's approach to working with each other or with their employees. Just as the second-generation siblings, John II and Anna, had generously supported their employees financially and emotionally, so did the third-generation brothers. Ken Reagan recalls that in 2006, he was only in his second year as vice-president of sales and marketing at State Garden when two unexpected events occurred, testing the brothers' commitment towards their employees and customers. First, Ken suffered a heart attack and was unable to work for several months. Mark III told him to focus on his health and ensured that he never missed a paycheck. That same year, the United States Food and Drug Administration issued a massive recall of fresh spinach packaged by Natural Selection Foods Company. The spinach was determined to be tainted with Escherichia coli and had caused illness in over 200 consumers and three deaths.[14] While State Garden's items were not implicated in this infectious outbreak and their traceability practices could prove their product was not at risk, it chose to comply with all recommendations and removed all spinach items from the shelves. This move cost it several million dollars in 2006. Nevertheless, at the end of the year, all employees received a small bonus as the brothers noted that the recall "was not the fault of our employees." Such caring gestures are deeply embedded in the memory of State Garden's employees, leaving the DeMichaelis family with a highly motivated and committed management team willing to do anything to ensure the success of their company.

As State Garden grew, the brothers began to broaden the managerial breadth by recruiting senior non-family members from their networks and past relationships. For example, Skip White, the current chief operating officer, was quite emotional when sharing how he came to work at State Garden. In 2007, he was a senior category manager at Shaw's Supermarket,[15] a large north-eastern grocery chain he had worked at for 34 years. State Garden was their supplier and he knew that John II was highly respected in the industry for his honesty and integrity. He also enjoyed a good working relationship with Mark

III, whom he found to be a willing partner in creating new products and efficiencies. When Shaw's was acquired by another company, Skip was suddenly and unexpected laid off. Next day, he got a voice mail from Mark III and the two met. At this meeting, Mark III wrote Skip an offer to work at State Garden on a cocktail napkin. While the exact work Skip was to do at State Garden was unclear at that time, Mark made it clear that he was going to work there and wanted him as part of the team.

Within a few days, Skip was working at State Garden. His first task was to analyze the business to identify opportunities to become more efficient while also enhancing their customer service. State Garden had already transitioned into the fast-growing pre-washed salad category and was located in the east, which was the largest market for processed fresh salads. Due to the nationwide spinach recall of 2006, traceability and stricter food safety regulations had become exceedingly important. The government and State Garden's largest customers demanded more visibility as to where their products were grown and by whom. Skip analyzed the supply chain process. With warmer weather and longer growing seasons, the produce was grown in the west coast of the country. The industry norm was that food processors would package the produce close to the growing sources in the west and transport the packaged products in trucks to the consumer outlets.

State Garden was an outlier. Although it too purchased the produce from the west coast, instead of packaging it close to the source as per industry norms, it would transport the unpackaged produce in tightly packed pallets in trucks that drove across the country to the company's processing facility in east. This was an efficient approach for two reasons. First, as freight is restricted by weight and it was possible to load 16,000–17,000 pounds of unpacked produce on a 30-pallet truck, as opposed to 6,000–7,000 pounds of packaged produce per truck, State Garden enjoyed freight savings advantages. Second, as the loaded trucks took five days to travel across the country, samples could be taken from every pallet for pathogen testing and sent to the lab. By the time the trucks would arrive in Boston, the test results were ready. If any issues were detected with the produce, it could be destroyed upon arrival under United States Department of Agriculture supervision, if needed, without incurring the time or expense of packaging.

Skip continued to analyze the internal operations and found the DeMichaelis brothers to be "very close and humble… All are different but value the differences. Kevin is quick to decide, black and white. Johnny is thoughtful and takes a couple of days to think through. Mark is logical and the voice of reason." With some more acquisitions and internal growth, State Garden rapidly evolved from a 15 million dollar revenue company in 1998 to a 100 million dollar revenue company by 2008. While some internal processes and systems had kept pace, others needed upgrading. Skip worked on those projects over the years and in 2018 he was appointed the chief operating officer.

While John III and Kevin III worked with Skip and the rest of their management team to ensure their current operations ran smoothly and customer needs were met with State Garden's customary high standards, Mark III turned his attention to exploring new business directions. A visionary yet cautious entrepreneur, he was always working on some project and looking for ideas. Good at calculating the advantages of different business models, he would take time to process and analyze different options. He would either present something special to his brothers and their management team or abandon the idea to explore other possibilities. For his part, Mark III shared that while the previous generation members, John II and Aunt Anna, seemed to have an "efficiency itch," he feels:

> a product development itch… [as I] catch a rush from figuring out the next idea before it is really an idea. [I] can be restless at times if [I] know there is an idea has not yet formed, it's an itch [I] cannot scratch. [I] just feel something has to be done.

The family-shared patient approach to decision making was evident as State Garden evolved into the organic produce business. John III notes that since the mid-1990s, Mark III has been aware of the shifting consumer preferences and would learn about these shifts through conferences he attended, conversations he would have at industry association meetings where he was in leadership roles, growers he visited and brainstorming sessions with leaders in the retail food industry. However, he also recognized that to be competitively viable in this space they had to simultaneously develop a consistent supply chain of high-quality organic produce, find compelling ways to differentiate this segment from their conventional produce segments and ensure their processing standards exceed the expectations of food safety authorities and organic consumers.

When State Garden purchased Noreast Fresh in 1998 there was no brand or label for the company's organic product offerings. The only label used was the Noreast brand and it looked very similar to the conventional product offerings. There was very little graphic variation. The challenge the organic industry had in its infancy was differentiating it from conventionally grown product. From his college days in Vermont, a state known for its leadership in ecological sustainability, Mark III knew that those interested in organics were more discerning customers. Knowing where their food came from and how it was grown was more important to them than the price paid for it. This distinct customer could not be grouped in with the traditional shopper and needed a brand to call their own. However, finding the right name and image for the organic pre-packaged produce proved to be a struggle for State Garden and its team. State Garden wanted to reach more than just the environmentally conscious consumer. It wanted to stress environmental sensitivity but also strived to appeal to the family shopper looking for the healthiest options available. The brand would need to stand out on the shelf with a simple attractive name and a memorable image. The brothers were also aware of their septuagenarian father's keen desire to systematize and institutionalize their charitable giving focused on children in their community. Ideally, they wanted their new product line to satisfy organic customers and honor the legacy wishes of their father. John III described those intentions as follows:

> Dad [John II] didn't want this to be perceived as a marketing ploy. We sincerely wanted kids to start eating fresh, healthy and organic.

Wide open to branding ideas, State Garden retained a graphic artist who was given free artistic reign. Mark III shared the futility of this exercise as they ended with "a museum of bad ideas. Nothing connected 100%" with what they were trying to accomplish. Finally, Aleta Bransfield, a member of State Garden's management team, said to him:

> I'm kind of sick of watching you fumble around for a good name. Isn't your daughter's name Olivia? Isn't Olivia's Organics a nice name?

Figure 7.2 *A sample of Olivia's Organics products*

As Olivia is the only female DeMichaelis in the fourth generation, it was settled. Their organic brand, "Olivia's Organics" (Figure 7.2), and the corresponding charity "Olivia's Organics Children's Foundation,"[16] were established in 2005. A portion of the proceeds of sales from Olivia's Organics went directly to the foundation to support community-based charitable programs aimed at enriching the lives of children in regions where State Garden's products were sold. Autism Speaks, Kids Clothes Club, the Greater Boston Food Bank, Food Bank for New York City and Toys for Tots are a few of the many programs supported by this foundation.

Just as it took time to establish the concept of a brand that resonated with the DeMichaelis family and the consumers, State Garden needed to build a reliable organic supply chain before it could move primarily into this market segment. Reputational risk was high as the organic customers were extremely conscious about food safety and the integrity of the products. For conventional farmers, despite the ever present downward pressure on their prices due to the commodity nature of the product and increasing market interest in organic tender leaf greens, shifting to organic farming represented a risky change. Growing organically is demanding. Growers must forgo production on a field for three years to turn it into an organic field that qualifies for related certification. Moreover, they could not use synthetic fertilizers and pesticides, like their conventional counterparts, leaving them vulnerable to threats of losing their crops from weather and insect-related pressures during growing season. Finding proper seed varieties that were adaptable to different growing climates was also challenging. Thus, establishing a network of reliable growers was essential to success in the organic produce segments.

In addition to working with its supplier network, State Garden also piloted experimental organic growing on the east coast. To explore new ways to grow the organic produce, Mark III engaged his long-time friend from college, Mark Pins (known as Pins in the company). Now serving as the director of marketing and sustainability, Pins joined State Garden in 2009. In recounting how he joined his friend's company, he shared that the two of them had met on their first day of college and remained good friends. Pins enjoyed a successful career in the ski industry managing Ragged Mountain Ski Area. When that company was acquired, he asked his friend Mark III for a reference as he was going to apply for another job in the ski industry. Instead, Mark III convinced Pins to join State Garden as his experiences could be helpful for them. Upon joining the company, Pins was made responsible for customer service and was charged to explore new growing techniques in the organic produce segment. He and Mark III looked at different types of greenhouses, vertical farms and technology businesses. Ultimately, State Garden purchased a company called "Locally Known" in Maine and leased farmland in Florida in an attempt to bring the supply chain closer to the customer base. This would eliminate the need to bring the product across the country. These experiments were tried for three years but climate and soil conditions prevented State Garden from scaling up these growing operations.

It was clear that State Garden would need to expand its supply chain with its grower partners in the west. In order to do so, the family traveled west several times to meet its growers. It took a few years to convince its growers to farm organically. Mark III shared the argument they would make in an attempt to convince their growers to transition to organic as follows:

> I can pay you $1 per pound for conventional, but I can pay you $1.30 per pound for organic. This is what my customers are asking for and I, am in turn, asking you for it.

In a world of shifting preferences, excess supply of conventional produce, the ever present climate risk and most importantly trust in the DeMichaelis family, some growers were willing to change to better align their production with the shifting markets. Typically, State Garden was dealing with small and medium-sized farms whose land holdings were split in several locations. This enabled it to use a phased approach to convert to organic farming by dedicating selected locations for conversions. Pins noted that the efficient logistics and high safety standards differentiated State Garden from its competitors. It cut no corners on food safety and exceeded the industry standards. If a grower could not meet the high standards and specifications, they would lose their business with State Garden. The company was well aware that it had raised the bar significantly for its growers and was willing to pay more for products if its standards were met. It always treated its growers fairly keeping its end of the bargain in a handshake business.

Alongside efforts to build a supply network, State Garden worked with grocers to develop its organic salad program relying on the 4Ps of marketing – product, price, placement and promotion. Crush-proof rigid plastic packaging, vibrantly colored labels, vertical displays and private label options further solidified State Garden's relationship with its grocers while building recurrent demand for the growers. These packaging innovations remain the best solutions to maintain the integrity and quality of baby leaf lettuce.

Increased emphasis on Olivia's Organics and State Garden's pre-washed salad business also necessitated adjustments to the physical facilities of State Garden. As there were limits to its ability to retrofit the bays, investment had to be made in building its own facilities with state-of-the-art washing, sorting and packaging machinery. The bays in the New England Produce Center were increasingly underutilized, bothering their frugal aunt Annie, whose last request to Mark III before she died in 2011 was to "Get rid of the darn bays!"

By 2013, they had exited the wholesale business and sold off bays to other fresh produce businesses.

While John II and his wife had previously spent time in Florida during the winter, health issues caused them to forego their winter Florida trips to be close to the high-quality health care available in Boston. John III assumed the role of caretaking for their parents, who were increasingly unable to care for themselves. This resulted in a shift of responsibilities between the brothers and an increasing role of their management team, as Mark III focused his attention on growing the organics markets. John II passed in 2017.[17]

David Bernstein joined State Garden in 2019 as the chief financial officer after having worked several years in the corporate hedge fund and accounting industry, and as a consultant for the company for several months. In sharing his impressions of State Garden when he joined, he observed a high level of commitment in people working here and a real pride in working for the brothers, who worked with such humility with their team. He noted:

> ***Even though some jobs are not exciting, and expectations are exacting, there is a greater feeling of mission that pushes everyone to do the right thing.*** **It's something transformative.**

Bernstein also observed that while the DeMichaelis family was financially frugal, it was not afraid to spend money sensibly on items that did not have immediate payoffs but helped to improve the quality of its products for its customers or workplace for the employees. For example, State Garden established "above market and above specification food safety standards, such that its products are tested and held for pathogens for 24-hours before going to market." State Garden management is unaware of anyone else in the industry adhering to these strict standards and commitment to its valued consumers.

Ken Reagan reiterated that State Garden had the best safety program and protocols in the industry. Growers are subjected to an extensive food safety vetting process which could last up to a year before being able to supply State Garden with fresh products. When the Olivia's Organics brand was launched in 2005, only 5 percent of State Garden's total sales came from the organic segment. By 2019, the ratio had completely flipped as 95 percent of sales came from its organic products and 5 percent came from conventional products. State Garden was getting its supply from growing partners in 12 regions in the west. The company did not own any farmland and contracted with its farmers on an annual basis. Farmers were ensured a fair price and if any farmer needed more money, the family paid more money. The family viewed it as a partnership that worked well for all involved.

2020 AND THE FUTURE

State Garden has established itself as the leading provider of organic baby leaf lettuce in eastern USA. The produce is bought from dozens of independent growers in the western regions, transported across the country in contracted refrigerated trucks, tested for pathogens along the way and washed and packaged in state-of-the-art facilities in Boston. This fresh produce industry is rampant with risk factors, as explained by Mark III:

> There are a million things that can go wrong. Weather, timing, trucking. If you can limit the controllable risks better than the other guy, then you will perform better than your competitors.

Three generations of the DeMichaelis family have relied on their integrity and hard work to cultivate and nourish family and non-family relationships to be successful for over eight decades. What started as one man supported by his young family buying a day's worth of celery, washing, cleaning and hand packaging it in their basement in 1938, is now one of the leading processors and distributors of organic fresh produce in eastern USA. Over 900 employees were gainfully employed in State Garden's 170,000 square foot complex with cutting-edge processing facilities, cold and dry storage areas and head office.

The company presents itself to the public as a "family-oriented" company, viewing its customers, growers and employees as part of their "extended family." Relationships with key stakeholders, often extending over decades or generations, provide a strong foundation, enabling the company to evolve with the changing needs and preferences of its customers. As a third-generation family business, family and non-family leaders and managers continue to seek an appropriate balance between the family values of humility, obligation and altruism, as they continue to grow with innovative products and fine tune their systems and processes. Larger opportunities may present themselves through their now well-recognized brand built on a family member's name and its charitable leadership in the community. Third-generation DeMichaelis brothers, John III, Mark III and Kevin III, oversee the operations along with their carefully selected and trusted management team. Ken Reagan, vice-president of sales and marketing, summed up the current operations as follows:

> [Internally] it's like clockwork every day. No one misses a beat. We pride ourselves on communication. Everyone takes pride in their job. Nobody wants to disappoint anybody… everybody is like family here and we have a lot of employees.

The State Garden experience of the fourth-generation family members varies considerably from the experiences of their fathers who worked closely with the second-generation siblings, John II and Anne, contributing muscle and insight to the packaging and reselling of their legacy celery and spinach business. Acutely aware of these differences, the brothers are trying different ways to prepare the next-generation members for their State Garden-related responsibilities. John III's children have graduated from college, work in the business and report to Ken. They are expected to respect the chain of authority and play by the same rules as all other employees. Ken's charge is to identify the natural abilities and interests of each fourth-generation DeMichaelis member, provide opportunities to develop and test their skills and guide their career development. His experiences with John III's eldest sons provide an early insight into how this process is evolving:

> Justin is the analyzer, a numbers guy. And, his brother John IV is the "outside guy" who excels at events and retail using his marketing skills and personality. (Ken Reagan, Vice-President, Sales and Marketing)

Mark III's children are in middle and high school and are gaining familiarity working with the charitable endeavors of the business. Kevin III's children are even younger but participate in company-sponsored events and activities. Attention is being devoted to prepare the fourth generation of the DeMichaelis family for their role in State Garden. Mark III explained that efforts are under way to ensure there is a "back-up for a back-up for every part of their operation from the growers in the west to each sequence of the step till their products are consumed in people's homes." Jim Landry, a seasoned team builder from a successful larger company in the region, has been brought in as State Garden's new culture officer and charged with the important task of ensuring that contingency plans for all important roles and tasks are in place.

As the leadership of the business has evolved to incorporate more non-family members and as the fourth generation of the DeMichaelis family is being integrated in the company, the ongoing market viability of organic versus locally grown segments dominates concerns for the future. Consumer interest in these two segments is often confounded and difficult to ascertain. State Garden's local presence is strongly embedded with its buyers – the grocery chains – and the company's charitable work in its region, while its organic produce is grown in the climatically advantaged western regions of the country and transported to its processing facility in the east. Consumers concerned about the carbon dioxide emissions in transporting goods over long distances favor locally grown produce, whereas those troubled by harmful health issues caused by the chemicals used in conventional farming prefer organic produce. Unfortunately, for the climatic challenged regions of eastern USA, the ideal combination of locally grown organic produce limits the possibilities for State Garden. Until the 2020 Covid-19 pandemic redirected the consumers' attention towards health safety issues, the recyclability of clam-shell packaging was an important concern. Chief financial officer, David Bernstein, noted that while cognizant of their usage of plastic to ship their products, their industry continues to struggle with packaging given the perishability concerns. Relying on their entrepreneurial itch, the State Garden leaders continue to explore opportunities to convert post-processing waste into usable assets including vegetable juices, frozen products and variations of fresh packaged produce.

The DeMichaelis family leaders express and live sustainability through the longevity and health of their family and the extended family of employees, growers and customers, as succinctly stated by Kevin III:

> **Relationships are a root to sustainability.**

This resolve was once again tested in 2020 when the Covid-19 pandemic engulfed the world forcing stay-at-home orders. Although State Garden was deemed an essential business that could operate, the health authorities mandated the company to follow additional precautions to ensure safe distancing in their operations. Instead of laying off any employees, the company chose to reduce production to 60 percent and change the rotations so that all employees could be retained, albeit with reduced hours for many.

For John III:

> Societal sustainability means generational stability within a company and working toward a common goal. Whether it is success or failure, sticking together as one.

And, Mark III summed it up as:

> Going beyond just environmental to environment and health. Organics [are] embraced by environmentally conscious. So, we [can] reach out to customer interested in environment and health.

The key stakeholder relationships cultivated by the DeMichaelis family over the past eight decades, their authentic leadership laced with humility and dedicated hard work, combined with the non-scratchable entrepreneurial itch in the family's DNA, is likely to propel State Garden to its 100th anniversary celebrations in a few years.

KEY INSIGHTS

- State Garden's transformation from conventional to organic fresh produce that simultaneously alleviates environmental and health concerns has been paved by fair dealings with key external and internal stakeholders including customers, suppliers, competitors, employees, the local community and family members.

- The singular pursuit of three generations of family leaders to meet and exceed customers' needs and expectations enabled several entrepreneurial pivots as consumers' behaviors changed over eight decades.
- Equality of compensation of family owners and unanimity in key strategic decisions has enabled the DeMichaelis family to stay focused on growing the family enterprise without dysfunctional distractions.
- Frugality in personal spending and continuous reinvestments enable the timely pursuit of entrepreneurial opportunities.
- For the longevity of a family enterprise across generations, it is critical to continuously manage the trilemma of ensuring the financial viability of the company (profits), care for its customers, employees and farmers (people), and the health benefits of its products (planet).

ACKNOWLEDGMENTS

We appreciate the research assistance-ship provided by three Grossman School of Business students during the first two of the three rounds of data collection. These are: Shanna Clement and Kyle DeVivo (undergraduate students) and Bharagavi Mantravadi (sustainable innovation MBA student).

NOTES

1. This case is based on three separate rounds of interviews in 2013, 2019 and 2020. In the first round, Rocki-Lee DeWitt and two undergraduate research assistants visited the State Garden premises for two days to interview four family members of the second and third generations: John II, John III, Mark I and Kevin I, and three senior non-family members, Son Le (production supervisor), Tony Bordieri (chief financial officer/chief operational officer) and Michele Bordieri (human resources manager). By the second round of interviews, John II had passed, Son Le had retired and the Bordieri husband and wife team had left State Garden. Both authors and their graduate research assistant visited State Garden to interview three family members – John III, Mark I and Kevin I – and the non-professional top executives – Skip White (chief operational officer), David Bergstein (chief financial officer), Ken Reagan (vice-president, sales and marketing), Mark Pins (vice-president, sales and customer services), Jim Landry (vice-president, culture and human resources). The last round of interviews was conducted by telephone with John III, Mark I and Kevin I.
2. The actual names of family members are John M., also known affectionately as Johnny (second generation), John S. (third generation, John M.'s son), John J. (fourth generation, John S.'s son) and John C. (Mark's son). For parsimony and convenience of readers, we use John II (for second generation), John III (for third generation) and John IV and John IV, Jr. (for fourth generation). Mark

III and Mark IV, and Kevin III and Kevin IV are used to denote the third- and fourth-generation family members with the same first names.

3. Located near the waterfront and today's Government Center in the heart of Boston, Massachusetts, Faneuil Hall first opened in 1743. The project was initiated and gifted to the city of Boston by a generous wealthy merchant, Peter Faneuil. It was meant to be a meeting place and a market for trading. A National Historic Landmark since the 1960s, this has been the site of several historic American gatherings including major speeches by American presidents.
4. For ease of reading, the company is referred to as State Garden in the case although the official name change from State Garden Celery Inc. to State Garden Inc. did not take place till 1998.
5. Kathy Means. 1987. "Anna celebrates 50 years." *Packer Magazine*.
6. www.nepctr.com
7. Gersick, K., Davis, J. A., Hampton, M. M. & Lansberg, I. (1997). *Generation to Generation: Life Cycles of the Family Business*. Boston, MA: *Harvard Business School Press*.
8. https://beef2live.com/story-states-produce-food-value-0-107252
9. Guthrie, J. F., Zizza, C. & Raper, N. (1992). "Fruit and vegetables: Their importance in the American diet." *Food Review*, 15(1): 35.
10. www.agmrc.org/commodities-products/vegetables/lettuce, sourced 12/15/2019.
11. Noreast Fresh Inc. v. Commissioner of Revenue, No. 98-P-1917, decided October 27, 2000. Caselaw.findlaw.com/ma-court-of-appeals/1469357.html
12. Also known as the BOGO program – buy one, get one free.
13. For parsimony, we refer to the company by its shorter name – Noreast – in this chapter.
14. www.cdc.gov/ecoli/2006/spinach-10-2006.html
15. www.shaws.com
16. http://oliviasorganics.org/foundation/
17. His wife and life partner, Marion, passed in 2018.

8. Griffith Foods: Nourishing the world

Stuart L. Hart

INTRODUCTION

In 1919, E. L. Griffith, and his son, C. L., took the first bold steps toward improving America's food industry with the founding of Griffith Laboratories. At the time, the nation's food supply couldn't be trusted. Upton Sinclair's *The Jungle* had exposed the unhealthy conditions of the Chicago stockyards in 1906, but rancid beef, inedible sausages and unpurified spices continued to find their way into American homes. Both C. L. and E. L. Griffith wanted to help change that by introducing food science to the food industry. They believed they could improve food safety and help create healthier, better-tasting food using new technologies, food science and innovative manufacturing processes.

The grandson of E. L. Griffith, Dean Griffith, began his career with Griffith Laboratories in 1950. In the ensuing decades, he was the principal visionary who expanded the company overseas, building the global presence that it continues to grow today.

Like E. L and C. L, Dean's *Methodist upbringing imbued him with strong ethics and values which fed his sense of moral responsibility when it came to business – that the company his family had founded and led since its inception should provide a place for employees to learn and grow.* Dean also felt strongly that the *company should be a "vehicle for the greater good."*

Dean and his spouse Lois Jo Griffith were also very philanthropic, and these guiding principles made a lasting impression on their son, Brian, and guided Griffith Laboratories into the twenty-first century.

Fast forward to 2019. Brian Griffith serves as executive chairman of the company which now realizes annual sales in excess of 1 billion dollars and operates in over 30 countries around the world. Brian's rise to the company's senior leadership was propelled by his ability to connect the core values and philosophy of his predecessors, particularly his father, to the pressing societal challenges faced by the world in the twenty-first century – environmental degradation, social inequality, hunger and malnutrition (see Figure 8.1 for a family tree of the key family players).

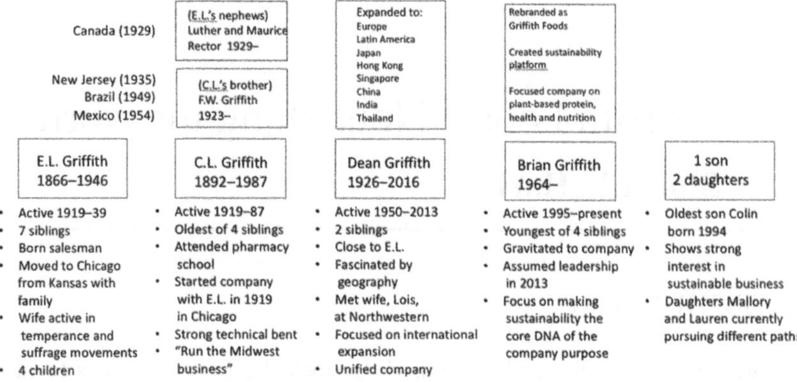

Figure 8.1 *The Griffith family tree*

In 2015, the company's name was changed to Griffith Foods to better align with its newly stated purpose: "We blend care and creativity to nourish the World." The intent was to leverage the legacy and values of the Griffith Family to embed sustainability into every aspect of Griffith Foods, making environmentally sustainable and socially inclusive development its core mission and strategy.

THE FAMILY ROOTS

The Griffith Family first arrived in the American colonies from Wales in the early eighteenth century.[1] The family migrated from Maryland to North Carolina, where they settled near Winston-Salem. Over time, they came to own substantial real estate holdings including a brick factory and a wagon factory. The family was also deeply spiritual, helping to build the Methodist community in the area. Unfortunately, the Civil War took its toll and their holdings were mostly lost after the war.

Pioneer Origins: Enoch Luther (E. L.) Griffith

E. L. Griffith, born in 1866, had seven siblings. Two of his older brothers migrated to the new state of Kansas and homesteaded near Dodge City. Later, the remaining members of the family loaded a couple of wagons and migrated to Missouri. Eventually, they were able to secure a farm, settle down and go to work. Unfortunately, after just a few years, E. L.'s father was killed in a farm accident, leaving E . L., his siblings and his mother to fend for themselves. At the time he was only 10 or 11 years old. As a result, they migrated to Dodge City, Kansas, where E. L.'s older brothers had homesteaded.

Shortly after their arrival in Kansas, E. L. and his mother staked out a claim in 1880. Unfortunately, at the time, women were unable to homestead – only a male could stake a claim. E. L., who was around 14 at the time, went before the judge to plead the case on his mother's behalf. The story goes that the judge commented: "Young man, you are very eloquent, and I'm convinced today to give your mother this land grant." As it turned out, E. L. Griffith was a born salesman, brimming with charisma and "superb, innate people skills" – skills that would serve him well in the years to come.

During their time in Dodge City, E. L. found a way to attend and graduate from college – an incredible feat in what was essentially a Wild West environment. After graduating from college in 1888, he began teaching school in a one-room school house, got married and started a family. Eventually he began selling school supplies and discovered his true calling as a salesman.

In the early 1890s, he moved his young family to Chicago in search of better opportunities. His first job involved selling grocery items he had bought from a food wholesaler to local stores in the neighborhood. He later became sales manager at the Short Milling Company and helped to start the First Methodist Church in Englewood, Illinois.

E. L. married into the Ladd family, which originally came from Indianapolis. His wife, Clara, was a very independent woman – she started the first kindergarten in Chicago and was an activist in the Temperance and Women's Suffrage movements. She was accustomed to protesting in the streets in pursuit of her desired social and cultural goals.

The Science of Food: Carroll Ladd (C. L.) Griffith

E. L. and Clara had four children – each raised in an environment stressing hard work, frugality, integrity and honesty. C. L. Griffith, born in 1892, was the oldest of the four siblings. His sister Lois, died of whooping cough in childhood. A second sister, Dorothy (Dot), was a bit of a maverick, eventually moving to the west coast in search of adventure and more freedom. C. L.'s younger brother, Francis Willard (F. W.), would be the only other sibling to become actively involved with the new company.

Given the family's farming background, C. L. was interested in pursuing studies in agronomy at the University of Illinois. A neighbor, Mr. Pattison, however, made an offer that would change the trajectory of C. L.'s life – and that of the Griffith family: Pattison owned a small pharmaceutical business which was set to close unless he could find a successor (neither of his own sons was interested). So, when C. L. graduated high school, Pattison made the following offer: "I will give you my business if you will get a degree in

Pharmacology." C. L. accepted this offer, went to Northwestern for his degree – and the rest is history.

After graduation, C. L. served in the United States (US) Army Medical Corps during the First World War. After returning from the service in 1919, E. L., who had attended to the pharmacy business during C. L.'s absence, approached him about bringing his knowledge of science and pharmacology to a new company – what would become Griffith Laboratories. Over the years, E. L. had sold everything from books to pickles to specialty flour. He recognized that, in the wake of the First World War, the food industry in the US was very backward. His idea was to start a business with his son that would serve the meat-processing and baking industries. C. L., 27 at the time, had the technical knowledge; E. L., at 53 years of age, had the experience and the selling skills. And so, Griffith Laboratories was launched.

The business began on the south side of Chicago in an old storefront, with the sale of specialty flour for the meat industry – a product that the elder Griffith had prior experience with selling. C. L.'s brother, F. W. Griffith, joined the company in 1923, along with his friend Mervyn (Merv) Philips, both of whom were instrumental, along with the elder Griffith, in rapidly expanding Griffith's sales. Indeed, E. L.'s personal commitment and willingness to spend time on the road helped expand the company to be national in scale.

E. L. blended entrepreneurship and education throughout his career. He taught Griffith's customers about the company's scientific approach to food production and nutrition. C. L. focused on product development and assigned quality control to his former chemistry classmate, Lloyd Hall, an African American scientist. The Hall and Griffith families were also friends who shared dinners and attended opera performances together. Dean Griffith, C. L.'s son, later said he was raised to "believe that people are all the same, regardless of race."

C. L. was also an instinctive educator. He *viewed the business as a platform to "bring new ideas, concepts and processes and teach them to our customers.*" This also extended to the Griffith family of associates. C. L. often asked employees to read articles and report back to him for discussions. As one impacted individual noted, "C. L. was ahead of his time where effective, continuing education was concerned." And when it came to food science, he "knew his stuff and couldn't be bamboozled." Known for his spirituality and generosity (which would shape his vision for philanthropy), C. L. Griffith also built three Methodist churches, two in Illinois and one in Wisconsin.

For all of his intellectual prowess, however, C. L. was never interested in expanding the company beyond its midwestern origins: he was content to manage the business in Chicago, think up new ideas and develop additional customers in the Midwest of the US. It was E. L. who led the way in national and, ultimately, international expansion. E. L. convinced the two sons of his sister – Luther and Maurice Rector—to begin a Griffith business in Canada. In 1929, Griffith Canada was chartered as a separate company with its own stock, with E. L., F. W. and C. L. all owning significant shares in the new company

Figure 8.2 *C. L. Griffith, E. L. Griffith and F. W. Griffith (left to right)*

(Figure 8.2). When E. L. died, his shares were split between his four children – an ownership structure which would ultimately create complications and conflicts that were not foreseen at the time the company was formed.

E. L. (along with F. W.) also led the way in expanding Griffith beyond the US and Canada – to Mexico, South America and beyond: it moved into Central and South America in the 1940s under F. W., followed by the incorporation of the company's first plant in Mexico in 1954. Even after Griffith's operations in Cuba were shut down during Fidel Castro's revolution, C. L. Griffith kept his father's aspirations alive by preserving the company's international footprint. These early international expansions typically started as low-cost sales offices, then, after some time, expanded into general offices and a blender, which facilitated the ability to provide local supply for existing Griffith products. Once sufficient demand was established, these offices were converted into new companies with separate ownership structures. This was "wild west" entrepreneurship at its best, with little governance or central control from Chicago.

During the Great Depression, many of Griffith's customers struggled to stay in business. Yet, Griffith did well because it developed creative ideas to help customers cut costs and make better-quality, safer products for less money. Griffith developed a reputation for being most creative when times were difficult. Griffith focused on improving the food industry with new processes such as meat cures, revolutionary ingredients like liquid seasonings and innovative machines like the Mince Master©, which transformed the production of ham, bacon and sausages. The Mince Master© was an adaptation of a German agricultural machine made for grinding animal feed which a Griffith salesperson in Germany had taken note of. C. L. worked to adapt and perfect the machine for the making of sausages, frankfurters and bologna, and secured patents for the new innovations.[2] Once perfected, Griffith saturated the market with the machine; the only problem was that the machines never wore out, so there were few replacement sales other than for replacement parts. So, together, C. L., E. L. and family began expanding Griffith with a simple philosophy:

Help the customer prosper, and Griffith Laboratories will prosper.

Going Global: Dean Ladd (D. L.) Griffith

C. L. and his wife Sylvia had two children – a daughter, Maxine, and a son, Dean. The son, Dean Ladd Griffith, was an introverted child. A naturally reserved and quiet individual, Dean's days were often spent in the public library near his childhood home on the south side of Chicago, learning about topography, climate and unique natural resources in distant locations such as Africa and Australia. This lifelong interest in geography no doubt fueled his later drive to travel the world and expand the company internationally.

This spirit of adventure was fueled by his close relationship with his grandfather, E. L. Griffith. In the summers, E. L. occasionally picked Dean up to spontaneously take a train trip around the US or to Canada. Closer to home, the two would visit the local forest preserve which forged Dean's love of trees and botany. His grandfather remained a mentor, teacher and source of emotional support throughout Dean's adolescent and teenage years.

Upon graduating from high school, Dean enlisted in the Army in 1945. While he was reserved and accommodating by nature, his Second World War training taught him the necessity of fighting to survive. He completed his officer training program just as the war in the Pacific drew to a close. In 1946, Dean was on a three-day pass from Fort Knox and decided to visit Northwestern with a friend. That weekend he met Lois Falkner who had grown up near Milwaukee, Wisconsin. After Dean's military discharge, he started classes at Northwestern in January 1947. Dean and Lois began dating regularly. It wasn't long after that they realized they were in love and got engaged on Valentine's Day 1949; they exchanged their marriage vows in June 1950… and the rest is history!

Dean dreamed of overseas travel and adventure but ultimately chose the path of majoring in business and beginning his career at Griffith. He worked his way up through a variety of roles, including an internship where he worked directly with the men in a meat-processing plant. From this experience he vowed that he would help the people who worked at Griffith develop their skills, grow their competencies and find fulfillment in their work.

These experiences as a child and young adult, especially the value of learning, listening and adaptability, shaped his leadership and the trajectory of the company. His religious upbringing also instilled in him the strong belief that the company should be more than just an instrument to make money. Instead, as his son Brian would later recount, he believed that it should be a:

place where people can learn and grow.

Dean not only imbued the company with a strong set of values around learning, growth and good works, but also presided over the internationalization of the company. While early expansion under E. L. and C. L. was primarily organic and expanded through F. W., Dean's uncle and cousins, the Rector family, one of Dean's enduring legacies was consolidation of the many far-flung enterprises that had been accumulated into a coherent international company and ownership structure.

Because of the war in Europe and Asia, the US had the most advanced food-processing industry in the world in the post-war years. This presented a great opportunity for Griffith to take its innovative products abroad. The first forays abroad were focused on exporting from the existing bases in the US,

Canada and Latin America. Not surprisingly, Dean met with resistance when he first proposed starting overseas companies since such a strategy would effectively kill the export market.

Ultimately, however, Dean won out and during the 1960s–80s, Griffith opened new companies in Belgium, Colombia, Costa Rica, England, Japan, Hong Kong, Spain, Singapore and France. And during the 1990s–2000s, Dean presided over the opening of new companies in Brazil, China, Korea, Thailand and India, along with Innova which was the company's savory flavor business. In addition, two companies – Custom Food Products and DM Foods (focused on soup, base, sauce and gravy offerings) – were acquired to enhance the competency portfolio of Griffith Laboratories. The combination of Custom Food Products and DM Foods was later rebranded as Custom Culinary.

This expansion, starting in the 1970s, changed Griffith from a US company with an export division into a truly international company. From local plants, Griffith was offering new services to new markets, which meant adapting to the different cultures it served. Dean initiated this expansion using relatives as managers, but quickly discovered that hiring family was counterproductive. As the international expansion progressed, it was becoming increasingly clear that the split ownership among all these disparate entities had led to a "dysfunctional company." The various owners were more competitive than cooperative. As Dean noted: "To become a truly global company, it was necessary to unify these fragmented parts." And unifying the company meant it was necessary to buy out some of the relatives as well as some of the larger non-family shareholders.

As was the case with the initial proposal to internationalize, the idea of consolidating ownership was not initially well received among the various family factions, including Dean's father, C. L. As a starting point, Dean engaged Kuhn Loeb & Co., an investment banker, to determine a fair value for the various entities. Once a consolidation plan had been put together, it became clear that F. W. and one of C. L.'s cousins had enough shares to sell the business out from under everyone else! Through a private placement with five institutional lenders, Dean locked in for ten years enough funds to make the buyouts. He then began the delicate process of negotiating the deals with all the relatives who wanted to sell.

After orchestrating a complex series of family buyouts, Dean successfully restructured the company in 1978, making other large stock purchases from major shareholders. It proved to be a turning point for Griffith, which allowed the company to place additional emphasis on hiring international employees with a deep understanding of native flavors as well as the needs of nearby customers. It's the primary reason why today Griffith Foods does business in over 30 countries and is capable of tailoring customized products – like vegetable- and cereal-based namkeen snacks in India or nutrition-packed soft-meat products for the elderly in Japan – to meet the food cultures and needs of the local communities it serves.

For 15 million dollars in stock purchases, Dean had secured the private future of the company. It was also a good investment for the Employee Stock Ownership Plan (ESOP) and the remaining shareholders. Indeed, for more than 30 years, Griffith Stock has outpaced the S&P 500 stock index (see Figure 8.3).[3] In fact, when great-grandson Brian ultimately became executive chairman of the company in 2015, he commented that because of his father (Dean), he was the beneficiary of a "much cleaner, better structured company."

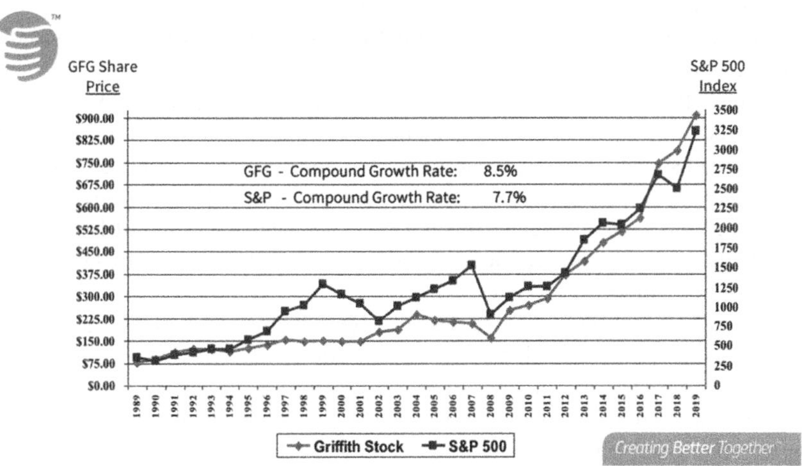

Figure 8.3 *Griffith Foods stock price versus S&P 500 Index, 1989–2019*

This consolidation included much cleaner ownership, achieved through the establishment of a dual class stock voting and dividend structure. The dual class stock structure offered to all shareholders the ability to exchange their existing shares for either Class A with one vote per share with a dividend equal to 11 times that of the Class B shares; however, if one selected B shares they received 10 shares for every one share tendered of existing Griffith shares. In the end, all shareholders other than Dean's immediate family selected the Class A shares with the higher dividend while Dean's family selected the Class B shares and the ability to increase its voting power by a factor of 10.

CREATING BETTER TOGETHER

Griffith Foods is fueled by the enduring belief that change is never created in isolation.[4] Countless global partners rely on the company for seasonings, spices, coatings, sauces and more, while its sustainability efforts support local and regional food eco-systems around the world. As we will see, Griffith Foods' contemporary initiatives stem from a simple but revolutionary idea: that a business can be a vehicle for the greater good.

A Revolution in Taste, Texture and Food Safety

At the outset, C. L. and E. L. Griffith sought to infuse speed, safety and reliability into a flawed food system. They named their company Griffith Laboratories to underscore their focus on food science and got to work creating flours and liquid seasonings. Their decision to secure the American rights to a product developed in Germany called Prague Powder in the 1920s set the company on its current path.

Prague Powder, a mixture of sodium nitrate and sodium nitrite, radically improved the curing process for meats. By writing a curing handbook and teaching customers how to properly use the powder, the Griffiths did nothing less than revolutionize the American meat industry. Griffith's innovations enhanced the taste and safety of food products, reduced cost and food waste and helped to speed up production. Then, as now, Griffith grew by helping its customers to grow.

Virtually overnight, slabs of bacon, often flabby and malodorous due to time-consuming sweet pickle cures, could be dry-cured, making them flavorful and crisp. Sausage production, once a hit-or-miss proposition, became more dependable and efficient thanks to liquid seasonings. Griffith's adoption of artery pumping, once an overlooked process, cured hams in as little as 12 days instead of three months, leading to a reduction in spoilage rates of pork products.

These changes played a key role in preserving meats for American families during the Great Depression. Additionally, under chief scientist Lloyd Hall, Griffith pioneered methods to kill micro organisms in many foods and ingredients, including K-rations for soldiers fighting in the Second World War.

New epochs created new needs. As families fanned out into suburbs after the Second World War, quick meals and convenience became priorities, increasing interest in frozen foods, ready-made dinners and boxed cake mixes. Using soy protein concentrates, Griffith helped pack nutrients into breakfast cereals and ushered in the age of Salisbury steaks, while the company's iconic Mince Master® equipment allowed customers to produce sausages at an astounding rate of 500 pounds a minute.

Soon, flavor boosters made from vegetable proteins, like Vegamine, added body and umami to once-pallid soups. Bottles of natural smoke and Pepperoyal seasonings infused bold tastes into the otherwise bland diet of 1950s and early 1960s America. These innovations supported the viability of Griffith's unique business model, which aided its partners by ensuring consistency and improving the quality of its products.

Today, Griffith Foods' efforts to nourish the world take on a variety of new forms. Innovations abound, ranging from the development of gluten-free coatings made from chickpeas, navy beans and rice for people with food allergies, to specially formulated protein-packed porridges that nourish impoverished communities. And looking forward, entirely new technologies like plant-based proteins and 3D printing will be harnessed to address the challenge of sustaining nutritious and affordable food for the 10 billion people expected to inhabit the planet by 2050.

Continuous Innovation

The push for continual innovation has been a Griffith hallmark since founding. Griffith built its first research kitchen in 1937, but its contemporary chef-driven culinary program came much later, in the 1960s. That's when Griffith chef Otto Schlecker – who helped the US bring home a number of prizes from the 1967 Culinary Olympics (now the IKA International Culinary Competition) – worked to ensure greater collaboration between the company's culinary teams and food scientists. This led to the formation of an affiliate of the US business known as Chefs' Associates. This entity, which was independent for several years, was ultimately integrated into the Griffith operating units.

This blending of knowledge from first-rate chefs and food scientists was an innovative move at the time, and allowed Griffith to expand into the restaurant industry and further improve the quality of its products. Indeed, Griffith has acted as a "development partner" in the creation of some of the most iconic fast food and fast-casual creations ever produced with customers like KFC and McDonalds.

Whenever a Griffith innovation became commonplace, the company turned to the next unmet need. During the 1990s, that meant anticipating the public's desire for a wider array of food options, whether it was more authentic ethnic flavors or healthier low-fat options that arose out of baby boomers' growing interest in examining food labels.

Griffith acquired Custom Food Products® located in Chicago in 1991 and a few years later Custom Food Products acquired DM Foods located in Ohio. Subsequently, Custom Food Products was rebranded into Custom Culinary. Custom, which was originally acquired to expand Griffith's soup, base, sauce and gravy offerings, then launched its Innova® Flavors division in 1997, which greatly diversified its catalog of natural flavorings. In time, generic flavors became a distant memory. Griffith worked with partners to create authentic regional flavors as diverse as its expanding footprint, from red Thai curries and shawarmas to chimichurri and tandoori pastes.

By the 2000s, Griffith had formed truly multi-disciplinary teams. While its regional chefs ensured authenticity, its food scientists developed novel ways to replace monosodium glutamate (MSG), reduce sodium, eliminate transfats and create clean-label products. Meanwhile, sensory scientists calibrated textures and aromas throughout the process and Griffith's consumer insights and marketing specialists researched the trending dishes, consumer preferences and flavor profiles around which its customers could build new products and recipes.

The creation of cross-functional teams, such as the Global Innovation Council and the Global Culinary Council, ensured ideas were openly exchanged and integrated across the company's international operations. Griffith believes that greater change comes from blending together diverse approaches and points of view.

GRIFFITH FAMILY VALUES: A FORCE FOR THE GREATER GOOD

Even in its early days, the Griffiths viewed the company as a vehicle for serving the greater good.[5] Originally, making better meat and bakery products through enhancing flavors, improving food safety and creating faster and more efficient processing were the primary goals for the company. "If you look at our history, being a vehicle for the greater good has been the ethos of this company," said Brian Griffith: "This unstated idea was instilled in the company over many, many years, and specifically during the tenure of Dean Griffith, my father, who spent over 60 years with the company."

The business has always been a private and family-owned enterprise, a component that is incredibly important to the Griffith family. "We are a fourth-generation, family-owned business and there's a lot of commitment from the family, but we know our success is truly due to the commitment of our employees," said Griffith. "Brian's stewardship has been vital to translating values from generation to generation," shared T. C. Chatterjee, who was named the company's chief executive officer (CEO) in 2016.

The Conversation that Changed Everything

Yet, Brian Griffith's rise to becoming executive chairman of the company was by no means pre-ordained. As a child, he and his three older siblings would spend time at their family's summer property on a lake outside Chicago. Brian's older brother Scott and two sisters Lori and Carol were 12, 9 and 5 years his senior, so it should come as no surprise that the eldest Griffith was looked to first when it came to pass the torch in the family business.

There was a key conversation, however, between Brian and his father that changed everything. Brian recounted it this way:

> One summer, when I was ten years old, I vividly recall a moment on the dock at the lake with my Dad. He was talking about his philosophy for the company and how important he thought it was that working at Griffith be a gratifying experience for employees – that it should be a place where people learn and grow. He emphasized that we all have a spiritual need to be part of something bigger than ourselves, and that he had a responsibility to see that the company fulfilled this need… And then he said something I will never forget: *That the company should be a vehicle for the greater good.* I remember thinking that that was pretty cool; it was not an abstract idea and I was intrigued and proud of that aspiration. At the time, I was actively working with local veterinarians in what I thought was my future vocation but that exchange with my Dad planted the seed that business could be much more.

A few years later, in his early teens, Brian went on a series of business trips over a couple years with Dean and Lois that took him to Europe, Latin America, Australia and New Zealand. Like his parents, he remembered being absolutely fascinated by the rich cultural traditions, diversity of foods and unique challenges faced in working across different geographies and entities, but most importantly his interest in what he would later call "organizational culture" was piqued.

By the time he was applying to college, he faced the choice of whether or not to prepare himself to join the company or pursue other endeavors. In a short but seminal conversation, Brian informed his father of his plan to pursue a liberal arts degree, work for another company for five years, get an MBA and then join Griffith. And that is what he did (Figure 8.4).

Defining Moments

After graduating from college, Brian joined Kraft Foodservice as a corporate trainee, was promoted to procurement manager and spent four years in the field, gaining valuable experience with food service distribution channels. He then left Kraft to pursue his MBA. Brian and his wife, Sue, had their first child, son Colin, during his MBA studies. Upon completing his MBA in 1995, he joined Griffith Laboratories as a marketing manager in Europe. During his time in Europe, Brian and Sue had two more children – daughters Mallory and Lauren.

The move to Europe was an important formative experience for Brian's family. Sue's willingness to move abroad – and key role she played while living there – enabled Brian to travel extensively and gain crucial first-hand experience with foreign operations, both in Europe and in Asia. As Brian put it: "You can't work effectively with an unhappy spouse." Sue threw herself

Figure 8.4 *Brian Griffith (top) and his parents, Dean and Lois*

into the education and well-being of the Griffith children, and established a circle of friends and contacts that were crucial to the family's adaptation to its new environment.

The Griffith family moved back to Chicago in 2000 when Brian became vice-president of marketing for an acquisition made in 1991, Custom Food Products. A key defining moment in his career at Griffith came in 2001, when it was clear that Custom Food Products, despite its strong profitability, needed a radical change in strategy to move from a private label to a branded company in the rapidly consolidating broadline food service distribution channel. During the 1990s, broadline food service distributors such as Sysco, Kraft Foodservice (eventually US Foodservice) and Gordon Foodservice (among others) pursued aggressive roll-up or fold-out strategies that put pressure on food companies that used distributors to get their products to market. His experience at Kraft positioned him to rise to the challenge as general manager of Custom Food Products and lead the repositioning and reorganization of the company that would become Custom Culinary.

It was at this time that Brian also hired T. C. Chatterjee from Unilever to join him at Custom Food Products in what would become the beginning of a long and fruitful relationship between the two. The transformation that was necessary at Custom Food Products required not only a gifted functional leader in strategy and marketing but a like-minded "forward thinker" that could be a trusted partner in the process. In a family enterprise it is essential to have great talented partners within the family but more importantly throughout the business. Said Brian: "I can say that Griffith Foods would not be where it is today without the great partnership that I have with TC. Our relationship is one that is based on a depth of trust derived from competence and character that we both bring to the table." It is this type of relationship that enables successful family businesses to thrive during next-generation transitions and the step-function growth required to not only compete effectively for the future but to thrive and deliver on the company's purpose.

When Brian moved abroad once again to become president of Griffith Foods Asia Pacific in 2005, T. C. was promoted to general manager/president. Early in 2011, Brian became a multi-regional president with the three presidents of Asia Pacific, India/Middle East and Latin America reporting to him. Later in 2012, the additional role of vice chairman was added to Brian's responsibilities and he essentially took over leading the company's board.

In 1999, Dean appointed Herve de la Vauvre, another non-family member, to be CEO of Griffith Laboratories Worldwide – the fifth in a string of non-family-member CEOs which started in the 1980s. The new CEO shared many of the Griffith family values but was primarily focused on the profit and loss and financial performance which during his tenure significantly improved. This set the stage for a second, truly seminal moment for Brian Griffith – the moment when sustainability rose to the fore as the defining focus for the company's future.

The year was 2013. Several of Griffith Laboratories' biggest customers had been inquiring about the company's philosophy and strategy with regard to sustainability. Dean Griffith, while a nature lover in his personal life, never connected his passion for geography and nature to the purpose or strategy of the company. And the CEO saw little need to do anything beyond responding to basic customer expectations and being in legal compliance with regard to sustainability.

At a senior management meeting when the topic of customer sustainability surveys was treated as a pesky nuisance, it struck Brian to the core: "I felt we had lost our way at that moment." And while Brian, by his own admission, had only a "general awareness" at that point of what sustainability in a business context might actually entail, he sensed its potential to reinvigorate the company's family values and humanistic approach to management:

> **I sensed sustainability was a powerful connection to the idea of being a "vehicle for greater good." I realized that sustainability could be *the way* in which we could demonstrate this ideal.**

The stage was set and Brian seized the moment; he clearly remembers looking at the CEO and saying "I got this." He immediately assembled a team consisting of T. C. Chatterjee, regional vice-presidents and functional leaders in supply chain, human resources, marketing, strategy, finance and operations and began work on the sustainability model for Griffith. Brian's son Colin, who was a student at Colorado College at the time, majoring in environmental science, aided and abetted this process of learning. "He was giving me books and articles to read," said Brian, "by authors like Bill McDonough, Paul Hawken, Michael Pollan, and Stuart Hart."

At the next senior management meeting in May 2013, Brian wanted to honor his father in the process of linking the idea of Griffith "as a vehicle for greater good" to sustainability. While Dean did not utilize the modern vocabulary of "sustainability," Brian asked him to speak first about what the company represented to him – Dean spoke of the importance of responsibility, of being engaged in something bigger than one's self, and of using the company as a vehicle for the greater good.

Brian then stood up and introduced the triple-bottom-line model – people, planet and performance – that the sustainability team had drafted together. He made the case that confronting the environmental and social challenges associated with "sustainability" – malnutrition, supply chain transparency, soil loss, energy and water use – actually captured the essence of Griffith's commitment to be a force for the greater good – that it represented "who we are." It was, in short, the bridge to the future. And, it represented the sort of company that the next generation of Griffiths could be proud of – and potentially be attracted to.

He made the case with conviction and passion. It was a moment, in his words, of "authentic leadership" spoken by a family member with true concerns regarding his family's long-term business legacy. And it was at that moment that the leadership of Griffith Laboratories was passed to the great-grandson. Brian had his father's blessing along with the approval of the board, and he never looked back. He kept the non-family CEO in place until 2016, while the company prepared T. C. Chatterjee to become the next CEO.

Since that fateful day in 2013, Griffith Foods has been on a journey of learning and transformation, led by Brian's personal passion and commitment. He insisted that sustainability be organized as a "platform" for the company and not as an initiative or separate department. All initiatives are attached to and live inside one of the three pillars of people, planet and performance across the platform. Brian said: "The triple bottom-line essentially gave form and structure to the idea of a vehicle for greater good. For the first time in our history we formally organized ourselves for impact." This unleashed a torrent of interest and passion among people already in the company. And the company's sustainability journey was under way.

SUSTAINABILITY AND PURPOSE

Dean Griffith continually reinforced the importance of preserving Griffith's legacy as a change maker. He insisted that there were always opportunities for Griffith to improve local and global food chains if the company remained focused on what it did best: elevating partners brands', leveraging innovation and being true to company values. Looking forward, the emerging challenges of global sustainability had become the key drivers of purpose and innovation. But like everything else at Griffith, it was forged from the idea that twenty-first-century food companies could achieve healthy profits while serving as ethical stewards of its people, the planet and the performance of all of its stakeholders.

The Sustainability "Platform"

Following that fateful meeting in 2013, Brian Griffith led a team to create the sustainability platform for the company. A stakeholder engagement process was initiated which included dialogue with customers, suppliers and external experts in the food and agriculture space. A materiality assessment was also conducted in 2014 which led to the identification of several issues that were both important to key stakeholders and had potentially important business impact and implications.

Based upon this work, a set of metrics was established focused on "People, Planet, and Performance (3BL – Triple Bottom Line)." Key metrics that were tracked included:

- People: employee safety, employee engagement, ethical employment, talent development, family support and community involvement.
- Planet: solid waste reduction, energy efficiency, water conservation, emissions reduction, transportation efficiency, and sustainable sourcing.
- Performance: customer growth, financial improvement, food safety, risk management, ethics/integrity and healthy, nutritious and innovative products.

Once the platform was established, Brian stepped back and realized that the company was missing a clearly articulated purpose that answered the higher-level question of "why we exist." He felt there was a real need to articulate the connection between what was unique and authentic about Griffith and the significant needs in the world that the company could address. A participatory process was set in motion in 2015 and Brian asked T. C. Chatterjee, now chief operating officer of Griffith Laboratories Worldwide, to lead the "Purpose Project" as the future CEO and engage the employees in the development of a concrete expression of Griffith's purpose, which was ultimately articulated as:

> **We blend care and creativity to nourish the world.**

The new company purpose also led, in 2015, to the development of a framework known as the Griffith Foods' "house" (see Figure 8.5). The house built upon Griffith's new purpose, pulling together the stakeholder engagement, materiality assessment and triple-bottom-line work, and visually reinforced the importance of sustainability as the core platform for the company's future. Indeed, as Brian emphatically stated:

> **sustainability became the lens through which Griffith Foods sees the world and the "filter" that informs all our decisions.**

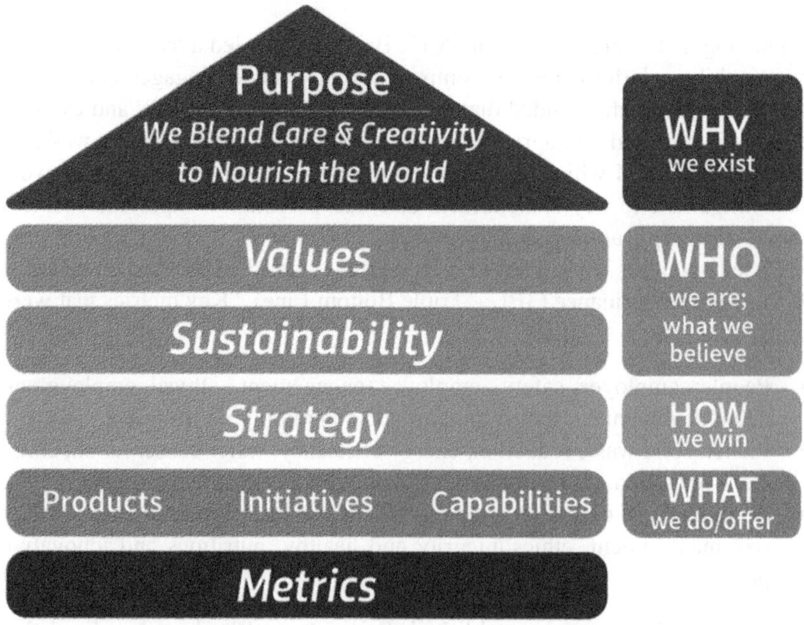

Figure 8.5 *The Griffith Foods "house"*

The "house" came to serve as an important expression of Griffith Foods' core values and became a key communication tool emphasizing the importance of sustainability to the company's future. Brian Griffith elaborated on the importance of the purpose to the company's focus on sustainability:

> Everything flows from our Purpose – "why we exist." Griffith Foods' values and sustainability platform, together with our new brand, define "who we are & what we believe." Sustainability ensures that what we do to succeed leads to the responsible growth of our customers' and Griffith's business. Our "House" is holistic, integrated and synergistic; it is how we operationalize and cascade purpose into action and impact.[6]

Griffith Sustainably Sourced

One of the critical areas of focus associated with the people, planet and performance metrics was the company's supply chain, which manifested itself in the Griffith Sustainably Sourced (GSS) Program (see Figure 8.6).[7] Like all of Griffith's innovations, it is a program based on mutual benefits to stakeholders, in this case, farm-level integration of the supply chain. By offering support to farmers and spice cultivators around the world, Griffith has helped producers generate higher yields and safer work environments and provided fully traceability and transparency for customers.

Figure 8.6 *Griffith Sustainability Sourced*

The program was conceived in 2009, on a road trip with Shyam Mohan (then president of Griffith India/Middle East), during a discussion around proactively addressing challenges with the Indian red chili supply. Griffith decided to vertically integrate its red chili supply as one of the largest buyers in the world of the commodity. It began by working with a trusted on-the-ground partner in India to establish and organize direct relationships with the farmers. It became evident that there were multiple, far-reaching benefits beyond risk management, with farmer income, sustainable agricultural practices and community development being the most important. It also knew a fully traceable and certified sustainably grown product was key. So, the company then approached one of the best-known certifications familiar to consumers – the Rainforest Alliance – and asked them to include spices and herbs along with its well-known coffee work.

The Rainforest Alliance readily embraced the opportunity to expand its certification framework and the program was under way. By 2015, the company was sourcing the majority of its chili peppers, a highly used ingredient in Griffith's recipes, from Rainforest Alliance-certified farms in India. The chilis are sustainably grown using integrated pest management to limit the amount of pesticides used, enable water conservation and protect the soil from erosion. Farmers in the GSS India Chilis program are trained to follow sustainable cultivation practices which are guided by the Sustainable Agriculture Network standards, and receive other benefits such as access to medical facilities.

The program also utilizes mobile apps to track and manage the use of pesticides, and has introduced soil and water testing to maximize return. These tactics are not only more environmentally sustainable, they have also resulted in value-added products for Griffith's customers. Additionally, through Griffith Foods' purchasing practices of tracking the chilis from their time in the field until use in a recipe, the farmers receive a higher return through the elimination of intermediaries, transportation to market and commission to selling agents.[8]

These methods help producers protect their crops from insects and disease while ensuring Griffith can source a steady supply of natural high-quality ingredients. The GSS program has expanded the number of naturally sourced products Griffith can produce for its partners, who, in turn, enjoy the added benefits of a transparent, fully traceable supply chain. The "sweet spot" for identifying spices and herbs that are most suitable for the GSS model are raw materials where smallholder farmers are the primary growers and where Griffith sources large volumes with inconsistent quality. GSS earned Griffith and its partner farms a number of Rainforest Alliance certifications while yielding more authentic flavors, stabilizing costs and boosting the standard of living for local communities. These initiatives are both a validation of Griffith Foods' past successes and a clear signal of its future ambitions, an essential step in its continuing push to blend care and creativity to nourish the world.

Most recently, the Griffith Food's sustainable sourcing initiative has led to the launch of a new company – Terova – focused not only on sustainable sourcing for Griffith but also improving the livelihoods of the smallholder farming communities from which raw materials and spices are sourced. By aiming to serve not only Griffith Food's own captive needs, but also expanding the broader external market for sustainably sourced, Terova enables the company to multiply its positive impact in farming communities around the world – and create a new revenue source at the same time. Through Terova, Griffith aims to engage 2,000 farmers by 2020, 7,000 by 2025 and 10,000 before 2030. Ultimately, the aim is for Griffith to source 100 percent of selected spices, herbs and botanicals from Terova.

Rebranding for Purpose

In 2016, Griffith Laboratories became Griffith Foods. Changing the name was a deliberate move directly aligned with the new purpose. While the "Laboratory" designation spoke to the company's first century of food science and product development, the new name spoke more directly to the diverse capabilities and aspirations that differentiate the organization and what customers were looking for in the future.

But before the company began the exercise to create a new identity, it knew the importance of fully understanding and describing "Why We Exist" – the company's purpose:

> **When the Griffith family decided to articulate its Purpose, the primary factor was that the inspiration for it had to come from within the company, not externally; it had to be as true to us today as it was 97 years ago, and if we had it right, would be as true a hundred years from now. (T. C. Chatterjee)**

"'Foods' captures who we are as a company today. The new brand identity resonates across the world in more than 30 countries where Griffith operates," continued T. C. Chatterjee.

It was also crucial that the Griffith Food's purpose capture the spirit of the company in an authentic way. As T. C. Chatterjee said, "the most important question we asked was, does it feel like Griffith? Multiple levels of the organization were involved, and it took about nine months from start to finish to develop a statement which captured the essence of what has guided the organization for almost a century." The new company purpose and name informed the development of a new identity and rebranding, including a new logo (see Figure 8.7): in the new Griffith Foods logo, the "hand" represents care and the reverse image, a "fork," represents creativity, with the sweeping green stroke across the top representing the company's commitment to "nourishing the world."

Brian Griffith believed that the company purpose would be the most powerful lever of change and driver of innovation. Said Griffith: "Over the past decade we have significantly improved our financial performance… and for

Figure 8.7 *Griffith logos: old and new*

some, our newly articulated purpose was simply a broad affirmation of 'business as usual' but with more soul. But by virtue of its ambition, it was setting the stage for significant change and transformation." Indeed, the new name and brand identity were developed not only to capture what the company is and what it stands for, but also how it aspires to help its customers – and the world – in the future.

Purpose-Driven Strategy

In 2015, Brian Griffith rose to become the executive chairman of Griffith Foods and T. C. Chatterjee became CEO of Griffith Foods Worldwide in 2016. To complement and reinforce the work on the sustainability platform, purpose and the house, Chatterjee initiated a process to translate Griffith Foods' purpose and sustainability commitments into a portfolio of new strategies and capabilities worldwide.

The Purpose-Driven Strategy initiative kicked off in February 2016, beginning with a scenario planning process. Business leaders throughout the company confronted the global challenges in food and agriculture by considering the implications of four plausible but very distinct future scenarios based upon varying levels of food production capacity and food delivery to consumers: Healthy Abundance, Happy but Unhealthy, Fat and Frustrated and A Perfect Storm. Business units and local partners worked to collect data relevant to each of the four scenarios. The process culminated in two strategy sessions held in November 2016 and February 2017 involving business leaders from across the company.

A strategy working group comprised of business leaders from all the regions then assumed the responsibility of coalescing the results of these sessions and began communicating the findings and expectations for next steps over the summer of 2017. Local business units then began to work with regional leadership to develop new products, launch new strategic initiatives and build new capabilities from the ground up. Said Chatterjee: "We have made a commitment that everything we do as a company will be driven by and connected to our Purpose. And our Purpose driven strategy has focused the organization on 'where to play' and 'how to win' to best serve our Purpose."

The Purpose-Driven Strategy leveraged the existing Griffith Foods' capabilities of consumer insight, culinary, food and sensory science, but also sought to build new layers of competence for the future through work streams focused on health and nutrition, leveraging technology, shared value and partnerships/ecosystems. Examples of strategic initiatives associated with these four work streams included:

- Health and nutrition: nutritional products, botanicals; plant-based/alternative proteins.
- Leveraging technology: 3D printing, blockchain, artificial intelligence, Internet of Things.
- Shared value: affordable nutrition for the underserved at the base of the pyramid, building smallholder famers' capacity and knowledge along with local processing capabilities and community development.
- Partnership eco-system: customer partnerships, startups and venture investments, waste stream/food loss commercialization.

The Purpose-Driven Strategy has now become a key driver of the company's future growth and expansion strategy. The goal is that these four work streams and their associated initiatives should account for no less than 25 percent of Griffith's revenues and profits by 2022, with continued geographic expansion into underserved markets.

SUSTAINABILITY 2.0

When Brian Griffith rose to his current position as executive chairman in 2015, his aspiration was to introduce healthier products, focus on affordable nutrition, redefine industry norms and improve local and global food eco-systems. Accordingly, Griffith is developing new ways to improve the taste and texture of plant-based proteins in hopes of nourishing the world in a way that the planet can sustain itself; new oven-based Never-Fry coatings are also being developed to preserve essential textures and flavors without the need for unhealthy oils. And partnerships with new customers and food industry incubators, like The Hatchery in Chicago, have been initiated to support the next generation of food entrepreneurs who will further revolutionize the industry.

With purpose as his compass, Brian Griffith is dedicated to building a profitable and sustainable twenty-first-century company – one that is a better investment for its owners, a better environment for its employees, a better citizen in its communities and a better steward of the planet's resources. Yet to truly achieve the goal of industry transformation, it would be necessary to expand upon the existing Sustainability Platform to integrate sustainability into the very fabric of the company – to elevate the world challenges of sustainable agriculture and affordable nutrition to be the focus of the company's core strategies, and to align the organizational structure, systems and processes accordingly. This would mean making bolder moves and longer-term investments, building new capabilities and committing to aspirations, goals and metrics that are transformative in character.

Griffith Foods seemed to be particularly well positioned to take on this challenge. Indeed, as Brian Griffith stated:

> **we don't have the problems faced by publicly held companies – a couple of down quarters and you are forced to abandon your long-term game plan. As a privately-held and family-owned company, we have no excuse not to do the right thing. We have the capacity, and it is our duty to tackle these challenges. It is our family's legacy that is at stake; we are compelled to do so.**

Beginning in 2017, Griffith Foods began working with Enterprise for a Sustainable World (ESW) – a non-profit focused on sustainable business – to help them pursue Sustainability 2.0. ESW began by facilitating workshops with the board and the senior leadership team aimed at developing a deeper understanding of and shared perspective about the sustainability drivers and world challenges that would drive core strategy in the future, beginning with the Sustainable Development Goals (SDGs).

Sustainable Development Goals Assessment

In 2016, the United Nations adopted 17 interconnected SDGs in a universal call to action to end poverty, protect the planet and ensure that all people enjoy peace and prosperity. These included 169 consensus targets and sub-goals that were directly relevant to business. ESW surveyed key senior leadership and staff to assess their perceptions of Griffith Food's current sustainability platform and initiatives in relation to the SDGs, and their implications for long-term strategy and opportunity identification. The results were discussed in a workshop aimed at identifying the most relevant and important world challenges upon which to focus the company's attention.

Transformational Sustainability Benchmarking

An initiative with ESW was launched in 2018 to benchmark the leading-edge "next" practices in companies focused on sustainability as a core strategy. The project was designed to focus on the "outliers" – a sample of those companies in the world pushing the envelope when it comes to truly transformational sustainability. Ultimately, a sample of 15 companies was selected for further study. The companies were examined collectively in order to identify patterns and to create a model for presenting the key elements and "next practices" for transformational sustainability.[9]

The results revealed that a strong sense of *purpose* was indeed important when it came to embedding sustainability as a core strategy. However, a societally relevant purpose was insufficient to the task of focusing company attention on the actual, on-the-ground challenges that the company seeks to address. For this, another layer of specificity seemed to be required to embed lofty purpose in operational reality – Aspirations and Quests. Aspirations and Quests bring purpose to life and serve as the "connective tissue" for goals and metrics, as well as rewards and incentives.

Building on transformational sustainability benchmarking, Griffith aims to develop a set of aspirations and quests looking out to 2030 to provide clarity as to where the company is heading and the positive impacts it seeks to create in the world through its business. The aim is not to just increase employee "engagement" in the traditional sense – a motivational gambit to increase the level of "discretionary effort" so as to boost financial performance. Instead, as Brian Griffith so aptly put it, the objective is to increase the level of *fulfillment*: to harness the power of positive impact to make good on Dean Griffith's commitment that the company provide the opportunity for people to learn and grow, and to serve the greater good.

Turning Metrics on Their Head

Most companies adopt sustainability goals and targets as a set of commitments separate from their primary goal, which is *financial* performance. For Griffith, however, Sustainability 2.0 means turning this logic on its head – making the company's sustainability-based aspirations its primary objective. Financial metrics are subordinate and serve to support the societally driven purpose. As Brian Griffith puts it:

> Purpose and sustainability are the primary objectives. Our aim is to do the right thing in the world, to use our knowledge and capability to make the world a better place. We are organizing for impact. Goals that measure progress in this regard are really our effectiveness measures – they tell us how well we are doing as a company.

> Financial measures are indicators of how efficiently we are pursuing these societal objectives – how well we are converting societal needs into business reality. They are target locating tools, means to an end. They are not the end in themselves.

With this philosophy in mind, Griffith committed to the use of science- and context-based metrics in tracking its progress toward its strategic/sustainability goals wherever possible. Mark McElroy, one of the pioneers in this emerging method, was engaged to work with Griffith Foods to develop these metrics. As a first step, the aim was to develop a fully customized Multicapital Scorecard for each of Griffith's existing ("current reality") goals and targets – those associated with the Sustainability Platform.[10]

In 2019, Griffith Foods also hired a dedicated and experienced staff person to lead its Sustainability 2.0 initiatives – Kathy Pickus – who had previously served as chief sustainability officer at Abbott. To assist and inform this process, Griffith Foods also formed an external advisory council to work directly with the board on embedding sustainability into every aspect of the company. As work on Sustainability 2.0 continues to evolve and the additional set of aspirational goals are developed to reflect the company's future direction, a second stage of "future aspiration" metrics will also be developed to measure and track company progress toward them.

ALL IN FOR THE FAMILY

Since Griffith Laboratories was co-founded by E. L. and his son, C. L. Griffith, there was a natural transition of leadership to C. L. once his co-founder father stepped away.[11] As we saw, C. L. Griffith ultimately turned leadership of the company over to his son, Dean Griffith. Unfortunately, this leadership succession was anything but smooth. By the 1960s and 1970s, there were numerous members of the extended family who had ownership stakes in the company. Relationships grew tense as competing family factions had conflicting views about how the company should be run, and as the various factions fought for power and control the question surfaced: should the company remain private, go public or be sold?

All of this came to a head during the 1970s. Dean's father, C. L., was not particularly interested in the international operations of the company, so as the international presence grew, Dean took it upon himself to negotiate with the different family factions to consolidate the various independent entities around the world and reorganize them into a single, international company. Other family members involved with the company did not necessarily agree with Dean's approach and made their displeasure known. As Brian Griffith remembers it: "My dad [Dean] was a sensitive man who was naturally conflict averse. But with uncles, aunts and cousins arguing about the future of the company, and some of them trying to force the sale of the company, Dean realized that he needed to take action to deal with the situation."

Joe Maslick, who worked as an executive for the company for over 50 years, played a key role in the evolution and development of the company. Over that time span, he developed a special and unique relationship with each of the Griffith family members. As his relationships blossomed, Joe grew to be not only a loyal and trusted business partner to the Griffiths but also a valued advisor to the business and the family. Joe retired from the company in December 2017 but today continues to serve as a Griffith director, trustee of the company's retirement plans, trustee of the company and family charitable foundations. He also continues to provide advice and counsel to Brian and his family. During his career, he served the company in many roles and most recently, before his retirement, as executive vice-president and chief financial officer of the company.

During Joe's tenure he assisted both C. L. and Dean with tax and strategic organizational planning which laid the foundation for the reorganization and consolidation of the business. He also negotiated various acquisitions and divestures including the largest single divesture in the company's history in 1999. The sale of this non-food-related business provided critical financial resources to grow the food business and capital to further consolidate the voting control of Dean and Brian's family.

Joe, having worked with three generations of Griffith family members, reflected on the numerous similarities that ran through the three family generations. These included deep moral and ethical principles, high energy and tireless work ethic, religious beliefs, dedication and love of the Griffith business, its employees, customers and suppliers, and love of their lake house and the environment.

There was one other passion that ran through the three generations – their generosity and philanthropy which manifested itself through their love for sharing with others, paying it forward and helping those who were less fortunate. Dean was so passionate about his giving and paying it forward that he developed a guiding principle for the company that each Griffith unit would give back to each of the communities in which Griffith does business. In order to do this and to fund this giving program, each Griffith unit is required to target 1 percent of its operating income to give back to the unit's respective community. The giving could consist of cash donations or product produced in a Griffith facility donated to local charitable organizations.

Brian has followed in his grandfather and father's footsteps with his generosity and philanthropy by continuing the Griffith principle of setting aside 1 percent of worldwide operating income with a commitment for each unit to support local organizations with a special focus on hunger and food banks. Brian also believes that just writing a check is easy, but the real "gift" of philanthropy is personal engagement and volunteerism, which is the most meaningful and satisfying way to pay it forward. Brian established a program where employees can volunteer their time during work hours to support local food banks in packing and distributing meals and other charitable endeavors.

So, three generations of Griffith family members believed and were committed to "paying it forward" and the belief "that if you take care of the Company it will take care of you," and most importantly that the company was founded to be "a vehicle for the greater good." But when it came to family conflicts and differing views on whether the company should remain private, go public or be sold, Dean was convinced that the only solution was to buy them out and secure control of the voting stock by implementing a dual class stock ownership structure.

As one might imagine, the time during which all of these negotiations were taking place regarding the consolidation of the company and the buyout of family relatives was quite tense. But given Dean's well-honed negotiation skills, he was able to weather these turbulent times and accomplish the ultimate goal of consolidating the ownership and operations of the business under his immediate family's control. This arrangement preserved the option for the next generation to find the best person to lead the company after Dean retired.

"Although Griffith Foods is technically a fourth-generation family company, it really looks more like a second-generation organization since the company in its current form started with my father. Dean emerged from the family struggles as the *one* family leader for his generation" (Brian). And when it became clear that Brian shared Dean's values and ethos for the company (as described above), he became the chosen family member to lead the company for the next generation. The same mechanisms that Dean used to buy out relatives in the late 1970s were also used to provide liquidity to the rest of Brian's immediate relatives – a process that continues to this day.

The net result is that today Brian, his mother and the family trusts own approximately 80 percent of the voting control of the company with approximately 9 percent of the voting control dedicated to the ESOP (every US-based employee has a stake in the company) and the remaining approximately 11 percent of voting control still held by various family members and former employees. In addition to the ESOP, the company sponsors a 401(K)-retirement plan for active employees. When employees decide to retire or leave the company they can choose to sell their Griffith shares back to the ESOP when they leave. Given the consolidated corporate structure there is currently no family council, although this is a tradition that Brian would like to establish. As a family member, you are either in the business or you sell your shares.

The company has a family business specialist on the board, and Brian has given his three children the power to manage key aspects of the Griffith family's lake property as a "training environment" to cultivate a collaborative decision-making process around managing a place that they care deeply about and represents five generations of environmental stewardship.

All three members of the fifth generation – Colin, Mallory and Lauren, now in their 20s – have had exposure to the business both domestically and in particular when living abroad in Paris and Hong Kong as young children. During annual family meetings, executives from the company periodically brief them on business initiatives and in one-to-one meetings regarding specific areas of interest. The door is open for all three to join the business: youngest daughter Lauren is currently in college at the University of Colorado. Middle daughter Mallory is pursuing interests in interior design. Oldest son Colin has so far shown the most interest in becoming engaged with the family business. With a degree in environmental science, he has already interned with Griffith, is currently working for a sustainability-oriented company on the west coast and is considering an MBA focused on sustainable business.

The ultimate goal for Brian is to ensure great owners for Griffith Foods moving forward, whether or not the fifth generation works directly in the business or in various other roles (e.g., the board, a future family council to include the unborn sixth generation) that are best suited to the talents and interests of the three children.

ISOMORPHIC OR ICONOCLASTIC?

As part of the interviews done with Brian Griffith for this case, a final question was asked regarding the importance of family ownership to the company's ability to be truly committed to purpose, sustainability and the greater good. It was noted that publicly held companies are often influenced into becoming what institutional theorists called "isomorphic" – mimicking the "best practices" of peer companies you want to be associated with so as to be viewed as legitimate, both by Wall Street and key stakeholders.[12]

Academics applying this theoretical perspective emphasize that a key to realizing isomorphism is imitation: rather than necessarily optimizing or innovating their strategies and practices, organizations look to their peers for cues as to appropriate behavior. For "corporate sustainability," this often means being ranked highly by the "right" outside evaluators (e.g., Dow Jones SAM, MSCI, Sustainaytics, EcoVadis), adopting industry standards in structure and metrics (e.g., Global Reporting Initiative, SASB, Carbon Disclosure Project) and working with highly visible and accepted partners, consultants and non-governmental organizations.

When asked if this logic necessarily held for Griffith Foods, Brian Griffith replied:

> While this is not our ultimate goal, we must adopt where appropriate the best practices and metrics associated with these certifications and organizations in addition to our aspirational goals that epitomize our Purpose in action. We are interested in learning everything we can from the experience of others, but at the end of the day, our goal is not legitimacy or acceptance – we are not ruled or controlled by Wall Street or other financial stakeholders. Instead, our goal is to be true to ourselves – to do the right thing. We are duty bound to step out – to innovate – for the betterment of society and the world.

Asked if this looked more like being iconoclastic than isomorphic, Brian responded simply, "Yes."[13]

KEY INSIGHTS

- A father–son founding team with expertise in sales and science can provide the necessary skill sets to embed scientific mindset and entrepreneurial pragmatism in a new venture.
- When business is viewed as a "vehicle for greater good," a company moves past the concerns of legitimacy or acceptance by others, in a realm of feeling duty bound to innovate for the betterment of society and the world.
- Exploring new ideas, concepts and processes to help customers to prosper translates into the prosperity and growth of a company.
- A workplace that provides opportunities for employees to learn and grow, without leaving, establishes a strong community of engaged motivated contributors.
- Clearly articulated stretch goals like sustainable sourcing from 10,000 farmers before 2030 anchor an organization towards a meaningful future.

NOTES

1. This section and case study is adapted from: Griffith, D. (2006). *The Griffith Story: Memories, Reflections, Visions*. Alsip, IL: Griffith Press; https://nourishingtheworld.com/narrative-type/heritage/; and personal interviews conducted July 2019–April 2020 with Brian Griffith, T. C. Chatterjee and Joe Maslick.
2. For details, see: www.mincemaster.com/about/mincemaster-history
3. Griffith stock value is based upon a combination of sales and profit growth and peer group financial performance, benchmarked against the S&P 500.
4. This section is abstracted from: https://nourishingtheworld.com/narrative-type/heritage/

5. This section is adapted from: "Creating better together." *Thebossmagazine.com*, March 2017, and personal interviews with Brian Griffith, conducted July 15–16, 2019.
6. "Creating better together." *Thebossmagazine.com*, March 2017.
7. This section is abstracted from: https://nourishingtheworld.com/narrative-type/heritage/
8. "Creating better together." *Thebossmagazine.com*, March 2017.
9. The overall results are summarized in Hart, S., Napolitan, K. & Dasgupta, P. (2018). *Transformational Sustainability Benchmarking*. Ann Arbor, MI: Enterprise for a Sustainable World.
10. Thomas, M. & McElroy, M. (2016). *The MultiCapital Scorecard: Rethinking Organizational Performance*. White River Junction, VT: Chelsea Green Publishing.
11. This section is based upon personal interviews with Brian Griffith, conducted July 15–16, 2019.
12. See DiMaggio, P. J. & Powell, W. (eds) (1991). *The New Institutionalism and Organizational Analysis*, pp. 1–38. Chicago, IL: University of Chicago Press.
13. As I finished the writing of this case study in early May 2020, the world – and Griffith Foods – was in the grip of the Covid-19 pandemic. It is heartening to know, however, that as one might hope, the company has been able to resiliently take this crisis in its stride – at least so far: it took steps prior to the crisis to have sufficient stores of raw materials and supplies to maintain production levels; given its range of customers and products, it has been able to maintain sales by flexibly adapting to market conditions; and perhaps most importantly, it has been able to guarantee continuing wages, salaries and benefits for all employees while at the same time instituting new practices to prevent the spread of the Covid-19 virus. As of this writing, there were zero Covid-19 cases among Griffith employees.

9. Royal Van Wijhe Coatings: Sustainability over four generations

Judith van Helvert and Rosemarie Steenbeek

INTRODUCTION

> A modern sustainable future cannot exist without a substantial dose of innovation. (Marlies van Wijhe, fourth-generation Chief Executive Officer, Royal Van Wijhe Coatings)

Royal Van Wijhe Coatings (Van Wijhe), based in Zwolle, The Netherlands, is a fourth-generation family-owned business in the Dutch coatings industry. Traditionally referred to as the paint industry, this industry was a laggard in transitioning to an environmentally friendly economy. In 2020, Van Wijhe, a well-known medium-sized company, was the third largest brand in decorative coatings in The Netherlands. Its two major competitors – PPG (supplier of brands like Histor and Sigma) and AkzoNobel (Flexa and Sikkens) – were publicly listed companies. Van Wijhe was in a unique market position as it was an industry leader in environmental sustainability not only in its products and production processes, but also in helping others transition towards ecologically friendly production.

Sustainability was always important to the Van Wijhe family, even though the meaning of this term changed with each generation (see Table 9.1). For the founding and the subsequent generations, sustainability meant survival and an ability to pass a healthy family firm onto the next generation, and a focus on the social dimension (people and community). For the third generation, the attention shifted towards the environment and producing better, and less toxic products. The current leadership of Van Wijhe remained focused on survival, the environmental impact of its products and enabling others in the coatings industry in its journey towards sustainability. Alongside the evolution of sustainability, the core business changed as well. What started as a Dutch producer and wholesale supplier of paints in 1916 became a business with its own production, laboratory facilities and a fully developed trading department, operating at both national and international levels.

Table 9.1 *An overview of Van Wijhe*

	Key products	Business activities	Strategy	Governance	Meaning of sustainability
Generation 1	WIJZO cold water paint	Wholesale	Survival	Partnership of Derk Vermeulen and Dirk Hendrikus Van Wijhe	Continuity
Generation 2	WIJZONOL system paint	Wholesale and production	Survival and growth	Partnership of Dirk Hendrikus Van Wijhe and sons Bertus and Jan Van Wijhe	Caring for others
Generation 3	High solid paint; color tinting system	Wholesale, production, technical color advising and research and development	Positioning through focus on sustainability	Advisory board and Shares Trust Office	Caring for the environment
Generation 4	SolidLux	Wholesale, production, technical color advising and extended research and development activities	Market transformer through focus on sustainability	Supervisory board and Shares Trust Office, B Corp	Impact on environment (United Nations Sustainable Development Goals)

Note: The Shares Trust Office is a special construction found in many family businesses in The Netherlands. In this form of organization a distinction is made between the share certificates and the controlling rights. Only the holders of the share certificates have rights to dividends and value appreciation/depreciation. The controlling rights are transferred to the board of the "stichting administratiekantoor (STAK)" – a Shares Trust Office. The STAK articles include clauses concerning the appointment of board members.
Source: FBNed (2003). *The Family Business Governance Report: Practices and Recommendations*. Tilburg.

This chapter[1] describes the evolution of Van Wijhe with an emphasis on the last two generations of chief executive officers (CEOs) and their role in the strategic focus on sustainability. While the fourth-generation leader, Marlies Van Wijhe, continued to win prestigious awards like Businesswoman of 2010 by "prix veuve clicquot" and the "Best for the World 2019" in the environment category three times in a row by B Corp, she was determined not only to spread the word concerning Van Wijhe's sustainability efforts, but also to be the frontrunner in improving the workings and image of the chemical coatings industry.

THE HISTORY OF ROYAL VAN WIJHE COATINGS: 1916–2020

Van Wijhe received the "Royal" predicate in 2016 when it celebrated its 100th anniversary as a successful independent Dutch company in the paint and coatings industry. Innovation and sustainability were deeply embedded within the rich history, culture and values of the family firm and were reflected in how 54-year-old Marlies Van Wijhe ran her family's company. As the third largest Dutch brand in decorative coatings and colorants, Van Wijhe had grown significantly since its start in 1916 as a wholesale paint business. By 2020, the company had its own production facilities and a trading department with 15 stores. It invested significantly in research and development (R&D) activities focused on decorative paints and intermediate materials for the paint industry. Predominantly engaged in business-to-business sales to stores, wholesalers and industrial customers, Van Wijhe also catered for DIY (do-it-yourself) stores. Although the Dutch market remains its focal point, most of its growth was realized abroad through its export department – Ralston Colour & Coating – named after one of Van Wijhe's main brands.

GENERATION 1: SUSTAINING BY ADAPTING

Van Wijhe was founded in Zwolle during the First World War, also known as the Great War. Dirk Hendrikus Van Wijhe, Marlies' great-grandfather, and his colleague Derk Vermeulen decided to start their own firm. Both Dirk and Derk were in their 40s and had worked for a local drugstore and wholesaler in paint products for several years. In 1916, the two men decided that they wanted to be more independent and opened their own wholesale firm, which they called Fa. Van Wijhe en Vermeulen. They both took a mortgage and a bank loan to launch their new business with borrowed capital. Ownership was shared equally in this partnership. Customers whom they had served while working at the local drugstore now became their clients in the new firm. Unfortunately, many products were not available during the war, so they began trading in available items like chemicals, pharmaceutical goods including baby powder and eau-de-cologne, and raw materials for paint. Later, they added ready-to-use paint products. The agility of the family firm was already visible in its early days as they acted and responded to the changing circumstances to overcome difficulties and keep the business healthy.

In 1928, Derk Vermeulen passed away. Dirk continued without him and it was his wish to work with his two sons and continue as a family firm. At that time, the sons were expected to join their family's firm and, consequently, the eldest son Bertus was the first one to start working with his father. Panic struck when Dirk's second son, Jan-Tijmen (Jan), was invited by an acquaintance to run the office of a Dutch shipping company in Latin America. Jan was interested and confused about this opportunity because he suddenly had to choose whether or not to join his family's firm. Much to his father's relief, he decided to decline the offer and joined the family business. Once both sons were in the company, its name was changed to Van Wijhe & Sons. In those days, it was common for painters to make their own paint. Dirk and his sons perceived an opportunity to serve painters. So, although the firm's product range still varied considerably, the business established itself more and more as a wholesaler in raw materials for paint and paint producer for professional painters. In 1935, the trio invented and started producing their first unique paint product they called WIJZO Koudwaterverf (cold water paint) – a name based on their family's name Wijhe and the Dutch word for sons – zonen.

GENERATION 2: SUSTAINABILITY THROUGH COMPASSION

Sons Bertus and Jan took over the company in 1941. Just like the first generation, they found themselves in the middle of a war, the Second World War. To survive, they employed 20 additional persons to the 10 already working at Van Wijhe during the war to package polish for coal stoves, a product that they had in storage in large quantities. They had to improvise to survive as important raw materials for the production of paint, such as linseed oil, were only available in small quantities through a special voucher system. This shortage jeopardized production and, therefore, the firm made a trade deal with fishermen based in Urk, a small village in The Netherlands. They exchanged linseed oil vouchers for homemade jenever, a traditional juniper-based liquor also known as Dutch gin. This improvisation and persistence enabled them to get through yet another war.

After the Second World War, Van Wijhe & Sons grew steadily. In 1946, it launched its second self-invented product, WIJZONOL – an aggregation of three Dutch words: Wijhe, zonen (sons) and olie (oil). Based on colored carbolineum and primer, this oil-based paint was useful for painting raw wood. The timing of the introduction of WIJZONOL to the market was perfect as demand was high because of the post-war reconstruction of The Netherlands.

In those days, the meaning of sustainability involved having an obligation towards society[2]. Right after WWII, there was no national pension scheme for workers. The workers' old-age provision depended on altruism of the employer. Marlies recalls that her grandfather Jan tried his very best to provide his employees with decent retirement provisions, which was not that common at that time. Compassion for others was something that came naturally to the Van Wijhe family.

In 1960, tragedy struck for the Van Wijhe family. Bertus, who did not have any children, died unexpectedly leaving Jan alone in the firm. While Jan and his wife had one son – Dick – they had never discussed the possibility of transitioning the leadership and ownership of the firm to him. The family firm was hardly a topic of conversation at home and without consulting his parents, Dick decided to study chemical technology in Delft. He had thoughts of working for a company like Shell and traveling the world. Three weeks after the sudden death of his uncle Bertus, Dick phoned his father to talk about the future of the firm. Dick was in his final year at college and when he asked his father if he wanted him to join the business the answer was a short but resolute "Yes, please." Dick thought that if he had not asked the question, he would probably not have ended up working for his family firm. He recalled that phone call as his shortest job interview. Jan was delighted with the entry of his only child. Not only would it help him with his workload, but it would also secure the continuation of their family firm. Dick gave himself 10 years in the company and promised himself to reevaluate whether he wanted to stay longer after that. But he fell in love with the job and never thought of doing anything else.

In 1962, Dick became a director of the company, and father and son worked together for 10 years. Dick recalled enjoying working with his father as follows: "We had many discussions about important strategic decisions. We both had our own opinions. And sometimes we decided to do it his way and sometimes we decided to do it the way that I had suggested." In 1965, the firm was relocated to an industrial area outside Zwolle with many possibilities to expand.

GENERATION 3: SUSTAINABILITY THROUGH CARING FOR THE ENVIRONMENT

In 1971, Dick officially succeeded his father and merely a year later changed the name of the company to Van Wijhe Coatings B.V. By then, the family firm had developed into a substantial paint factory. Business went well. Thanks to the success of WIJZONOL paint, Jan left Dick a thriving company. The Netherlands was in a phase of reconstruction after the war and the building of new houses reached a peak. WIJZONOL was exactly the product that painters needed as it had the right composition and features. This product helped boost Van Wijhe to become a dominant player in a market known for its high quality.

During his time as CEO from 1971 to 2000, Dick focused on increasing volume to create efficiencies of scale and expanded product range through innovations and acquisitions, including that of the American brand Ralston by Sherwin Williams. These expansions opened the DIY and maintenance markets for Van Wijhe. Using his knowledge and skills, gained through his education in chemical technology and on-the-job discussions with his father, he directed his focus to inventing new products aimed towards environmental sustainability. These efforts resulted in a number of revolutionary products and process improvements, two of which were particularly significant. First was their unique system to mix colors. This pathbreaking system made it possible to create every color with just two base paints – white and colorless – instead of ten different paints used at that time. This invention resulted in an enormous boost in inventory management as it significantly reduced storage and transportation costs. The second major innovation was the "high solid" paint, for which Dick received an innovation prize. This paint uses fewer solvents and is therefore less harmful to the environment. Unfortunately, the painters were not very fond of this new product so it did not catch on commercially. Investments, made in R&D for the product development and of course for the production of the paints, were lost. Possibly, more or better market research would have prevented this failure. However, it was important to Dick to show to himself and others the possibility of producing a more environmentally friendly paint product. According to Marlies, the product came too early for its users. She explained: "We were the first firm that offered a more environmentally sustainable wall paint, but the time was not right. Only now it is becoming more important. For example, we have a customer in Ireland, who wants to do business with us because we work so hard on sustainability."

Dick's passion for nature found its way into the family firm not only through newly invented products, but also through relationship management practices. He would give away books about nature and the environment to important customers, suppliers and other stakeholders. He was enthusiastic about a Dutch book series on nature, so he purchased many of them and convinced the publisher to add a preface by him. Marlies, the current family leader, refers to these books in her presentations to employees, customers and industry associations (Figure 9.1). In the early 1980s, Van Wijhe launched a television commercial to educate viewers about the environmental benefits of its water-based paints. Unfortunately, the commercial did not run for long because the foundation of the Dutch Commercial Code banned it. It was argued that although water-based paint was less harmful to the environment, it was still not very environmentally friendly as producing water-based binders required more energy in comparison with solvent-based binders. Ironically, a 2000 Dutch legislation deemed the same products as environmentally friendly paints and required professional painters to use water-based paints indoors. This legislation was initiated by the Federation of Dutch Trade Unions because the use of solvent-based paints can cause health issues.

Dick's focus on environmental sustainability in the firm originated from his passion for nature. Environmental sustainability played a significant role at home and developed into a joint family value. He talked about the importance of nature and the environment with his two daughters, Marlies and Marijke,

Source: Poruba, M. et al. (1981). *De grote bossengids van Van Wijhe Verf BV*. Zwolle: Uitgeverij Thieme.

Figure 9.1 The Great Forest Guide of Van Wijhe Paint

when they were young. He would buy books and take them outside to explore birds, plants and flowers, teaching them about natural phenomena. Marlies recalls that her father was always busy with birds even though it did not mean much to her as a young girl. He was intrigued by the Club of Rome, a group of scientists, politicians and business leaders who raised awareness on resource depletion by publishing a report entitled "The limits to growth" in 1972. While this report received great attention upon its publication, most people soon lost interest in it. But not Dick. He knew intuitively that the issues that were mentioned in this report, including resource depletion, the population growth rate and pollution, would become extremely important for society, as would the role of his family's firm in the economy. He photocopied the book for his daughters and retains a copy of the book to this day. As a consequence, good treatment of nature and people came naturally to the Van Wijhe family and is deeply embedded in its business.

It is important to note that Dick's devotion to and focus on nature and environmental sustainability in the firm was quite exceptional at the time. The Brundtland Report, also known as *Our Common Future*, was published much later, in 1987.[3] Until the 1990s, sustainability meant voluntarily taking responsibility for society in a way that went beyond legal prescriptions.[4] Since the 1990s the concept of "sustainability" has begun to include the natural environment, which shows just how progressive Dick was for his time.

In 1989, Dick sat down with his two daughters to talk about the future of Van Wijhe. The reason for this was that he had received an attractive offer from another company to buy their family firm. He felt that it was time for his daughters to make a decision on whether they could picture a future for themselves in the family business or not. The sisters were still studying and did not work at the business at the time their father asked this question. So, they asked for three weeks to think about it, after which they answered: "If you think we can do it, we would like to succeed you." Subsequently, Marlies and Marijke bought 100 percent of the ownership shares from their father by using a subordinated loan and paid off this loan with profits made by the firm over a period of 10 years. Marlies and Marijke became the owners of Van Wijhe at the age of 25 and 22, respectively. The shares were divided equally between the two sisters. Reflecting back on that moment, both of them indicate that they did not feel pressured to make this choice. Instead, they very much liked the idea of taking over the business. A couple of years later Dick found not being the owner anymore "as boring as watching paint dry." He asked his children if he could buy back 10 percent of the shares as he missed being involved in the firm. Nowadays, Dick comes to the office every Monday and is the representative of the family on the supervisory board.

GENERATION 4: SUSTAINING BY STRATEGIZING

In 1989, at 22, Marijke was the first of the fourth generation who started working in the family business. At that time, Van Wijhe did not have a marketing department but that was something Dick aspired for. Together with a colleague, Marijke started her first challenging marketing activities at Van Wijhe and found she would never want to leave the firm. Reflecting on her experience when she started working she shared, "I was young when I entered the family business and it was not always easy. Because I am a Van Wijhe family member, people will treat you differently." Now, in her 50s, it does not bother her anymore as she has learned to put things in perspective. Unlike her older sister, she did not have an ambition to become the CEO. So, there was no discussion as she was clear she did not want the top job and related responsibility. Today, she continues enjoying her charge of corporate marketing activities in the marketing department.

Marlies entered the business a few years later, in 1994, and started working in the export department. She was always fascinated with biology and felt this interest may have evolved from her father's interest in nature. However, the idea of working at a laboratory for the rest of her life seemed off-putting, so she decided to take a master's program in business administration. After her studies, she worked at Royal DSM, a Dutch multinational active in chemicals, for five years, after which she decided to enter the family firm. Looking back on this decision, Marlies is glad she started her career outside Van Wijhe as she learnt a lot in her first job, both pleasant and unpleasant, that was very different from her family firm. In 2000, Marlies officially succeeded her father to become the first female family member to officially run Van Wijhe as the CEO and the strategic decision maker.

Marlies and Marijke represent the fourth generation of the family. While Marlies is the CEO, she consults her sister and father before making key decisions. As owners they meet up to five times a year to discuss their business and their ownership strategy. Marlies and Marijke's mother, Thea Van Wijhe, acts as the chief emotional officer in case of any disagreement between the family members. Marlies explained:

> My father and I can be stubborn. Sometimes I want to go this way and he wants things to go the other way and then we clash. Then, my mother comes in and makes sure we can act as adults again. It does not happen often that we disagree, but sometimes it obviously does.

Marlies reports to a supervisory board of three external members and her father, and Marijke takes notes at the meetings. Thus, the three family members were equally informed. This, in turn, helped to enable fast and flexible decision-making processes.

Being a family member played a key role in how Marlies ran the family business. Her focus on environmental sustainability could be traced back to her roots. In her words, "Through the focus on environmental sustainability I see that the two worlds of biology and the family business merge and I think that is really cool." She shared that her interest in biology never ceased. The latest Intergovernmental Science-Policy Platform on Biodiversity and Ecosystem Services report published in 2019 on the deterioration of nature and biodiversity further inspired Van Wijhe's corporate philosophy, which guides its corporate strategy and, in turn, its business objectives and activities. Marlies recalled her delight when she was asked to chair the board of "Future for Nature" as this opportunity provided her with access to another world. Future for Nature is a Dutch foundation supporting young nature conservationists (up to 35 years old) committed to protecting species of wild animals and plants. Annually, three conservationists are awarded by this foundation. Marlies' role as chair of the board is to supervise the selection processes and the organization of the award event.

Marlies dreamt of a time when paint could be safely flushed through the sink without harming people and the environment. She believed this goal could be accomplished through innovation as "without it a firm was valueless." Under her leadership R&D became even more important as it enabled the family firm to produce sustainable products. Also, pioneering new products became one of the core values at Van Wijhe. Various approaches were used to reduce the environmental impact, but the strategies of redesigning products and reducing the material used dominated production processes. Redesign renders coatings less harmful for the environment and reduction eliminates toxic ingredients while developing longer-lasting coatings.

Marlies continued to invest in activities aimed at developing innovation, even during times when Van Wijhe had to cut costs in other areas. For example, in 2010, during the financial crisis, Marlies thought it was essential to keep her R&D and sales employees as these people were a great asset to her firm. Through working more efficiently in other departments of the firm, she was able to modernize and renovate the laboratory during the crisis. Two years ago, after having worked with other R&D managers, Marlies appointed Ron Hulst to manage the two R&D departments of the company (Figure 9.2). Ron is an experienced, energetic and creative chemist with a great track record in the industrial chemical sector. The regular R&D department was comprised of about 20 employees who focused on innovating and developing paints and related areas. This was the core business of Van Wijhe. Marlies regarded these employees as the heart of the family firm and encouraged them to develop innovations needed for their industry. People working in this department came from varied backgrounds, education and experiences, thereby forming a remarkable mix. Some of them were painters interested in working for the Van Wijhe R&D department and educated themselves accordingly. According to Ron Hulst, the R&D manager, one of the best people in the department was a former bookkeeper with an accounting background.

In addition to the regular R&D department, Marlies decided that more fundamental research was needed to adapt and co-shape the future of Van Wijhe and the coating industry. She believed:

> **You cannot grow in a world that has reached its limits. Growth in terms of turnover and volume is not sustainable.**

So, a second department, the WYDO laboratory, focused on R&D, was established with about 10 employees. The name WYDO is an aggregation of "Wijhe" and "daughters" (Wijhe/dochters). At WYDO more fundamental research was conducted, primarily by microbiologists. It was expected that this department may develop new ideas and innovations that were not related to the paint and coatings industry. The R&D manager explained that "If, for

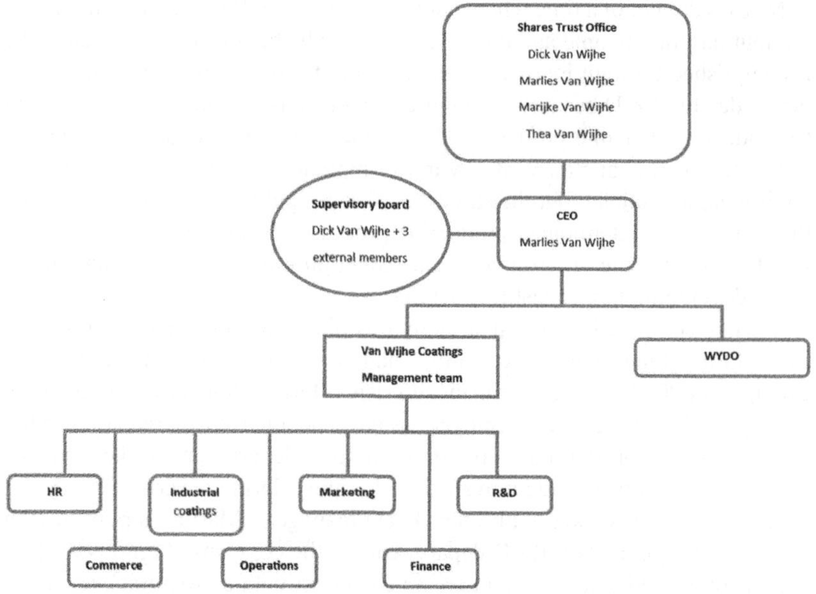

Figure 9.2 *Organization structure of Van Wijhe Coatings*

example, at WYDO we found a solution for the micro-plastic problem, which is caused only for a very small part by paint, that would be fantastic and fully in line with its purpose." An example of current fundamental research at WYDO involves exploring the possibilities of making a water-resistant paint from lemnoideae, better known as duckweed.

WYDO has already delivered its first successful product, SolidLux – a patented floor coating, free from solvents, that immediately hardens by UV light. Marlies explained that while it was initially developed to reduce disturbance on gallery floors in museums, it was later discovered that it could also be used in cold stores and freezer rooms without having to defrost the place. She believes that "the best thing about innovations is that something you had never thought of being possible becomes a reality," and hoped that SolidLux was the first step in many product developments to come. While SolidLux coatings are free from solvents, they are still made of chemicals. So, the next focus is to improve this by changing the composition of the product. Van Wijhe has always worked with raw materials that are least harmful. Often, these materials are not the cheapest. But they persevere until new solutions are found. SolidLux is the payoff from the patient capital investment that Van Wijhe has made available for product development and innovation. Marlies shared her thoughts on investment in innovations aimed at reducing the environmental impact as follows:

> This patient capital enables us to invest money in developments that we believe in. Choosing the right focus in these innovative projects is not a rational choice, it is a gut feeling.
>
> **We have to invest a lot of money in these innovations, without knowing if or when we will earn it back.**
>
> For example, the development of SolidLux has taken eight years and it has been on the market for two years. It will still take a while before we start making money. Obviously, we are still looking for new application opportunities.

One of Ron's challenges was to manage the "regular" R&D department and WYDO simultaneously and ensure that each unit concentrates on the right issues and creates the right type of innovations. There is a significant distinction between the two departments. Research at the regular R&D department should be more focused than that at WYDO, where the employees should be able to think more freely. A balance between creativity and focus is therefore needed in the two research departments. Ron seems to be able to harmonize both just fine. Being one of the first PhD candidates of Nobel Prize winner Ben Feringa at Groningen University, he learned the art of harmony between focus and creativity from the best: "without being able to find the right balance, you would never win a Nobel Prize."

Van Wijhe works with the 17 Sustainable Development Goals (SDGs) of the United Nations as a basis for all of its activities. Ron explains:

> **It is not possible to choose just two of three goals to work with. Then you are basically saying that you want to drive electric, but you ignore those little children mining the heavy metals to do so. Every goal is important and, therefore, we incorporate all of them in our endeavors.**

So, for every new recipe, Van Wijhe wants to improve on each of the 17 SDGs. This means that a supplier in bio-based materials has to be able to tell where the raw materials come from, how they are being mined, etc. One employee was dedicated to developing and implementing a new in-house software called Wij Corp to gather and incorporate information related to the 17 SDGs of the United Nations from the various stakeholders that Van Wijhe works with. As a result, some suppliers ended their cooperation with Van Wijhe because they did not want to share this kind of information, while others demanded exclusivity to be considered innovation partners of the company.

Even though not everyone who works at Van Wijhe is as closely involved in the sustainability initiatives as Marlies or Ron and his teams (R&D and WYDO), every employee is expected to embrace a certain passion for nature and the environment and identify with sustainability as the Van Wijhe family does. Pursuing this, Marlies set up a "green team" – a group of three or four young employees who ceaselessly work to devise ways to encourage sustainability within Van Wijhe. The green team has organized events like an internal competition for the most sustainable idea and an annual theme week to stimulate the awareness of climate change for the annual Dutch "warme truiendag" (warm sweater day).[5] In return, members of this team have the opportunity to participate in the "Nudge Global Impact Challenge." Nudge is a Dutch social enterprise and a B Corp like Van Wijhe. It offers leadership programs and consulting services and collaborates with businesses, non-governmental organizations, scientific institutions and governments to firmly root sustainability in their business models, governance and leadership. It also offers an eight-month development program in which leadership, sustainability and impact creation are addressed, and during which young professionals can shape their own sustainability impact plan. This program ends with a four-day education program during which knowledge, inspiration and skills are provided to the participants to become a force of change.

Besides working on environmental sustainability in terms of production and involving employees, Van Wijhe also focuses on other aspects of the business. For example, it calculates its carbon footprint of products sold. Marlies explained: "Once you have a baseline measurement, that can be a starting point for making a plan to reduce your impact in the coming years." Additionally, Van Wijhe focused on making its packaging and transportation activities ecologically friendly. In an attempt to make the plastic wall paint buckets more sustainable, Marlies and her team collaborated with a waste management company and a plastic bucket manufacturer to develop a bucket made from recycled plastic waste. A reevaluation of transportation activities revealed that they could pile four layers of buckets on one pallet rather than three. Marlies explained:

> It sounds simple, but we had to do a lot of research to figure this out. The buckets have to be made of the appropriate material and they need to be piled and secured correctly. As a result, we can now pile more volume per pallet and we have reduced transportation expenses.

Moreover, Van Wijhe devoted efforts to render its building as sustainable as possible, for example by using a geothermal heating system that reduced carbon dioxide emissions by 94,000 kilos annually. It also switched to naturally sourced solar power reducing carbon dioxide emissions by another 40 percent. As a result of all of these efforts, Van Wijhe received the B Corp certificate[6] in 2016. This is an international classification for sustainable and profitable firms. Other firms that have received this certificate include Ben & Jerry's, Tony's Chocolonely, Patagonia, Danone and Triodos Bank. To receive this certificate, firms not only have to score on the ecological dimension of sustainability in their products and production processes, but also on social dimension of sustainability in terms of contribution towards people. Van Wijhe was the first in the world in the chemical industry to receive the B Corp. It reinforced that it was on the right track and helped the family firm to continue on its sustainability journey.

When asked about the position of Van Wijhe in the coatings industry and the strategy of her company, Marlies explained that her family's belief in environmentally sustainable products was essential for the continuity of their family firm. The two coating giants – PPG and AkzoNobel – operated on a global scale and generated annual revenues of 13.2 and 9.2 billion euros, respectively.[7] As these companies focused on low prices and high sales volumes, smaller and medium-sized companies like Van Wijhe had to carve specific niches in an industry that had declined by 30 percent in eight years. This reduction was caused by the fact that the durability of coatings had increased from six to twelve years over two decades.

As a medium-sized player and the third largest paint brand in The Netherlands, the family owners of Van Wijhe had the freedom to make their own strategic decisions and invest in long-term projects they believed in, without pressure from external shareholders. Instead of focusing on low prices and high volume and always losing to PPG and Akzo Nobel, Marlies and her family viewed the climate change crisis and the loss of biodiversity as an inspiring opportunity to distinguish their company in the marketplace. When she joined her company, it was clear to the Van Wijhe leaders that their industry had to develop environmentally friendly products. But they were unclear on how to achieve this. Marlies shared, "In those days [the 2000s], sustainability was not very fashionable yet. And when we were in the middle of the economic crisis, about ten years ago now, I decided I should focus on it. A kind of sustainability through the continuous improvement and innovation of our products."

As innovation had been the cornerstone of Van Wijhe since its founding, the establishment of the WYDO laboratory came naturally as a critical part of the future strategy. Making a chemical company sustainable was a challenging undertaking. With 500,000 tons of annual carbon dioxide emissions, there was considerable room for improvement in the Dutch paint industry. Marlies saw it as her duty to take the lead in transitioning the coating sector towards the overarching aim of becoming climate neutral by 2025. Van Wijhe made substantial investments of energy, time and money to develop high-quality environmentally sustainable products from renewable resources that do not compete with the food industry.

It was a risky move, however, as the outcomes were unclear. Together with her family, management team and the supervisory board, Marlies took the risk as she never wanted to look back and wish they had done it. It was a calculated risk, she stressed: "With all the knowledge that you have, you prepare a well-developed business case. Sometimes a decision will not lead to a good result, but you can only know this after you've tried it." Being a family-owned business means that the family is able to act quickly and be more decisive. The freedom from not having to consult shareholders only interested in dividends or focused on share prices has made it easier to pursue the family's mission of patient capital and ensures that Van Wijhe maintains a healthy and sustainable firm.

By 2020, Van Wijhe had successfully carved a market niche with its environmentally sustainable high-quality coating products. Next to these newly developed sustainable products, the company continued to continuously improve its traditional paints, with every new batch of paints being a bit more sustainable than the batch before. The company was the market leader in terms of life span of new paints, as its paints lasted for 12 years in comparison to the industry norm of eight to ten years. The annual carbon dioxide emissions of the Dutch coating industry in 2020 were equal to a city with roughly 130,000 people. Marlies considers this a huge problem and that is why Van Wijhe has set the objective to operate in a climate-neutral fashion in 2025. Van Wijhe challenges its competitors to join it.

The chemical industry was and still is a very polluting industry. But ignorance also negatively affects the reputation and image of the paint and coatings industry which can be difficult and frustrating for companies like Van Wijhe that are working hard to develop environmentally sustainable products. For example, while chemicals are considered harmful, they can also help to limit the impact on the environment. Chemicals just sound like something damaging, even when products are completely bio-based. In nature, many elements are protected by a coating, providing important ideas for their industry. Ron explained that:

> the coatings help to protect the wood used for window frames. A wooden window frame can be re-painted over eight thousand times before the paint used on it has a more substantial negative impact on the environment than the micro plastics in an artificial window frame.

SAPEA, an advising body to European commissioners, argued that there was a need to inform societal actors, such as manufacturers, food retailers, citizens and scientists, of the relative assessment of plastics and coatings on nature and society.[8] Marlies believed that the solution to this negative perception should come from the industry itself. Towards this end, she started the national campaign WIJ ZIJN NU[9] ("we are now") to raise awareness of pollution due to the coatings industry. This campaign stressed that to leave a better world for the next generation, by 2050, all 10 million buildings in The Netherlands must use long-lasting durable paint made from bio-based renewable materials using circular-economy processes to reduce the carbon footprint.

Van Wijhe is very serious about changing the industry, which is reflected in its strategic focus on sustainability. Being as sustainable as possible has always been important to the Van Wijhe family. Marlies has even integrated this in the corporate strategy and slogan:

A country that is livable for the next generation exceeds any economic interest.

Looking at the current state of the sector, there is still a lot to gain. A sustainable company in the chemical industry still sounds like a paradox. However, the family's experience and drive to innovate have helped Marlies to find a way to transcend this paradox and to make it work. It is also this kind of entrepreneurship that made Marlies win prestigious awards. For example, in 2019, she was recognized for 25 years of exceptional service to the community and her commitment to sustainability and innovation in the coating sector with the Knight Order of Orange-Nassau.

For Van Wijhe, sustainability involves more than looking after the environment. As the company has shown since the first generation of family involvement, continuity of the firm is key to sustainability. Being a family firm, Van Wijhe aims to pass a healthy and thriving business onto the next generation. That is why Marlies made some changes to further professionalize the firm. A renewed mission, vision and strategy were formulated for the years to come and new supervisory board members were selected, allowing for their potential support of sustainability and innovation. As a consequence of this renewed strategy, Marlies changed how Van Wijhe talked about its products. They are no longer referred to as paint solutions but as coating solutions. "Coating solutions" refers to much more than only paint. She noted that while everyone was still talking about paint, with a 30 percent decline in sales and longer product life spans, the industry is changing rapidly. Nobody knows if paint will still exist in 50 years' time. Van Wijhe tried to position itself to conquer the new market realities.

GENERATION 5: WHAT DOES THE FUTURE HOLD?

Bob (22) and Fleur (19), the children of Marijke and her husband Robert, represent the fifth generation of the Van Wijhe family. Fleur is taking a master's program in business administration and Bob has already started working at the firm. He works part time as junior brand manager in the marketing department. Fleur works at Van Wijhe during the holidays and recently joined Marlies on a business trip to find out what it is like to be a CEO. History is not repeating itself, so the two children of Marijke do not have to make a choice about their future in the business at an early stage of their life. Succession has not yet been a topic of discussion. There is still time for them to decide what they would like to do. However, they do have to make a decision at some point. Marlies explains:

> We have always told them that they are free to choose whether they want to be involved in the firm or not. But, at some point they have to make up their mind. The family firm is here, whether they like it or not. We cannot change that and family succession is something you cannot control. The next generations must be willing, and able, to do it.

At this moment there are no signs that Fleur and Bob would not like to work in the family business in the future. "I do think they would like it if the company remains in the family," Marijke says. But only the future can tell. For now, both sisters, Marijke and Marlies, encourage the children to spread their wings elsewhere because "it is better to make your first mistakes somewhere else."

KEY INSIGHTS

This chapter paints a picture of how the meaning of sustainability at Van Wijhe has evolved from a focus on continuity to sustainability as a strategy. The following insights are derived from this case:

- *The meaning of sustainability is context- and time-dependent.* During the last century the meaning of sustainability shifted from focusing on continuity during the two World Wars to calculating the impact on the environment by using the United Nations SDGs in the twenty-first century. Sustainability as a concept is constantly evolving and will continue to do so. Being flexible and creative is necessary to adapt.
- *Sustainability through innovation.* In making the transition to a more environmentally sustainable company, it is necessary to keep up with developments. This transition requires the redesign of current products or the decreased use of a product altogether. Innovation is necessary for redesigning and creating new sustainable products.
- *Strategic partnerships are essential.* High-quality knowledge is key for a thriving business. Relevant partnerships and skilled personnel can make a difference in being able to take on a leading role and to come up with the appropriate innovations.
- *Having a family-owned business.* This means being free to make decisions that fit the mission and vision of the family. The short communication

lines result in the ability to respond quickly and decisively to a changing environment.

- *Patient capital.* The unique resource of patient capital enables the decision makers to take calculated risks and to invest with the prospects of having long-term returns instead of quick wins.

These characteristics have resulted in a healthy, thriving and sustainable family-owned business which can be passed onto the next generation.

NOTES

1. This case study is based on data collected from in-depth interviews with Marlies Van Wijhe (three times), an interview with Marijke Van Wijhe, Dick Van Wijhe and R&D manager Ron Hulst, over a 12-month period. In addition, information from news articles, videos and Van Wijhe's website was used. More details of research methods including interview transcripts are available from the authors.
2. Bowen, H. R. (1953). *Social Responsibilities of the Businessman.* New York: Harper and Row.
3. World Commission on Environment and Development (1987). *Our Common Future.* https://sustainabledevelopment.un.org/content/documents/5987our-common-future.pdf
4. Jones, T. M. (1980) "Corporate social responsibility revisited, redefined." *California Management Review*, 22(3): 59–67.
5. Warm Sweater was started in 2007 by the Climate Alliance (Klimaatverbond) as a reminder of climate change and the commitments made in the Kyoto Protocol to reduce emissions and stop global warming. Research indicates that lowering central heating by one degree Celsius saves 6 percent energy, reducing carbon dioxide emissions by 6 percent as well. Thus, Greenchoice calculated that if everyone in The Netherlands would turn the heat down by one degree Celsius, it would reduce carbon dioxide emissions by 6,300 kilograms.
6. https://bcorporation.net/about-b-corps
7. Verbraeken, H. (2019). "Kleine verfbedrijven zoeken de niches in een krimpmarkt." *Het Financieele Dagblad*, March 21.
8. SAPEA, Science Advice for Policy by European Academies (2019). *A Scientific Perspective on Microplastics in Nature and Society.* Berlin: SAPEA. https://doi.org/10.26356/microplasticsSAPEA
9. www.wijzonol.nl/over-wijzonol/duurzaam

10. GMA Garnet's circular economy: Jebsen & Jessen's leadership in environmental sustainability

Marta Widz and Vanina Farber

Jebsen & Co. was founded in 1895 as a trading company when Jacob Jebsen and Heinrich Jessen, who later became brothers-in-law, left their home waters of Aabenraa in modern-day Denmark and established themselves as merchants in Hong Kong. Their forefathers, courageous sea captains and ship owners since the eighteenth century, sailed the coasts of Europe, South America and Asia, first reaching Hong Kong in 1861.

Inspired by the creed of Chinese philosopher Mencius in the third century BC, "Within the four seas, all men are brothers," the group acted as a bridge between continents and cultures and suppliers and consumers.[1] As a trading house, Jebsen & Co. initially commercialized tobacco, ginger, oils, cotton and satin. It entered its first partnership in 1897 with BASF, the German chemicals giant, to trade indigo, and in 1898, it established its first joint venture in China to sell cement, nails, ironware and glass. In order to facilitate the procurement of goods, Jacob Jebsen and Heinrich Jessen opened their own European purchasing office in 1909 and named it Jebsen & Jessen Hamburg.

From those modest beginnings, a powerful group – Jebsen & Jessen Family Enterprise – emerged. In 2019, the group was managed and owned by the descendants of Jacob Jebsen and Heinrich Jessen. Under the leadership of the third generation's two principal family shareholders – Hans Michael Jebsen and Heinrich Jessen[2] – the company generated over 3.1 billion euros in sales and employed over 7,100 people.[3] Its international footprint spanned 20 countries around the globe, from Europe to South-East Asia, Australia, the Middle East, the United States (US) and Latin America. The firm consisted of many legal entities organized around four principal business entities (Figure 10.1):

- Jebsen & Co., established in 1895, based in Hong Kong, primarily owned by Hans Michael Jebsen.
- Jebsen & Jessen Hamburg, established in 1909, based in Germany, equally owned by Hans Michael Jebsen and Heinrich Jessen.

- Jebsen & Jessen (SEA), established in 1963, based in Singapore, primarily owned by Heinrich Jessen.
- GMA Garnet was initially established in 1991 as a joint venture between Ketelsen Enterprise and Jebsen & Jessen Hamburg and was then gradually integrated into the Jebsen & Jessen Family Enterprise's portfolio. Based in Perth, Australia, it is primarily owned by Hans Michael Jebsen and Heinrich Jessen, who both hold equal stakes. GMA Garnet is the world leader in mining, processing, distributing and recycling of industrial garnet. As it achieved the most significant social innovation of the whole group – a circular business model – it acts as the role model for other Jebsen & Jessen Family Enterprise entities.

Figure 10.1 Four principal business entities of Jebsen & Jessen Family Enterprise

In this chapter, we elaborate on how the shared determination of the Jebsen and Jessen families to build and sustain enduring partnerships and maintain an entrepreneurial spirit, facilitated by their governance system and accelerated by their purpose-driven leadership, has enabled the Jebsen & Jessen Family Enterprise to become a global leader in the social innovation of a circular business model at GMA Garnet.

JEBSEN & JESSEN FAMILY ENTERPRISE

Partnerships, Entrepreneurship, Governance and Leadership

History has taught the Jebsen & Jessen Family Enterprise that its entrepreneurial spirit, values-based partnerships and governance-supporting, purpose-driven leadership are the reasons for its continuing existence. The current third-generation family owners turned the legacy of founders into their purpose:

> **Today, the Jebsen & Jessen Family Enterprise continues its mission to build a sustainable business and preserve an entrepreneurial spirit. Together, the group's members focus on strong partnerships and an unwavering dedication to our customers.**[4]

Values-Based Partnerships

The Jebsen & Jessen Family Enterprise was started on a partnership ethos and philosophy, when Jacob Jebsen and Heinrich Jessen joined forces in 1895. Born into two established families of captains and shipowners, who hailed from Aabenraa, a small yet renowned historical town in Denmark steeped in age-old seafaring traditions,[5] they referred to themselves as two cousins, even though they were not blood relatives. Heinrich Jessen's uncle was married to Jacob Jessen's aunt but there were no descendants who would share either Jebsen's or Jessen's blood. They later became brothers-in-law, but what united them was their shared destiny and a history of over 125 years.

The shared experience of their partnership, which extended over several generations, allowed the Jebsen & Jessen Family Enterprise to master enduring relationships. Helmuth Hennig, a past managing director of Jebsen & Co. who worked for the group for nearly 40 years[6] and whose father and grandfather were also long-time employees, noted:

> **The enduring success of the Jebsen & Jessen Family Enterprise is based on the sustainability of their relationships.**

The longstanding transgenerational relationships with employees and their families is an example of the ability of the Jebsen & Jessen Family Enterprise to sustain partnerships. And the company's relationships with other stakeholders, such as business partners, are just as enduring. An example is their 65-year partnership with the Porsche family, for which Jebsen & Co. has been a distributor since 1955, when the first Porsche was introduced in mainland China. Similar partnerships are found in Jebsen & Jessen (SEA)'s many 50/50 joint ventures, such as with Air Liquide (JJ-Lurgi Engineering) or Lapp Group (JJ-Lapp). As Helmuth Henning stressed:

> These relationships are just as positive and just as important to us as they were on day one… [showing] the desire of the owners to build long-term relationships that lead to a long-term success.

When asked for the secret to enduring partnerships, Hans Michael Jebsen, the third-generation principal shareholder and leader, replied:

> One cannot institutionalize or legislate relationships; they evolve from the complexities of individuals.

Shared values are, therefore, paramount to sustaining relationships, and the partnership of the Jebsen and Jessen families has been based on common values of trust, prudence, commitment, entrepreneurship and partnership.

Heinrich Jessen, the third-generation principal shareholder, explained:

> **That goes back to our shipping roots. As the captain of a ship, you *trust* the people you are working with; it takes a certain amount of *entrepreneurialism* to go to far away places around the world, *prudence* to make sure you can weather a storm, *commitment* to your crew and your customers, and *partnerships* with the traders in the Far East from whom you buy the goods that you bring back to the West.**

These values proved to be "the best glue" for the relationship of the two families that have worked together for three generations, while maintaining their differentiated identities. As Hans Michael Jebsen stressed:

> A good metal is made of different components, going through heat and shock treatment to become one. That is an analogy for what forged our family partnership.

Entrepreneurial Spirit

When Jacob Jebsen and Heinrich Jessen formed the original Jebsen & Co. partnership, they adopted the coat of arms of their hometown, Aabenraa – the three mackerels – for their company's logo (Figure 10.2):[7]

> The mackerel is a fighting fish, which moves fast when chasing its prey… Unlike most fish, it is not equipped with a swim-bladder (which would make it weightless in the water) and it must be on the move at all times to avoid sinking to the bottom![8]

Staying in motion to remain afloat reflects the mackerel's character as well as the extreme entrepreneurial spirit of the Jebsen & Jessen Family Enterprise.

This spirit has been tested generation after generation, as the consecutive family leaders have successfully found ways to rebound and reinvent the firm to ensure its continuity and longevity. According to Heinrich Jessen:

> Near-death experiences put each generation back to the pioneering stage. We have never gone into the comfort-zone holding pattern that can be observed sometimes in subsequent generations of family firms.

Source: Jebsen & Jessen Family Enterprise: www.jebsenjessenfamilyenterprise.com/; Miller, L. and A. C. Wasmuth (2008). *Three Mackerels: The Story of the Jebsen and Jessen Family Enterprise*. Hong Kong: Hongkongnow.com, p. 1.

Figure 10.2 The Three Mackerels: the Jebsen & Jessen Family Enterprise current (left) and original (right) logos

The first generation endured the complete destruction of the company and the personal repercussions during the First World War (1914–18). As Aabenraa was part of Germany at the time, Jacob Jebsen – who held a German passport – found himself labeled an "enemy" in the British colony of Hong Kong and was interned in a prison camp, first in Hong Kong and later in Australia, for more than four years. All treaties, agreements and conventions concluded with the German Empire were declared null and void. As a consequence, Jebsen & Co.'s Hong Kong operations were seized and ships were confiscated, never to be returned to its owners. Heinrich Jessen, who found himself in Jebsen & Jessen Hamburg at the beginning of the war, saw all of his senior employees drafted into the German armed forces. When the two partners were reunited after the war in Aabenraa, they discovered that all that was left of their pre-war business was a pile of rubble. Undeterred, they rebuilt a better company starting from revitalizing the Hamburg operations, establishing a new branch in Aabenraa, and then redeveloping the Asian operations, as soon as they received a telegram saying that marketable goods were needed in China. No objections were raised about them re-establishing their operations in China and Hong Kong because they were newly recognized as Danish nationals, as a result of a post-war referendum that made Aabenraa part of Denmark.

The 1920s and 1930s saw the entry of the second generation into the management of the business, with Heinz Jessen and Michael Jebsen playing a crucial role in establishing new ventures, such as taking the agency for the Danish Maersk Line and introducing Mercedes-Benz's diesel vehicles in China. Later on, their younger brothers, Hans Jacob Jebsen and Arwed Peter (AP) Jessen, also joined the business. After the Second World War, which wreaked havoc on the company similar to the First World War, they all had to join forces to rebuild the company. As soon as the Second World War broke out, Jebsen & Jessen Hamburg closed, and in 1940 – when Germany invaded Denmark – all Danish citizens of German-occupied countries residing in British territories were declared "technical enemies" by Britain.[9] Luckily, drawing on the experiences of their senior generation during the First World War, the second generation had moved almost all its activities from British Hong Kong to Chinese Shanghai in the first months of the war, which enabled the survival of the firm. Although "battered and bruised, with hugely diminished business activities and a skeleton of staff,"[10] and forced to shift its operations back to Hong Kong from Shanghai as a result of the Chinese Civil War and the Cultural Revolution, the company rebuilt itself out of the great post-war opportunities, alongside the regeneration of Germany's economy and the rise of Hong Kong to greater global prominence.

The Jebsen and Jessen families seized every opportunity to resume former connections and represent German industrial enterprises, not only in Hong Kong, but also in Singapore, where the business branched out as Jebsen & Jessen (SEA) in 1963, first in the role of an agent trading other companies' goods and later as a manufacturer of its own goods, for example industrial cranes. Heinrich Jessen explained that at that time, cranes were imported from Germany and Japan and not manufactured in Singapore. Jebsen & Jessen (SEA) signed the manufacturing license agreement and 20 years later entered into a 50/50 joint venture to create MHE-Demag, which became a dominant player in crane production, service, repair and refurbishment and built over 20,000 industrial cranes.[11]

After a century of trading other manufacturers' products, moving up the value chain to manufacture cranes was a bold entrepreneurial step by the second-generation family leaders and the beginning of a new trend that has been accelerated by the third generation. Embracing the opportunity to serve the needs of a newly emerged middle class in China, Jebsen & Co. moved boldly down the value chain and introduced its own brands, such as "Blue Girl" beer, the multi-brand lifestyle retailer "J-Select" and its own retail platform. Always on the outlook for new investment opportunities, the group has expanded its products and services in existing markets as well as new ones like Myanmar. Helmut Henning noted that resilience and adaptability are essential for thriving in a changing environment, while his partner Heinrich Jessen stressed:

> The only way to adapt is to keep yourself open to change, be willing to see things around you, develop and move with the times.

Enabling Governance

Over the course of their 125-year partnership, the Jebsen and Jessen families have established four intriguing governance principles that reflect the spirit of their forefathers and the determination of the current generation at the helm of the company.

First and foremost is the founding principle of a "principal shareholder" for each family, based on the "one captain–one ship" mentality. The two principal third-generation shareholders are Hans Michael Jebsen and Heinrich Jessen. They are the majority shareholders in their respective companies, that is, Hans Michael Jebsen is the principal shareholder in Jebsen & Co. and Heinrich Jessen is the principal shareholder in Jebsen & Jessen (SEA). For the other entities, the "hand in glove leadership" principle with equal cross-shareholdings and consensus-based decision making is applied. These principles have helped to maintain the closeness between the two families as noted by Hans Michael Jebsen, "We are each other's executors of wills and trusted partners."

The second governance principle is the utmost independence of each business within Jebsen & Jessen's portfolio. With no overall holding company, the family enterprise is in fact a federation of businesses with flat organizational and decision-making structures. Hans Michael Jebsen explained:

> Our structure is tailor-made. The independently managed companies are local companies with local partners and local co-investors that enjoy maximum flexibility in this loose structure.

In order to align the goals of managers and owners, the ownership is temporarily extended to the managing directors of the business entities, just like the captains who not only navigated the ships but also – according to time-tested rules – often had to own part of the ship or cargo they transported. Upon retirement, the managing directors would sell the shares back to the principal family shareholders, thereby guaranteeing the sustainability of the family ownership.

According to Helmuth Hennig, a non-family temporary shareholder of Jebsen & Co.:

> Hans Michael Jebsen and Heinrich Jessen are the continuity from the historical as well as future point of view.

Heinrich Jessen explained how principal family shareholders steer the family enterprise through their positions on the boards of all the companies:

> Just like we don't have a structure above the four business groupings, we also do not have a holding structure from the board of directors' perspective. We meet informally all the time and formally at the board meetings of the different businesses in the Jebsen & Jessen portfolio.

The third governance principle is that only one person from each family could become a principal shareholder. Because shares are never inherited and can be bought only if the successor works in the business, that person has to be accepted by all other shareholders. The shares are acquired from the previous-generation owner and it may take decades to pay the predecessor. Heinrich Jessen underlined:

> I was asset rich and cash poor. It took me 15 years to pay off my shares with any dividends that came from my assets.

Other family members who want to join the business as directors and shareholders must buy their shares from their family's principal shareholder. If they wish to exit the business, these shares have to be sold back to the principal shareholder. However, as Heinrich Jessen, explained:

> The step from working in the business to shareholding is a big one. This is different to many other family firms, where family members become shareholders but stay away from the business.

Fourth is the low dividend appetite of shareholders and an absence of entitlement in the Jebsen and Jessen families. A strong desire to stay private and financially independent has encouraged the stewardship mindset of the family enterprise. The shareholder agreement is simple and practical, including the dividend policies, and regulates the maximum dividend level. As Heinrich Jessen explained:

> **The dividend appetite of the shareholders – and this goes across three generations – has traditionally been low. *We live the idea of putting the money back into the business.***

This enables patient investments in the business that may pay off over a longer term.

Hans Michael Jebsen explained the idea of the sustainable perpetuation of the business as follows:

> The company should not be subject to other agendas; it is there to be continued and not to be considered a personal asset that is disposable.
> **Corporate wealth does not equal private wealth.**

As a rule, there are only two family principal shareholders, but other family members can profit from the family wealth through various foundations, which support those who are in medical need, want to pursue an education or simply buy a house. The sustainability of this solution is guaranteed through the purchasing mechanism as the retiring principal shareholders are compensated for their shares by the incoming successors. The family foundations are fueled with funds from the retired shareholders.

Purpose-Driven Leadership

With its values-based, long-lasting partnerships, entrepreneurial curiosity and governance principles, which resulted in a very lean structure and enabled the Jebsen & Jessen Family Enterprise to stay agile, the company was ready to enter a new chapter of its history and integrate a sustainability agenda into the core strategy of the family enterprise. All the company needed was a purpose-driven leader to build on the families' inherent love of nature. Third-generation member Heinrich Jessen was to be that leader. He noted:

> The interest in the environment had always inherently been there. I grew up in Europe in nature, took walks in the forests and worked on farms very often. I see the same love for nature in Hans Michael Jebsen and in previous generations as well.

Even though the love of nature and respect for the environment was inherent in the family leaders, it was not fully embedded in their business until the late 1990s, when Heinrich Jessen, a tropical biologist by training, showed his mettle. He shared that "in many ways [he] was not supposed to join [his] family business." A graduate of an interdisciplinary environmental studies program in the US, he first worked at the World Wildlife Fund in Italy and then on a rainforest project in Papua New Guinea. While on the Pacific island, he read the book on the history of his family firm and was inspired by the entrepreneurial ventures of his grandfather. At that time, Jebsen & Jessen (SEA) was gradually moving away from distribution into engineering and manufacturing, with some of the latter activities involving hazardous chemicals with potential environmental impacts. He asked his father if the environment and business could be combined in the company and if they could start an environmental program. His father was supportive of this idea and helped focus the company's 1992 management conference on the theme of environmental sustainability. Prominent environmentalists and firms with active sustainability programs were invited to share their insights. Heinrich Jessen was among the guest speakers. It turned out to be a great way for him to be exposed to the top managers of the company, many of whom encouraged him to join the company and lead their pursuit to align environmental sustainability with their business goals and objectives.

To increase his knowledge of the field, Heinrich Jessen returned to the US to pursue a master's degree in industrial environmental management, with a particular focus on how to reduce a business's environmental footprint. Upon his return in 1995, he became the first environmental, health and safety (EHS) manager of Jebsen & Jessen (SEA), exactly 100 years after his grandfather and his cousin had founded Jebsen & Co. In his new role, Heinrich Jessen saw lots of "low-hanging fruit" and had to prioritize. He focused first on ensuring health and safety compliance across the group. The "Ingredients" business operated with hundreds of dangerous chemicals and lacked thorough processes to ensure safety. For example, tons of sodium cyanide were being stored in the vicinity of food ingredients. Even though it was not uncommon in the region and absolutely not against any law, Heinrich Jessen knew that this might cause contamination in case of spills or explosions. Proper storage methods, including segregation, isolation, separation, emergency response and prevention plans were developed and implemented.

"It was a great success," he said, as the EHS program demonstrated its economic impact in the form of lower insurance premiums upon instituting various risk-mitigating procedures such as fire-prevention systems and attracting increasingly EHS-minded chemical companies to work with Jebsen & Jessen (SEA) as their distributor. Numerous other EHS initiatives ensued: Jebsen & Jessen (SEA) was the first company in the region to ban shark fins at company dinners; it entered a new business of molded pulp packaging made of recycled paper, a biodegradable alternative to the standard protective plastic packaging; it exited a tropical wood furniture business using rainforest timber from Indonesia; although legal in South-East Asia, it ceased supplying tributyltin oxide – an ingredient in marine paints – because it had severe negative impacts on marine organisms. In the late 1990s, Jebsen & Jessen (SEA) was one of the first industrial companies in the Association of Southeast Asian Nations region to implement rigorous EHS protocols and to have all its member companies ISO 14001 and OHSAS 18001 certified.[12]

While EHS started as an ideological initiative, it quickly became institutionalized and considered a key part of the value proposition to its principals and customers, coordinated by a team of EHS experts. Heinrich Jessen's career progressed rapidly. He attended board meetings as vice chairman and in his day-to-day role cycled through several other operational functions, including manager of the recycled paper pulp packaging plant in Malaysia. This career journey helped him to understand the different company operations and prepared him for his ultimate job as the principal family shareholder and the chairman of Jebsen & Jessen (SEA) in 2004. He notes that "even while [his] role evolved, [he] continued to keep an eye on all of [the] environmental impacts."

For Jebsen & Jessen (SEA) integrating business and the environment – Heinrich Jessen's dream for over 25 years – became an inherent part of the business culture and business model.

It was the first industrial company in South-East Asia to employ a full-time carbon neutrality executive and the first to achieve full carbon neutrality in 2011. Since then, it has offset more than 400,000 tons of carbon dioxide and continuously monitored carbon levels with the help of tools developed in-house. It also implemented further emission reduction initiatives such as the installation of solar panels to generate power at one of its manufacturing facilities and converting to LED lighting in its offices.

Inspired by Heinrich Jessen's green legacy at Jebsen & Jessen (SEA), the sister company of Jebsen & Co. prioritized its environmental agenda and achieved carbon neutral status in 2013. One project involved collaborating with GE Jenbacher to deliver to the Hong Kong government the first high-voltage biogas-fueled combination heat and power generator, which has led to annual energy savings of 7 million Hong Kong dollars. Hans Michael Jebsen elaborated on the commitment to carbon neutrality as follows:

> The carbon neutrality benchmark has been very important for us because it cuts through the entire organization. Heinrich Jessen was instrumental in that because, with his educational background, he had a fresh look at the group activities. Since then, we have analyzed every single business and have seen that there is a footprint that can be optimized and that this is an on-going process. It is a matter of philosophy.

However, Heinrich Jessen admitted that it was not easy to implement environmental sustainability initiatives back in the 1990s. The changes required a purpose-driven leader, who would overcome hurdles from external and internal stakeholders. Sustainability initiatives were a novelty in the market, and there was, for example, an unwillingness to pay a premium for a responsible product like the organic cotton they were producing, so they had to stop that production and bear the sunk costs. Management teams were initially reluctant to implement EHS initiatives because the immediate benefits were not obvious. Furthermore, it was difficult for Heinrich Jessen, the son of the chairman and groomed successor, to collect honest feedback. He shared that:

> [he] had trouble getting feedback on [his] actions and judgment. When [he] decided to pursue a new strategy, [he] had to figure out for [himself] whether it was working or not. There was a lot of trial and error, but no one was telling [him] about [his] errors, so [he] had to discover them by [himself].

What helped Heinrich Jessen in his purpose-driven leadership were the time-proven strengths of the family in terms of entrepreneurship, partnerships and enabling governance. First, the entrepreneurial spirit helped turn many threats related to sustainability into business opportunities. For example, in Triton Textile – a business unit established in the 1960s to provide textile and apparel merchandising services, now integrated into Jebsen & Jessen Hamburg – one of the biggest areas of focus was social auditing, as textile production and merchandising of garments were too often associated with child labor and many poor practices. Heinrich Jessen noted that:

> [they] turned a challenge into an opportunity and now qualify, among hundreds of potential suppliers, as those that meet the strict standards of end customers.

Second, the legacy of values-based partnerships paved the way to the self-positioning of, for example, Jebsen & Co. as a nexus in a multiple stakeholder value chain:

> Having come a long way to evolve from a shipping agent to a specialized marketing and distribution organization, Jebsen relates itself with extensive stakeholders ranging from governments and customers to partners, shareholders, employees, non-profit organizations, environment and universities. We are part of a value chain in which every component is integrated and developed together. In view of this, Jebsen has committed itself to proactively address our stakeholders' diversified CSR [corporate social responsibility] needs, to achieve comprehensive and sustainable development together.[13]

Third, enabling governance, which was simultaneously decentralized and centralized, supporting agility and experimentation, emphasizing financial independence and patient financial capital, resulted in a total alignment of third-generation principal family shareholders around the value that "wealth is goodwill, not money in a bank," as underlined by Hans Michael Jebsen. They fully share the view that "the higher you want to grow, the stronger roots you have to have." Hans Michael Jebsen stressed that this results from a:

> deep conviction that we should only bite off as much as we can chew... Overconsumption and waste are the reasons for many disruptions in the world.

> A… wasteful lifestyle cannot and should not be a yard stick for any society. We, as a company with roots in a very green part of the world, have to contribute to the green agenda.

But the most spectacular example of the company's partnerships, entrepreneurship, governance and purpose-driven leadership in action was about to come as the biggest diversification in Jebsen & Jessen Family Enterprise's portfolio – the social innovation of a circular business model at GMA Garnet.

GMA GARNET

Garnet – a natural mineral product belonging to a group of silicate minerals – is known for its hardness, toughness and density making it an exceptionally efficient and effective industrial abrasive with excellent cutting capabilities.[14] The hardest industrial varieties are produced from the pinkish tinted almandine garnet. It was this garnet that Torsten Ketelsen, a Hamburg-born merchant with Danish roots, discovered in Australia in the 1980s, and he started to develop a market for it in the Middle East from his newly established Perth base, Ketelsen Enterprise. At that time, garnet was largely an unknown industrial commodity; other less-efficient, low-cost and hazardous products like silica sand and waste from the metal-smelting process were being used in the market.[15]

Torsten Ketelsen created demand for garnet by developing and cleverly marketing a series of differentiated products. He said that it was not the mining that was difficult. Instead, the challenge was finding and establishing a market for mined products. Developing the market for garnet in the Arabian Gulf and Middle East, where there is an abundance of sand and sand blasting was an industrial standard, required a big dose of determination in the 1980s. Torsten Ketelsen, the founder of Ketelsen Enterprise and co-founder of GMA Garnet, looked back:

> The first 20 years of my journey were the toughest; I kept bringing samples of garnet to a region where traditional abrasives, such as sand, were well established, very cheap and easily available. From the beginning we realized the only way forward was to offer a superior value proposition, including supreme efficiency and environmental safety. Initially, our customers were too busy sandblasting to even try our product; it was more expensive upfront, and profits only showed up later. But when they tried it, they usually fell for it quickly. They would often say, "Why didn't you come to me 10 years ago?"

By 2017, Torsten Ketelsen had successfully developed over 40 applications of garnet in the waterjet-cutting and abrasive-blasting industries, including those for cutting steel and marble in shipyards and aircraft production facilities. Ultimately, he established GMA Garnet as a garnet abrasives leader capturing 40 percent of the global market.

Torsten Ketelsen's industrial success was propelled by the unfettered support of the controlling shareholder, the Jebsen & Jessen Family Enterprise. GMA Garnet's history had been deeply intertwined with that of the Jebsen & Jessen Family Enterprise since 1991 when Torsten Ketelsen formed a 50/50 joint venture with Jebsen & Jessen Hamburg to sell garnet in Europe. At the time, Jebsen & Jessen Hamburg was trading mainly in chemicals and textiles between Asia and Europe. Garnet was a complete novelty for them, but they were driven by entrepreneurial curiosity and welcomed diversification. Additionally, the first application of garnet was in shipyards – a sector the firm was familiar with due to its multi-generation seafaring history. The Jebsen & Jessen Family Enterprise was functionally organized as a federation of independently managed businesses, many of them established as entrepreneurial partnerships with leading global brands. This newly established joint venture was embedded in Jebsen & Jessen Hamburg's offices and was named GMA Garnet (Europe) GmbH.

The journey to the full integration of GMA Garnet into the Jebsen & Jessen Family Enterprise had begun. After 10 years of distributing the product, in 2001 Garnet International Resources was established with a purpose of making a bold entrepreneurial move up the value chain and purchasing a number of mining activities in Australia, the US and South Africa. Heinrich Jessen commented:

> When you are familiar with the business for 10 years because you are distributing the product and are responsible for the technical sales, then the step from there to securing the supply is not such a big step to take. It is a coherent one.

Garnet International Resources was fully integrated into the Jebsen & Jessen Family Enterprise on terms similar to other operating entities, exemplifying the entrepreneurial leanings and governance; the main ownership was equally shared by the two family principal shareholders, Hans Michael Jebsen and Heinrich Jessen. Torsten Ketelsen and Wolfhart Putzier, the non-family shareholder and managing director of Jebsen & Jessen Hamburg, shared a minority interest in Garnet International Resources, remained operationally involved in the company and enjoyed a great deal of latitude to develop the business. The shareholders were bound by a lean, standard shareholder agreement, which established, among other things, the maximum dividend level, reflecting the low dividend appetite of the shareholders.

The final step into the full ownership integration of GMA Garnet took place in 2015, as a result of the retirement plans of Torsten Ketelsen and Wolfhart Putzier from the GMA Garnet Group. The chief executive officer and chairman positions were filled by two external, professional non-family managers. GMA Garnet was fully integrated into the family business, which, according to Torsten Ketelsen, offered much better prospects for the long-term success of the Group than the alternative of an external sale to a leading global private equity firm. "The decision to keep GMA Garnet in the portfolio of Jebsen & Jessen Family Enterprise had grown naturally," explained Hans Michael Jebsen, and this was based on the shared values, Danish and German origins and strong roots in the Hamburg area. As Torsten Ketelsen reflected:

> We are all Hanseatic merchants with high business ethics and morale.[16] For us the value of the word is high; we still do business with a handshake, long-term goals are supreme and trust and partnerships are key. Hans Michael Jebsen and Heinrich Jessen act on what they say.

Purpose-Driven Leadership at GMA Garnet

The entrepreneurial spirit of Torsten Ketelsen and the concentrated ownership with shared values and governance principles of the Jebsen & Jessen Family Enterprise enabled the successful integration and success of GMA Garnet, which soon became the world's largest producer and distributor of industrial garnet. But the real test of putting the entrepreneurship, parentship and enabling governance into action was about to come with a move down the value chain and the sustainable recycling of garnet. According to Torsten Ketelsen:

> A big driving force for the success of GMA Garnet is that as a private company you can maintain much more of an entrepreneurial spirit and the flexibility to create and grasp business opportunities.[17]

Hans Michael Jebsen reflected that "the garnet recycling opportunity was not driven by any legislation but by our entrepreneurial curiosity and fueled by our experimentation." The exceptional qualities of garnet – particularly its extraordinary hardness and toughness – means that it retained most of its abrasive characteristics after use, and it turned out that it could be recycled several times. As Heinrich Jessen explained:

> Recycled garnet shows slightly different characteristics. But because we have so many different sources of garnet, we are able to blend it or use it for many other applications and sell it back to the market.

However, marketing garnet recycling proved difficult in the beginning because customers did not see the immediate value added. The future of garnet recycling was dependent on Torsten Ketelsen's purpose-driven leadership. He recalled:

> **When I started the recycling concept 20 years ago, everyone said I was crazy to promote recycling because we would sell less virgin garnet. Instead, in the long run, the customer base has increased greatly due to the additional product value and cost savings for the customers.**[18]

The time-proven partnerships, entrepreneurship, governance and purpose-driven leadership of the Jebsen & Jessen Family Enterprise led to unlocking the sustainability strategy, this time at GMA Garnet. Indeed, GMA Garnet pioneered the concept of sustainability in mining, with a clear commitment to environmentally friendly mining practices and a circular business model, acting as an example to the industry (Figure 10.3). Heinrich Jessen explained:

> What is inherently interesting for the GMA Garnet business, is that the environmental, health and safety credentials are strong in the entire value chain, from mining, through processing and up to reprocessing and recycling.

Figure 10.3 Sustainability credentials in the circular economy model of GMA Garnet

Three Phases of the GMA Garnet Circular Economy

Garnet belongs to a group of silicate minerals, the processing of which occurs in three phases. In the first phase of mining and processing, garnet is extracted using an open-cast surface mining technique. The minerals are extracted from an open pit. Excavators extract the dune sand using front-end loaders and carry it in dump trucks to the "wet plant" so the heavy minerals of garnet and ilmenite can be separated from the residual materials like sand, seashell remains, stones and sediment. The resultant wet concentrate contains 90 percent garnet. It is stock piled in huge pink heaps to allow excess water to drain out before being dry processed in large gas-fired rotary dryers to extract the remaining moisture. After the process of magnetic separation and screening, the various GMA Garnet products are either packed or transported as loose bulk to GMA's port storage.

GMA Garnet implemented exceptional mining, waste and land management standards, exceeding Australian environmental compliance. For example, before beginning to mine, the company collects the top soil and plant seeds. The garnet and other heavy minerals are then mined and separated and the residue materials are trucked back to the mine and dumped into the mined crater and shaped into the original contours. The original top soil and seeds are then returned. Heinrich Jessen explained this approach as follows:

> When mining… is completed in years to come, there will be no visible signs that there has ever been any such activity, and sheep and kangaroos will share the grazing land as they have done for decades. The topography changes a bit because the landscape is a bit lower but that doesn't have any adverse environmental impact.[19]

GMA Garnet uses environmental measures in its wet processing of garnet. Relying on gravity, magnetism and centrifugal forces, only water is used to clean the extractions and separate minerals from non-minerals. This is an environmentally safer approach than traditional chemical processing.

The second phase of the GMA Garnet circular economy is logistics and application. In this phase, garnet and ilmenite are shipped by sea to customers and distributors around the world. As garnet is heavy and, thus, when used as a blasting agent does not create dust, it is a much cleaner and safer material to use than traditional abrasives like silica sand that are banned or heavily restricted in most countries because the dust created by these materials is linked to silicosis – a fatal lung disease. Garnet is also preferable to other alternative abrasives such as coal and copper slags, which are associated with environmental and health hazards. Thus, garnet is a far cleaner non-polluting solution. Torsten Ketelsen described it with a very illustrative example:

> Just outside Hamburg, located on the river Elbe, there is a beautiful island full of apple and cherry trees. On that island there is a small shipyard, which was using a copper slag sandblasting abrasive. Its dust was constantly contaminating beautiful antique houses. The owner of the shipyard bought, one by one, all the old waterfront houses to stop the complaints. He was one of my first customers in Germany! A few

> years later, he told me that garnet really changed many aspects of his business. Because garnet does not produce dust, the owner of the shipyard was able to sell the houses back to the market at significant profits!

The third phase of the GMA Garnet circular economy entails the recycling and reprocessing of the mineral. It is in this phase that GMA Garnet implemented its most notable social innovation, thereby differentiating itself from other garnet producers. The used garnet is recovered, reprocessed to separate the garnet grains from residue and contaminants, packed as special recycled grade material and fed back into the distribution system. Reprocessing is done using recycled water and a slime extraction unit in the wet plant. To reprocess the used garnet bought back from customers, GMA Garnet established the recycling facilities close to major customer centers in order to minimize transportation. In 2020, five large industrial-scale recycling plants, located across Asia Pacific, Europe, the Middle East and the Americas, were operating successfully. GMA Garnet had established itself as the innovative industry leader for developing garnet recycling technologies and offering an eco-friendly solution to its customers for the disposal of used garnet.[20] Garnet recycling proved to be a novel market solution to a global environmental problem as it helped to maximize the life span of a non-renewable natural resource thereby reducing the need to extract more garnet from nature. For garnet users, recycling provides a cost-effective and environmentally responsible disposal option for their industrial waste.[21]

GMA Garnet's social innovation spurred similar efforts across other operations of the Jebsen & Jessen Family Enterprise. Heinrich Jessen described one such example:

> Our biggest industrial ecology story is at an ilmenite mine in South Africa where the Jebsen & Jessen Family Enterprise has mining rights. In the mining process of ilmenite there, garnet was a waste product and it was going right back to the mine after the ilmenite was extracted. We managed to convert a waste product into a finished product by giving it another run and extracting the garnet before the rest goes back into the mine.

Adding the garnet recycling and transforming the production process to become circular led to the full vertical integration of GMA Garnet:

> GMA is the only global garnet supplier to manage the complete supply chain from source and processing to international distribution. We have invested significantly to expand our sources of supply and production capacity to incorporate alluvial, crushed and recycled garnet. Our team of dedicated sales and technical experts work with our customers to understand their priorities and challenges. We deliver specialist advice and distribute a complete range of premium abrasive products to

> more than 80 countries from our own warehouses and a network of more than 100 distributor outlets.[22]

Indeed, as Torsten Ketelsen pointed out, GMA Garnet does not consider itself primarily as a miner anymore because the company is selling a technical product and creating its own market.[23] In his words:

> We are a global distribution company that produces its own products, an ever-growing suite of branded garnet products, and distribute these through our own logistics and distribution network from the mine to the end users all over the world.

Heinrich Jessen wraps up the GMA Garnet story by saying, "The Garnet story is such a good story, from the entrepreneurial, the business case and environmental point of view."

With the strong environmental and social sustainability credentials and strong materiality along the whole value chain, GMA Garnet contributes to the following United Nations' Sustainable Development Goals:

- Goal 9: Build resilient infrastructure, promote inclusive and sustainable industrialization and foster innovation.
- Goal 12: Ensure sustainable consumption and production patterns.
- Goal 15: Protect, restore and promote sustainable use of terrestrial ecosystems, sustainably manage forests, combat desertification and halt and reverse land degradation and halt biodiversity loss.

GMA Garnet's social innovation of a circular business model has become a role model within the Jebsen & Jessen Family Enterprise illustrating how value-based partnerships, an entrepreneurial spirit, enabling governance structures and purpose-driven leadership coalesce to pioneer a sustainability strategy within the industry. For his entrepreneurial drive and ability to establish a completely new market for garnet, Torsten Ketelsen was recognized with the 2008 Australian Entrepreneur of the Year Award in the Technology and Emerging Industries category, and in 2015 with E&Y Australian Entrepreneur of the Year Award in the mining category.

The Jebsen & Jessen story continues; 125 years since the creation of the first company, an unbroken chain of three generations has been committed to ensuring the founders' legacy of connecting East and West.[24] The Jebsen & Jessen Family Enterprise continues on its mission to build a sustainable business and preserve its entrepreneurial spirit.[25]

KEY INSIGHTS

The Jebsen & Jessen Family Enterprise case illustrates how two entrepreneurial families used their values-based partnership and carefully structured governance principles to enable trail-blazing entrepreneurial opportunities around environmental sustainability principles, generation after generation. These fundamentals helped to pioneer the sustainability strategy first at Jebsen & Jessen (SEA) and then across the whole group, including GMA Garnet where the circular economy concept was brought to life across the whole value chain and became a role model in the garnet mining and processing industry. The following ideas implemented by Jebsen & Jessen Family Enterprise are particularly noteworthy:

- *The three mackerels: staying in motion to remain afloat concept.* This concept reflects the time-tested entrepreneurial spirit of the Jebsen and Jessen families to rebound and reinvent the firm to ensure its continuity and longevity.
- *The "one captain–one ship" principal shareholder concept as a base for enduring partnership.* Each family – the Jebsens and the Jessens – would normally have only one principal family shareholder, who would accumulate the majority of each family's shares. Further, the principal family shareholder is a majority shareholder in his respective company, i.e., Hans Michael Jebsen is the principal shareholder in Jebsen & Co. and Heinrich Jessen is the principal shareholder in Jebsen & Jessen (SEA). As Jebsen & Jessen (SEA) and Jebsen & Co. are a composite of several autonomous companies, the principal family shareholder of each is the primary decision maker in the companies that are part of his respective portfolio. For other entities, including GMA Garnet, the "hand in glove leadership" principle with equal cross-shareholdings and consensus-based decision making is applied.
- *The temporary ownership concept.* For goal alignment between owners and managers, the ownership is sometimes temporarily extended to non-family managing directors of business entities, just like captains who not only navigated the ships but also – according to time-tested rules – often had to own part of the ship or cargo they transported. Upon retirement the managing directors sell the shares back to the principal family shareholders, thereby guaranteeing the sustainability of the family ownership.
- *The sustainability journey may begin with the low-hanging fruit* tied to core business challenges like eliminating toxic chemicals or plastics, but it needs a leader who believes in the sustainability purpose and who continuously keeps social innovation on the radar. In time, as owners and managers develop a level of comfort that environmental and social

initiatives do not affect economic performance negatively, they build the momentum for more meaningful social and environmental initiatives with greater impact. The impactful social innovation initiatives may be fully implemented outside of the core business first and adopted to the legacy and core business in later stages.

- *Sustainability initiatives often require customers and other stakeholders to be "educated" about the win-win benefits.* Even though garnet delivers superior performance for customers, can be reprocessed and reused, is cleaner and safer and has no negative health effects compared to traditional sand blasting, it still took decades to educate and convince customers about the superiority of the product. Again, purpose-driven leadership and entrepreneurial endurance played a crucial role. Breaking a "business-as-usual" mindset requires engaging with stakeholders.
- *Social innovation* in one business sparks similar initiatives in other businesses within the family group of companies, leading to industry-level leadership, differentiation and competitive advantage.

NOTES

1. Miller, L. & Wasmuth, A. C. (2008). *Three Mackerels: The Story of the Jebsen and Jessen Family Enterprise*. Hong Kong: Hongkongnow.com, p. 5.
2. This chapter was developed based on (1) the interviews with: (i) Hans Michael Jebsen, third-generation principal shareholder of Jebsen & Co, in Aabenraa, Denmark, August 2016, by Benoit Leleux and Marta Widz; (ii) Heinrich Jessen, third-generation principal shareholder of Jebsen & Jessen SEA, in Singapore, September 2016 by Benoit Leleux and Marta Widz; (iii) Helmuth Hennig, Jebsen & Co. non-family managing director, in September 2016, phone interview by Marta Widz; (iv) Torsten Ketelsen, founder, shareholder and ex-chief executive officer of GMA Garnet, in Zurich, Switzerland, May 2017 by Marta Widz; (2) desk research by Marta Widz; and (3) on the following case studies: (i) Leleux, B. & Widz, M. (2017). Jebsen & Jessen Family Enterprise: A Hong from the Cold, IMD-7-1859; (ii) Leleux, B. & Widz, M. (2019). GMA Garnet: Partnering for Environmental Mining. IMD-7-2075; (iii) Widz, M. (2016). Jebsen & Jessen South East Asia: Building a Sustainable Environment for Good Business. FBN-Polaris case study.
3. Jebsen & Jessen Family Enterprise: www.jebsenjessenfamilyenterprise.com/en/AboutUs
4. Jebsen & Jessen Family Enterprise: www.jebsenjessenfamilyenterprise.com/about-us/
5. Miller, L. & Wasmuth, A. C. (2008). *Three Mackerels: The Story of the Jebsen and Jessen Family Enterprise*. Hong Kong: Hongkongnow.com, p. 8.
6. Helmuth Hennig joined the Jebsen Group in 1983 and was the group managing director of Jebsen for 20 years, from 2000 to 2020, when he handed over the role to Alfons Mensdorff: https://en.prnasia.com/releases/apac/jebsen-group-appoints-new-group-managing-director-278699.shtml

7. Miller, L. & Wasmuth, A. C. (2008). *Three Mackerels: The Story of the Jebsen and Jessen Family Enterprise*. Hong Kong: Hongkongnow.com, p. 5.
8. Jebsen & Jessen (SEA): www.jjsea.com
9. Miller, L. & Wasmuth, A. C. (2008). *Three Mackerels: The Story of the Jebsen and Jessen Family Enterprise*. Hong Kong: Hongkongnow.com, p. 57.
10. Ibid., p. 59.
11. In 2019, in its quest to capture an unprecedented opportunity and grow boldly into new strategic ventures, the company exited the crane manufacturing business by selling it to another family business – KONE.
12. The ISO 14001, International Organization for Standardization, certifies that the company designs and implements an effective environmental management system and that its environmental impact in operations, such as adverse changes to air, water or land, is being measured and improved; the OHSAS 18001, Occupational Health and Safety Assessment Series, certifies that the company designs and implements an effective occupational health and safety management system and that it strives to ensure safety internally in the workplace by getting both workers and management involved in risk reduction.
13. Jebsen Group Corporate Social Responsibility Report 2015, p. 22.
14. Garnet scores 7.5 to 8 on the Mohs scale, on which the hardest mineral, diamond, scores a perfect 10. Unlike diamond, which is friable, garnet is very tough, and does not break down on impact. Garnet is also very dense: the specific weight of garnet is 4.1, which means it is over four times heavier than water. Its three characteristics – hardness, toughness and density – make garnet a very effective abrasive.
15. "GMA Garnet." *Business First*, 2015. www.businessfirstmagazine.com.au/torsten-ketelsen-gma-garnet-group/11738/
16. The Hanseatic League, also known as Hansa, was a medieval commercial confederation of merchants that initially united the northern German towns of Lübeck, Hamburg and Bremen and then spread across the Baltic and the North Sea to dominate the maritime trade for several centuries. Hanseatic merchants were known for their high ethical standards in business; those virtues continue to be cultivated by the Honourable Society of Hamburg Merchants.
17. "Smooth transition for GMA Garnet." *Business News: Western Australia*, July 2015. www.businessnews.com.au/article/Smooth-transition-for-GMA-Garnet
18. "GMA Garnet." *Business First*, 2015. www.businessfirstmagazine.com.au/torsten-ketelsen-gma-garnet-group/11738/
19. Miller, L. & Wasmuth, A. C. (2008). *Three Mackerels: The Story of the Jebsen and Jessen Family Enterprise*. Hong Kong: Hongkongnow.com, p. 174.
20. www.gmagarnet.com/en-au/about-gma
21. GMA Garnet: www.gmagarnet.com/en-au/sustainability-(1)
22. www.gmagarnet.com/en-au/about-gma
23. "GMA Garnet." *Business First*, 2015. www.businessfirstmagazine.com.au/torsten-ketelsen-gma-garnet-group/11738/
24. Jebsen & Jessen (SEA): www.jjsea.com
25. Jebsen & Jessen (SEA): www.jjsea.com/about-us/our-history/

APPENDIX: JEBSEN & JESSEN FAMILY ENTERPRISE AND GMA GARNET

Jebsen & Jessen Family Enterprise	GMA Garnet
Partnerships and entrepreneurship (the *why*)	
Values-based partnerships were reinterpreted to reflect the self-positioning of the family business as a nexus in a multiple stakeholder value chain: "We are part of a value chain in which every component is integrated and developed together. In view of this, Jebsen has committed itself to proactively address our stakeholders' diversified CSR [corporate social responsibility] needs, to achieve comprehensive and sustainable development together." The values of *trust, prudence, commitment, entrepreneurship* and *partnership* that go back to the shipping roots as well as an inherent love for nature were reinterpreted to include sustainability: "Wealth is goodwill, not the money in a bank." *Entrepreneurial spirit*, reflected in the company's logo and in the motto of "staying in motion to remain afloat," was reinterpreted to turn many threats related to sustainability into business opportunities, such as Triton Textile adding social auditing services to its portfolio of merchandising services. New initiatives around sustainability were approached with entrepreneurial curiosity, such as the appointment of Heinrich Jessen as the first EHS executive.	*Values-based partnerships*: Torsten Ketelsen's partnership with the Jebsen & Jessen Family Enterprise spanned some 25 years; it began with a joint venture in 1991, followed by the creation of Garnet International Resources Ltd (GIRL) in 2001 and then the full ownership integration of GIRL into the Jebsen & Jessen Family Enterprise in 2015. The four shareholders of GIRL shared similar German–Danish roots and values: "It was a meeting of minds. We are all Hanseatic merchants with high business ethics and morale." GIRL turned out to be a "concentrated ownership with similar views." *Entrepreneurial spirit*: Torsten Ketelsen, upon discovering garnet, created over 40 garnet applications and achieved a 40% global market share by replacing traditional abrasives, which were hazardous to health and the environment. Garnet recycling "was not driven by any legislation but by our entrepreneurial curiosity."

Jebsen & Jessen Family Enterprise	GMA Garnet
Governance and leadership (the *how*)	
Enabling governance: *Concentrated ownership* enabled quick decisions, influenced directly by one principal family owner. The *low dividend appetite* enabled the introduction of the first points on the sustainability agenda way before the market was ready to pay a premium for it. The lean and agile structure of the local companies – with *no overall holding structure* – enabled "a great deal of latitude given to the management." That latitude facilitated decentralized experimentation with the sustainability agenda at the local level. *Absence of entitlement* in the family together with the *succession rules* dictated that one family member from every generation from both the Jebsen and Jessen families had to bring something to the table to be a shareholder. Environmental sustainability was Heinrich Jessen's seal that revived full commitment to the sustainability agenda. *Purpose-driven leadership*:Heinrich Jessen pursued a master's degree in industrial environmental management, with a particular focus on how to reduce a business's environmental footprint. He became the company's first EHS manager, exactly 100 years after his grandfather and his cousin had founded the Jebsen & Jessen Family Enterprise. He was trusted by the second-generation family leaders to combine environment and business and to start the environmental program in the company, but he had to overcome various hurdles from internal stakeholders, such as the management team, and external stakeholders, including an unwillingness by the market to pay a premium for a responsible product. Heinrich Jessen implemented EHS measures that demonstrated its economic impact (e.g., lower insurance premiums upon instituting various risk-mitigating procedures such as fire-prevention systems). Sustainability became an inherent part of the business culture and business model in all groups at the Jebsen & Jessen Family Enterprise. As underlined by Hans Michael Jebsen: "The carbon neutrality benchmark… is a matter of philosophy."	*Enabling governance*: The *latitude* given to Jebsen & Jessen Hamburg enabled the creation of the joint venture with Ketelsen Enterprise to distribute garnet in Europe. The newly established joint venture was named GMA Garnet (Europe) GmbH and was fully embedded in Jebsen & Jessen Hamburg's offices. The establishment and development of GIRL, a predecessor of GMA Garnet, exemplified the governance of Jebsen & Jessen Family Enterprise: (1) two family principal shareholders (Hans Michael Jebsen and Heinrich Jessen) equally shared control of the company; (2) two non-family shareholders (Torsten Ketelsen and Wolfhart Putzier) shared the minority interest, remained operationally involved and enjoyed a great deal of latitude to develop the business; (3) the shareholders were bound by a very lean, standard shareholder agreement, which set, among other things, the maximum dividend level, reflecting the low dividend appetite of the shareholders. The full integration of GIRL into the Jebsen & Jessen Family Enterprise's portfolio had grown naturally, as a result of the long partnership and common values, when Torsten Ketelsen executed his almost full ownership exit. *Purpose-driven leadership*:GMA Garnet offered a superior value proposition: first, supreme efficiency of garnet; and second, environmental safety. "Initially, our customers were too busy sandblasting to even try our product. But when they tried it, they would often say, "Why didn't you come to me 10 years ago?" Torsten Ketelsen showed extreme determination to first, establish a market for garnet; second, to position it as a technical product; and third, to step into garnet recycling, even though the customers did not see the immediate value: "They said I was crazy to promote recycling because we would sell less virgin garnet," but garnet, thanks to its hardness and toughness, could be recycled several times.

Jebsen & Jessen Family Enterprise	GMA Garnet
Sustainability strategy (the *what*)	
Jebsen & Jessen's *inward-looking sustainability strategy* included many EHS measures (e.g., implementing EHS protocols; ISO 14001 and OHSAS 18001 certifications). It drove investment and de-investment decisions (e.g., entering a new business of molded pulp packaging made of recycled paper; exiting a tropical wood furniture business; ceasing supplying tributyltin oxide) and the decision to achieve full carbon neutrality by its two main business entities: Jebsen & Jessen (SEA) and Jebsen & Co. in 2011 and 2013, respectively. Additionally, Jebsen & Jessen (SEA) was the first industrial company in South-East Asia to employ a full-time carbon neutrality executive and invest in solar panel solutions to generate power at one of its manufacturing facilities in Singapore. The *outward-looking sustainability strategy* included supply chain transparency and social auditing at Triton Textile (part of Jebsen & Jessen Hamburg), sustainability reporting of Jebsen & Co. along five "bottom lines": financial, business partnership, staff well-being, philanthropy and environmental conservation, as well as investing in green projects in Asia such as delivering to the Hong Kong government the first high-voltage biogas-fueled combination heat and power generator.	*Circular business model at GMA Garnet*: The full vertical integration of GMA Garnet enabled pioneering the concept of sustainability along the whole value chain, from mining (exceptional mining, waste and land management standards), through processing (using only water to clean the extractions and separate minerals from non-minerals) up to reprocessing (garnet recycling). The environmental and social footprint of garnet was much lower compared to other products. First, the amount of extracted garnet was reduced; what otherwise would be considered an industrial waste was turned into a new product and the life span of this non-renewable natural resource was maximized. Second, garnet did not cause any lung diseases such as traditional sand abrasives and was a much cleaner solution as it did not pollute. With its strong materiality, GMA Garnet contributes to the following United Nations' Sustainable Development Goals: Goal 9: Build resilient infrastructure, promote inclusive and sustainable industrialization and foster innovation; Goal 12: Ensure sustainable consumption and production patterns; and Goal 15: Protect, restore and promote sustainable use of terrestrial eco-systems, sustainably manage forests, combat desertification and halt and reverse land degradation and halt biodiversity loss. GMA Garnet's *sustainability strategy* spurred similar efforts *across other operations*: "Our biggest industrial ecology story is at the ilmenite mine in South Africa where Jebsen & Jessen Family Enterprise has mining rights" (Heinrich Jessen), and where it converted the waste resulting from ilmenite extraction into a finished product by adding one more production step and extracting garnet from what would be considered industrial waste.

11. Tahbilk: A fifth-generation Australian family wine business's journey to sustainability

Michael Browne, Chris Graves and Francesco Barbera

INTRODUCTION

Tahbilk, a fifth-generation family business, is regarded as one of Australia's "greenest" wine businesses.[1] Tahbilk is proud of its sustainability credentials, including the carboNZero[2] accreditation featured in its marketing materials. These credentials have been recognized by the Royal Agricultural Society of New South Wales who awarded the company a President's Medal for outstanding contributions to the Australian environment using the triple-bottom-line (TBL)[3] approach. In addition, the Banksia Foundation,[4] a not-for-profit organization known for its sustainability awards, nominated Tahbilk as a finalist in its 2015 awards for the Small to Medium Business Sustainability Leadership Award.

While the Australian wine industry is regarded as a leader in sustainability today,[5] this has not always been the case. In the past, this industry received significant criticism for its lack of attention to environmental issues, such as an excessive reliance on chemicals, poor land maintenance practices, the overuse of water that is a scarce resource in Australia and its substantial carbon footprint.[6] Tahbilk could once have been painted with this brush. However, the commitment of the Purbrick family, owners of the Tahbilk Estate and business for nearly 100 years, to the environment and sustainability over the last 25 years have seen it recognized for its leadership in sustainability in the Australian wine industry. From humble beginnings, fourth-generation family member and chief executive officer (CEO) Alister Purbrick commenced Tahbilk's journey to sustainability in 1995 with the introduction of the "wetlands project" because he saw it as the "right thing to do." With his leadership and fifth-generation family member Hayley Purbrick's championing of Tahbilk's Environment Plan and Sustainable Business Model (Figure

11.1), Tahbilk provides insights as to what it takes for a family business to be a champion in sustainability.

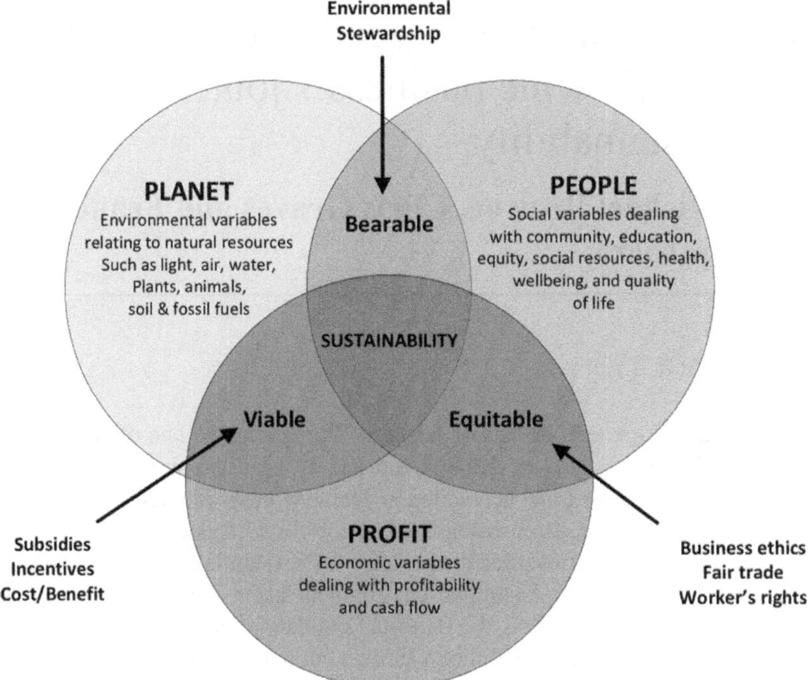

Source: Tahbilk (2019). *Tahbilk Environment Plan 2017–2010.*

Figure 11.1 Tahbilk Sustainable Business Model

The Tahbilk Sustainable Business Model encapsulates *Tahbilk's approach incorporating the concept of TBL where environmental initiatives must be both bearable on the people it affects and viable on the business.*

As such Tahbilk embraces the view of sustainability espoused by Australian Grape and Wine Inc.,[7] that while a business must be profitable enough to take advantage of new opportunities, it must also protect and enhance the image of wine through its commitment to the environment and social responsibilities.[8]

Tahbilk's Sustainable Business Model brings together the family's values and its understanding of what it means to operate a significant business and be the custodian of a unique piece of land. This is set out on the first page of the Tahbilk Environment Plan:[9]

> It was recognised by previous generations of the Purbrick family that we are ultimately farmers whose produce is affected by a changing climate. We need to do our part to ensure that we are assisting to maintain a moderate growing climate for our product, to ensure its longevity and quality continues. As custodians of the Estate, we have an environmental responsibility to leave a sustainable legacy for those family members to come. (Hayley Purbrick, fifth-generation family member)

The Purbrick family understands that for Tahbilk to avoid adverse impact on future generations, sustainability must be part of every aspect of the farm and business. Thus, its belief is well aligned with the sustainability objectives in production, processing and packaging set by the International Organisation of Vine and Wine. These include efforts towards the conservation of water, energy and biodiversity, as well as the management of waste and human talent.[10] These objectives encourage strong performance on social, environmental as well as economic dimensions.[11] Tahbilk has been successful in each of these dimensions while growing to become one of Australia's largest wine companies, ranked 21st by production volume, 16th by export volume and 11th by dollar turnover.[12]

THE THREE KEY FACTORS IN TAHBILK'S SUCCESSFUL APPROACH

Three key factors have enabled Tahbilk to be successful in its pursuit of environmental sustainability. The first is the uniqueness of the land on which the business operates. The second is the drive of the Purbrick family, whose commitment and pursuit of family values has enabled the business to grow and prosper over five generations. The third factor is society's changing attitude to the environment.

The Land

The land Tahbilk operates from is referred to by the family as the Tahbilk Estate. It is a 1,200 hectare property that has 11 kilometers of frontage to the Goulburn River. The property contains wetlands spanning 8 kilometers that create a meso-climate ("climatic variability within a wine-growing region"[13]) within the Nagambie Lakes region resulting in an environment that is significantly "cooler than anywhere else in the Goulburn Valley."[14] The Tahbilk Estate is one of only six locations in the world and the only region in Australia where the meso-climate is influenced to this extent by an inland water mass. In addition to the specific climatic conditions, the soil on the Tahbilk Estate has a "very high Ferric-oxide content,"[15] which has a positive effect on grape quality and adds a distinctive regional character to the wines. This soil type is replicated in only one other region in Victoria.[16]

While the Tahbilk story started in 1860, 65 years before the Purbrick family purchased the estate and business, fifth-generation member Hayley Purbrick notes that the significance of the property can be traced back in history to the indigenous clan of Daung-wurrung, the first peoples[17] who referred to the property as "Tabilk" – a place with many waterholes.[18] Hayley Purbrick also notes that European settlers referred to the land as being "pristine" and having "an abundance of the natural environment."

Whether it is the Daung-warrung clans, the early settlers, the previous owners of the property or the current owners, the Tahbilk Estate has always been regarded as special. The Purbrick family owners have embraced the opportunity that the land provides and believe that to maintain it, they must keep "giving back to the environment."

Whether they are directly or indirectly involved, all family members embrace the unique nature of the property, understanding that the unique characteristics associated with the property positively impact on the quality of the wines and offer a significant point of difference in a crowded wine market.

The family's commitment to sustainability could not be more evident than in the Tahbilk Environment Plan (discussed below) and its Sustainable Business Model (Figure 11.1). Both acknowledge the uniqueness of the land and the impact that the family as farmers can have on it. They were each developed from the understanding that as custodians, the Purbrick family must adopt policies that preserve and nurture the land now and into the future, because to do otherwise would be both commercially and environmentally irresponsible and unsustainable.

The Purbrick Family

To understand how the Purbricks reached their current position as leaders in environmental and sustainability practice some understanding of the history (Figures 11.2 and 11.3) of the family and its association with Tahbilk is necessary, as is its approach to governance, the importance of family values and the contribution of future generations.

History of Tahbilk

While the Tahbilk story commenced in 1860, it was 65 years later that the Purbrick family's association with Tahbilk commenced. Reginald Purbrick, a wealthy Australian who lived in England,[19] purchased the Tahbilk Estate in 1925. It was dilapidated, a far cry from its current pristine state. Reginald, a competitive, risk-taking entrepreneur,[20] saw it as an investment opportunity fully expecting to sub-divide the land into smaller dairy farms for a profitable sale. He only visited the property once.

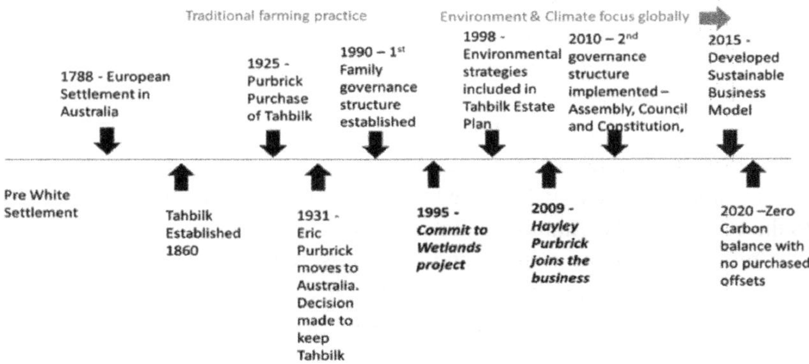

Figure 11.2 Timeline of significant events

Figure 11.3 Abridged Purbrick family tree

Nearly 100 years on, a period that included the industry corporatization of the 1980s, when many of Australia's family wine businesses were swallowed up,[21] the Tahbilk Estate and business remain in the Purbrick family's hands. That it does is attributable to the commitment of the family to the business, which is no more evident than in Reginald's son, Eric. It was Eric who convinced his father that the property should not be sub-divided as it could be rehabilitated. His father agreed on the condition that Eric move to Australia from the United Kingdom (UK) permanently to run the property, which Eric did in 1931 in the midst of the Great Depression. Although he knew little about farming and wine making, he turned the business around and was fundamental to the survival of the Tahbilk Estate. It was Eric's hard work and perseverance that re-established the winery and Tahbilk's reputation.[22] Mark Purbrick, Eric's grandson and the current chair of Tahbilk, is sure that the business would not have survived the Great Depression without his grandfather's commitment and tenacity.

Although today Tahbilk is known as a winery for the majority of Tahbilk's history, excluding a golden period during the 1870s and 1880s when Tahbilk became the third or fourth largest winery in the colony, wine has played second fiddle to broad acre farming.

As a farming property, the land was worked hard, with little regard for environmental and sustainability practices. Native vegetation was cleared from large parcels of land on the estate and in the post-Second World War period farming techniques, including those employed on the Tahbilk Estate, became more sophisticated with an emphasis on maximizing crop yields through the application of fertilizers and chemicals. However, during the 1990s, there was a growing appreciation of the importance of the environment that permeated agriculture and society generally. As Hayley Purbrick notes, farmers became acutely aware of the importance of the environment and sustainability in their agricultural activity, and Tahbilk altered their farming practices accordingly.

There was also a desire by Alister Purbrick for their "estate grown operation" to pursue an ambitious wine-based growth strategy which required decisions about the traditional Tahbilk business as well as the future direction of the business.

In 1990, the family, consisted of second-generation Eric, third-generation John and the fourth generation, addressed how to balance its desire to grow, preserve the reputation of its estate and maintain family ownership and control. It decided to maintain the small boutique family winery reputation of Tahbilk and establish a broader Tahbilk Group (Figure 11.4) through which the family entered into a series of joint ventures. Those joint ventures related to the vineyards, wineries, contract wine making, packaging and brand creation. The Tahbilk Group now consists of 13 operating entities, 11 of which are wholly owned by the Purbrick family.

Figure 11.4 The Tahbilk Group: major joint venture entities

The decision by the family to create the Tahbilk Group enabled the family to pursue an aggressive growth strategy, where business decisions were more attuned to objectives of growth and profitability, while also keeping the traditional "priceless" family business and the land upon which it operated in its revered position. Alister Purbrick notes that the Tahbilk brand remains the "sacrosanct jewel in the family crown, even though from a turnover perspective, [it] probably only makes up about 15 to 20% of the Group."

The role of family governance

To oversee the duality of maintaining the legacy of Tahbilk and pursuing ambitious growth, the Tahbilk Group is overseen by an advisory committee made up of family and non-family members, who effectively run the operations of the whole business. However, from a governance viewpoint, the Tahbilk board of directors that consists of Mark Purbrick as chair, Alister Purbrick as CEO and Deborah George (nee Purbrick) is ultimately in control. An overview of the organizational structure is set out in Figure 11.5.

Mark Purbrick reflects on the strength of the governance focus, saying that he and his brother are "best mates," but that at the board of directors and advisory committee meetings it is clear that "there is a difference between family and business." He sees the ability of family members to separate their roles as family members and business leaders as a strength of the Tahbilk business.

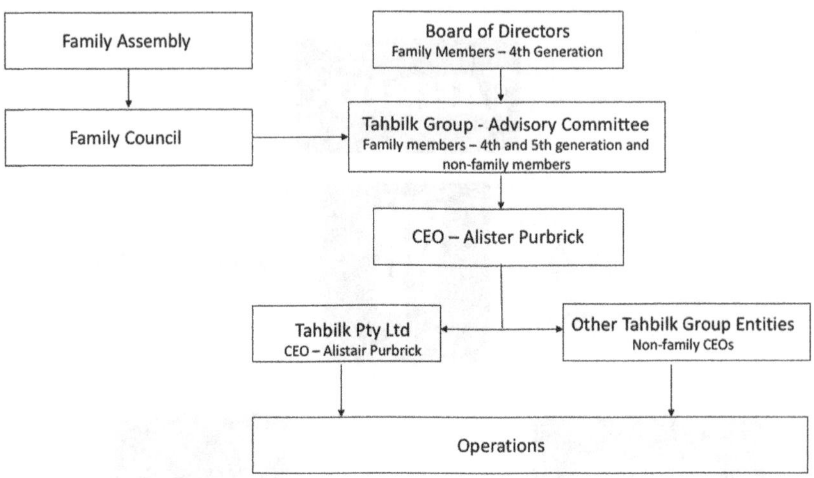

Figure 11.5 Tahbilk Group structure

The governance approach was ratified through a series of family meetings in the 1990s (the family's first governance structure) and then confirmed by resolutions of the Family Council and Family Assembly and enshrined in the Family Constitution in 2010 (the family's second governance structure).

The formalizing of the Family Council, Family Assembly and establishment of the Family Constitution, in the words of Alister Purbrick:

> helped dramatically increase the knowledge of particularly the "next gens," about not only Tahbilk, but the Group as well, and has given them a forum to be able to have lots of input.

The Family Assembly provides members with an opportunity to meet annually to receive information about the Tahbilk business, raise issues and ask questions as well as to vote on the make-up of the Family Council. All family members are eligible to attend and vote, with adults having a full vote and those aged between 14 and 18 having a half vote.

The family has made it clear through resolutions at the Family Assembly and Family Council that both Tahbilk Pty Ltd and the Tahbilk Estate are to be preserved as they are where family history resides. Those resolutions are supported by a legal trust structure which houses Tahbilk Pty Ltd and the Tahbilk Estate. First and foremost, this means that ownership of these prized assets will remain with the Purbrick family. However, securing the land in family hands requires more than the legal steps taken of placing it into a trust. In Victoria, Australia, there is a limit on the life of a trust with the result that the assets within the trust, including all shares in Tahbilk Pty Ltd, the owner of the estate, will vest in the beneficiaries in the middle of this century. The family has investigated options for seeking to formalize ownership beyond this date, however, legal and taxation rules make this practically impossible. As a consequence, the family has also made a commitment within the Family Constitution to hold land in perpetuity. This commitment to being custodians of the land through the Family Constitution has added significance when considered alongside the commitment by the family to Tahbilk's environmental and sustainability initiatives.

Embedding the family's values

The family's values, governance and commitment to the environment and sustainability have also come to the fore, in a recent proposal by the fifth generation, that funds earmarked for a dividend be directed towards sustainability rather than distributed to the family. The proposal was raised in a family forum and then subsequently ratified by the company.

The proposal is consistent with the family's *"no greed"* philosophy that has permeated the business culture.

There is no desire by any member of the family to put financial pressure on the firm; preferring financial resources to be devoted to long-term initiatives rather than a desire for a short-term return on investment. As Mark Purbrick says of the family values:

> I think one that jumps out is that as a family, it's never been about personal gain or greed, and I think if you look at the environmental side, you know, generally people who abuse the environment, do it for personal gain and greed.

The Purbrick family's willingness to forgo a dividend in favor of what they consider to be a higher purpose is one of many examples of the significance of the family's values as they pursue their sustainability journey. Another is Alister Purbrick's recounting of how the formal journey to sustainability commenced with the regeneration of a portion of the wetlands on the estate in 1995:

> In 1995 we decided that we would return about 350 acres, which we now call the Wetlands and Wildlife Reserve, to its former pristine self.

The land was not high-performing farming country so while the motive was altruistic, it was believed to be the decent thing to do. As the wetlands project progressed, it became evident that there could be a commercial benefit to the decision. The establishment of the wetlands enabled the business to take advantage of the growing interest in the environment and eco-tourism. As Alister noted, it did not "cost us a lot." Further, he reflected:

> We've been aided as a family with our ambitions… because [the environment has] become so topical globally.

The decision to open up the wetlands and with it embrace elements of the growing trend to sustainability and eco-tourism enabled Tahbilk to differentiate itself from the plethora of other wineries and cellar doors in Australia. It quickly discovered that the wetlands project offered an economic benefit that led to the opening of the Wetlands Café in 2005, offering wetland boat tours/cruises and the promotion of eco-trail walks. So, from what was initially driven from a value-based altruistic sentiment centered on the desire to return some of the estate to its former pristine self, Tahbilk also reaped a financial benefit.

The family has and continues to get an economic benefit from these environmental and sustainability initiatives. However, the family's focus of giving even more of the land back to wetlands regeneration and land revegetation as part of its commitment to sustainability is also consistent with the family's acknowledgment that it has a custodial role. As Mark Purbrick says:

> we are caretakers of the business… [we have] no intention of selling while we are walking on this earth… The result is, it doesn't matter how much the business is worth because it's going to be there for the future generations.

It is a view consistent with the family's values. Alister Purbrick says the backbone of the business is the family values of "integrity," "transparency," "ethics," "morality," and "honesty," making the point that these are the obvious ones. He believes that the business's ability to demonstrate that it lives these values *is* "what attracts people [to Tahbilk]." They are inculcated in the way Tahbilk does business.

The family and business have a long-term commitment to the community and the industry in which they belong. Alister says:

> My family over the generations has been very much of a mind to give back to our industry or community.

The family and business take pride in their role as a significant local contributor to the community. It is the largest employer in the region. Tahbilk is a founding member of "Take-2," a sustainability initiative of the Victorian government.

The next generation champion of sustainability

The final element in a discussion about the Purbrick family's commitment to the environment and sustainability is the contribution of the next generation. In the words of Alister, fifth-generation family member, Hayley Purbrick, joining the business saw Tahbilk "turbocharge" its commitment to the environment and sustainability.

Hayley Purbrick says:

> my purpose is wrapped up in environmental sustainability… I've always loved nature and the countryside from a young age. I just love trees, animals and open spaces. I grew a love of gardening through working in the garden at Tahbilk and pondered viticulture on leaving school but landed in landscape architecture [moving] into agriculture at the end of my first year and loved the resource management subjects. Back then, environmental sustainability was not its own thing.

On graduating from university, Hayley joined global accounting and consulting firm Ernst and Young and had ambitions to be an early member of its environmental consulting arm. A year or so later she says:

> I decided to leave and join Tahbilk. We had started tree planting and works on the wetlands when I started at Tahbilk, so I think I just grabbed the chance to drive it because I love nature! I feel this deep connection to the Tahbilk landscape, which is hard to describe.

Hayley's leadership has turbo-charged Tahbilk on its sustainability journey, one she considers they are about 70 percent along from a business culture perspective. Hayley sees herself as the de facto role model and responsible for leading the cultural change. She is responsible for implementation of the Tahbilk Environment Plan that involves detailed emissions minimization programs, the expanded revegetation and biodiversity programs, the LEAN Thinking program and facilitation of Tahbilk's carboNZero accreditation, all of which is fundamental to Tahbilk's sustainability commitment and builds upon the early foray of her father into the wetlands project in 1995. Each of these programs is discussed further below.

Society's changing attitude to the environment

The last of the three factors in Tahbilk and the Purbrick family's journey to sustainability is the growing awareness of the importance of the environment and sustainability in Australia. The family's commitment to first open up the wetlands coincided with an increasing awareness of the importance of the environment. Its subsequent decision to embrace the full thrust of the carbon reduction strategy shortly after Hayley Purbrick joined the business in 2009 coincided with a time when it appeared that a carbon pricing mechanism would be introduced in Australia. For political reasons, Australia has not adopted a formal carbon pricing mechanism. However, this did not diminish the focus of businesses such as Tahbilk in their focus on environment and sustainability practices. Within Australia, various incentives are available to businesses focused on sustainability. Tahbilk has and continues to take advantage of various grants and programs targeted to enhance its ongoing environment and sustainability program.

Tahbilk has on occasion been ahead of its key stakeholder groups in its sustainability journey. Early on, Tahbilk identified that a significant segment of its customer base was not as far along the sustainability curve as the company was. At that point, Hayley Purbrick instituted a survey of key stakeholders to ensure that as Tahbilk embarked upon its sustainability and environment initiatives, it was doing so in step with its stakeholders' expectations. There was no desire to alienate any of its customer base, as to do so would impinge on the viability element of the Sustainable Business Model.

Regular surveying of its key stakeholders has enabled Tahbilk to tailor its corporate social responsibility (CSR) approach and messaging to ensure they are all part of the firm's CSR journey.

Outcomes include the development of a sustainability blog to communicate to its various customer channels and the use of packaging and marketing materials which meet or exceed customer expectations and resonate with new markets including younger age groups and Scandinavia.

THE ENVIRONMENT PLAN: TAHBILK'S PATHWAY TO SUSTAINABILITY

Family leaders are all aware that while they have absolute control over the business, they understand that they operate within a professional governance system that necessitates formality and complete alignment throughout the business to its sustainability strategy. The governance structure led Tahbilk to develop an Environment Plan and Sustainable Business Model that apply the principles of the TBL. Tahbilk's commitment to the TBL has just one modification, the addition of quality:

> There are the four things that underpin everything we do. It's around people, community, the environment, over-delivering on quality and obviously sustainable financial results. (Alister Purbrick, fourth-generation family member)

The plan sets out a pathway for protecting and investing in activities that will enhance the Purbrick family and Tahbilk's reputation as leaders in sustainable practice. It is focused and comprehensive and is key to the successful operation of the Sustainable Business Model. It is inclusive, having the buy-in and support of the family, the employees and the community. Tahbilk understands that it needs to bring all its stakeholders along its CSR journey.

The Plan is a function of both the external and internal drivers providing a documented framework and a reference point for decision making and accountability for now and into the future. The first steps in the establishment of a standalone plan occurred with the inclusion of environmental strategies in the overall Tahbilk Estate Plan in 1998, and it became a standalone document in 2013. The Sustainable Business Model was incorporated into the Environment Plan in 2015.

The Environment Plan's stated purpose is to outline "the pathway for Tahbilk to achieve its goal of protecting and investing in activities which minimize human impact and deliver positive environmental outcomes within the sustainable business framework." It sets an overall strategy, objectives, the steps to be taken and reports against the objectives using financial and quantifiable energy savings as a meaningful attempt to quantify its performance towards its goal of zero carbon emissions without the need to purchase carbon offsets by 2020. Zero carbon emissions is an objective the business considers to be fundamental in meeting its sustainability commitment of "leaving a sustainable legacy for [future] family members" and the broader community.

The Plan is championed by Hayley Purbrick, whose role as environment, business improvement and digital manager sees her as the main driver of the cultural change and alignment that is necessary for the successful implementation of the Environment Plan. Her activities are conducted under the watchful eye of CEO, Alister Purbrick, and approved by both the Tahbilk advisory committee and board of directors. The following examples from the Environment Plan demonstrate how Tahbilk is working towards meeting its objective of a sustainable business model.

Carbon Accreditation

Tahbilk undertakes regular carbon audits to provide independent verification of its performance and program to confirm its net zero balance for carbon emissions. Tahbilk has certification of its status via Enviro-mark Solutions and under the carboNZero accreditation. Hayley Purbrick says Tahbilk takes pride in being:

> the first and only winery in Australia to be certified carboNZero at the organisation and product level [and] one of only eight wineries in the world to have achieved full certification.

She goes on to reinforce Tahbilk's environmental credentials and commitment to sustainability within the wine industry, saying that this program is important because it shows that Tahbilk:

> meets and exceeds international standards and best practice; the accreditation is recognised in over 60 countries, and it is the only body which accredits businesses under the PAS2050 standards outside of the UK.

It is vital to the business that it achieves these outcomes while at the same time meeting the overall objectives of the Sustainable Business Model for which Tahbilk requires that it is bearable. That is, it delivers benefits to the people (staff and the community) and the planet while at the same time giving Tahbilk a significant advantage in the highly competitive global wine market.

LEAN

LEAN is an internal program which includes training and education initiatives within the business to encourage the achievement of business sustainability through the adoption of a cost-benefit approach that reduces "waste" and minimizes Tahbilk's carbon footprint. The LEAN program is incorporated into manager key performance indicators to maintain focus beyond the training program. A regular newsletter showcases sustainability initiatives, and there is an internal awards program to recognize a commitment to lean values and achievements within the business. A leadership group incorporating all team leaders oversees and monitors the ongoing commitment to, and achievement of the environmental and sustainability objectives that underpin the LEAN initiative. One example of Tahbilk's waste reduction initiatives is its projects aimed at reducing packaging materials brought onsite by suppliers and the composting of grape and winery waste as well as food waste from the café. Tahbilk is also undertaking projects to return wastewater to the environment.

To emphasize the bearability and viability elements of the Sustainable Business Model as it impacts upon the commitment to reduce waste, Hayley Purbrick comments:

> we wouldn't just do something that's environmentally conscious, for example "No waste is to come onto the property, full stop," because that wouldn't be a bearable expectation on our employees or the business... It's being mindful that the environment is not the only part of the picture, you're also working with people, and so you can't just make a change for the sake of one element of the three-circle approach, you need to consider all elements before you go ahead and do something.
>
> It doesn't mean that, say, we can't have a target to have no waste coming onto the property, but it just means it doesn't happen overnight. It might be a five-year target and the way we get there is, we work with everybody in the business to achieve that target, rather than just making the change purely from an environmental perspective

> and not considering the elements of the business that it might impact. Which also [goes to] the viability of the business. If we stopped all waste coming onto the property overnight, we would also lose quite a lot of money, and we'd have no suppliers.

Revegetation

Tahbilk has undertaken a Carbon and Biodiversity Assessment to assess the capacity that exists for carbon sequestration through revegetation of the site. Since the initial assessment in 2012, the revegetation program has incorporated new plantings on existing plots, and the addition of further plots, all of which are having a positive impact on carbon sequestration. Tahbilk is also working with the Goulburn Indigenous Seedbank to establish seed production sites for the purpose of ensuring that there is a continued supply of native plant species that were previously at risk. This program is "directly influencing the health of native insects, birds, amphibians, fish, reptiles and mammals that rely on healthy, diverse and functioning ecosystems to survive." The revegetation plan continues, and Tahbilk is exploring ways to promote its success.

Biodiversity

From the time of its wetlands project, Tahbilk has taken steps to ensure its natural environment is healthy and biodiverse. Tahbilk's Environment Plan refers to the positive benefit of undertaking initiatives that include the capacity of the local environment to recover from unpredictable weather events, contribute to climate stability, pollution breakdown and absorption, nutrient storage and recycling. Tahbilk's contribution to improved biodiversity includes programs using its billabongs to support rare and endangered species, using debris from a local road construction program to re-snag areas of the Goulburn River that abut the estate to slow erosion and the provision of a secure environment for local amphibians and fish. Tahbilk has installed spillways on the estate to allow a more efficient passage for fish between its billabongs and the Goulburn River. Tahbilk, in conjunction with the local catchment authority, has conducted a trial release of the threatened Southern Pygmy Perch in the lagoons and billabongs on the estate in the hope of establishing a breeding program for this threatened species. If successful it will add to the food chain and provide a food source for larger fish including the Murray cod, the Goulburn perch and local birds. Tahbilk has also acted to understand and mitigate the potential impact of its own business on the local environment. It has incorporated acoustic monitoring of areas around the wetlands, established buffers between its vines and the natural waterways and sewn thick grasses, straw and reeds at the outlets to trap solid waste.

The Environment Plan also includes a commitment to continue the development of partnerships with local indigenous communities, the University of Melbourne and other relevant industry groups to enhance Tahbilk's work in the area of biodiversity.

Energy

The business has adopted strategies to reduce emissions wherever possible. The goal of having a zero carbon balance without the requirement to purchase carbon offsets has seen the business incorporating more extensive use of solar power as well as implementing technology solutions to reduce energy consumption.

In addition to the areas highlighted from the Environment Plan, the Plan incorporates measures to monitor and reduce chemicals, fertilizer and fuel. Tahbilk's latest Environment Plan states:

> Since 2014 Tahbilk has implemented a range of projects in the area of revegetation, water, waste, energy and continuous improvement [that has led to a reduction of more than 25 percent in Tahbilk's carbon dioxide emissions] notwithstanding the organisation has increased production while keeping overhead costs low and "doing good" for the natural environment.

The result is that Tahbilk pursues the creation of value while being mindful that each element of the TBL must work together for the family to create and capture the value that it desires:

> To me [Hayley Purbrick], the planet component is more around environmental sustainability, but it's also got to be bearable. If we have an environmental outcome, it has to be bearable on our people. We can't be doing it at the sake of all else; it's also got to have a profitable outcome.
>
> It's about looking after your people but also making sure that you're fair and equitable in all that you do in your business.
>
> At the core of our business, we're not about pushing people to the nth degree, just to get a profit.

The result, Hayley Purbrick says, is that "you can't just make a change for the sake of one element of the three-circle approach, you need to consider all elements before you go ahead and do something."

THE FUTURE

Family leaders understand that they have an ongoing responsibility, and it is one that is not without its challenges. Hayley Purbrick believes that the family, board and employees are only about three-quarters of the way along the journey of embedding the cultural change necessary to ensure Tahbilk meets its objective of operating a Sustainable Business Model.

Hayley feels that the business will have met its objectives in achieving its Sustainable Business Model when she is no longer required to be the driver of environmental accountability within the business. After all, as Hayley Purbrick says, "isn't that what we all desire to ensure our legacy is lasting?" Hayley Purbrick encapsulates the present and future expectations for Tahbilk by saying:

> I think there's a great sense of pride in what Tahbilk is achieving. I also think it comes back to the family business's social responsibility that's very strong across all generations… It is [pride in being] part of something that is doing good for other people and for the environment, for the community… [It is] my understanding from my cousins that the reason why they love Tahbilk and love being associated and attached to Tahbilk is that it feeds into their values and it gives them a sense of contribution to the community.

ACADEMIC AND PRACTICE INSIGHTS FROM THE TAHBILK CASE STUDY

Tahbilk has responded to society's demand for businesses to adopt "more socially responsible business models."[23] By adopting the Sustainable Business Model (Figure 11.1) that flowed from ad hoc steps in the 1990s when the family reclaimed unproductive farmlands turning them into wetlands, the business is driven by the belief that "sustainability involves everything you do on a farm."[24] Tahbilk's progression along the CSR path has enabled it to differentiate itself in the market, enhance its reputation and over the long run generate a suitable financial return.[25]

The Tahbilk case study enables us to see how the Purbrick family, the multi-generational family owners of one of Australia's largest wine businesses, has adopted proactive environmental and sustainability strategies. Those strategies have manifested themselves in a business model focused on the creation and capture of value that aligns with the TBL approach to sustainability. The TBL concept has an accounting element that seeks to quantify outcomes.[26] It offers a performance measure for sustainability in a social, ethical and environmental context.[27] For Tahbilk, the quantification of results is more than financial; it also seeks non-financial outcomes that deliver benefits to both people and the planet.

Table 11.1 Corporate social responsibility (CSR) values mapped to socioeconomic wealth (SEW)

CSR values	SEW dimensions and attributes
Family involvement	SEW dimension of family control
Commitment	SEW dimensions of emotional connection and binding social ties
Identification	SEW dimensions of identity and binding social ties
Collectivism	Extended view of SEW
Perpetuation	SEW dimension of renewal of family bonds
Obligation	SEW dimension of emotional connection
Altruism	Extended view of SEW

Sources: CSR: Marques, P., Presas, P., & Simon, A. (2014). "The heterogeneity of family firms in CSR engagement: The role of values." *Family Business Review*, 27(3): 206–27; SEW: Berrone, P., Cruz, C., & Gomez-Mejia, L. R. (2012). "Socioemotional wealth in family firms theoretical dimensions, assessment approaches, and agenda for future research." *Family Business Review*, 25(3): 258–79 and Miller, D., & Breton-Miller, L. (2014). "Deconstructing socioemotional wealth." *Entrepreneurship Theory and Practice*, 38(4): 713–20.

The Purbrick family's approach to the Tahbilk wine business could be referred to as a "devoted" winery[28] with its approach to sustainability evidenced by its investment in its employees (e.g., the LEAN program), customers (e.g., customer surveys) and the community (e.g., biodiversity programs and sustainability blog). There is congruence between the corporate, management and family vision in the pursuit of its environmental and sustainability objectives. The family's desire to produce a TBL with a focus on the delivery of both financial (profit) and non-financial outcomes (people and planet) aligns with the concept of socioemotional wealth (SEW),[29] that is the affective utility that accrues to a family from decisions and actions of the business in the pursuit of non-financial objectives.

Academic Insights

The Tahbilk case study provides an opportunity to demonstrate how family values can foster a family's commitment to pursue CSR initiatives in a sustainability context within the business and how the pursuit of those initiatives aligns with the desire to preserve and enhance the SEW.

Table 11.1 maps the CSR values embodied in the CSR initiatives taken by Tahbilk against the SEW dimension (FIBER[30]) and attributes (restricted and extended[31]). In doing so, it provides a way to consider SEW as something broader than solely the collective affective utility derived from the CSR initiatives taken by the Purbrick family in the operation of Tahbilk.

When mapping CSR against SEW, we utilize FIBER, a term which has become accepted in the family business literature to signify the five dimensions of SEW that reflect the drivers for the actions a family takes to accrue affective utility within the family business. We also utilize the restricted or extended view of SEW. The restricted view of SEW is where the affective utility accrues to the immediate family. In contrast, in an extended view of SEW, the affective utility accrued extends beyond immediate family to a broader group that includes the extended family and stakeholders.

In the discussion that follows, we highlight how the CSR values relate to the dimensions of SEW, and how CSR values apply to only the extended view of SEW.

Family involvement: the SEW dimension of family control

We understand that to be a family business, family involvement is central.[32] For businesses committed to CSR, "family involvement" manifests itself through "family characteristics, values and culture" and "managers' personal characteristics,"[33] which via the family's control of the business exert influence over the direction of the business.

The Purbrick family has its "footprint" all over this business. The family influences the strategic direction of Tahbilk through its involvement in own-

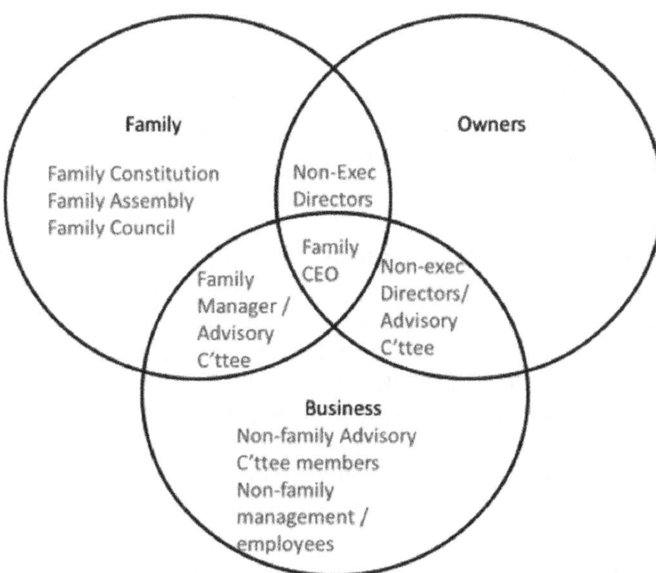

Figure 11.6 The Tahbilk business mapped against the three-circle model

ership, business and family sub-systems of the three-circle family business model[34] (see Figure 11.6). Through its controlling influence, the family is able to ensure that its shared values are reflected in the way it does business and has been central to the successful implementation of the Tahbilk Environment Plan and the Sustainable Business Model.

Family commitment: the SEW dimensions of emotional connection and binding social ties

The family is committed to keeping the business in family hands for the long term. The business and the land are sacrosanct, and the family sees itself as the custodian. There is no plan to build the capital worth of the business for resale; as Mark Purbrick says, the financial value is not relevant because there is no intention to sell it. That does not mean the family owners are not interested in the financial performance of the business or in seeing it grow. It does mean, however, that by not being focused on short-term returns or setting the business for sale that the Purbrick family can take a long-term view.

There are no external demands on the business, no desire to build the asset for imminent sale or demand for excessive dividends by "greedy" family members. We know that the adoption of long-term strategies is a characteristic of family business.[35] It is the Purbrick family's willingness to set and implement its environmental and sustainability strategies through the Environment Plan, adoption of the Sustainable Business Model and its understanding of its role as custodian that has enabled the building and maintaining of patient capital within the business,[36] and enhanced its stock of SEW within the business.[37] That stock of SEW can be observed in family members' pride in being associated with the business, their emotional commitment to the business and the sense of contribution that binds them to the community and industry to which they belong.

Family identity: the SEW dimensions of identity and binding social ties

We understand that one of the unique characteristics of a family business is that the family's own identity is inextricably linked to the business.[38] And, that a sense of identity with the family business is a characteristic common to those family businesses that pursue CSR initiatives.[39]

The Purbrick family has a passion for its employees, customers, visitors, "the land, foundations and history upon which it is built."[40] In this, it seems the current custodians of Tahbilk are no different from earlier generations for whom Tahbilk "was the only thing"; it is "part of our family fabric."[41] For Tahbilk, the evidence is clear. From the moment that Eric Purbrick convinced his father, Reginald Purbrick, not to sell the Tahbilk land, the Purbrick family's identity and that of Tahbilk have been inextricably linked. The link remains today, such that family members, whether directly involved in the business or not, enjoy the strong association of the family name with the business. That is the family derives SEW from being strongly identified with the business.[42]

Adoption of sustainability initiatives in the form of the Sustainable Business Model is consistent with the family wanting to be favorably linked to a business operating in a manner that minimizes the impact on the environment and committed to delivering a sustainable legacy for future generations and the community at large.

That the family identifies with the business may also be a reason for the family adopting strategies orientated toward Tahbilk's stakeholders.[43] This is consistent with a key dimension of SEW – binding social ties.[44] Through the generations, the Purbrick family, via its involvement with the Tahbilk business, has developed a strong sense of community as a significant regional employer, and as committed industry and community representatives.

Each has been a significant element in the family operating its business sustainably. The family is committed to its employees, evidenced by both the requirement that strategies and initiatives adopted within the business are bearable on the workforce and align with the objectives of the LEAN program. The family has built strong relationships with industry groups whose focus is on improving business culture and sustainability practices (e.g., APC) and with community groups whose prime goal is land care (e.g., Land for Wildlife and Landcare Victoria). At a broader and altruistic level, its actions in improving the biodiversity of the environment around the estate offer a broad range of benefits to the community to which it belongs.

Collectivism: the extended view of SEW

Tahbilk has embraced collectivism through its no-greed philosophy that sees a low focus on taking money out of the business. A recent example of this is the preference, particularly from the "next-genners," for funds to be applied to CSR in the form of environmental and sustainability initiatives, rather than being paid out to the family. It is the collective view of the family to pursue these environmentally sustainable-focused initiatives, enabling the business to pursue a "generational investment strategy."[45] This is enhanced by a governance structure that will keep the business in family hands for the long term. Formalizing the governance structure at the family level, through the Family Assembly and Family Council, ensures that the family voice is perpetuated across multiple generations. That collective view reflects an extended view of SEW where those benefiting extend to a group of family members and perhaps even a broader group that includes non-family stakeholders.[46] The family sees the business as sacrosanct and as such is "collectively invested" in ensuring its future prosperity. It is more than an "emotional connection."

Perpetuation: the SEW dimension of renewal of family bonds

As is evident in each of the elements of the family business system, the family has enshrined family involvement through the ownership, family and business sub-systems. Through family involvement in each of these sub-systems, the family's commitment to perpetuating the business is clear. The Purbrick family has taken steps to ensure that future generations will be involved in the Tahbilk business. These steps provide the "Renewal of family bonds"[47] in the FIBER dimensions of SEW, with the Purbrick family's next generation already enthusiastically and passionately involved in the business.

Obligation: the SEW dimension of emotional connection

A family's sense of obligation to the business is an important attribute of businesses that pursue CSR initiatives.[48] The regular reference in the interviews with Purbrick family members to their role as custodians reflects an element of their emotional connection to the land and business. The family's actions in respect of the Tahbilk business and the Tahbilk Estate is evidence of that obligation.

Altruism: the extended view of SEW

The family members' understanding that they are custodians has led them to take an altruistic stance in their approach to sustainability initiatives as they fulfil their CSR responsibilities. That altruistic approach is evident in their past and features in their plans for the future. The question has been posed as to whether it is genuinely altruistic if there is a payback for the actions taken. In the Tahbilk situation,[49] it is evident that their CSR initiatives have had both a financial and non-financial payback. These initiatives in the form of their commitment to sustainability have delivered a competitive advantage to the business by providing a point of difference. The initiatives have and will, over time, deliver financial benefits by way of cost reductions. However, the family is looking to other elements of the TBL philosophy. It is adopting strategies that are financially viable, bearable on its staff and sustaining and enhancing the environment in which it and the community operate. Tahbilk's TBL approach is aligned to the "extended view of SEW" where the family business looks to the delivery of affective utility to a broader group of stakeholders that extends beyond the immediate family.[50]

KEY INSIGHTS

- Tahbilk believes that its demonstrated commitment to the environment and sustainability has provided a point of competitive advantage that builds on the intrinsic values of family business, namely, trust, integrity and a long-term commitment to quality. It believes that all of these elements fit together and that if one of them were to be removed, the business would lose something.

- The family business's commitment to the TBL approach to the environment and sustainability is pragmatic. The business understands that for its environmental and sustainability strategies to be successful in the long term and to meet the stated objective "to leave a sustainable legacy for those family members to come,"[51] the strategies implemented must be both viable, that is financially responsible, and bearable, that is not onerous on the people who work in the business.
- At the macro level, the focus on sustainability by the company has coincided with a greater focus on the environment by society at large. Its approach is delivering an economic benefit over the long term and a competitive advantage in a cluttered Australian wine market.
- The Tahbilk case study provides insights into how a multi-generational family business has implemented CSR strategies that embrace environmental and sustainability objectives. It illustrates how the Tahbilk business under the guidance of the Purbrick family has embraced and championed both external and internal drivers in the family and business commitment to sustainability.
- In the Tahbilk case study, we see how the pursuit of a Sustainable Business Model enables this family business to pursue the TBL objectives of planet, people and profit in a bearable and viable manner. It illustrates that the pursuit of sustainability and environmental initiatives makes good sense for the business. This case demonstrates how sustainability (combined with the traditional elements of a family business) creates a business model with authenticity and differentiation from competitors. It also demonstrates how the pursuit of environment and sustainability can assist business families in achieving their SEW objectives.

NOTES

1. Winetitles Pty Ltd. (2018). "Preserving nature: Tahbilk's innovative eco-approach," *Australian and New Zealand Grapegrower and Winemaker*, 648. https://search.informit.com.au/documentSummary;dn=347870331426056;res=IELNZC
2. CarboNZero is a certified trademark of Manaaki Whenua Landcare Research. www.landcareresearch.co.nz/resources/business/the-carbonzero-programme
3. Kenton, W. (2019). "Triple bottom line (TBL)." Investopedia. www.investopedia.com/terms/t/triple-bottom-line.asp
4. Banksia Sustainability Foundation and Awards, Australia. http://banksiafdn.com/about/
5. Santini, C., Cavicchi, A. & Casini, L. (2013). "Sustainability in the wine industry: Key questions and research trends." *Agricultural and Food Economics*, 1(1): 9.
6. Knight, H., Megicks, P., Agarwal, S. & Leenders, M. (2019). "Firm resources and the development of environmental sustainability among small and medium-sized

enterprises: Evidence from the Australian wine industry." *Business Strategy and the Environment*, 28(1): 25–39. doi:10.1002/bse.2178
7. Australian Wine & Grape Inc. (previously known as the Winemakers Federation of Australia) "is the peak national body for the Australian wine industry." www.wfa.org.au/about-australian-grape-and-wine/
8. Pratt, M. A. (2012). "Comparison of sustainability programs in the wine industry." *Proceedings of International Conference in Innovation and Trends in Wine Management*, Burgundy School of Business, Dijon.
9. Tahbilk Pty Ltd. (2019). *Tahbilk Environment Plan 2017–2010.*
10. OIV Resolution CST 1/2008-OIV, cited in Flores, S. S. (2018). "What is sustainability in the wine world? A cross-country analysis of wine sustainability frameworks." *Journal of Cleaner Production*, 172: 2301–12.
11. Norman, W. & MacDonald, C. (2004). "Gettting to the bottom of 'triple bottom line.'" *Business Ethics Quarterly*, 14(2): 243–62.
12. Winetitles Pty Ltd. (2017). *The Australian and New Zealand Wine Industry Directory*, 35th edn. Adelaide: Winetitles Australia.
13. Van Leeuwen, C. & Seguin, G. (2006). "The concept of terroir in viticulture." *Journal of Wine Research*, 17(1): 1–10.
14. Winetitles Pty Ltd. (2018). "Preserving nature: Tahbilk's innovative eco-approach," *Australian and New Zealand Grapegrower and Winemaker*, p. 79.
15. Tahbilk Pty Ltd. (2019). *Tahbilk Environment Plan 2017*–2010, p. 4.
16. Woodhouse, F. (2010). *Vintage Stories: A 150 Year History of Tahbilk*. Victoria: Tahbilk.
17. "First peoples" refers to the Aboriginal and Torres Straight Islanders who inhabited Australia prior to the European settlement of Australia.
18. "Welcome to our place." www.Tahbilk.com.au/
19. Woodhouse, F. (2010). *Vintage Stories: A 150 Year History of Tahbilk*. Victoria: Tahbilk.
20. Ibid.
21. Allen, M. (2012). *The History of Australian Wine: Stories from the Vineyard to the Cellar Door*. Melbourne: Melbourne University Press.
22. Lofts, G. (2010). *Heart and Soul: Australia's First Families of Wine*. Brisbane: John Wiley & Sons Australia.
23. López-Pérez, M., Melero-Polo, I., Vázquez-Carrasco, R. & Cambra-Fierro, J. (2018). "Sustainability and business outcomes in the context of SMEs: Comparing family firms vs. non-family firms." *Sustainability*, 10(11): 1.
24. Ohmart cited in Santini, C., Cavicchi, A. & Casini, L. (2013). "Sustainability in the wine industry: Key questions and research trends." *Agricultural and Food Economics*, 1(1): 2.
25. López-Pérez, M., Melero-Polo, I., Vázquez-Carrasco, R. & Cambra-Fierro, J. (2018). "Sustainability and business outcomes in the context of SMEs: Comparing family firms vs. non-family firms." *Sustainability*, 10(11).
26. Pojasek, R. B. (2011). "Triple bottom Line." In N. Cohen & P. Robbins (eds), *Green Business: An A-to-Z Guide*. Thousand Oaks, CA: Sage.
27. Norman, W. & MacDonald, C. (2004). "Gettting to the bottom of 'triple bottom line.'" *Business Ethics Quarterly*, 14(2): 243–62.
28. Santini, C., Cavicchi, A. & Casini, L. (2013). "Sustainability in the wine industry: Key questions and research trends." *Agricultural and Food Economics*, 1(1): 2.
29. Gómez-Mejía, L. R., Haynes, K. T., Núñez-Nickel, M., Jacobson, K. J. & Moyano-Fuentes, J. (2007). "Socioemotional wealth and business risks in

family-controlled firms: Evidence from Spanish olive oil mills." *Administrative Science Quarterly*, 52(1): 106–37.
30. Berrone, P., Cruz, C. & Gomez-Mejia, L. R. (2012). "Socioemotional wealth in family firms theoretical dimensions, assessment approaches, and agenda for future research." *Family Business Review*, 25(3): 258–79.
31. Miller, D. & Breton-Miller, L. (2014). "Deconstructing socioemotional wealth." *Entrepreneurship Theory and Practice*, 38(4): 713–20.
32. Chua, J. H., Chrisman, J. & Sharma, P. (1999). "Defining the family business by behavior." *Entrepreneurship Theory and Practice*, 23(4), 19–40.
33. Marques, P., Presas, P. & Simon, A. (2014). "The heterogeneity of family firms in CSR engagement: The role of values." *Family Business Review*, 27(3): 206.
34. Tagiuri, R. & Davis, J. A. (1996). "Bivalent attributes of the family firm." *Family Business Review*, 9(2): 199–208.
35. Sirmon, D. & Hitt, M. (2003). "Managing resources: Linking unique resources, management, and wealth creation in family firms." *Entrepreneurship Theory and Practice*, 27(4): 339–58.
36. Berrone, P., Cruz, C. & Gomez-Mejia, L. (2014). "Family-controlled firms and stakeholder management: A socioemotional wealth preservation perspective." In L. Melin, M. Nordqvist & P. Sharma (eds), *The Sage Handbook of Family Business* (1st ed., pp. 179–95). Thousand Oaks, CA: Sage.
37. Cennamo, C., Berrone, P., Cruz, C. & Gomez-Mejia, L. R. (2012). "Socioemotional wealth and proactive stakeholder engagement: Why family-controlled firms care more about their stakeholders." *Entrepreneurship: Theory and Practice*, 36(6): 1153–73.
38. Berrone, P., Cruz, C. & Gomez-Mejia, L. R. (2012). "Socioemotional wealth in family firms theoretical dimensions, assessment approaches, and agenda for future research." *Family Business Review*, 25(3): 258–79.
39. Marques, P., Presas, P. & Simon, A. (2014). "The heterogeneity of family firms in CSR engagement: The role of values." *Family Business Review*, 27(3).
40. Winetitles Pty Ltd. (2018). "Preserving nature: Tahbilk's innovative eco-approach," *Australian and New Zealand Grapegrower and Winemaker*, p. 78.
41. Lofts, G. (2010). *Heart and Soul: Australia's First Families of Wine*. Brisbane: John Wiley & Sons Australia, p. 63.
42. Berrone, P., Cruz, C. & Gomez-Mejia, L. R. (2012). "Socioemotional wealth in family firms theoretical dimensions, assessment approaches, and agenda for future research." *Family Business Review*, 25(3): 258–79.
43. Bingham, J. B., Dyer, W. G., Smith, I. & Adams, G. L. (2011). "A stakeholder identity orientation approach to corporate social performance in family firms." *Journal of Business Ethics*, 99(4): 565–85.
44. Berrone, P., Cruz, C. & Gomez-Mejia, L. R. (2012). "Socioemotional wealth in family firms theoretical dimensions, assessment approaches, and agenda for future research." *Family Business Review*, 25(3): 258–79.
45. Sirmon, D. & Hitt, M. (2003). "Managing resources: Linking unique resources, management, and wealth creation in family firms." *Entrepreneurship Theory and Practice*, 27(4): 343.
46. Miller, D. & Breton-Miller, L. (2014). "Deconstructing socioemotional wealth." *Entrepreneurship Theory and Practice*, 38(4): 713–20.
47. Berrone, P., Cruz, C. & Gomez-Mejia, L. R. (2012). "Socioemotional wealth in family firms theoretical dimensions, assessment approaches, and agenda for future research." *Family Business Review*, 25(3): 258–79.

48. Marques, P., Presas, P. & Simon, A. (2014). "The heterogeneity of family firms in CSR engagement: The role of values." *Family Business Review*, 27(3).
49. Ibid.
50. Miller, D. & Breton-Miller, L. (2014). "Deconstructing socioemotional wealth." *Entrepreneurship Theory and Practice*, 38(4): 713–20.
51. Tahbilk Pty Ltd. (2019). *Tahbilk Environment Plan 2017–2010.*

PART IV

Institutional leadership for sustainability

12. The role of family values in institutional change toward sustainability in the Bordeaux wine industry

Sanjay Sharma, Tatiana Bouzdine-Chameeva and Joerg S. Hofstetter

> Organic "is the future" for Bordeaux, declared Guillaume Halley, owner of Château de La Dauphine in Fronsac, at a dinner held in London to discuss innovation and change in the prestigious French wine region. "It's hard work but it's necessary," he said. "At the moment, 7% of the Bordeaux estates work like this, but it was only 3% ten years ago." He says he expects 100% of Bordeaux to be organic within 30 years from now.[1]

> Starting with the 2019 vintage, every bottle of St.-Émilion wine will have been made from grapes grown with sustainable farming methods, such as organic or biodynamic viticulture. The local wine council for four Bordeaux appellations has passed a measure mandating sustainable farming. Any wine not farmed sustainably may only be bottled as generic Bordeaux. The decision impacts nearly 3.85 million cases of wine made annually within the St.-Émilion, St.-Émilion Grand Cru, Lussac St.-Émilion and Puisseguin St.-Émilion appellations.[2]

The above quotes from two popular wine industry magazines indicate that in 2013 there was discussion about an organic future for the wineries in the Bordeaux region and only 7 percent of Bordeaux estates had adopted sustainable farming. At that time the target for 100 percent organic farming was estimated to be 30 years into the future, by around 2043. A short four years later in 2017, media reported that four appellations in Saint-Émilion *mandated* sustainable viticulture for 100 percent of the wineries within these appellations. How did this rapid institutional change come about? Our study was motivated by questions that were unanswered by media reports about institutional change toward sustainable farming in the Bordeaux region: was the institutional change indeed as rapid as media reports suggest or the culmination of a gradual process? What factors precipitated the decision by Saint-Émilion appellations to take the lead in this institutional change? Was this change driven mainly by external forces or also by internal values and motivations of the owners/leadership of the estates? Given that the winery industry in the Bordeaux region is dominated by family-owned estates (approximately 85 percent of the total), did the business families play a role in this change?

Our study was based on in-depth interviews with key stakeholders of the Bordeaux wine industry including representatives of the Bordeaux Métropole – the metropolitan council centered in the city of Bordeaux and covering the Gironde department of France; the Institut des Sciences de la Vigne et du Vin (ISVV) of the University of Bordeaux and a multi-disciplinary higher education, research and development center; the Bordeaux Wine Council or Conseil Interprofessionnel du Vin de Bordeaux (CIVB), the industry association that represents the winegrowers, wine merchants and brokers; the owners and estate managers of three family-owned left-bank wine estates in the Bordeaux appellations of Pauillac, Margaux and Pessac, two right-bank family-owned estates in the appellation of Saint-Émilion and two family-owned estates in the Bordeaux Supérieur Appellation. These in-depth interviews (details of respondents and length of interviews are in Table 12.1) enabled us to get a perspective on the origins of the sustainable viticulture and viniculture initiatives, the main actors, the external and internal driving forces, the institutional process of adoption, the various sustainable agriculture and winery certification systems and the role of family-owned wineries in the process of institutional change. The interviews were supplemented by secondary data from the websites of the wineries, the CIVB and news articles in the most respected industry press outlets including *The Wine Cellar Insider*,[3] *Decanter* and *Wine Spectator*.

THE BORDEAUX WINE REGION

Bordeaux is one of the largest and most popular wine regions in the world, selling its wines to consumers and collectors on all continents, attracting visitors from all over the world and playing a central role in the formation of the world's wine professionals: growers, wine makers, consultants, traders and critics. The total planted estates in the Bordeaux wine region cover more than 115,200 hectares and include around 6,000 chateaux (wine estates) that make more than 9,000 different Bordeaux wines of every vintage that total over 900 million bottles of wine a year. This constitutes around 1.5 percent of the global wine production. The industry has consolidated in recent years with a decline of chateaux from around 9,500 in 2010 to around 6,000 in 2018. The average size of an estate is 19 hectares of vines. During the 1990s, very few estates had more than 100 hectares of vines. Today, there are close to 50 different properties consisting of more than 100 hectares, indicating the level of consolidation.

French wines are structured within the French Appellation d'Origine Contrôlée (AOC) system, also known as appellations. The Bordeaux wine region is organized into 57 AOCs. This system goes back over 500 years, initially to ensure a product's origin. Since 1935 the French AOC system is governed by the Institut National de l'Origine et de la Qualité (INAO) and has been embedded in European law since 1992. For each AOC the geographical region for production and origin of raw materials and farming and processing methods are precisely specified and constrained. The INAO enforces these definitions with rigid controls and tough penalties. The AOC regulates the grape varieties, maximum yield, density of vine planting, minimum alcohol level, cultivation methods and wine-making techniques and quality controls.

Bordeaux's global reputation as a producer of high-quality wines is in large part the result of its long history of wine exports, trading by merchants and the classifications of the *Grands Crus Classés* – classified growth wines established in 1855. However, these prestigious wines represent less than 5 percent of the total volume of wine in the region. The 1855 classification serves as an indication of the potential for the quality of the wine but was initially based on the price evaluation of wines. The resistance to changes in this classification motivated wine regions like Saint-Émilion and Sauterne to establish their own quality classification.

In the 1855 classification, the most prestigious and highest priced, and with perceived highest quality, are the five first growths (Premiers Crus): Haut-Brion, Lafite Rothschild, Latour, Margaux and Mouton-Rothschild. These are followed by Saint-Émilion's three Premiers Grands Crus Classé A: Ausone, Cheval-Blanc and Pavie; Pomerol's top estates: Lafleur, Le Pin and Pétrus; and Sauternes' Grand Premier Cru Château d'Yquem.[4] These attract the most attention in the media as well as by tourists. Just below the level of Grand Cru Classé is the classification of Cru Bourgeois, first established in 1932 and which recognized the quality and value of red wines produced in the eight appellations of the Médoc region.

Unclassified Bordeaux wines can sell for as little as 3 euros a bottle. For the sake of the global image of Bordeaux wines, several AOCs have a goal of increasing production of more differentiated and expensive wines. Amongst AOCs, Saint-Émilion is the second largest annual producer of wine in hectoliters. The main markets are China, which imports around 532,000 hectoliters annually, the United Kingdom (UK) (traditional and most important market), which imports 225,000 hectoliters a year but re-exports a significant portion, and the United States (US), which imports around 159,000 hectoliters. While China imports more in terms of volume, the US imports more in terms of value.[5]

DATA COLLECTION

Representatives from the following organizations, associations, institutes and family-owned estates were interviewed jointly by all three authors. Table 12.1 provides details of respondents.

Bordeaux Métropole encompasses 28 localities around Bordeaux city. Sustainability is core to its mission including preserving natural areas, supporting sustainable agriculture and mobility, renewable energy transition, local food, sustainable water management and waste reduction. Patrick Faucher has been the director of energy, ecology and sustainable development since 2006.

ISVV is a multi-disciplinary higher education, research and development center, founded in 2009 to bring together research, training and technology transfer teams to meet the challenges facing the wine industry of tomorrow. Two hundred and fifty researchers contribute to ISVV projects and the institute welcomes around 500 students as future enologists annually. Alain Blanchard, professor in microbiology, has been the director of ISVV for five years.

CIVB is a private association under the Ministry of Agricultural Affairs. It was founded in 1948 when there were approximately 50,000–60,000 growers in Bordeaux, and it was important for people to work together to defend their interests and the industry. Today CIVB represents the interests of nearly 6,000 Bordeaux wine producers and wine growers, and about 400 wine merchants and wine brokers. It is one of the most influential wine industry bodies in France, with three missions: to promote Bordeaux wine in the French and international markets; collect statistics and data about production and the markets and share that knowledge with members; and improve the Bordeaux wine industry's technical understanding relating to the production and quality of wine. The presidency of CIVB changes every five years from wine producer to wine merchant, and, at the time of data collection, the president was Allan Sichel from Maison Sichel, wine merchants.

The SME Association (Système de Management Environmental du Vin de Bordeaux) is an association of wine growers and wine producers in Bordeaux based on voluntary participation, mutualization and sharing experiences focused on sustainability and collaborative efforts in vineyards. It was set up in 2010 by 28 family-owned wineries with support from CIVB to unite their efforts in their transition towards sustainable viticulture.[6] It is composed mainly of wine producers (92 percent), with several wine cooperatives and wine merchants. The SME Association facilitates the environmental management system (EMS) collective certification process for its members. Today it has more than 800 members with 246 members certified in ISO 14001. The 10 areas of focus of the SME Association include water management, reduction of energy consumption, carbon footprint reduction, waste management,

Table 12.1 Respondents for primary data collection

Organization	Category	Name (hours)	Title
Bordeaux Métropole	Government	Patrick Faucher (2 hours)	Director, Energy, Ecology & Sustainable Development
Institute of Vines and Wines (ISVV)	Research institute	Alain Blanchard (2 hours)	Director
Bordeaux Wine Council (CIVB)	Industry association	Allan Sichel (2 hours)	President 2014 –2019 (Member of Sichel family, Bordeaux wine merchants)
		Christophe Chateau (2 hours)	Director of Communications
		Laura Esperandieu (2 hours)	Director, Environmental and CSR
SME Association	Industry association	Agathe Minot (2 hours)	Director
Vignoble Bardet, Saint-Émilion *Family owned*	Sustainable farming	Phillipe Bardet (3 hours)	Owner: Les vignobles Bardet, Member of CIVB, Former President of the Technical Commission of CIVB, Member of the Regional Comission of INAO; President of Système de Management Environmental du Vin de Bordeaux
Château La Grâce Fonrazade, Saint-Émilion *Family owned*	Organic/biodynamic	Francois-Thomas Bon (2 hours)	Owner; Vice President of Système de Management Environmental du Vin de Bordeaux
Château Pontet-Canet, Pauillac *Family owned*	Biodynamic winery	Jean-Michel Comme (3 hours)	Technical Director/Estate Manager
Château d'Esther, Bordeaux Supérieur *Family owned*	Biodynamic winery	Eva Fabian (2 hours)	Owner with husband Thomas
Château Le Noble, Bordeaux Supérieur *Family owned*	Organic	Maria Bonnefon (3 hours)	Owner, Chief Executive Officer and Head of Marketing
Château Haut-Brion, Pessac-Léognan *Family owned*	Haute Valeur Environnementale/ traditional	Barbara Wiesler-Appert (2 hours)	Director, Estates Public Relations
		27 hours of interviews	

reduction of the use of pesticides via the implementation of best vineyard practices, protection of biodiversity and preserving landscapes, preserving healthy environment for the populations living and working in the area, participating in training and sharing of best practices and supporting innovations for sustainable environment.

Family-Owned Estates

The family-owned estates selected for data collection were based on selective sampling of the heads of families of the two estates that took leadership of the institutional change process in the four Saint-Émilion appellations with classified growths and premium pricing (Vignobles Bardet – organic and Château La Grâce Fonrazade – biodynamic); one large prestigious fifth-growth classified premium pricing family estate that was a pioneering leader in biodynamic wines (Pontet-Canet) outside the Saint-Émilion appellation in Pauillac where there was no mandate for organic or biodynamic practices; two smaller pioneering biodynamic (Château d'Esther) and organic (Château Le Noble) family estates in the Bordeaux Supérieur appellation who were leading in the development of a mandate for organic/biodynamic practices; and one of the most prestigious first-growth classified (one of the original five) family estates (Château Haut-Brion) in the Pessac-Léognan appellation with super premium pricing that had not adopted either organic or biodynamic practices and pursued traditional farming and wine making. Since corporate wineries in the region are less than 15 percent (as compared to 85 percent family estates) and most corporate wineries are owned by banks and insurance companies located in Paris with little connection to the land, they tend to be followers rather than leaders in organic and biodynamic practices. Hence, corporate wineries were not a part of data collection.

Vignobles Bardet is a family-owned winery on the bank of the Dordogne river in Saint-Émilion, which traces back its history to 1704. The previous generations of the Bardet family were merchants and brokers, though they had a vineyard and were making wines for their own needs. They were mainly *gabariers* (commercial transporters) to transport wines on the river. With the arrival of the railway the *gabariers* gradually ceased their activity. Philippe Bardet, the current owner since the 1980s, decided to focus mainly on wine producing and extended the winery from 9 to 90 hectares, of which 55 hectares are under the Saint-Émilion Grand Cru AOC and 35 hectares in the Castillon and Côtes de Bordeaux AOCs. Being an active member of the CIVB as president of the Technical Commission, he is strongly involved in sustainable development projects and is a pioneer in the movement of the SME Association.

Château La Grâce Fonrazade in Saint-Émilion is a family-owned winery owned by the husband and wife team of François-Thomas and Benedicte Bon. They bought the property in 2010 in a deteriorated and half-abandoned state. In 2013, the property started its second life with new modern cellars and meeting the technical requirements of biodynamic certification. François-Thomas Bon has over 20 years of international experience in Chile and Argentina, Australia and China in wine making and consulting. He has a strong concern for environmental preservation and is actively engaged with the SME Association.

Château Pontet-Canet is a family-owned wine domain of 81 hectares located on the left bank of the Garonne river in Pauillac. It is classified as 5th Grand Cru. The property has known three different families of owners: until 1865, Jean-François de Pontet, the governor of the Medoc; the Cruse family, a rich family of Bordeaux merchants, and since 1975 the Tesseron family. Château Pontet-Canet is the pioneer among the classified growth wines of Medoc with biodynamic certification and has been followed by other classified growth wine domains such as Château Latour, Château Durfort–Viviens and Château Palmer in biodynamic certification.[7]

Château d'Esther, a family-owned winery in the Bordeaux Supérieur AOC, was acquired by Thomas and Eva Fabian in 1993. The estate has been engaged in organic agriculture since 2002, with a focus on biodiversity. The estate has been certified biodynamic by Demeter since 2013. Its wines have won several prizes, helping to change the public perception of biodynamic wines to be wines of excellent taste and quality. The family works closely with social organizations to provide individuals the opportunity to reconnect to nature by helping with harvesting.

Château Le Noble, a family-owned winery in the Bordeaux Supérieur AOC, was acquired by Marie and Thomas Bonnefon over 10 years ago, when both quit their positions in banking and marketing companies, respectively, in Paris. Thomas' family has a background in wine making and he broke with tradition to pursue a career in finance, but came back to the land over 10 years ago. The property has 30 hectares, of which 15 are planted vines constituting the vineyard at the origin of the production of its high-quality wines since the beginning of the nineteenth century. The family has a commitment to sustainability and has been certified organic since the 2013 harvest as a manifestation of its passion for natural wines to express the uniqueness of the terroir.

Château Haut-Brion, Pessac-Léognan, a multi-generational family-owned winery, introduces itself as the world's first luxury brand. It is considered to be one of the oldest vineyards in France, dating back to the first century after Christ. In 1660, the English King Charles II defined Haut-Brion as royal supplier, creating a high demand for these wines by London's upper class. At that time, Haut-Brion had revolutionized wine by introducing its innovation of "long-keeping wines" (New French Claret) and by also operating the highest-priced gourmet restaurant in London. In 1787, when becoming president of the US, Thomas Jefferson made Haut-Brion the White House's wine. In 1885, the estate was officially recognized as one of four grand cru classé wines. In 1935, the estate was acquired by Clarence Dillon, a New York banker, and still is in the Dillon family's hands as the only grand cru estate in non-French ownership. Château Haut-Brion, certified Haute Valeur Environnementale (HVE) in 2012, operates 51 hectares of vineyard located within Bordeaux in close proximity to residential areas. The Delmas family has served the Dillon family (owners) as the estate's wine makers for three generations, that is, three generations of the Delmas family have served three generations of the Dillon family.

SUSTAINABILITY IN THE WINE INDUSTRY

The production of wine consists of two stages: viticulture and viniculture (also known as enology). Viticulture concerns all elements of farming, ending with the harvested grapes. Viniculture concerns all elements of making wine, starting with the selection and reception of grapes and other input material and ending with the wine in its final packaging ready for the consumer market.

Sustainable Viticulture

Sustainable viticulture includes the fostering, maintaining and enhancing of a healthy eco-system with soils rich in beneficial micro organisms and organic matter by using animals such as sheep and birds to control weeds and pests, cover crops to promote biodiversity and richer soils, drip irrigation and process ponds to conserve water, improve air and water quality, preserve local eco-systems and wildlife habitats and environmentally friendly inputs.

Three different approaches toward sustainable viticulture dominate the Bordeaux wine region: EMS, organic and biodynamic. EMS in the region is characterized by the SME du Vin de Bordeaux of the SME Association and is certified either via ISO 14001, the international standard, and/or HVE, a core element of the French government's environmental certification scheme for agriculture. While ISO 14001 does not state specific environmental performance criteria, the intended outcomes include the enhancement of environmental performance, the fulfilment of compliance obligations and the achievement of environmental objectives. HVE covers well-defined criteria on biodiversity conservation, plant protection, managed fertilizer use and water resource management. The EMS approach allows a reasonable use of some non-organic crop protection materials and fertilizers.

Organic farming is the growing of grapes without using any non-organic or petrochemical-based crop protection materials and fertilizers. European

Union (EU) regulation and French national organic laws define practices and substances that are allowed or restricted. Biodynamic farming treats the vineyard as a closed loop, employing organic practices and natural alternatives for eliminating waste and promoting a healthy eco-system. While organic and biodynamic differ from generic forms of sustainable farming, these are considered very different philosophies of farming. The biodynamic farmers are often very passionate about following an exacting approach and methods as developed by Rudolph Steiner in 1924 based on a philosophy that soil fertility, plant growth and livestock care are ecologically interrelated, and the approach emphasizes spiritual and mystical perspectives.[8]

Sustainable Viniculture

The production of wine generates a large amount of wastewater and organic waste that must be treated adequately to avoid contaminating the eco-system. The vinification process affects the properties of the generated waste or residual material. Sustainable enology is the process of reduction of residues and their subsequent treatment in the elaboration of the wine, the reduction of resource use including energy, fresh water, glass, cork, labels, packaging and wood; the reduction of pollution, such as greenhouse gases or wastewater; and the elimination of chemical aids, such as sulfites. Attention is also given to energy use in buildings and machinery and social issues, including working conditions and community support.

Certifications

Wines produced according to organic standards must follow strict EU regulations, including the inputs and resource efficiency, and cannot have more than 10 parts per million of sulfites injected into wine to prolong shelf life. Wines produced according to biodynamic standards must follow the certification standards of organizations such as Demeter or Biodyvin. The Demeter Biodynamic Certification established in 1928 as the first label for biodynamically produced foods is used in over 50 countries.

Organic certification, unlike biodynamic certification, is undertaken by individual national organizations. In France, the most commonly used certification is Agriculture Biologique (AB). In 2012, the EU established Terra Vitis, an organic certification for wines. This organic wine label can only be used on products when they contain at least 95 percent of organic ingredients and respect strict conditions for the remaining 5 percent. While certifications such as Terra Vitis often go above and beyond what is required by HVE's highest level 3, only those estates that have followed the criteria for HVE 3 can be certified starting in 2020.[9]

The ISO 14001 certifies that a winery has specified and implemented structures and processes put in place for the continuous improvement of environmental impact indicators such as emissions, wastes and energy usage and acts in full compliance with those. The HVE 3 certification established by the French Ministry of Agriculture in 2011 for farmers and wine growers, in addition to examining the processes of continuous improvement under ISO 14001, assesses performance on biodiversity and use of fertilizers and chemicals to treat vine diseases.

The mandate for sustainable farming, starting with the 2019 vintage in the Saint-Émilion AOCs, provides estates with the option of adopting and certifying a range of farming methods: biodynamic, organic, HVE 3 or ISO 14001. While ISO 14001 certifies a generic process of continuous improvement toward environmental goals, these goals are voluntary and vary individually for each winery. At the same time, there is no assurance that the goals will include the elimination of chemicals and the adoption of organic practices. A winery may decide only to focus on goals of reduction of water and energy use and a gradual reduction of chemical use against which the certification will measure progress. However, in order to achieve a 100 percent mandate for the four Saint-Émilion AOCs within a short time frame, this option had to be made available to wineries in the region that were unable to achieve HVE 3, organic or biodynamic certification in the immediate period of time. Table 12.2 provides an overview of different certifications adopted in the Bordeaux wine estates. The data in the table are from 2017.

INSTITUTIONAL BARRIERS FOR SUSTAINABLE WINE MAKING

Weather

The coastal humid weather in the Bordeaux region creates a high risk of fast-spreading pests and diseases. It is much more difficult to adopt organic or biodynamic practices in such a climate as compared to wine regions that have drier weather, such as Provence in southern France, Chile or Australia. High and frequent humidity in the Bordeaux region can lead to aggressive mildew infestations which can destroy an entire, or most of the, untreated crop. In 2018, due to heavy rains, the region experienced aggressive mildew. While the estates that treated the vines with sulfur and chemicals managed a normal yield, the rapid infestation substantially destroyed crops of wine estates that were biodynamic and did not use any chemicals to control the rapid attack. Hence, Bordeaux is an interesting context to examine motivations for adopting sustainable viticulture against the backdrop of high risk of crop failure and resulting financial stress.

Table 12.2 *Sustainability certifications in Bordeaux wine estates*

Data on Bordeaux region (Gironde dept.)		**Product certification**		**Company certification**			
		Organic	**Biodynamic** DEMETER, BIODYVIN	**ISO 14001**	**Terra Vitis** (equivalent HVE 2)	**HVE 3** (3 levels)	**SME** (equivalent HVE 2)
Number of certified companies		532	45	26	62	850	306 (900 engaged)
	%	10%	1%		~35% (including the companies in process of certification)		
Number of hectares		10,817 ha	984 ha		About 45,000 ha		
	%	10%	1%		~50%		

Past Success and Reputation

Centuries of great success and the high reputation of Bordeaux wines have reinforced the current established strategies and practices. Any reduction in demand by some markets such as Europe and the UK that have demanded more sustainably produced wines has been compensated by growing demand in the Chinese market that has no such requirements.

Pricing

The public perception of Bordeaux wines is dominated by the classified wines that sell at high prices. However, most wineries in the Bordeaux wine region are not classified and sell their wines at relatively low prices. While a new winery can start as organic or biodynamic, Bordeaux is a centuries-old region and the transformation of a traditional vineyard using conventional farming to an organic or biodynamic vineyard is at least a three-year process. Many wineries lack the financial reserves and capital to reduce production and yields for this period. A larger estate can undertake the transformation in sections but it is harder for a smaller estate.

Public Perceptions of Quality

As recently as the 1990s, biodynamic and organic wines had a reputation for lower quality compared to conventional wines. This perception still persists amongst some influential consumers and markets and classified Bordeaux wineries are able to sell conventional wines at good prices. In fact, our study found that some high-priced biodynamic wines did not signal their biodynamic practices on their label and marketing materials, probably because they did not want to risk alienating long-standing customers who bought the wines based on quality and were not concerned about them being organic or biodynamic. However, these estates' websites clearly described the practices.

INSTITUTIONAL DRIVERS FOR SUSTAINABLE WINE MAKING

The CIVB, its related partner organization the SME Association and the French government are very active in increasing participation of wineries in various sustainability initiatives. According to Christophe Chateau, the communications director of CIVB:

> Two years ago, the French government made a decision – in 2030 we want all the AOCs to be linked with sustainable development certification. Nowadays, in

> Bordeaux 60% of the vineyards are engaged in sustainable development. Our goal in Bordeaux is 100% by 2025. We have a new strategic plan for 2025.

There are two main institutional drivers most relevant in explaining the mandating of sustainable farming practices in the Saint-Émilion AOCs:

- Macro drivers: societal norms, reputational risks, market demand and the push to differentiate the AOCs in global markets to obtain higher prices for wines by enhancing the image of the AOCs.
- Micro drivers: institutional entrepreneurship and values-led leadership by individual family-owned estates motivated by their family values about healthy eco-systems, enriched soils and elimination of all non-organic substances for higher-quality fruit and wine and for human health. Individual families acted as change agents in shaping the macro-level environment at the AOC level.

Macro Drivers

Societal norms

A number of societal forces and norms have affected the French consumers' demands for food grown with organic, biodynamic or sustainable farming practices. The Food Sustainability Index (FSI) is a global study on nutrition, sustainable agriculture and food waste which collects data from 67 countries across the world to highlight best practices and key areas for improvement in relation to the United Nations' Sustainable Development Goals. The FSI for 2017 and 2018 ranked France number 1 in the world in terms of food sustainability.[10] The report cites France's progress in tackling food waste and the adoption of sustainable farming. The national strategy has been implemented all over France at the departmental level. In Gironde, the department within which the Bordeaux region is located, there has been a special push by the ex-mayor of Bordeaux and ex-prime minister of France, Alain Juppé. As per Patrick Faucher, of Bordeaux Métropole, explains:

> More people ask for organic wine, in general for organic alimentation. A special service department on energy, ecology and sustainable development was created [at Bordeaux Métropole] in 2006. Now it is 50 people focused on energy savings, the department's [Gironde's] energy production, and renewable energy. Our goal is to be able to produce the same amount of energy as we consume by 2050. The climate is changing and in Bordeaux even more than in other parts of Europe and this is also a reason why sustainability has become an important issue.

Christophe Chateau of CIVB agreed:

> Knowledge has increased and thinking is changing. And we have a huge pressure from government, journalists and people [society], and high pressure from consumers too. With this big change in thinking of the people and especially the new generation, the winemakers are trying to become more organic... The ecological party did well in the last elections in France for Europe... we don't want to destroy the planet.

Reputational risk

Listed as a UNESCO World Heritage site since 2007, Bordeaux is the second most visited city in France after Paris. It enjoys a unique prestige in the heart of the wine country and attracted around 7 million tourists in 2017.[11] Saint-Émilion, also listed as a UNESCO World heritage village, attracts about 70 percent of all wine tourists visiting the Bordeaux region, followed by Medoc. Many wineries welcome visitors, offer guided tours on their estates, access to their impressive castles, wine tastings, restaurants, hotel rooms or participation in harvesting. Such personal experiences aim at deepening visitors' loyalty, raising their quality expectations and increasing wine consumption. The Bordeaux wine region, and in particular Saint-Émilion, has attracted substantial investments into wine-related offerings from investors around the world.

Bordeaux is also a major center for research and education in wine. For a successful career in the global wine industry, work experience in the Bordeaux region is almost considered a prerequisite. Many of the leading wineries and merchants in Bordeaux benefit from the talent of young wine growers, wine makers and traders that apprentice in the practices and philosophy of wine making. It is the home of academic organizations on wine such as the ISVV, wine consultants, enologists and wine critics. It has substantial influence in the global wine industry.

Around 2008–2009, Bordeaux wines began to suffer a loss of reputation by trendsetters among sommeliers and merchants in Europe, and subsequently by general consumers concerned about the drastic increases in retail prices. Consumers began to weigh the relationship between the high price of Bordeaux wines and their quality as compared to wines from other regions in France and, in particular, countries such as Italy and Spain. The fast-rising demand from China allowed the Bordeaux wine business to make up for these losses for some time. The fall in reputation was also because of changing consumer preferences due to increasing consumer unwillingness to stock wine for a decade or more versus the comfort of drinking it young. The stories and histories of the estates about the vines and wines became less interesting for the average consumer.

In 2015, a year of spectacular vintage for Bordeaux in terms of produced volume and quality, "Bordeaux bashing" gained significant momentum in France due to a court trial against two estates accused of intoxicating school children in Villeneuve-de-Blaye with their crop protection practices.[12] A growing number of stakeholders focused public attention on the practices of Bordeaux wineries and vineyards. Confronted with growing mainstream and best practices in organic agriculture in general and in other French wine regions, Bordeaux's reputation stood the risk of being seen as the world capital for outdated industrial wine making, painting all estates with the same negative brush regardless of the fact that some family-owned estates were very advanced in their sustainable business practices. Hence, the move toward sustainability was also a move by leading family-owned estates as institutional change agents to salvage the reputation of the Bordeaux region. This was more important for the family estates that sold higher-priced wines, especially in more prestigious AOCs of Saint-Émilion.

Markets and consumers

Bordeaux as a global leader in the wine world has been under pressure to defend its position against both traditional and emerging rivals. Wine regions across the world such as Italy, Australia and the US have substantially increased the quality of their offerings. New stories and tastes have been introduced by wine makers from other regions and countries, altering consumer preferences. Some wine regions have become center stage for both wine lovers and speculators; Burgundy wines sell at higher prices and now only three wines from Bordeaux remain among the 30 most expensive wines.[13] Some wine regions (e.g., in Spain, Australia and South America) sell good-quality wines at substantially lower prices.

The decade-long multi-stakeholder engagement process around sustainable farming and organic food in France has led to increased consumer awareness and preferences and demands for organically produced wine. All the respondents we met cited the increasing demands for organic wine by French consumers. According to Alain Blanchard of ISVV:

> The French market is already demanding organic wines, and also northern European countries such as Scandinavian markets, German market and the Belgian market a bit.

Christophe Chateau:

> First, it [the demand for sustainable development] comes from the government, which imposes rules, easy rules to follow, but then the signal comes from the market. With the governmental decision they [wine producers] could hesitate as "the cost must increase, it will give me trouble." But when consumer demands, then it

changes everything. And now winemakers are asking even for stronger [and] harder rules.

Micro Drivers

Family values: institutional entrepreneurs and lone pioneers

According to Allan Sichel, the president of CIVB, regardless of the philosophy, the main focus should be minimization of harmful molecules in the soil and in nature:

> Organic or not organic is not the issue. The issue is how do we reduce the dependence on pesticides. It's very important to be inspired by all the experiments, whether they be organic, whether it be biodynamic or whether it be chemicals, we want less molecules in the air, we want less molecules in the soil, we want less accumulation of various molecules in the soil, again whether it be natural or whether they be chemical. What's important is more how nature can absorb these molecules outside their usage to protect vines and grapes.

Individual families approach this philosophy differently. Motivations for the adoption of sustainability practices by individual families included: (a) the threat of climate change to the volume and quality of the grape harvest; (b) increasing demand of organic/biodynamic by sommeliers, traders and consumers; (c) intensifying "Bordeaux bashing" that endangered demand for, and the reputation of, the Bordeaux wines in general; (d) depleted and damaged fertility of soil in the region due to excessive chemical use in the past; and (e) growing health concerns of the family and workers living in and around the vineyards.

Hence, the motivations of individual Bordeaux wine estate-owning families range from achieving sustainability on their own estate – we classify these as *lone pioneers*; to leadership in institutional change toward sustainability at the regional or AOC level, to societal change to address issues such as climate change and clean water – we classify these as *institutional entrepreneurs*. The motivation and strategic responses of families focused on their own estates is in the embedding of organic and/or biodynamic practices in alignment with the family's values and convictions. Those focused on the sectoral or AOC level believe that their ability to succeed and compete by embedding sustainability in their estates depends on the performance and reputation of all estates in an AOC such as Saint-Émilion. These families adopted the role of institutional change agents to bring other families on board to adopt sustainable practices. These families use arguments ranging from making a business case to the importance of improving the image and public opinion about the Bordeaux wine region.

Some families are driven by family values that go beyond achieving collective change at the AOC level toward a more sustainable world, restoring eco-systems and biodiversity and addressing climate change. Concerned about the damage already done to the natural environment by traditional chemical-based wine-making practices, they are driven by the desire to save the planet by reducing pollution and resource use, and the conviction that to achieve their aspired objectives collective action beyond the AOC is mandatory to build the capacity for change and scale up for impact via collective action.

The families that took leadership for institutional change at the regional/AOC level were driven by increasing discomfort with the non-sustainable practices of many estates in the same AOC that affected the reputation of all families in the region. They chose to lead and show by example that change was not only possible but also beneficial for all in the AOC/region. They organized meetings and gatherings of families leveraging their leadership in CIVB and other bodies to overcome inertia of laggards by forcing them to take the first small steps via ISO certification and build up momentum and scale across the AOC.

Whether an individual family chose to focus on transforming their own estate toward sustainable farming and wine making or undertook leadership for institutional change at the AOC/regional level depended on the extent to which they took leadership positions in association bodies such as CIVB and thus acquired political and persuasion power; and their own competitive position in the market. The lone pioneers with a premium price and a strong image and reputation (such as Grand Cru Classé) adopted biodynamic practices to improve the quality of their wines to maintain and improve premium pricing and did not feel motivated to carry the laggards along and help them build their capabilities for sustainable farming and certification. The most proactive and rigorous practices such as organic and biodynamic were adopted by estates that were driven by family values for eco-system and human health.

FAMILY ESTATES AS INSTITUTIONAL ENTREPRENEURS

Table 12.3 highlights the motivations of the individual family estates that we studied. Around 85 percent of the estates in the Bordeaux wine region are family owned, several for multiple generations and for as many as 500–600 years. A few families (Bardet and Bon) played a leading role as institutional entrepreneurs in leading the political process to obtain a consensus for a mandate toward sustainable certification in Saint-Émilion or Bordeaux Supérieur. Other families led as lone pioneers by example in adopting and implementing cutting-edge organic and biodynamic sustainability practices

Table 12.3 Motivations for the adoption of sustainable practices by Bordeaux family estates

	Founded	Current ownership since	Hectares	Certifications	Primary motivations
Vignoble Bardet (Bardet family)	1704	1979	90	HVE 3; SME	*Institutional entrepreneur* Personal values for preserving environment Lead societal change toward sustainability
Château La Grâce Fonrazade (Bon family)	Nineteenth century	2010	11	Organic	*Institutional entrepreneur* Changing consumer preferences Personal values for environmental preservation Lead institutional change for AOC reputation
Château Pontet-Canet (Tesseron and Comme families)	1705	1975	81	Biodynamic	*Lone pioneer* Personal values for preserving eco-systems Harmony in nature Lead societal change toward sustainability
Château Le Noble (Bonnefen family)	1806	2009	30	Organic	*Lone pioneer* Changing consumer preferences Personal values for preserving environment
Château Haut-Brion (Dillon and Delmas families)	First century AD	1935	51	ISO 14001; HVE	*Traditional* Maintain quality and premium prices

and strategies in other AOCs such as Pontet-Canet in Pauillac. The examples of these lone pioneers showed other estates in the AOC that embracing sustainability was associated with enhanced quality of wine, premium pricing and enhanced prestige of their vintages.

The Bardet Family

The Bardet family has been involved with the wine business since 1704. Starting off as river traders and vineyard owners, the family's major foray into wine making was the founding of Château du Val d'Or, a Saint-Émilion Grand Cru, in the 1920s. In the 1960s, Château Pontet-Fumet was established. Philippe Bardet, became the head of Vignobles Bardet in 1979. Phillipe has a decades-old track record of leadership in sustainable practices in the industry. As far back as 1994, he became active within the Forum of Responsible and Environmentally Friendly Farmers. He has a passion for growing wine and a deep respect for the terroir.

Phillipe and his wife Sylvie continue to focus on preserving their family heritage and transferring it to their four children. Their two oldest sons, Paul-Arthur and Thibault Bardet, who are studying winery management, are ready to take over. In 2008, Philippe took over Château Franc le Maine, another Saint-Émilion Grand Cru. In 2013, they acquired the prestigious Château du Paradis, also a Saint-Émilion Grand Cru. In recognition of their family history as river traders, the gabare river boat became the emblem of Vignobles Bardet. The outline of the boat with its wind-filled sail on course for the future symbolizes the Bardet family's entrepreneurial business philosophy. The motto of Vignobles Bardet is:

> **Respect for the terroir and the ambition to pass it down.**[14]

This reflects the values of sustainability and patient capital for the long term.

In discussing the family's motivation for taking the lead on building a consensus around sustainable farming in the Saint-Émilion AOC, Phillipe Bardet explained how and why he was driven to begin the process of becoming an institutional change agent:

> Our house is on the bank of the Dordogne river and I observe this river since my very early days. The pollution of the river over the years started disturbing me and finally pushed me to engage into the analysis of the levels of macro pollutants including effluents in the river and micro pollutants which are pesticides and other wastes and discharges. We have been successful in the collective management of macro pollutants in the form of river effluents. However, there is strong inertia over

> micro pollutants – certainly there are pesticides but also medicines or drugs or other chemical pollutants. And there is work to be done collectively by the estates.
>
> We began working on this about 15 years ago... and that was collective work on communications and work with the State – we managed to receive financial subsidies for that project. First the analysis was performed on the creek nearby, and that allowed us to communicate and to insist that it was necessary to change the behavior by the estates. Then the analysis was performed in Dordogne river. The collective action by all estates is successful and now the analysis shows that there are no pesticides in the river.
>
> For the analysis of the river, I was a leader... I was among those who provoked that collective movement. The issues on the pollution have been brought forward by the winemakers, by technical people. My engagement in the system is related to the environment.
>
> **To protect the environment, we can't do it solely just in our corner playing a star role. We need to start with small measures, and then generalize them.**
>
> What I am the most proud of is something for which I am not responsible. In our village, Vignonet, the winemakers asked me to join their initiative. They created a center for collective cleaning of pulverisators [fine pollutant particles]. This is the first one in Gironde, my village, without my participation or motivation. That is what I am proud of. This means that the message has passed through!

Bardet also reflected on his family's deep and enduring values for the preservation of the terroir and the eco-system that motivated his leadership of the institutional change process:

> **The difference of engagement (for eco-system preservation and the terroir) in the actions comes from the family. It is tacit knowledge, know-how from experience.**
>
> In the family we discuss during table time, talk about wine and our decisions, our clients. It is also transmitting the traditions and process. Knowledge management.

Reflecting on enduring family values and alignment of values between family members and employees, Bardet stated:

> In my company, in terms of human resources policy, I am the captain or a leader. However, it is not like a situation where there is a chef and subordinates who expect the orders from the chef. No, it is impossible in our case.
>
> **It is not even as an orchestra and a conductor, it is more as an organization of a music quartet for example. Everyone takes the leadership on certain subjects or at certain moments.**
>
> Even when they are not from the same family, they understand, they have same values and take leadership on certain issues. We have two other families who lived here when we extended the vineyard and bought those parcels. Their grandfather lived here, their father and now we have the son who is doing his training with us. It is a kind of relationship full of good will and caring inside the family-owned company. These relations are stronger than with standard employees, based on mutual respect and honor – the honor of belonging to a group.

Commenting on the respect for the land and the terroir that cements the values for environmental preservation:

> It is possible for those producing the Airbus to come from another world and take over the process. For taking over the nature in the vineyard it is impossible. There is too much tacit knowledge and for understating it you have to be here, to live in the fields.

The Bon Family

Francois Thomas Bon worked with Phillipe Bardet to manage the political process of consensus amongst Saint-Émilion AOCs for the sustainable certification mandate. Bon inherited the farm from his father who worked for Hennessey in Paris and acquired the land in Saint-Émilion as an investment. However, instead of leaving the land unused, his father planted fruit trees and farmed sheep and cattle on the land. Francois came back after studying in the UK in 1992 and began to plant vines. At that time, he felt that "they would never make grand cru classé wines, never sell at the high price, but would make great wines." In 2010, with his wife Bénédicte, Bon took over a property whose last harvest was in 1980. At what is now known as the Château La Grâce Fonrazade, Saint-Émilion Grand-Cru, the couple completely restructured its vineyards and cellars and between 2013 to 2016 converted the estate to production of organic wine classified Grand Cru. In 2017, they revealed the first organic vintage. According to Bon:

> **It took time to become organic since it required three types of investment: a long-term investment in building up knowledge, heavy investments in cash, and substantial technical investments. And then, the most challenging, human resources – finding well-trained people for doing a good and productive job for organic winemaking is difficult. Not enough people are trained, not enough practiced in the world in general.**

In addition to working with Phillippe Bardet to obtain consensus on sustainable certification in the Saint-Émilion AOCs, Francois has played, and continues to play, an important role as an institutional change agent as a consultant on organic viticulture and enology for a number of estates in the region.

In reflecting on family values:

> **We have to teach our children and explain that sustainable viticulture is an interesting path to be taken.**
>
> To make organic wines you need knowledge and finding good people is tough. I prefer to find them among my neighbors who know the terroir. Learning organic viticulture has been the most difficult for me. I hope that my daughter will follow

> me and I want to say to her that organic is also a business and you have to make good wine. And it is a most difficult thing for me to combine organic and business.

Thus, both Bardet and Bon emphasized that the capabilities, knowledge and human capital for organic and biodynamic viticulture is a bottleneck and not easy to find. Hence, the tacit knowledge of the family connected to the land and the terroir, and its transmission across generations, is important for success.

The Consensus-Building Process for Institutional Change at the AOC Level

The political process for consensus building was led by Philippe Bardet of Vignobles Bardet and Francois Thomas Bon, of Château La Grâce Fonrazade, both leaders of family-owned wineries. Aided by Bon, Bardet adopted a double-pronged approach for obtaining consensus: personal persuasion and outreach to the estates in the Saint-Émilion AOCs and being elected co-chairman of the industry association CIVB's technical commission and member of the regional commission of INAO. Bardet and Bon working with CIVB held a number of town hall meetings with wineries in the Saint-Émilion AOCs over a couple of years to obtain consensus on the sustainable farming mandate. Over this period, they convinced the wineries about the importance of the business and reputation but also about the importance of health of their families and workers and the long-term eco-system health of the Bordeaux terroirs. At the same time, in order to get consensus within the AOCs in the short time frame and given the wide range of capabilities of the Saint-Émilion wine estates, flexibility was essential. Bardet explained:

> For the system to put in place in St.-Émilion, we agreed on a spirit of diversity. St.-Émilion does not want to control all the certifications. The idea is that everyone must be certified. And everyone chooses a certification according to their own sensibility. The challenge is as for any team, or a sport team, it is necessary that the best are sufficiently strong for managing the injured or handicapped. You know the commandos in the army when they have a wounded soldier they will not move with the speed of an injured person, they will carry him to walk quicker. It is important to have an ambition where the strongest could carry the others.

Allan Sichel, the president of CIVB, agreed:

> Sustainability is much broader than only organic certification. CIVB is geared toward the reduction of the use of pesticides, being careful of what pesticides and how much, and applying them in small doses and only as needed and when needed.

Bardet and Bon adopted a leadership role in CIVB's training and certification process. Bon explained:

> Some family estates have, since a long period of time, felt that making efforts to protect the environment are necessary and taking care of the environment is important. Others have focused on the commercial effect (profits), which is necessary. **However, if you have negative social impact and generate pollution and show that you are not respecting the environment and health, it could have negative impacts on your commercial side.**
>
> The first group of people are the rare people who believe that it is vital to look after the environment, but they lead others who find their own interests.

According to Allan Sichel, the president of the CIVB:

> The SME process started in 2008, and the first group started in 2010 with 25 companies that participated (note: the first ones that stepped forward voluntarily). It took a few years to get the first certifications… Now there are 800 companies involved but only 246 or 247 that have gone as far as for full HVE 3 certification. SME is just a tool of continuous improvement.
>
> The Association de Vin de Bordeaux, the Le Premier Association SME, was accredited with the possibility of gaining HVE 3 certification on a collective basis, which puts a lot of pressure on the whole group because if during the audit one company is not accredited, it can have repercussions on the whole group, so everyone loses their certification. There's a lot of pressure to make sure that everyone is kept up-to-date continuously. We have internal audits to make sure that those companies going for certification are actually all of a sufficient standard and that they're not bringing a risk to the whole association. There's a lot of internal discipline. So, it's not because you're part of the SME that you qualify for certification, you have to show that you have the ability to achieve the right stage so you're not putting the certification of others at risk.

The differences in sustainability adoption amongst the wineries are due to different philosophies, financial capacity and the unique terroir and histories of family estates. Nevertheless, due to the efforts and leadership of families such as Bardet and Bon, sustainable development has become the common denominator and the individual wineries have combined forces to help each other achieve this goal.

According to Christophe Chateau of CIVB:

> St.-Émilion was the first appellation, which decided that all their members need to be sustainable. They changed the appellation rules. We don't want to fight and not make quick progress by insisting that all estates be organic or biodynamic. There are good or bad points in each choice, so we accept these differences. You can make your own choice depending on your knowledge, your money, your appellation.

LONE PIONEERS' FAMILY ESTATES OUTSIDE THE SAINT-ÉMILION AOCS

The section above highlights the family values-driven institutional entrepreneurship of Phillipe Bardet and Francois Thomas Bon as agents of collective change toward sustainable viticulture and viniculture in Saint-Émilion. They led the movement to get estates in the Saint-Émilion AOCs to develop respect for, and begin the process to preserve the terroir that is a part of the estates' family heritage and future. At the same time, we found out that the Bordeaux Supérieur AOC was the pioneer in mandating sustainable farming in 2017 and there are many estates outside of Saint-Émilion that have converted to 100 percent organic or biodynamic even though there is no mandate within their AOC for such a change. Their practices have been driven by deep-rooted family values and passion not only for the terroir but an abiding belief in the high quality of wine produced in an eco-system that is healthy, vibrant, resilient and sustainable.

Philippe Bardet explained the motivations of family estates in Bordeaux in general:

> The major difference is that if a family lives in Bordeaux on their property, that is most important. The origin of the family does not matter. We have extremely rich families who invested in St.-Émilion, their children went to school in St.-Émilion and they are certainly more involved in sustainability than those families who are just financial investors. I too need to look at the bottom of my annual balance sheet, but the financial investors mainly solve investment problems from the top of their balance sheet. We are from different worlds.

It is evident that such family values dominate over the societal and market forces for the estates that adopted organic and biodynamic practices long before there was societal or reputational pressure or an AOC mandate and very small niche markets existed for such wines. For example, Domain Paul Barre in Fronsac adopted biodynamic practices in the 1970s. Many estates that are the most proactive in their sustainability practices do not market their wines as organic or biodynamic in the belief that the quality of their wines is superior and consumers will pay premiums and consumers focused on organic/biodynamic will be able to assess their practices from the details on their websites.

Château Pontet-Canet, Pauillac

Château Pontet-Canet is a prestigious and well-known estate with a long history that was granted fifth-growth status in the 1855 classification. Pontet-Canet has remained one of the largest Bordeaux wine-producing estates in the Pauillac appellation. At the time of the purchase by the Tesseron family in

1975, the vineyard was in poor condition and in need of a lot of replanting. Guy Terrerson was also involved in Cognac and owned Château Lafon Rochet in the St. Estephe AOC in the Bordeaux region. His son Alfred Tesseron took over running the estate in 1994. The recent success of Pontet-Canet can be attributed to the current management of the estate by Alfred Tesseron and the technical director and estate manager, Jean-Michel Comme. The property has continued to improve. Judging from market prices for their vintages, even though Pontet-Canet is a fifth growth, they are producing wines at the level of the best second growths and, in some vintages, as good as the firsts.

The estate has been a pioneer in biodynamic farming. In 2010, Château Pontet-Canet became the first major Bordeaux wine producer to earn the official AB organic certification. Other certifications include organic certification awarded by Ecocert and biodynamic certification from Biodyvin. Jean Michel Comme, the technical director and estate manager, helped bring Alfred Tesseron to see the value in biodynamic farming. The first experiments with biodynamics at Château Pontet-Canet began with 14 hectares of vines in 2004. Today, they are 100 percent biodynamic.

Jean-Michel believes that if the vineyard and soils are healthy they can protect the vines against disease, naturally eliminating the need for chemicals. Instead of traditional green harvesting, hedging and leaf thinning, the estate reduces the number of buds per vine by pruning. All these efforts result in grapes that are evenly distributed, with good ventilation, maximum sun exposure and improved ripeness. Of course, the non-use of chemicals and fertilizers means that yields are less than 35 hectoliters per hectare in most vintages and below average (which is 45–55 hectoliters per hectare) at other estates that use chemicals. However, both Alfred and Jean-Michel believe that this is made up by higher quality and higher prices.

In keeping with a comprehensive sustainability philosophy and values, the estate shuns tractors and uses horses to turn the soil. Since horses never step in the same place twice, they aerate the soils in different places adding oxygen to the soil versus the identical allotted paths that tractors follow. Jean-Michel believes that horses are gentler and lighter than tractors when they churn the soil. The horses are considered to be willing and happy when they work in the vineyard since they enjoy eating grapes.

Starting with the 2017 vintage, all the grapes are now destemmed by hand in order to eliminate machinery and reduce the environmental footprint. The estate continues to strive to eliminate the need for electricity in the cellars which have no wall sockets. This alters how the wine vinifies as there are no pump overs. Lighting is powered by geothermal energy from boreholes that were dug into the vineyards to circulate water. The reduction of electricity use includes the elimination of computers to make harvesting or fermentation decisions. The family's philosophy is that a healthy eco-system is more apparent visually than with technology. Determining the perfect time to pick grapes, rather than based on technology as with many large estates, is based on Jean-Michel walking through the vines looking for deeply colored skins, brown stems and, most importantly, no rot. If the fruit looks good, he tastes. When the grapes are ripe, he picks. Unlike most Bordeaux Grand Crus, Pontet-Canet does not believe in making a second wine since they feel that every vintage tells a different story, and all wines should taste like the vintage.

The process of complete elimination of all chemicals takes a few years and 2007 was the last vintage when chemicals were used. Jean-Michel Comme, who started with Pontet-Canet in 1989, is not only the technical force but also the philosophical and values-based champion for biodynamic farming. He is a passionate advocate of biodynamic farming and believes that it is irresponsible to farm in any other way on the terroir:

> you have the crops and the diseases, and in between you have the farmer that creates a protection to suppress the diseases, he wants to kill the enemy. The enemy is the disease and the enemy wants to kill you and the only option it to kill it first. With the conventional way, you send a nuclear weapon to the enemy – because you are sure it is very powerful and don't care about the repercussions of this weapon because you only focus on the result. When you are organic, you have the same state of mind, you want to kill the enemy, but you are not allowed to use the nuclear weapon because the nuclear weapon is very damaging. So, you use arrows to try to damage the enemy. But the idea is the same, you try to kill the disease before being killed. So that's why we tried to find another way, biodynamic.
>
> We have organic certification and we applied for Biodyvin, from the beginning, and since 2014 we also have the Demeter certification. Because we have our own cows from the estate and we wanted to prove, if necessary, that we produce our own biodynamic preps, we can prove it. But we do not promote or advertise on the biodynamics certification.

As per Jean-Michel Comme and other families that have adopted biodynamic practices, the philosophy is very different from the dominant one in Western civilization which considers the diseases as a problem to be cured. Biodynamics sees a problem as a normal reaction to an imbalance created in the vine because of the environment, which is closer to the philosophy of the Chinese medicine as per Comme. The difference that he sees between biodynamics and the other approaches in viticulture is so dramatic that he was not convinced by organic methods:

> We were not convinced by the organic philosophy, because the organic philosophy has the same relationship with the disease as the conventional… we have never been organic and I have never considered myself as an organic producer.

Even though Pontet-Canet has multiple biodynamic certifications, Comme does not believe in labeling that signals their practices for marketing. He expresses discomfort with the extremely high prices of some wines that only the rich and collectors can afford:

> A pure marketing approach cannot last. I do not forget that we are a commercial company, and we need to make money. The best approach to do so is to make the best wine. Being a certified growth, we have higher prices and the goal for us is to have the highest price.
>
> **Sometimes people invest in the wrong ideas: focus on the return on your investment instead of quality of wine. But, if you invest for quality in the grape growth, you can get back much more.**
>
> So, the cost of production is something secondary to me. If you invest with a good idea you will be able to get back much more. If you invest nothing you will have nothing back.

According to Jean-Michel Comme, the high hot humidity in 2018 led to a sudden onset of mildew that damaged more than half the harvest. This resulted in a major financial loss for the chateau. While other estates saved their harvest by applications of chemicals, Jean-Michel with the consent of Alfred decided not to disrupt the biodynamic and healthy eco-system that had built over 14 years and also not to ask workers to leave their families to work on a Sunday. Jean-Michel and Alfred believe that the financial loss in 2018 is offset by the many good years in the past and the future. Comme highlighted that the support he got from the Tesseron family in the year of substantial financial loss would not be forthcoming from a corporate winery focused on the bottom line:

> The 3 estates certified as biodynamic in the Médoc have almost the same yields, and all three lost 2/3 of their crops [in 2018]. And Latour, that is organic certified, lost half of the crop. Last year, [2018] I was not able to provide a real crop to my owner, I feel guilty even if I made no mistake. The owners [family] however fully understand the conditions and they are motivated to keep going on that way.

According to Alfred Tesseron:

> I am not a winemaker. My team members are not winemakers either. As most of the work is done in the vineyards, we are growers. Our success and achievements at Pontet-Canet are due to our efforts in the vineyards, not the wine making. At the end of the day, our goal is to produce unique vintages of Pontet-Canet that are for drinking, not just for wine tasting.[15]

The risks of biodynamic viticulture are high and require an unwavering faith. As confirmed Alain Blanchard of the ISVV:

> In the bad years as 2018, the wine estates that use biodynamic techniques did 1/4th of what they do in general. They could balance that with the next year. They

> managed to get good wine by reducing the crop. If in the next year they have bigger harvest, they make more wine and they keep the same price. With expensive wines it is feasible but how many smaller chateaux can afford that? It is very difficult financially. When the price for a bottle is much lower, you can't afford to do that.
>
> If you go organic in Bordeaux, you do not get better prices, but you increase risks. If you go for organic, you can try to save your crop but you need to be able to treat the whole vineyards in the time window of 6 hours, even on the weekends. That means that you have to be ready to go to the fields with all your workers to treat quickly… You increase the risks.

The family philosophy is to tend the vineyard and vinify the wines on a parcel-by-parcel basis and to do as little intervention as possible in order to develop a resilient and healthy eco-system. As compared to the institutional change leadership of Bardet and Bon in Saint-Émilion, the Pontet-Canet estate has chosen to lead by example, through its consistently high-quality vintages and premium pricing, to show other estates that the adoption of biodynamic farming methods is risky but possible in the challenging humid weather and also contributes to high quality and prices.

These pioneering sustainability practices have established an example for mimetic institutional change since several other estates have imitated and adopted this practice. Among the estates that have followed the example of Ponte-Canet are some of the most prestigious and premium wine-producing classified estates: Château Latour in Pauillac, Château Margaux in Marguax and Château Clinet in Pomerol.

The Tesseron family wine business includes Alfred's nieces Mélanie and Phillipine Tesseron, daughters of his late brother Gerard. The family vision is to pass on the history and the healthy terroir and eco-system to future generations and secure the future of Château Pontet-Canet. In 2016, they purchased the very large 600 acre estate of the late comedian, Robin Williams, in the Napa Valley, renaming it Pym-Rae. The close connection between the Tesseron and Comme families extends into the future as Jean-Michel Comme's son now works on the California estate. Jean Michel Comme and his wife Corinne also own their own biodynamic vineyard, Champ des Treilles in the Sainte Foy appellation.

Château Le Noble, Bordeaux Supérieur

Château Le Noble domain consists of 30 hectares of which 15 have been planted with vines since the beginning of the nineteenth century. Located in the town of Saint Germain du Puch, halfway between Bordeaux and Saint Émilion, Château Le Noble is on the left bank of the Dordogne. The owners are Maria and Thomas Bonnefon. Thomas represents the fifth generation of a wine-making family with its roots in Languedoc and the south-west of

France. He is a graduate of the prestigious Bordeaux-Blanquefort school of viticulture and viniculture. His studies were complemented by advanced internships in several Bordeaux chateaux, including a year at the Grand Cru classé Château Rauzan-Ségla appellation Margaux in Médoc.

The Bonnefons are passionate about the terroir and have followed organic farming practices since 2013. They give special attention to soil treatment with light plowing and natural enrichment during planting. The pruning processes are varied according to the grape varieties, aiming for quality rather than quantity. According to Maria Bonnefon:

> Organic wine is a phenomenon which is now important in global markets. I would say that China, Japan and Malaysia and Asia are changing. Our wine is sold now in Singapore and Taiwan just because we are organic, and they are very much interested… for me, and Thomas, we did not have vacations, for several years now. It's very important what we created. Thomas brings our children every day to the winery. It is important for them to see if they would be interested to continue, it would be wonderful. It would be a tremendous decision.

Based on our research, it was quite clear that the family-owned estates took leadership of the process to achieve a sustainability mandate in the Bordeaux region, both by setting an example through the practices they adopted at their estates and obtaining persuasive power by taking on leadership of industry organizations such as CIVB and SME.

CONCLUSION

Our study confirmed the role of family-owned estates as agents of institutional change for sustainable viticulture and viniculture in the Bordeaux region. Contrary to the media reports (for example, see the opening quotes at the beginning of this chapter), we found that the process of mandating sustainable farming and wine making was not sudden and rapid but had already started in 2008 in the Bordeaux Supérieur AOC. However, the progress was slow and gradual until Bordeaux bashing gathered momentum, especially after the 2015 court trial of two estates accused of intoxicating school children in Villeneuve-de-Blaye with their chemical spraying.[16] At the same time, societal norms, regulations and national movements in France strengthened sustainable farming in all sectors, and market demand for organic and biodynamic wine accelerated in France, Scandinavia, Germany and Japan. As these institutional forces coalesced and reinforced each other, estate-owning families such as Bardet and Bon, who already held strong family values for eco-system health, environmental preservation and biodiversity, took the institutional leadership-building consensus by leveraging their leadership in industry associations and by holding town hall meetings of estates within Saint-Émilion.

While individual family-owned estates had been adopting organic and biodynamic or other sustainable farming practices for over two decades, it is quite likely that without the macro-institutional forces such as changing societal norms in France and market shifts, the mandate may not have happened. The estate-owning families also emphasized the link between their values for preservation of the environment and their attachment to place, that is, they saw themselves as stewards of the terroir, eco-system health and biodiversity for the future generations. The families expressed the importance of tacit knowledge that was transmitted during informal interactions and conversations between different generations of the family. Thus, while societal norms, reputational risk and market forces were catalysts, the family values toward sustainability enabled them to become passionate institutional change agents.

An interesting philosophy that emerged was Ponte-Canet's passion for biodynamic viticulture and viniculture, not in response to societal and market forces but based on a radically different view of the wine business. Jean-Michel Comme expressed clearly that while many wineries saw the vine as an industrial plant from which they could extract maximum production and profits, their own perspective of the vine was a part of a healthy living eco-system whose by-product was exceptionally good-quality wines. He saw disease in the vineyard as a symptom of an unhealthy eco-system and not as something to be cured via a nuclear approach of bombarding with chemicals.

Besides New Zealand, the Bordeaux region is one of the most challenging major wine regions in the world with high humidity and rain and a very high risk of aggressive mildew that has to be treated within a window of six hours to avoid losing most of the crop and financial disaster. Under such conditions, family-owned estates, not only large estates with premium pricing of between 100 to 200 euros a bottle such as Pontet-Canet, but also small estates that sell at low prices of between 10 to 12 euros a bottle such as Château d'Esther, have been biodynamic for more than a decade and a half, based on family values. As described above, in 2018, during a bout of aggressive mildew affecting the vines, Pontet-Canet and other biodynamic estates chose not to spray chemicals and undo years of developing a biodynamic healthy eco-system. They absorbed the major financial stress. While Château Pontet-Canet commands premium prices and can make up the loss in years of good harvest, Château d'Esther sells at much lower prices and has also managed to stay biodynamic in the challenging weather. Similarly, winery estates in New Zealand have built globally renowned expertise for high-quality organic and biodynamic wines in very humid weather. The lesson for other winery regions that face much less challenging weather conditions is that if the New Zealand and Bordeaux winery regions can become sustainable, so can all other wine regions of the world. This could result in the complete transformation of the global wine business with positive impacts on eco-system health and biodiversity.

NOTES

1. Mercer, C. (2013). "Organic 'is the future' of Bordeaux wine." *Decanter*, September 16. www.decanter.com/wine-news/opinion/the-editors-blog/organic-is-the-future-for-bordeaux-wine-15716/
2. Mustacich (2017). "Bordeaux's St.-Émilion Mandates Sustainable Viticulture." *Wine Spectator*, November 9. www.winespectator.com/articles/st-emilion-mandates-sustainable-viticulture
3. TWCI (2019). *The Wine Cellar Insider*. www.thewinecellarinsider.com/wine-topics/bordeaux-wine-production-facts-figures-grapes-vineyards/
4. Balter, E. (2019). "The ABCs of Bordeaux." *Wine Spectator*, March 27. www.winespectator.com/articles/modern-abcs-of-bordeaux-3490
5. TWCI (2019). "Château Pontet-Canet Pauillac Bordeaux wine, complete guide." www.thewinecellarinsider.com/bordeaux-wine-producer-profiles/bordeaux/pauillac/pontet-canet/
6. SME (2019). www.bordeaux.com/fr/vignoble-engage/labels/le-systeme-de-management-environnemental-du-vin-de-bordeaux-sme
7. Ginestet, E. (2018). "Jean-Michel Comme (Pontet-Canet) 'la vigne est ma seule passion sur terre.'" *Idealwine*, February 7.
8. Kristiansen, P. & Mansfield, C. (2006). "Overview of organic agriculture." In P. Kristiansen, A. Taji & J. Reganold (eds), *Organic Agriculture: A Global Perspective*. Collingwood, AU: CSIRO Publishing.
9. Millar, R. (2019). "Terra Vitis to include HVE certification in 2020." *The Drinks Business*, September 20. www.thedrinksbusiness.com/2019/09/terra-vitis-to-include-hve-certification-in-2020/
10. WEF (2018). World Economic Forum. www.weforum.org/agenda/2018/11/france-is-most-food-sustainable-country-u-s-and-u-k-faltering
11. BTC (Bordeaux Tourism and Conventions). (2019). http://presse.bordeaux-tourisme.com/en/bordeaux-by-figures
12. Petijean, S. (2015). "Epandage près d'une école à Villeneuve (33): la plainte classée." *Sud Ouest*, October 9.
13. Liv-Ex. (2019). www.liv-ex.com/services/data/
14. www.idealwine.net/jean-michel-comme-pontet-canet-la-vigne-est-ma-seule-passion-sur-terre/
15. Petijean, S. (2015). "Epandage près d'une école à Villeneuve (33): la plainte classée." *Sud Ouest*, October 9.
16. Petijean, S. (2015). "Epandage près d'une école à Villeneuve (33): la plainte classée." *Sud Ouest*, October 9.

13. The Wallenberg family of Sweden: Sustainable business development since 1856

Sarah Jack and Mattias Nordqvist

BACKGROUND

The Wallenberg family business story started when André Oscar Wallenberg (1816–86), who had made a successful career as a naval officer, helped a friend to find the financial resources to expand a sawmill in the region of Dalarna, north of Stockholm in Sweden. He subsequently moved to Stockholm and pursued an entrepreneurial career, founding Stockholms Enskilda Bank (SEB) in 1856. André Oscar Wallenberg came from a family of priests, teachers and government officials mostly active in the south of Sweden. From the start of the Wallenberg family's business operations, it has worked hard to support enterprise and research in Sweden and internationally.

The Wallenberg family has always been concerned with supporting companies of Swedish origin that are looking to grow their operations in international markets. In building and developing its interests, the family tradition has primarily been to focus on innovation and long-term sustainability through financial vigilance. This focus has continued and today the fifth generation of the family, led by Jacob, Marcus and Peter, Jr. Wallenberg (Figure 13.1), continues to work to support enterprise and research through its historical roots and embedding the traditions which have been used to generate much of its long-term success. The general model is that family representatives do not work actively in the companies or other organizations under their control, but they exercise their involvement, direction and control through positions in the boards of directors.

In 2020, the Wallenbergs' interests comprised 15 non-profit foundations – the Wallenberg Foundations – and the industrial holding companies Investor AB (public) and FAM AB (private, owned by foundations controlled by the family) with their respective holdings, including ABB, AstraZeneca, Atlas

Source: www.wallenberg.com.

Figure 13.1 *Jacob, Marcus and Peter Wallenberg, Jr.*

Copco, Electrolux, EQT, Ericsson, Nasdaq, Saab AB, SAS, SEB, SKF, Stora Enso, Wärtsilä (all public) and Höganäs and Mölnlycke (private).[1]

THE WALLENBERG FAMILY TODAY

In addition to the three fifth-generation cousins Jacob, Marcus and Peter, Jr., four other fifth-generation cousins are involved mainly in the governance of the family's not-for profit activities: Caroline Ankarcrona (director on the board of Knut and Alice Wallenberg Foundation), Andrea Gandet (director on the board of Marcus and Amalia Wallenberg Foundation), Mariana Risberg (director on the board of Marcus and Marianne Wallenberg Foundation) and Celia Pilkington (Figure 13.2).

Celia Pilkington and Peter Wallenberg, Jr. lead an educational program for members of the sixth generation to be introduced to the family's sphere.

A guiding principle for the family's work in terms of how it organizes its influence in the foundations and the business holdings is "Like the generations before us, we are working on a long-term basis for the betterment of our country." Other core principles that guide the Wallenberg family are:

- *"Sweden is – and will always be – the base of the family's activities"* – long-term commitment toward Sweden.
- "*esse non videri*" – to act, not to seem to be. That is, focusing on getting the job done.

- "*To move from the old to what is about to come is the only tradition worth keeping*" – focus on innovation and renewal.
- "*No business is so bad that it cannot be put back on its feet with the right leadership, but no business is so good that it cannot be destroyed by a bad leader*" – placing the right person in the right place at the right time.
- "*The lesson learned from crises is to always maintain financial vigilance and strong liquidity positions.*"
- "*Focus is on having ownership positions in sound companies that are, or have the potential to become, the leaders in their industry or global leaders*" – leading companies and excellence in research.

(a) (b) (c)

(d)

Source: www.wallenberg.com.

Figure 13.2 *(a) Caroline Ankarcrona, (b) Andrea Gandet, (c) Mariana Risberg and (d) Celia Pilkington*

THE WALLENBERG FAMILY AND SUSTAINABILITY

The Wallenberg family puts importance on sustainability as an integrated part of its core guiding principle "to act, not to seem to be." A long-term focus on its business activities is key to its sustainability approach. Every year, the Wallenberg foundations allocate significant grants to better understand sustainability from various approaches and academic disciplines. For instance, in 2016, the Knut and Alice Wallenberg Foundation gave a significant grant to the Stockholm School of Economics to establish the Jacob and Marcus Wallenberg Chair in innovation and sustainable development. The purpose was to facilitate new research into long-term business success and the role played by innovative managerial practices that involve customers, owners, employees and other stakeholders, and that take responsibility for societal impacts in this process.

Further, sustainability is an important concept for the Wallenberg family's industrial holding companies. For instance, according to the official communication from the publicly listed Investor AB:

> **Sustainability is fundamental to our business success and the success of our companies.**
>
> Investor has a long tradition of being a responsible owner and company, and firmly believes that a sustainable business approach is a pre-requisite for creating long-term value. We expect our portfolio companies to take on a proactive rather than a reactive and risk focused approach to sustainability.

Investor AB works with four focus areas within sustainability: (a) environment and climate, (b) people and communities, (c) innovation and research and (d) business ethics and governance (www.investor.com). Examples of how Investor AB works in these areas of social justice include having a whistleblowing system and anti-corruption policy and training procedure in all companies in which it invests. On the ecological dimension, 83 percent of its companies have signed the United Nations (UN) Global Compact and 74 percent of them contribute to the UN's Global Goals. Further, 100 percent of the electricity used in their main office in Stockholm comes from renewable sources.

A CONVERSATION WITH WALLENBERG FAMILY REPRESENTATIVES ABOUT SUSTAINABILITY

In order to better understand what sustainability means to the Wallenbergs as a family business and as active owners in many large companies, both private and publicly listed, we present below a conversation with Jacob, Marcus and Peter, Jr. Wallenberg:

> *What is your point of departure when it comes to sustainability?*
> **Sustainability is not only the environment, which some would say. It's much broader. From a company point of view, it's our relationship with society at large.**
>
> I define society at large as individuals in society. It's our employees, our shareholders, it's the universe that is part of the day to day work and we must have a relationship with all of them. That, to me, is really sustainability. Then you can dig into a number of verticals, the environment, the labor union relations, or the stock market and shareholder value maximization – and the consumer not to be forgotten!
>
> **The whole question about sustainability in its broadest sense, is fundamental to young people, so it's your future employees, your future customers, your future of many different things...**
>
> Sustainability is really about connecting people. (Jacob Wallenberg)

Jacob Wallenberg's cousin, Marcus Wallenberg, agrees and in a similar vein points out that when people talk about sustainability, the majority of the time they are focused on climate change. Marcus points out that if you are to run a business with a true long-term outlook, then sustainability is key to making it an attractive business. He continues:

> I think about the businesses in the sense that very often, publicly, people are talking about shareholders, as being number one. I would not say that shareholders are not important, but I would turn it around and say that for a business to sustainably deliver a return to shareholders and develop, it has to relate to all important stakeholders. Climate change is only one of the sustainability factors. If you're going to be a sustainable business, you have to innovate, you have to reinvent yourself, you have to deliver sustainable, positive advantages to customers and you have to be very careful when you select suppliers. You must understand the competitive forces, especially in a world where disruption is so pre-eminent as it is today. You must reinvent yourself not only in innovation, but also in your organizational structure and in how you design your business model for the future. This is happening today in every part of any business so if you're not able to cope with the times – and right now times are such that the science and technology is moving at an incredible speed – you will not be a sustainable business.

> *What does sustainability mean to you as a business family?*
> One part of our sustainability is long-term ownership. We are responsible owners. Today when people talk about sustainability, they ask "what do we as a family represent and what effect does this have on climate, environment and job opportunities?" There are really so many things you can put in the word sustainability. I work a lot with the sixth generation of the family. We have asked them what they would like us to focus on in the next couple of years. They all said... sustainability... Sustainability is what we do with our companies to see to it that they are companies with a mind, with a conscience, and do what they can when it comes to how they work with their employees, for the environment and for the general development.

> However, with the background and upbringing we have and the ownership we represent, sustainability is so much wider. Sustainability is the future. Being long-term responsible owners is really what we stand for and sustainability is inherent in this. **Without sustainability we would not be responsible, long-term owners. (Peter Wallenberg, Jr.)**

Working with the sixth generation's relationship and commitment to the companies and the foundations, the family organizes regular meetings with members from the fifth and sixth generations. It was through discussions at those family meetings that they realized sustainability is a key issue for the sixth generation. Marcus Wallenberg adds that they, as a business family, are often asked how it is possible that they are still around after five generations:

> I think it is about looking upon the business very long term. It is part of the sustainability concept. Moving with the times and being able to see what is about to come… and being ready to make changes is key in the sustainable way of doing business long term. Sustainable means actually that it is sustainable and it's not only climate change.

What attracts Jacob, Marcus and Peter, Jr. Wallenberg to this broader perspective of sustainability is that it fits with a long-term view of doing business in the "right way" and offers a way to invest in the future.

We invited Jacob, Marcus and Peter, Jr. Wallenberg to reflect on how their work on sustainability today is linked to the family in previous generations. They all suggest that it goes back in history to the main family members in business in the second generation: Knut and Alice Wallenberg (Figure 13.3). Knut and Alice, who did not have any children, started the family's largest foundation to support initiatives with social and other non-profit goals:

> They were extremely active outside of their daily job in looking at what was happening around them. They helped to finance the Stockholm Public Library, they helped people with disabilities, and they helped culture. Over a 100 years ago they were already thinking about how they could be part of developing society. Today this is part of our DNA. I'm an extremely proud member of the fifth generation. Every time I think about what Knut and Alice did, by starting their foundation, I feel it's amazing. (Peter Wallenberg, Jr.)

Jacob Wallenberg agrees and underlines that the family history (which goes back more than 160 years) is important to them because it means continuity in what they as a business family develop and prioritize. He points out that it relates to their human values and upbringing but also how Swedish society works and "colors" family life:

> When Knut Agathon launched the concept of "landsgangeligt," which is about supporting the country and the core of the Knut and Alice Wallenberg Foundation,

Source: www.wallenberg.com.

Figure 13.3 *Knut Agathon and Alice Wallenberg, founders of the largest foundation*

it says that all support should be for the good of Sweden. There is a bit of the liberal attitude, it's the country and the people of the country – that was important to them. Okay they didn't have any children, so it was easier to push in that direction, but it tells you something. Knut was the secretary of state during the First World War, he was a banker, and an industrialist. He had an engagement in society that was way beyond what was normal at the time. We have history to look back at. We have 16 different foundations in the family formed by, or in memory of, family members. This tells you something about the history, tradition that this family has been living by.[2]

How was sustainability introduced to you as a family member?
It's a little bit in our DNA. When our grandfather was alive and we were kids, the foundations were not really part of the discussion. The business was the focus, but the thinking was still around long-term responsible ownership. "Responsible" was a huge word that was used all the time. Our parents' generation, the 3rd generation, were very authoritative and clearly said what they expected you to do or not do. We try not to act like that today. It was a symbol of the times. Our introduction was more hands on every time we met grandfather or father in discussions around the table. It was just the way that they communicated, and we were brought up. We felt at a very early age that we were part of something which was meant to take responsibility. (Peter Wallenberg, Jr.)

Source: www.wallenberg.com.

Figure 13.4 *Marcus Wallenberg (1899–1982)*

In relation to how they were brought up and what values were emphasized as being important for their business activities, Marcus Wallenberg recalls his grandfather (also called Marcus Wallenberg), coining an expression that has become famous in Sweden. When the Wallenberg family discussed whether they would support the creation of the pan-Scandinavian airline SAS, their grandfather Marcus Wallenberg wrote to his brother: "moving from the old to what is about to come is the only tradition worth keeping." Marcus Wallenberg says that to him this expression captures an important part of sustainability:

> If you want the family business to continue, you must be on the move and adapt to what you think is about to come… It's all about people. If you want to run a sustainable long-term business, you must pay attention to the leader and be aware that certain types of leaders are suited to certain types of development in the company's history. Some people are fantastic at restructuring and reorganizing. Others are excellent at expanding and some people are very good at consolidating the position and moving forward. You must make sure that you have the right leader at the right time and at the right place.
>
> **And you must take care of people. My grandfather always said: "it's not their fault if you appointed them to a job – you did it."**
>
> So, you have the responsibility to move the person if it doesn't work out and to take care of them. It is not their fault. Try to help them into the next thing. If you're worried and you think it doesn't work out, you must be able to change the leader.

> *What does sustainability mean for the portfolio companies and their activities?*
> It's part of the survival. All our portfolio companies today realize that if they don't have a sustainability plan, they will not be part of what the next generation of employees want to work for. (Peter Wallenberg, Jr.)

Jacob Wallenberg explains that they have a network where chairpersons of the companies where they are shareholders meet regularly:

> We had a meeting a month ago. We meet and we have one or two items on the agenda. This time we had basically one: sustainability. We had a debate, for four hours, on sustainability. "What are you doing in your board? Are you engaged in this issue and are you in line with the rest of us?" or "ahead of us? Have you developed new ways of thinking?" "What does your board say?" It was an interesting debate because you can always judge by the question and the intensity of the debate how engaged people are.

Jacob, Marcus and Peter, Jr. Wallenberg follow up on this through their board work, ensuring that key questions are on the board's agenda. This helps to engage the management of the companies and ensure progress is being made in a responsible way:

> *Would you say that the role of sustainability has been changing?*
> As chairman of Investor, when I engage with shareholders at an Annual General Meeting or talk with journalists or when I go to Davos,[3] there is a lot of talk about sustainability. Everyone is interested. Everyone is asking questions. But you get very different answers… My personal judgement is that this is very straightforward. If you are engaged in global business, you have to deal with it. You have to deal with all the issues surrounding the world within the realm of sustainability. If you're going to be successful in the long run, you must be viewed as having a clear compass on a large number of different issues. This is a huge shift from where in the 70s your task was shareholder value maximization. (Jacob Wallenberg)

Agreeing with this view, Marcus Wallenberg adds that time is important if you are to do sustainable business, but you also have to be entrepreneurial and ready to invest in the long term.

For our final question we asked:

> *Would you consider yourselves as leaders in sustainability issues within your industries?*

Jacob Wallenberg responded, referring to the extent of their engagement with their view of sustainability:

> We're engaged in all these companies, and we've been running shareholder maximization and we're bankers. That's the general picture. In reality, we're fairly

> liberal and we've always been. We were the first to employ women. The bank was the first organization in this country that hired women in line duty. The bank was the first organization that offered a pension to its employees around the turn of the century. We were the leaders in several issues and we've always been. In different ways, engaged in society and relationship with employees. We have a history or a "compass" of a broader engagement. (Jacob Wallenberg)

SUMMARY

Through five generations, the Wallenberg family has worked to build and maintain long-term business sustainability and innovation through financial vigilance. This case study illustrates how these long-standing family traditions have been used as a platform to support enterprise and build sustainable growth and global expansion for companies of Swedish origin. Moreover, this long-term perspective to sustainable business activity has been driven through a family tradition of working for the advancement of Sweden and the progression of Swedish society through a vision of long-term responsible and sustainable ownership.

ACKNOWLEDGMENTS

The authors would like to thank Jacob, Marcus and Peter, Jr. Wallenberg for their help and support with the writing of this chapter.

NOTES

1. For further information about the Wallenberg family and their holdings, please visit www.wallenberg.com/index.php/en
2. Examples of important foundations supporting researchers and research projects: Knut and Alice Wallenberg's Foundation, Marianne and Marcus Wallenberg's Foundation, Foundation Marcus and Amalia Wallenberg's Memorial Fund, Berit Wallenberg's Foundation, Jacob Wallenberg's Foundation, Foundation for Jurisprudential Research, Dr Tech Marcus Wallenberg Foundation for Education in International Industrial Entrepreneurship, Marcus Wallenberg Foundation for International Scientific Collaboration and Peter Wallenberg Foundation focusing on economics and technology. The emphasis of funding is on medicine, technology and natural sciences, but the foundations also support social sciences, the humanities and archaeology.
3. Davos refers to the yearly World Economic Forum where political, business, cultural and other leaders of society meet to discuss current affairs (www.weforum.org).

Index

'Pramodita and Sanjay Sharma shine a light on successful family businesses that are at the forefront of sustainability. With purpose, innovation and a focus on the long term, these far-sighted enterprises are delivering for all stakeholders. This book offers important lessons for family businesses who want to create long term value and a shared prosperity for all. Well done.'

Alfonso Libano, COBEGA, S.A Spain and Family Business Network

'Recent crises have reinforced the need to ensure that we preserve our resources and organisations for next generations, the true meaning of good stewardship. This is all the more important for family companies where the family and the business are intertwined with each other. I am often asked whether I can suggest best practices for stewardship and sustainable development in a family business. The case studies presented here provide a wealth of insights on how to transform towards a sustainable organisation or design for it. And I was very impressed by the three cases of companies that championed the development of sustainable business ecosystems and thus brought along institutional change. They are impressive role models.'

Arnoud De Meyer, Stewardship Asia Centre and Singapore Management University, Singapore

'Take a trip around the world with Pramodita and Sanjay Sharma as they highlight 15 business families that have managed to combine purpose, profit and professionalism with deep commitments to sustainable development. An invigorating and enlightening look at what's possible in complex global environments.'

Judy Green, Family Firm Institute, USA

Printed and bound by CPI Group (UK) Ltd, Croydon, CR0 4YY
16/04/2025
14658432-0003